1004365118

HUBRIS AND HYBRIDS

A Cultural History of Technology and Science

Mikael Hård
and
Andrew Jamison

Routledge
Taylor & Francis Group

NEW YORK AND LONDON

Published in 2005 by
Routledge
Taylor & Francis Group
270 Madison Avenue
New York, NY 10016

Published in Great Britain by
Routledge
Taylor & Francis Group
2 Park Square
Milton Park, Abingdon
Oxon OX14 4RN

© 2005 by Taylor & Francis Group, LLC
Routledge is an imprint of Taylor & Francis Group

Printed in the United States of America on acid-free paper
10 9 8 7 6 5 4 3 2 1

International Standard Book Number-10: 0-415-94938-6 (Hardcover) 0-415-94939-4 (Softcover)
International Standard Book Number-13: 978-0-415-94938-5 (Hardcover) 978-0-415-94939-2
(Softcover)
Library of Congress Card Number 2005001698

Library of Congress Cataloging-in-Publication Data

Hård, Mikael.
    Hubris and hybrids : a cultural history of technology and science / Mikael
Hård and Andrew Jamison.
        p. cm.
    Includes bibliographical references.
    ISBN 0-415-94938-6 (hc. : alk. paper) -- ISBN 0-415-94939-4
(pbk. : alk. paper)
    1. Technology--History. 2. Science--History. I. Jamison, Andrew.
II. Title.

T15.H342 2005
303.48'3--dc22   2005001698

Taylor & Francis Group
is the Academic Division of T&F Informa plc.

Visit the Taylor & Francis Web site at
http://www.taylorandfrancis.com

and the Routledge Web site at
http://www.routledge-ny.com

For Aant Elzinga
and Sven-Eric Liedman
—teachers, supervisors, and mentors

CONTENTS

List of Illustrations   ix

List of Tables   xi

Preface   xiii

Introduction: A Need for New Stories   1

Part 1   The Roots of Technoscience

Chapter 1   The Scientific Reformation in Early Modern Europe   19

Chapter 2   The Industrial Transformation   45

Chapter 3   The Sites of Enlightenment and Innovation   71

Part 2   The Machine in the Mind

Chapter 4   Technocrats and Their Critics   97

Chapter 5   Eastern Minds Take on the Western Juggernaut   121

Chapter 6   Artistic Appropriations from Morris
              to *The Matrix*   145

Part 3   Machines and Knowledge in Action

Chapter 7   Mobility Mania and Its Material Manifestations   171

Chapter 8   The Cultural Forms of Communication
              and Information   197

Chapter 9   Public Works, Public Health, and Personal Hygiene   219

Part 4   Coping with Technoscience

Chapter 10   Making Technoscience Politically Accountable   245

Chapter 11   From Appropriate Technology to Green Business   269

Chapter 12   Conclusions: History as Cultural Assessment   293

Bibliography   309

Index   327

LIST OF ILLUSTRATIONS

Figure 1   The astronomer Tycho Brahe among his astronomical
            instruments. From *Tychonis Brahe Astronomiae
            instauratae mechanica,* 1598.   37

Figure 2   Political and cultural movements and
            scientific institutions.   43

Figure 3   Young James Watt playing with steam.   50

Figure 4   Waves of industrialization and cultural critique.   56

Figure 5   An early London coffeehouse, c. 1705.   75

Figure 6   Orville Wright's flight show on Tempelhof Field
            near Berlin 1908, organized by the newspaper
            Berliner Lokal-Anzeiger.   98

Figure 7   Construction site for the Three Gorges Dam,
            China, Hubei Province, c. 1990.   126

Figure 8   Charlie Chaplin in *Modern Times,* 1936.   159

Figure 9   Boy on street with sign, TITANIC DISASTER,
            1912.   172

Figure 10   British railway station.   176

Figure 11   Runners, cars, and cyclists on racecourse, Berlin
            Grunewald, 1920.   183

Figure 12   Poster for Telefunken Radios, c. 1930.   209

Figure 13   "The Compulsory Bath," illustration for
            Les Defauts Horribles, c. 1860.   231

Figure 14   Poster for Johns Volldampf washing machines,
            nineteenth century.   236

Figure 15   Hippies taunting police during the trial of
            the Chicago Seven, a group of radicals arrested
            during the protests against the Vietnam War at
            the Democratic National Convention, 1968.   248

Figure 16   Wind turbines and service roads dissecting
            a hillside, aerial, United States, c. 1990.   286

LIST OF TABLES

Table 1   The Cultural Appropriation of Technology
           and Science   14

Table 2   The Scientific Reformation as
           Cultural Appropriation   27

Table 3   Modern Science as a Form of Knowledge   39

Table 4   The Industrial Transformation as
           Cultural Appropriation   49

Table 5   Key Sites of Appropriation   76

Table 6   The Manifestations of Hygiene and Sanitation
           in the Public Sphere   228

Table 7   The Manifestations of Hygiene and Sanitation
           in the Private Sphere   229

Table 8   Changing Regimes of Power and Knowledge   252

Table 9   The Cultural Appropriation of Environmentalism   280

Table 10   The Dialectics of Sustainable Technology
           and Science   289

PREFACE

At a time when ever more money is spent on scientific research, and economic development is dominated by the search for ever more profitable technological innovations, it is striking how little all of this ingenuity and activity is doing to improve the human condition. The rhetoric and hype promise so much, but the reality so often fills us with anxiety and disappointment. While information and genetic technologies offer exciting possibilities in relation to communication and health care, and, more generally, in expanding our realm of experience and the scope of our imagination, the ways they are being developed have raised many difficult social and political challenges. These science-based technologies are threats, as well as opportunities, and they represent risks and dangers, as well as profit and potential.

How new is this situation? Are these dilemmas unique for our time, or are they recurrent themes in history? Can historical understanding provide any useful lessons in helping us resolve these contemporary contradictions? Can stories and reflections about the past contribute to assessing developments in the present?

The starting point for this book is the recognition that human societies have not always taken on new technologies and new scientific findings in ways that are "appropriate." Innovations—both factual and artifactual, scientific and technical—are double-edged swords that serve to transform relationships among people, as well as between human societies and our natural environments. Only through successful processes of cultural appropriation can we manage to tame or control the *hubris* that is fundamental to the innovative spirit. And only by becoming *hybrids,* combining the human and the nonhuman, the technical and the social, are we able to make effective use of our scientific and technological achievements.

This book is structured in four blocks. The first part presents the "roots of technoscience," by reexamining the so-called scientific and industrial revolutions, and following the central sites of knowledge production and innovation into the present. In the second part, "the machine in the mind," our focus is on the intellectual and artistic representations of science and technology, and we make a wide sweep, paying attention not only to European and North American, but also to Asian appropriation processes, including areas such as film and industrial design. The third block, "machines and knowledge in action," is about key areas of application and everyday appropriation—transportation and mobility, communications and media, sanitation and hygiene. Finally, in the fourth part, "coping with technoscience," we discuss issues of governance and politics, both in general terms and in relation to environmental issues. Our overall ambition is to lay the foundation for what we call a cultural assessment of technology and science, a process that might contribute to a future in which our machines and knowledge really do improve the human condition.

The book is based on many years of research and teaching in the history of technology and science, as well as in the interdisciplinary fields of science, technology, and society. We have long felt a need to counter the heroic stories of genius and invention that tend to dominate these fields with accounts that take broader social and cultural processes into consideration. The stories we tell are of "cultural appropriation," namely, the discursive, institutional, and daily practices through which technology and science are given human meaning. It is our hope that these stories might help provide a more balanced understanding of the contemporary relations between technology, science, and society.

We would like to thank our students and colleagues—at the University of Technology Darmstadt and at Aalborg University—for their help in developing the perspective that we present, and all of the authors whose works we have drawn upon. In a synthetic work of this kind we cannot claim specialist competence in all of the various topics that we discuss, and it goes without saying that the scholars we have referred to bear no responsibility for the use we have made of their work.

We dedicate this book to our Ph.D. supervisors, Aant Elzinga and Sven-Eric Liedman, who supported us in important phases in our careers and have continued to inspire us ever since. More specific thanks should be given to Aage Radman and Per-Olof Hallin, who gave us the opportunity to present a lecture series on the themes of the book at Malmö University College, and to all of those who discussed draft chapters at seminars and conferences.

Some of the material in chapters 4 and 11 has previously appeared in somewhat different form in the following copyrighted publications, which we gratefully acknowledge: *The Intellectual Appropriation of Technology: Discourses on Modernity,* edited by Mikael Hård and Andrew Jamison (The MIT Press, 1998), and *The Making of Green Knowledge: Environmental Politics and Cultural Transformation,* by Andrew Jamison (Cambridge University Press, 2001).

INTRODUCTION: A NEED FOR NEW STORIES

When we look at modern man, we have to face the fact that modern man suffers from a kind of poverty of the spirit which stands in glaring contrast to his scientific and technological abundance. We've learned to fly the air like birds, we've learned to swim the seas like fish, and yet we haven't learned to walk the earth like brothers and sisters.

—**Martin Luther King, Jr., "I Have a Dream"** (1963)

BEYOND ROMANCE AND TRAGEDY

The way James Watson told the story in 1968 in his controversial book, *The Double Helix,* the discovery of DNA was not particularly glamorous. In the early 1950s, he had been an ambitious young scientist, who had seen the task of describing the structure of the genetic "code" primarily as a way to make a name for himself—and win a Nobel Prize, which he did. Decoding DNA took a lot of hard work, a lot of questionable behavior in relation to other people, and, not least, a lot of educated guessing. The famous double-helix model was discovered, in Watson's account, not so much by following a tried and true scientific method as by following one's own well-trained intuition. It had involved suspense and competition, as Watson and his collaborator Francis Crick took on the American biochemist Linus Pauling to come first to the finish line. And it had its unpleasant moments, as Crick and Watson made use of the work of others for their own egotistical purposes. What made Watson's book especially significant was that the story was told in unusually colorful language, with Watson expressing strong opinions about other scientists, setting the characteristic tone already with the

1

opening sentence of the first chapter: "I have never seen Francis Crick in a modest mood" (Watson 1968, 15).

Watson's book helped to give science a human face, and it also helped to fashion a new kind of narrative about science and technology. *The Double Helix* served to bring the heroic scientist up to date. No longer alone with his thoughts in an ivory tower, seeking to discover the true nature of reality by means of logical inquiry and carefully designed experiments, the successful scientist, according to Watson's story, was a man of the world, just a bit more clever and ambitious than everyone else. He was strategic in his approach to research, competitive in his relation to other people, and rather uninterested in the broader social and ethical implications of his work. Like so many other scientists and engineers, he was driven by a kind of hubris, an almost unlimited will to power and transcendence over nature's limitations.

Thirty years later, Vandana Shiva, in her book *Stolen Harvest,* told a very different kind of story about DNA. At the turn of the millennium, the description of the genetic code had spawned the biotechnology industry, and food products based on the genetic manipulation of organisms had begun to be marketed. From the perspective of Shiva, a Western-trained Indian physicist turned environmental activist, the applications of Watson and Crick's discovery had become a threat to human health, to the viability of natural ecosystems, and to the survival of farmers in India and elsewhere. It was not so much that the science on which the new products were based was wrong or untrue; it was rather that the way that knowledge had come to be applied was filled with problems. In a country like India, disparities in income and opportunity meant that the vast majority of those who lived off the land would see their harvests "stolen" by the corporate manipulators of genetic material. According to Shiva, the handful of transnational corporations that were responsible for bringing the double helix to market were socially irresponsible, and it was difficult, if not impossible, to hold them accountable for their actions. "The conflict over genetically engineered crops and foods is not a conflict between 'culture' and 'science,'" she wrote. "It is between two cultures of science: one based on transparency, public accountability and responsibility toward the environment and people and another based on profits and the lack of transparency, accountability and responsibility" (Shiva 2000, 109).

Both stories deal with the same project, namely, the effort to understand the principles of genetics and apply that understanding to material uses. But the stories that Watson and Shiva were telling had very little else in common. In relation to the narrative forms discussed by Hayden

White (1987), Watson's story is a kind of romance, a heroic tale showing how youthful energy and ambition can lead to important scientific accomplishments. Shiva's story, on the other hand, is a tragedy, depicting some of the ways in which that same scientific accomplishment has had a number of very negative consequences. We argue that a proper understanding of the history of technology and science needs to make room for both kinds of stories, those that are told from inside the research laboratories and business firms in which knowledge and products are made, and those that bring in the wider social and cultural ramifications of knowledge making and artifactual production.

The stories that we tell in this book reflect the ambivalent character of technology and science in history. They show how, on the one hand, the hubris of engineering and science has opened up new possibilities for humankind, both real and imagined. On the other hand, they indicate that humans have continually needed to tame or control that hubris if the fruits of technology and science were to find appropriate uses. Such an approach is especially important at the present time, when the boundaries between technology and science are increasingly blurred, as are the boundaries between culture and nature. As biotechnologists consider cloning human beings, and as we communicate by means of cellular telephones and the Internet, implant mechanical devices in our bodies, and derive our nourishment from specially manufactured "functional foods," the very meaning of what it is to be human has come to change in subtle and complicated ways. We live amidst—and have to a large extent ourselves become—hybrids, entities that are neither purely human nor nonhuman, cultural, or natural (Latour 1991/1993). As such, technology and science no longer merely have impacts or consequences on our actions and behavior. Technological artifacts and scientific knowledge have become increasingly constitutive of what we do and what we think. In Donna Haraway's compelling metaphor, we have become *cyborgs,* beings that are, like humans, able to learn and feel and experience consciousness, but, like machines, increasingly "programmed" to learn and feel and experience things in certain ways (Haraway 1991).

Rather than considering technology merely as an extension of human capabilities, and science as a source of human enlightenment, we want to emphasize other elements that are at work in the making of scientific fact and technical artifact. By so doing, we want to try to carve out a middle ground between the polarized positions of the technological optimists and their cultural critics. For us, technology and science are not exclusively the unproblematic sources of material progress that they are for the promoters of commercial innovations. Nor do they represent merely the materialized interests of powerful social groups, as the critics of modernity would have it. We suggest that technology and science—or "technoscience," which seems to be a more fitting concept in the contemporary world—can be interpreted as both innovation and construction. Even more importantly, if we are to develop a cultural assessment of technoscience, and use our scientific and technological achievements appropriately, there needs to be a better historical understanding of the synthetic processes of reformation and transformation involved.

In this book, we tell the history of technology and science in terms of processes of cultural appropriation, by which new things and new ideas are made to fit into established ways of life. The development of technology and science involves not merely the proliferation of products emanating from corporate research laboratories and universities, a continual production of novelties, as the story line of innovation has it. And technology and science cannot be reduced to particular cases and projects that have their own contextual or situated logics, according to a story line of construction. There is an additional set of stories that need to be told, the ones about using and learning and interpreting and giving meaning, which follow story lines of appropriation.

Cultural appropriation is a process by which novelty is brought under human control; it is a matter of re-creating our societies and our selves so that new products and concepts make sense. It is in the mixing of different practical skills and knowledge traditions, of social roles and competencies, of visions and practices that we as human beings have come to make the worlds in which we live. The stories of appropriation are thus neither the romances that are dominant in production-centered accounts, nor the tragedies of victimization that are so common in the counternarratives of environmental destruction and globalization. They are rather dialectical stories of hybridization, of combination, both in terms of practice and identities, institutions and organizations, and discourses and disciplines.

It is important to recognize that appropriation is not merely a feature of the present era; already in the medieval period, eyeglasses and mirrors created opportunities for humans to experience a technically mediated reality, and, in the Renaissance, the use of machinery in fountains, religious practices, and printing inspired the mechanization and, later, "automation" of action and interaction, production and consumption. The cultivation of nature in gardens and parks was a way for humans to re-create their surroundings and also create new identities for themselves. In order to make use of our knowledge and artifacts, we not only have combined human and nonhuman entities, but also brought together previously separate social roles and identities, with their different skills and competencies, into new hybrid forms. In the seventeenth century, experimental philosophers represented a combination of what had previously been scholars and craftsmen, humanists and mathematicians; in the eighteenth and nineteenth centuries, engineers, entrepreneurs, and scientists developed as distinctive social types, combining the separate worlds of business and culture, technology and higher education; and, in the twentieth century, there have been shaped ever more hybrid identities, as technoscience has become fully integrated into our ways of life. To the older categories have been added the newer ones of managers, researchers, environmentalists, and, more specifically, risk assessors, research evaluators, and science journalists. We have also developed new forms of interaction with nonhumans, be they animals, plants, chemicals, or human-made artifacts. Through the centuries, human beings have become gardeners of plants, drivers of automobiles, operators of telephone exchanges, pilots of airplanes, information consultants, and, most recently, genetic engineers. In order to make use of our scientific and technological achievements, we are continually taking on new identities, changing our needs, and transforming our personalities.

What goes on in everyday life is connected to broader frameworks of perception and understanding, to ideas and visions about technology and science that are deeply embedded in our cultures. The contemporary fascination with space travel, artificial intelligence, and genetic engineering has led to the resurrection of the age-old visions of the transcendent power of artifacts and techniques to transform the human condition. We are constantly being presented with retellings of the classic tales of conquest and ingenuity that can be subsumed under the "myth of progress" (von Wright 1993). It is the "if only" syndrome, the eternal technical fixation that is deeply embedded in our underlying conceptions of reality. If only we could develop an even better instrument of production or destruction, if only we could tame another force of nature to provide us with unlimited energy, then our wealth and our capacities—the values by which we measure progress—would be so much greater. More than two millennia after the sun melted the wings of Icarus for coming too close, we are still under the spell of hubris, trying to fly higher and higher.

In the traditional story line, or "grand narrative," about technology and science, the idea of progress has been a central theme. Both the monastic orders and the millenarian movements of the Middle Ages had sought to establish a new kingdom of God on Earth, and, in the late Renaissance, their religious vision was translated into the utopias of science-based progress, from Tomaso Campanella's *City of the Sun* to Francis Bacon's *New Atlantis* and on to the scientific revolution itself. Later, in the period of industrialization, the positive philosophy, or, more broadly, the positivist discourse, portrayed technology and science as the very epitome of progress and human powers unleashed: "Prometheus unbound" (Landes 1969). It was through science and technology that ignorance could be defeated by enlightenment, that religious belief could be transcended by scientific truth, and that poverty and oppression could be eliminated by a technologically driven modernization. Machines became the determinant of social and economic development, the ultimate "measure of man" (Adas 1989). In the twentieth century, the all too obvious and visible failures of technology and science have brought into question the very idea of progress, and led to the articulation of new narratives, where overextension, overexpansion, and overkill are central. It is not merely that science and technology have failed in achieving many of their goals, or in solving the problems that their practitioners have attempted to deal with, it is that they are seen by many other people as forming an intrinsic part of their problems.

The narratives that began to be written in the 1960s have presented different story lines in relation to the history of technology and science. Hubris is a central theme in many of these stories, the ways in which scientists and their promoters have often gone too far in their ambitions. Hubris can be thought of as the visionary, superhuman aspect of science and technology, the attempt to transcend limitations and literally do the impossible. It is something like what David Noble (1997) has called a "religion of technology." As we shall see, it was a kind of hubris that inspired many of those who took part in the so-called scientific revolution of the seventeenth century, with its widespread search for fundamental laws of nature that could be valid everywhere, and to develop methods of investigation that would lead to a new enlightenment for humankind. It was also a kind of hubris that inspired the so-called industrial revolution of the late eighteenth century, when machines were infused into material production, and, in the process, destroyed ways of life and forms of social organization in the name of innovation and progress. In much the same way, it is a kind of hubris that leads contemporary governments to invest enormous amounts of money in the "life sciences" and in information and communications technologies while neglecting to fund properly many of the more prosaic, but humanly valuable, applications of scientific and technical ingenuity. Bill Gates and James Watson have become new cultural heroes, while the pursuit of adventure has been relocated to a virtual reality, far removed from the mundane problems that the vast majority of the world's population faces daily.

At the same time as this spirit of hubris is experiencing one of its periodic rejuvenations, the counternarratives, and the tragic tales of negative consequences and accentuating risks, are becoming more cataclysmic. In the horror stories of climate change and cloning, of environmental catastrophe and global terrorism, there is a growing sense of despair and despondency, a feeling that no one is any longer in control. The story of Frankenstein's monster, told by Mary Shelley in the midst of a first wave of industrialization, is being retold in the cultural critiques of genetic technology and global warming in books like Margaret Atwood's *Oryx and Crake* and films like *The Day after Tomorrow*. There is fear and foreboding, at the same time as there is fascination and technologically inspired fantasy. For most of us, our attitudes to technology and science fall somewhere in between the all too often polarized extremes. We tend to admire the ingenuity and appreciate the convenience, while, at the same time, we recognize the risks and uncertainties and try to learn to live with the dangers that surround us.

As such, we need new stories that can help us navigate through what the German sociologist Ulrich Beck (1986/1992) has labeled the "risk society," stories that can guide us in evaluating our technological options and assessing the quality of information that we are presented with. We need to fashion narratives that address the fundamental ambivalence that most of us feel toward technology and science, what the philosopher Raphael Sassower (1997) has characterized as "techno-scientific angst." We need stories that are neither purely romantic nor tragic, stories that address the ambiguities and explore the multiple lifeworlds of technoscience from a variety of different vantage points.

Our aim in this book is to provide a more balanced—and hopefully useful—view of the history of technology and science than is available in other surveys. The hegemonic story line of eternal evolution and progress has to be complemented with alternative stories communicating other messages. Technological and scientific innovations depend on entrepreneurs and competition, and the stories of James Watson and Bill Gates certainly have a place. But technology and science must also reflect other kinds of human values and relate to other lifeworlds if they are to fit into, and function within, the contexts in which they are put into operation. The stories told by Vandana Shiva and Mary Shelley also have a place in the total picture. For historians, the task is to provide a richer account of the past, to develop narratives that bring out our multifarious interactions with technology and science. There is a need for stories that can be shared, so that the benefits, like the costs, can be more equally distributed, and so that together we might be able to discuss how we can tame the wonders that wisdom and hubris have wrought. We need a history that can guide us in a world in which hubris is intensifying and hybrids are proliferating, a reflective history that can contribute to a cultural assessment of technoscience.

POINTS OF DEPARTURE

More than any other single contribution, it was the work by Lewis Mumford in 1934, *Technics and Civilization*, that initiated the kind of approach to technology and science that we are presenting. Written in an earlier period of polarization, when new artifacts—radio, airplanes, films, and automobiles—were giving inspiration to technocratic visions, and when economic depression was inspiring a range of reactionary and totalitarian responses, Mumford's book was one of the first efforts to try to capture the variety and complexity of sociotechnological transformations. Mumford tried to show the ways in which different beliefs and conceptions had combined to form a kind of technological mind-set, an instrumental form of rationality and behavior. He pointed to specific contextual factors—medieval monasteries, the invention of printing, the Protestant Reformation, mercantile capitalism—that had provided cultural conditions for what he termed the "ascendancy of the machine." Mumford also sketched the contours of a cultural assessment of technology, analyzing both the costs and the benefits in a long historical perspective and the forms of accommodation and adaptation that had emerged. While moving pictures, the radio, the airplane, and the automobile expanded human possibilities and enriched the experiences of life, they also posed threats to long-held values, to traditional patterns of behavior, and to the natural landscape and nonhuman beings. Both the threats and the opportunities, Mumford contended, needed to be taken into account in assessing technological change.

Mumford's book was complemented in the 1940s by the important study by the architectural historian Sigfried Giedion, *Mechanization Takes Command* (1948). Whereas Mumford had operated primarily on a "macro" level of generality with broad, all-encompassing frameworks of interpretation, Giedion focused his attention on particular material artifacts—the bathtub, the toothbrush, the stove, the electric lamp. He tried to show how the uses and meanings of particular technical artifacts had evolved simultaneously, that the economic development of technology was inseparable from the ways in which they were appropriated or domesticated into everyday life. At about the same time, the German sociologist Norbert Elias wrote his work *The Civilizing Process* (1939/1978), in which he disclosed how particular instruments had taken on meaning and contributed to the making of civilization in general and civilized human beings in particular. Using a terminology derived from the sociologist Max Weber, Elias explored the social values and norms, the forms of behavior and rationality, and the patterns of cultural adaptation that had been at work in early modern Europe.

As the history of technology and science was institutionalized in the postwar era, these formative, ambitious works tended to be supplanted, and eventually replaced, by more specialized studies, and the broader questions they had raised all but disappeared in the general enthusiasm over the new science-based products of the postwar era. Criticism tended to be marginalized, and the reflective role that people like Lewis Mumford had tried to play in society also was affected, as it became more difficult to pursue intellectual interests outside of the formal settings of academic life. Largely because of the role they had played in the war effort, scientists were given new social status and political responsibility in the period following the Second World War, and the study of the history of technology and science tended to become congratulatory, telling tales of triumph and success, rather than depicting the complicated and ambivalent processes of cultural and social appropriation.

Cultural approaches to technology and science tended to develop separately in the different historical subfields, and, in this book, we try to bring some of them together in an effort to provide a comprehensive account. In literary history, Leo Marx, for instance, sought to delineate a particular genre of "pastoralism" that had characterized the way in which key American writers and artists had represented technology in their works (Marx 1964). In recent years, many other literary and intellectual historians have focused on traditions of ideas, or discursive frameworks, as shaping influences for the development of technology. In medieval history, Lynn White investigated the longer-term historical roots of modern technology in a series of pioneering studies. The supernatural, and thus nonnatural, emphasis of Christian theology, and the artificial, and thus nonhuman, character of monastic life, provided the "cultural climate" for the emergence of technology in the Middle Ages (White 1978). Meanwhile, in the history of science and ideas, the modernist, or progressive, story line came to be challenged, in the 1960s and 1970s, by the writings of Frances Yates and others on the magical and mystical basis of modern science (Yates 1964, 1972).

Many early "scientists" were shown to be preeminently hybrid characters, combining new methods of investigation and new concepts and theories with older discursive frameworks, customs, and practices. Giordano Bruno, Johannes Kepler, and even the great Isaac Newton himself were much more complicated figures than had been previously realized. It was shown that they had pursued their scientific research, and carried out their scientific revolution, as part of a highly religious quest for revelation.

It was the enormously influential book *The Structure of Scientific Revolutions*, by Thomas Kuhn, that perhaps did most to challenge the heroic or congratulatory story line in the history of science. Kuhn argued that a sociological perspective was essential for understanding the development of science. Scientific ideas did not emerge in isolation from the broader society, but the influence of society on scientific development was not direct. Between the ideas of the scientists and the world outside there were mediating devices, discursive frameworks that had been essential in the period of the scientific revolution, as well as in many later periods of history. Kuhn called them "paradigms," by which he primarily meant the epochal achievements that served as models, or exemplars, for other scientists to follow. They were a kind of structure that served to organize scientific work, providing institutional identity and form, but also structuring reality into distinct and specialized frameworks of understanding. In responding to his critics, he later developed the notion of the "disciplinary matrix" to characterize what he had meant by the notion of paradigm: a set of methodological precepts and practical routines by which scientists were socialized into their disciplinary life-worlds (Kuhn 1970).

Whereas Kuhn by and large remained within an internalist tradition—focusing more or less exclusive attention on scientists themselves—the writings of British social historians, such as Christopher Hill, E. P. Thompson, and Eric Hobsbawm, provided very different sources of inspiration for the history of technology and science. Hill was one of several historians who had begun to complicate the dominant account of the scientific revolution, by investigating the human and social connections between the early scientists and broader political and economic processes (Hill 1965). Thompson and Hobsbawm brought into the understanding of the industrial revolution social and cultural factors that were often neglected. The stories that they told in their influential works were of resistance and rebellion on the part of those who had been affected by the changes taking place in British society. In their focus on the making of a working class (Thompson 1963) and the Luddite machine-stormers of the 1810s (Hobsbawm 1964), they were pioneers in the writing of history from below, from the losers' point of view. They brought the previously unheralded victims of technological change into the center of their narratives.

On a more theoretical level, the writings of the British literary historian Raymond Williams helped inspire a more ambitious and interdisciplinary approach to "cultural studies" by which technology and science have come to be examined in relation to patterns of behavior and networks of interaction, or what Williams termed "structures of feeling" and emergent "cultural formations" (Williams 1977). His own studies of communications technologies, in particular television, emphasized their uses rather than their production, showing the ways in which those uses were culturally shaped, and how television programming differed dramatically in the United States and England (Williams 1974). Williams also disclosed how our vocabulary—or what he called our "keywords"—had been constructed on the basis of particular historical contingencies; concepts had found their appropriate connotations over time, in contentions over usage and application and meaning (Williams 1976).

Even more influential in encouraging new approaches to the history of technology and science have been the works of Michel Foucault, who wrote specifically about the history of science, but also about some of the key institutions of appropriation—the hospital and the prison—while exploring, in both cases, the deep-seated "archeologies" of knowledge that lay concealed and underexposed in the dominant historical accounts (Foucault 1966/1970, 1975/1977). For Foucault and his numerous followers, it is not so much technology and science that is at the center of attention, but the discourses of power and knowledge that are constructed by and, in turn, serve to reconstruct the theories and concepts that inform both science and everyday life. Foucault's emphasis on power relations and on the use of disciplines and routines to exert social control has since come to be developed further by feminist historians, such as Evelyn Fox Keller (1985), and postcolonial historians, such as Edward Said (1993).

PROCESSES OF CULTURAL APPROPRIATION

The cultural turn in the social sciences and humanities during the past two decades, in which the works of Williams and Foucault have been major contributors, has influenced the history of technology and science in various ways. New questions have been asked and new research agendas have been introduced, alternative areas or social sites have been opened up for investigation, and neglected social groups have been brought out of the darkness of history. The history of technology and science had previously primarily been about inventors, engineers, and scientists, and research and development (R&D) activities taking place at public institutions and in private companies. Such design and production-oriented studies have mostly examined the cognitive and social conditions for new inventions and discoveries, and investigated how these have been turned into innovations and products. By comparison, the "demand" side was given only cursory attention, and, if investigated at all, it was largely in economic terms. Although not considered unimportant in principle, users and consumers tended to play the second fiddle in the historiography of technology and science.

The cultural shift in the history of technology and science can also be seen to reflect a new openness toward anthropological perspectives and ethnographic methods among historians more generally. This openness is most obvious in the history of the experimental sciences, where ethnographically inspired laboratory studies entered the field after the publication of Bruno Latour and Steve Woolgar's book *Laboratory Life* in 1979. At about the same time, historically minded anthropologists began to leave their exclusive focus on "pre-modern" societies and develop an interest in industrial culture. Pioneering in this regard was Anthony Wallace's prize-winning community study *Rockdale* (1978), which described changing living conditions in an industrializing town on the east coast of the United States.

Another important work was the study of the history of household technology *More Work for Mother* (1983) by the American historian Ruth Schwartz Cowan. Arguing that the introduction of new household technology had not necessarily eased the burden of work put on housewives, Cowan attacked well-established notions about the progressive character of mechanization. Although certain tasks had become easier to carry out by means of machinery, other tasks were added to the housewife's workload. Because washing machines made it possible to wash larger amounts of clothes, family members changed clothes much more often than they had previously. Although household appliances enabled the housewife to cook more effectively, the time spent in the kitchen was to a large extent compensated by spending more time in traffic jams on the way to the local mall or the cheapest supermarket.

Perhaps more than any other single contribution, it was Bruno Latour's *Science in Action* (1987) that brought out the decisive importance of social factors in the establishment of scientific facts. This book was based on two central premises of what can be called postpositivist philosophy of science: first, all observations of nature are to some extent dependent on a conceptual and cognitive framework; second, no scientific theory simply "reflects" natural phenomena, but always includes elements of interpretation and representation. In negating nature as the ultimate gatekeeper, Latour went further, however. Nature does not decide what is true or false; scientists do. Although a scientist has to refer to nature when amassing support for a certain theory, he or she in the last instance always has to convince other scientists about the validity of the theory. If he or she fails in constructing a network of supportive colleagues, the theory will not be accepted and probably fall into oblivion. Social status and material resources—for instance, in the form of a professorship at a reputable university or a new, expensive apparatus—can play important roles in the fight for acceptance.

While a range of cultural, or alternative, approaches have emerged in recent years in the history of technology and science, as well as in history proper, many of the new narratives that have been fashioned have been anything but grand. They have tended to be local, particular, and specific, and, as such, they have provided few opportunities for those who would like to make generalizations or try to apply them to other contexts. The cultural critics, and the victims for whom they sometimes speak, have too often been content with deconstruction and critique. Our ambition in this book is not merely to tell other stories, but to begin to develop alternative story lines that might help to create a better future. If, as Bruno Latour (1993) contended, we have never been modern, that modernity has been a justificatory tale, then it is not enough to be detached and ironic. We need to stress that modernity and the vast range of nonmodernities have coexisted and indeed must coexist, unless one group of human beings is to dominate the rest. But there also needs to be a common ground, where tales about technology and science can be debated and discussed.

Technology and science have marched through the centuries with a Janus face, smiling on some and frowning on others. What have customarily been seen as historically progressive achievements have invariably had their victims. While there can be no doubt that science and technology have helped make life more exciting, comfortable, and convenient for many people, there can equally be no doubt that science and technology have led to a variety of highly undesirable "side effects." If the history of technology and science is to be usable in the present, the stories that are recounted need to be more reflective, more critical, and more comprehensive.

In this book, we present the development of technology and science as multifaceted processes of cultural appropriation. What interests us are the ways in which technology and science have been given human meaning during the past five hundred years. We will discuss these appropriation processes both at a "discursive" level, where intellectual debates about technology and science have been conducted (Hård and Jamison 1998), as well as at a "practical" level of lifeworlds and micro contexts, where different people make use of technological artifacts and scientific facts in their own particular ways. While related to each other, these processes require different sorts of investigative methods for their understanding, and the stories about them are seldom connected. By bringing together the macro-level orientation on discourses and mentalities with the micro-level analyses of specific sites, or places, of appropriation, we hope to improve our collective competence in assessing and managing technological and scientific change.

In between, there is a level of institutions: the various rules and regulations, and the movements and organizations that connect the broader intellectual processes to the more mundane and practical processes of everyday life. Here we find what economists term systems of innovation and diffusion, that is, the companies, research laboratories, and state support agencies, as well as all the forms of governance and decision making that make up the realm of science and technology policy. This intermediary level is the "space" in our societies where broader cultural projects and visions, often starting as movements, tend to be linked to the particular practical spheres in which the projects are eventually implemented. By allocating funds to certain projects rather than others, by making various social innovations and creating new institutions, by producing and disseminating certain facts and artifacts rather than others, decisions are made about how technology and science ought to be used. These processes do not occur in isolation, nor do they occur all at once; as we shall see, they overlap and interact with one another in complicated ways (see Table 1).

TABLE 1. The Cultural Appropriation of Technology and Science

Analytical Level	Phenomenal Level		
	Facts and Artifacts	Systems	Structures
Discursive	**Semantics**	**Grammar**	**Language**
Assimilation	*Familiarization*	*Disciplining*	*Transformation*
Organizational	**Movements**	**Institutions**	**Rules, laws**
Mediation	*Dissemination*	*Incorporation*	*Professionalization*
Practical	**Behavior, identity**	**Routines**	**Procedures, customs**
Use	*Internalization*	*Domestication*	*Habituation*

Mechanization, electrification, automobilization, computerization, and genetic engineering, to take some typical examples, affect both the ways we talk and think, as well as the ways in which we carry out our practical activities. Our language takes on new words and alters old ones, as technical artifacts and scientific concepts are adapted to our discursive codes and frameworks. In our day, "information processing" and the "genetic code" have become central metaphors for all sorts of phenomena, and new words and concepts have entered our vocabularies while familiar ones have taken on new meanings. Our societies develop new forms of organization and interaction, of regulation and governance, as technologies impose their systemic and infrastructural requirements on the social order, or, more accurately, put new opportunities at our disposal. Technology and science do not determine cultural developments by imposing their logic upon us; rather they dispose our cultures to take on new possibilities. In the contemporary world, because of scientific and technological achievements in understanding genetics and genetic engineering, we now have genetic counselors and the scientific field of genomics, biotechnology companies, and genetic forensic experts. And in our everyday lifeworlds, we take on new identities and must learn new skills, as our practices are altered by technological and scientific innovations. We have to learn what is in the food we eat, and we have to reflect on the choices we make in the supermarket. Cultural appropriation is thus a variegated and highly differentiated set of reformation processes, and they are seldom discussed in an integrated manner.

While technology and science lead to changes in our ways of life, through processes of cultural appropriation we transform the facts and artifacts that we are continually confronted with. Our interpretations—the meanings we give to the products of technology and science—serve to transform them in fundamental ways, at the discursive, institutional, and political levels. In our day, information machines have been transformed into personal computers and cyberspace, as once horseless carriages were transformed into automobiles. We might hope in the future that genetic engineering can become transformed into green, environmentally friendly products. As we shall see in the chapters that follow, the reformation of culture and the transformation of technology and science have gone hand in hand, and our historical accounts of those processes should be told accordingly.

Part 1
The Roots of Technoscience

1

THE SCIENTIFIC REFORMATION IN EARLY MODERN EUROPE

It is idle to expect any great advancement in science from the superinducing and engrafting of new things upon old. We must begin anew from the very foundations, unless we would revolve forever in a circle with mean and contemptible progress.

—**Francis Bacon, (1620/1960, 46)**

THE IMPORTANCE OF THE DIGGERS

During the winter of 1648 to 1649, a failed tailor named Gerrard Winstanley had a vision. He was living in Cobham in southern England, trying to make ends meet, and in the spring he joined a small community on nearby St. George's Hill that had decided to take matters into their own hands and farm the land together. They were one of many such groups at the time, when England was in the throes of civil war, that combined a communalist set of beliefs, which they had largely concocted on their own, with an interest in performing experiments. The Diggers, as they called themselves, practiced collective forms of agriculture and animal husbandry as an intrinsic part of their particular version of Protestant religion. They were looking, as were so many others in those days, for new ways to attain revelation and find spiritual fulfillment in a chaotic world (Hill 1975).

Like many of the other "true levelers" who were active in England in the civil wars of the Interregnum period, when the king had been dethroned, the Diggers were egalitarians. But what was special about them was that their notion of equality extended to the realm of knowledge making. They took active part in the "great instauration"—the promulgation of useful knowledge—that had been proclaimed by Francis Bacon in the 1610s and that formed a central element in the activities of many of the participants in the civil war. When Winstanley published his protocommunist creed *The Law of Freedom in a Platform* in 1652, he articulated a visionary program for an egalitarian way of life, which included some rather far-reaching ideas about education and research. Knowledge making and technical development were to be carried out collectively, without any thought of profit or personal gain. The "Government under Kings," Winstanley wrote, had been based on "Traditional Knowledge and Learning" by which "both Clergy and Lawyer … by their cunning insinuations live meerly upon the labor of other men." In the "Common-wealth" to come, it was different:

> Therefore to prevent idleness and the danger of Machivilian cheats, it is profitable for the Common-wealth, that children be trained up in Trades and some bodily employment, as well as in learning Languages, or the Histories of former ages. … And in the manageing of any Trade, let no young wit be crushed in his invention, for if any man desire to make a new tryall of his skil in any Trade or Science, the Overseers shall not hinder him, but incourage him therein; that so the Spirit of knowledge may have his full growth in man, to find out the secret in every Art. (Winstanley 1652/1973, 126–27)

The Diggers and their social and political experiment lasted less than two years, and the broader experiment with democracy that they were a small part of lasted just a few years longer. By 1660, the king was back on the throne, radical groups and religious sects such as the Diggers had been outlawed, and Winstanley more or less disappeared from history. The Diggers, however, and some of the other groups like them who populated the country between 1640 and 1660 have lived on in the collective memory. In the ensuing centuries, Winstanley's text has had a significant influence in helping to fashion the counternarratives, or story lines of resistance and environmentalism. Even though the Diggers' experiment was unable to be sustained, and their activities were soon overwhelmed by other events, their story deserves to be included as one element in the reformation of science and technology in the sixteenth and seventeenth centuries.

The Diggers can be considered to be the victims of progress, and yet, without them, the very idea of science-based progress, and the grand narrative of modernity that has been derived from it, loses much of its meaning. In this narrative, groups such as the Diggers have served as antiheroes, people who might have had some good ideas, but who were ultimately unsuccessful and marginal to the main plots and stories of the so-called scientific revolution. Without the Diggers and the many other enthusiasts like them—the people, we might say, who experimented with their lives—it is hard for us to make sense of those who later established scientific experimentation as a legitimate, socially acceptable activity. The founding fathers of modern science, such as Robert Boyle and Isaac Newton, did not come from nowhere; rather they were part of a process by which political and social movements were transformed into an academic culture. Without the people's having planted the seeds and prepared the ground, it is difficult for us to imagine the culture emerging with its institutions and its practices, its discourses and its theories. Without the Diggers and the other groups like them, the historical account of the making of modern science and technology is one-sided and distorted.

In the process that we call the scientific reformation, there was an explicit narrowing of focus, a reduction of ends to means in the consolidation of an instrumental, or technological, rationality. There was a gradual sharpening of tools, both conceptual and practical, with the formation of concepts, methods, and instruments, and there was a formalization of the organizational activities, which came with the establishment of key institutions in the 1660s, such as the Royal Society and the French Academy of Sciences. In this world, the Diggers and others like them were unable to find a place. The social contract that was established in the seventeenth century, between the new-fangled "experimental philosophers" and their royal patrons, systematically excluded many of those who had previously wanted to be included in the reform of philosophy—women, in particular. To become acceptable to those in power, the scientists needed to renounce many of their earlier political ambitions. In the words of Lewis Mumford, "Under the new ethic that developed, science's only form of social responsibility was to science itself: to observe its canons of proof, to preserve its integrity and autonomy, and to constantly expand its domain" (Mumford 1970, 115).

MODERN SCIENCE IN FORMATION

In the seventeenth century, something fundamental happened in terms of how human beings went about enlightening themselves: there was a series of events that have come to be called a "scientific revolution." There was the simultaneous creation of new theories, methods, instruments, and organizations for the making of knowledge. And even though there is today a good deal more skepticism about the revolutionary character of what took place than there used to be, there is still general agreement that much of what we today call technology and science was significantly reformed at that time. Steven Shapin, for example, claimed that "there was no such thing as a scientific revolution," and yet he wrote a book about it, not perhaps because it was all that revolutionary but because it was formative for the present. Indeed, the scientific revolution was not considered all that revolutionary while it was happening; it was in retrospect that scientists began to refer to the events in the seventeenth century as something fundamental in relation to the making of modernity. In Shapin's words, "The very idea of the Scientific Revolution ... is at least partly an expression of 'our' interest in our ancestors, where 'we' are late twentieth-century scientists and those for whom what they believe counts as truth about the natural world" (Shapin 1996, 6).

In this chapter, we consider these events as an overlapping cluster of cultural appropriation processes. Modern science took shape—discursively, institutionally, and practically—through a complicated series of negotiations and contentions. Science provided ideas and techniques that could be used in society, but, in exchange for this useful knowledge, scientists, or natural philosophers as they called themselves at the time, demanded and eventually achieved status, legitimacy, and a degree of independence and autonomy: what has come to be called academic freedom. In some countries scientists established this social contract by making alliances and gaining support from absolute monarchs, whereas in other places scientists took part in the struggles of emerging capitalist elites. The reason that it is important for us to go back to the seventeenth century is that the links that were established between science and society in theoretical and practical terms were formative for the ensuing centuries. We might say that most of the meanings and many of the functions that science has in the contemporary world were constituted at that time.

On one hand, there was the emergence of a mechanical philosophy. This is what the dominant narratives have traditionally focused on: the story line of mechanization. From the ideas about mechanical motion articulated by Galileo Galilei in the early seventeenth century to Isaac

Newton's presentation of the theory of universal gravitation in his *Principia* of 1687 (in English, *The Mathematical Principles of Natural Philosophy*), nature came to be conceptualized in mechanical terms, with its operations described as mechanisms and its overall character likened to a machine. The great men of the seventeenth century had, with their original concepts of mechanical motion, gravitation, and infinite space and their analytical methods of calculus and differentiation, opened the closed world of the Middle Ages to systematic investigation. They had developed a new mathematics and a new cosmology that made it possible to analyze what had previously been separate spheres of reality and create what the Dutch historian E. J. Dijksterhuis called the "mechanization of the modern world picture."

The creation of the mechanical philosophy is central to what might be termed the foundational narrative of modern science, and of modernity. In the words of Herbert Butterfield, whose book *The Origins of Modern Science* played an important role in popularizing the story, "Since the rise of Christianity, there is no landmark in history that is worthy to be compared with this" (Butterfield 1965, 202). And even though there was more continuity with the physics of the Middle Ages than Butterfield's words suggest, the influence of mechanical philosophy on broader social and political discourses, as well as on language more generally, can hardly be exaggerated. We still talk about political "forces," social "pressure," and personal "attractions" as if human relations could be meaningfully characterized in the language of mechanics.

Central to the mechanical philosophy was the ambition to do away with all kinds of animist and vitalist theories, to take the life out of nonhuman nature. This is the other side of the coin, the tragic story that Carolyn Merchant presented in her influential book of 1980, *The Death of Nature*. Writing from an "ecofeminist" perspective, Merchant showed how the revolutionaries of the seventeenth century had turned the natural realm into an artificial world and a spiritual universe into one dominated by machinery. What had previously been conceptualized in terms of life forces was reduced to things that could be measured and that had no will or feelings of their own. The modern science that resulted from this revolution, according to Merchant, views nature as objects or resources that can be infinitely molded, or manipulated, for human purposes:

From the spectrum of Renaissance organicist philosophies ... the mechanists would appropriate and transform presuppositions at the conservative or hierarchical end while denouncing those associated with the more radical religious and political perspectives. The rejection and removal of organic and animistic features and the substitution of mechanically describable components would become the most significant and far-reaching effect of the Scientific Revolution. (Merchant 1980, 125)

At least as important as the mechanical philosophy in the forming of modern science was the growing influence of a particular way of thinking about knowledge and its functions in society, what Francis Bacon characterized as "useful knowledge." This was more of a social than a physical philosophy, and it was an important element in developing a language, or vocabulary, to talk about the various uses of scientific knowledge. For Bacon, the important thing was to separate the kind of knowledge that could actually be applied for the "benefit of man" from what he termed "idle" speculation and belief. All the old categories of thought had to be reconstituted, and a clear break had to be made with old prejudices, the "idols of the past," if knowledge were to be useful (Bacon 1620/1960).

The idea of considering knowledge making as something instrumental, or as means to achieve certain ends rather than as an end in itself, is an idea that fits well with an economic system based on commerce, in which, as Marx and Engels put it in their *Communist Manifesto* of 1848, all aspects of life were thrown into the "icy waters of calculation." To be able to be exchangeable in a commercial marketplace, material reality needed to be decomposed into its component parts and turned into commodities. Even more crucially, those parts needed to be evaluated and analyzed in quantitative terms: in short, reality had to be made measurable (Crosby 1997). Those activities that had an instrumental orientation, and could lend themselves to measurement and quantification, were given priority over those that were merely interesting or what we today might call qualitative.

In the seventeenth century, hubris had not yet achieved hegemony; there was still a kind of modesty about the scientific quest. A sense of wonder was combined with the experimental spirit among many of the leading practitioners of natural philosophy (Daston and Park 1998). Indeed, the methods of science were created, at least in part, to explain the fascinating oddities, or marvels, of the natural world. The early scientists collected strange things in a kind of religiously inspired appreciation of the awesomeness of God's creations. Gradually, however, the wondrous and the instrumental parted company as science grew into a professional and socially acceptable activity, and the wonders of nature were relegated to a popular realm of magic and superstition. In separating science from pseudoscience, the wondrous became, as it were, unexplainable once again, as science focused its energies on all that could be explained by its peculiarly rigorous methods. The resulting form of knowledge making has, of course, been extremely successful in relation to technological development, by limiting attention and interest to those aspects of reality that could be put to use, for either productive or, all too often, destructive purposes. As Max Weber put it in his famous lecture "Science as a Vocation," delivered toward the end of the First World War, science "leaves quite aside, or assumes for its purposes, whether we should and do wish to master life technically and whether it ultimately makes sense to do so" (Weber 1919/1958, 144).

For many historians of the scientific revolution, it is what might be termed the methodological plot, where René Descartes in France and Robert Boyle in England are given most attention, that is considered most significant. Indeed, Descartes's *Discourse on Method*—with its emphasis on mathematical logic and the famous reduction of ontology to epistemology, of being to knowing ("I think, therefore I am")—has for many historians come to be seen as the central feature of the entire revolutionary process. Unlike the methods of the Diggers, who were personally engaged in their experiments, the emerging scientific method constituted a fundamental separation between the knowing subject and the natural objects that came under investigation.

For all their differences, Bacon and Descartes, Newton and Boyle, and most of the other founding fathers (for there were no mothers of modern science) shared a common program. In their different ways, with their different contributions, they rewrote the book of nature by combining terminologies that had been part of separate discourses in the medieval world. The rigorous logical methods of argumentation that had been developed by the Scholastics were reformulated in such a way that they could be subjected to experimental testing. A new vocabulary was constructed that was absolutely essential for modern technology and science to find a place in society. It was a break with the classical ideals of knowledge, which were based on balance, harmony, and beauty. For the science and technology that was reformed in the seventeenth century, the idea of progress was to be the most important product of all.

The scientific revolution also had an important institutional side to it. To begin with, formally constituted academies of science were created and given a range of legal obligations and responsibilities within the nation-states that were beginning to emerge across Europe (Frängsmyr 1990). They proved to be exemplary institutions, in terms of their permanence and in what might be called their legitimation function. In their capacity to reform and expand their activities in the ensuing centuries, they also came to exemplify a general feature of cultural appropriation, which we can think of as incorporation. It was within the academies of science that the social roles, or social functions, of science came to be normalized and regulated. The academic culture, with the norms that Robert Merton characterized in the 1940s as "community, universalism, disinterestedness and organized skepticism," has provided an institutional home, or central operational site, for the growth of science ever since.

On the institutional level, there were other reforms, which took place in the course of the seventeenth and eighteenth centuries. What came to be considered the disciplines of scientific investigation gradually worked their way into university curricula, often in the wake of major conflicts between so-called ancients and moderns. In many countries, where the emerging nation-states had economic ambitions, new sites, or locations, for technological and scientific research were established: laboratories for mechanical and chemical experiments, and astronomical observatories and botanical gardens (Porter and Teich 1992). The scientific revolution was not merely a matter of new ideas and theories of nature; it was, even more significant, a process of social construction, of building a range of institutions and organizations, programs, and projects (Jardine 1999). In terms of cultural appropriation, what was involved was primarily a narrowing of what had previously been a broad religious and social movement into more professional and circumscribed institutional settings.

Finally, there developed a range of new personal practices and identities. What was often at work was the combination of activities that had previously been separated from one another: scholarship was combined with craftsmanship, philosophy was combined with experimentation. Hybrid, or synthetic, identities emerged in the academies, clubs, and salons of Paris and London, where broader and more general ambitions of technological rationality were internalized into new forms of practice. There were also reforms in the communication of results, most visibly perhaps in the printed proceedings of the academies but also within popular literature, as satirists and publicists—from Mandeville to Defoe—sprang up to disseminate the message of science-based enlightenment. Perhaps most important, the scientific reformation involved the construction of practices and identities related to the application of science, putting the theories to use. As Dava Sobel so colorfully described in the case of John Harrison's lifelong effort to make a clock that could tell accurate time at sea, the use

TABLE 2. The Scientific Reformation as Cultural Appropriation

At the Discursive Level
A semantics of utility
A grammar of mathematics
A language of mechanics
At the Institutional Level
Media of communication
Academic organizations
Professional norms and quality standards
At the Level of Practice
Hybrid identities
Routines for technical applications
Procedures for experimentation

of science was culturally and economically important (Sobel 1996). In short, there was a differentiated but interconnected series of processes that affected and influenced each other in complicated ways (see Table 2).

BEFORE THE REFORMATION

To appreciate what took place in the sixteenth and seventeenth centuries, we briefly recount some of the underlying factors that contributed to these multifarious appropriation processes. Around 1350, Europe represented merely one of several civilizations that existed in the world, and it was by no means the most dominant, in terms of cultural achievement, material well-being, or technical ingenuity. Many of the techniques that were used in Europe—in agriculture, energy, and everyday life—had come from elsewhere, and many ideas about nature that were to be found in Europe drew on intellectual traditions from other parts of the world, specifically from China, India, and the Middle East. The windmill had come into Europe from Persia, the compass had come from China, many fundamental mathematical concepts had come from India, and the idea of the university, an organized social space for learning, had been an Arabic innovation.

In Europe, as in most other parts of the world, the production of facts was separated from the production of artifacts. Scholarly traditions had developed in and around the medieval universities, and technical traditions had developed in and around the guilds of the skilled craftsmen. What was somewhat unique for Europe, however, was the number of conditions that proved important for their eventual combination during the scientific reformation process. Economic historians have stressed the climatic and geographical conditions and the challenges that a temperate environment meant for human survival, as well as the specific technological impulses that were fostered in the economic realm by such conditions (Mokyr 1990; Landes 1998). Others have emphasized the cultural climate, underlying metaphysical assumptions, and religious beliefs, as well as particular subcultures, such as those of the monasteries that encouraged particular combinations of scholarship and craftsmanship.

As in most historical processes, it was certainly neither exclusively the one nor the other that brought on the changes of the seventeenth century: there was, we might say, hubris and hybrids involved in the making of modern science. The economic or material factors were mixed with the cultural in intricate patterns of mutual interaction (Pacey 1974). In the centuries that followed the fall of Rome, the technological interest had been kept alive in Christian theology. And that conservation work, and eventually innovative activity, was, in large measure, carried out by the various denominations of Christian monks, who created their own artificial places, their orders, where they could honor their God with work and devotion. It was the waves of monasticism that provided the crucial cultural contexts for the eventual combination of scientific and technical knowledge and, more generally, of thinking and doing, knowing and acting. The monks' interest in discipline and order contributed directly to the mechanization of time and to the refinement of the mechanical clock; their devotion to manual labor contributed to the rationalization of agriculture and manufacture; their belief in faith and salvation led to the application of technics to philosophy, and even to art and music (Ovitt 1986). The medieval monasteries, we might say, provided key sites for hybridization.

It was primarily the monks of medieval Europe who devised agricultural and industrial methods, formulated religious theories and devotional practices, and built social organizations, in which technical artifacts were of central importance. To a large extent, it was their religiously inspired vision of a man-made world that eventually became dominant and universal. The different orders contributed somewhat different emphases. The Benedictines were the great promoters of manual labor, the Franciscans stressed gardening and animal husbandry, whereas the Cistercians emphasized mechanization, technical improvement, and manufacturing. But what they shared was a Christian, or supernatural worldview, a discursive framework that attributed to the artificial and artifactual a crucial mediating role in the activities of human beings.

The monks were artificial, in that they refused to take part in the most important natural function of the species; namely, reproduction. As David Noble (1992) put it, they lived in a "world without women," which has left its mark on science and technology ever since. As such, they can perhaps be thought of as the people who had the first significant hybrid identities. At least, the monks were one of the more influential groups of human beings whose identities were formed in direct interaction with nonhuman things of their own creation.

If the emerging European civilization that began to reach out and conquer the world after 1400 had a characteristic feature, it was the relative importance that had long been given to the continuous improvement of material artifacts (Ovitt 1987). Over several centuries, the technical interest had come to be put into practice and provide the material basis for the ensuing expansion. First, from about 600 to 900, there was a technologically induced transformation in agriculture, by which a system of innovations, including a new type of plough, crop rotation, and the use of the horse as a draught animal, had made for larger harvests and allowed for a revival of urban life (White 1962). There had also come a military revolution, with the use of cavalry, improvements in guns and cannons, and the social innovation of professional armies (W. McNeill 1982). Inspired by the Crusades— which, in its military aspect, was an especially important and all too typical kind of technological dialogue across civilizations—the stirrup was adopted, and more sophisticated forms of warfare on horseback contributed to the making of a feudal social order. Toward the end of the period, there had been a series of developments in relation to trade and shipping, as the zeal of Christian missionaries mixed with economic motives to fuel an "age of exploration" based, to a large extent, on improved ships, the new cosmological ideas, and a range of instruments for measuring time, space, and geographical position (Pacey 1990).

More generally, there was a kind of cultural dynamism afoot, mixing militarism with mercantilism, curiosity with enterprise, expansiveness with acquisitiveness, and, perhaps most significant in the long run, natural observation with religious devotion. In the second half of the fifteenth century, among the so-called artist-engineers of the Renaissance, that mixture of motivations served to inspire some of the greatest achievements that human beings have ever accomplished. They drafted and designed machines and weapons, experimented with medicines and materials, and applied the ideas of optics and mechanics to practical pursuits, in addition to producing the innumerable drawings and paintings and sculptures for which they are perhaps best known. Their pursuit of knowledge knew no bounds, and they were not concerned with boundaries or compartments. Science, art, philosophy, engineering, architecture, music, and even spiritual and mystical teachings were all drawn on and recombined as artist-engineers sought to infuse a new level of ambition and energy into Western civilization. It was a kind of hubris, in the sense that Leonardo, Michelangelo, Alberti, Brunelleschi, Dürer, and all the others were constantly trying to transcend their human limitations; there was more than a little influence from magic and from mysticism, but what was new was the level of craftsmanship and what might be called the innovative sensibility, or scientific spirit (Zilsel 1942). The Renaissance artist-engineers were never satisfied unless they could achieve something that had not been done before.

The artist-engineers developed, from our perspective, a new sort of hybrid identity, recombining, in their very persons, what had previously been, in Europe as elsewhere, separate lifeworlds, the learned world of the scholar and the practical world of the craftsman (Zilsel 2000). In Europe, the artist-engineers were able to bring those worlds together, not only because of their own personal talents and skills, which were substantial. More important, there were a range of new opportunities, especially in the highly competitive Italian city-states, which made it possible for their skills and interests to be combined in fruitful new forms (Grafton 2000). For one thing, patrons were willing to pay for their services, as trade brought a surplus that some, such as the Medici family, decided to use for projects of civic refinement and cultural creation (Jardine 1996). There were thus economic opportunities that made it possible for creative individuals to carve out new identities and ways of working. In redesigning their cities and glorifying their rule, the Renaissance patrons opened spaces in European societies, which were independent of the traditional institutions of feudal Christianity, for the enactment of new forms of artistic and scientific endeavor.

While those religious institutions had, in many respects, served to constrain creativity, they nonetheless had preserved the rich cultural legacies that had lain dormant for many centuries. And even more crucially, they provided some of the social spaces, or sites, within which the artist-engineers—and other Renaissance men—could innovate. In the monasteries and schools of the medieval Church, the resources of Greco-Roman antiquity and from the Islamic world had been translated back into Latin and commented on by generations of scholars. Because of the printing industry and, with it, an availability of books and accessibility of book learning, culture could be born again, communicated, and reinvigorated (Eisenstein 1983). Especially significant for innovations to happen, however, was the rise of a humanist sensibility, a freeing of the spirit from the dogmas and rituals of Christian theology (Mandrou 1973/1978). Man, or at least some men, could become once again the creator of his world rather than merely the believer in an all-powerful, superhuman Creator. The image of the magus, with an interest in magic and secretive knowledge, was a part of the humanist philosophy, or movement, as it made its way across Europe. And, as it spread, there came a renewal of that long lost sense of human creativity, which inspired new forms of artistic-scientific expression, from the utopian literary genre, invented by Thomas More, to the quest for realist representation in painting and sculpture.

In Europe, the relative weakness, and fragmentation, of political power made it possible for new social types to emerge. When the power of the Roman Church was directly challenged in the sixteenth century, it was essential that new sources of authority and new kinds of social identity be constructed. If political and religious authority were in need of reformation and overhaul, then innovation was also called for in the making of knowledge. What we today refer to as technoscience has its roots in that general movement of change and reform. And at its core was what might be termed a culture of hybridization.

In other parts of the world, the spheres of thought and action, scholarship and craftsmanship, and, for that matter, science and religion remained separated. The attempts to apply science to practical work were few and far between, and the barriers across society—in status, prestige, income, and class—were stronger and more or less insurmountable. Joseph Needham, who discussed these matters at length in his pioneering studies on Chinese science and technology, emphasized the difference in contextual locations between scholars and craftsmen in China and Europe. The scholars in China were primarily imperial bureaucrats—the so-called mandarins—with very different identities than the humanists who were beginning to emerge in Europe. The craftsmen, on the other hand, were constrained by the authoritarian and centralized state, as well as by the kinds of economic opportunities that were available in Chinese society. As a result, the possibilities for entrepreneurship were weak. And there was little incentive, and far less encouragement, for the scholars and craftsmen to meet, let alone combine in new social spaces and in new hybrid social types (Needham 1969, 1981).

Europe had other advantages, as well—not least economic, because of the interurban trade networks that developed in the Middle Ages

(Cipolla 1976). The autocratic and highly competitive character of European societies meant that there was greater room for initiative and enterprise than elsewhere. There was also a strict separation in Western Christianity between the human and nonhuman realms; with a supernatural God, Christians, Jews, and Muslims shared a narrative of creation that permitted intervention and technical exploitation. But the Christian story, particularly as interpreted by some of the founders of medieval monastic orders, went further, in making God into something of an engineer, and making technical improvement a kind of holy calling. For the artist-engineers and the humanist philosophers of the Renaissance, that devotion to manual work was given extra significance by being connected to certain indigenous beliefs in magic and prediction that had come to be cultivated in Europe following the black death and the other disasters of the fourteenth century (Thomas 1971).

However it is to be explained, it took two centuries before the new kind of knowledge making that the artist-engineers embodied began to find more stable and collective forms—in both theory and practice. New institutional arrangements and organizational settings, social roles and personal identities, learned discourses and academic philosophies, and facts and artifacts came to be constructed. What Jan Golinski termed "making natural knowledge"—the forging of disciplinary identities, the articulation of instrumental discourses, and the construction of experimental practices—was no easy or straightforward process (Golinski 1998). It was rather a series, or cluster, of interacting activities that were strongly influenced by the contexts in which they took place, nationally and locally.

FROM MOVEMENTS TO INSTITUTIONS

In his classic work from 1904 *The Protestant Ethic and the Spirit of Capitalism,* Max Weber suggested that the religious movements of the fifteenth and sixteenth centuries had released a new kind of human value system, or ethos, into Europe, which emphasized the importance of manual labor—and of technical improvements—in the expression of religious devotion. Like science, Protestantism represented, in Weber's famous phrase, an attempt to "disenchant the world," the recovery, or recognition, of humankind's natural surroundings out of the realms of mysticism, superstition, and supernatural faith. And as the Protestant ethic spread across Europe, working its way into different lifeworlds and ways of life, it stimulated more rational approaches to the investigation of nature: direct observation and experimental interaction, as well as new ideas about using natural materials for human purposes as part of capitalist enterprise (Hård 1994). There was the publication of a new technical literature that depicted the techniques of mining and metallurgy, of pumps and machines, and there were books, as well, that presented the procedures of various trades and skilled practices (Grafton and Blair 1990). In the sixteenth century, with printing and the journeys of exploration, there was a kind of all-encompassing opening up of the European culture to new experiences and ideas, out of which modern technology and science were eventually constituted and circumscribed.

It is possible to identify at least two rather different waves of appropriation in the making of modern science. The first wave was a clustering of social and intellectual movements, which were intimately connected to the Protestant reformation, and the second wave was the so-called revolution of the seventeenth century. In the historical literature, it was Frances Yates who did most to bring out the difference between the different waves (Yates 1964). By identifying some of the key transition figures and movements in the sixteenth and seventeenth centuries, she challenged the main view of the scientific revolution that had dominated the history of science. In the general enthusiasm over science that developed after the Second World War, many historians had looked back at the seventeenth century as the "moment at which the world was made modern; it was a Good Thing, and it happened sometime during the period from the late sixteenth to the early eighteenth century" (Shapin 1996, 1). The story line of modernity began with the great men of the seventeenth century, who had rewritten the laws of nature and provided the methods that scientists still use today for discovering truth. And while this grand narrative proved to be highly influential in the development of the history of science as an academic discipline, it seemed to neglect too much of what had actually happened in the early modern era.

When historians such as Yates wanted to write about people such as Giordano Bruno, for whom scientific ideas were inextricably linked to religious and political ideas, they needed a somewhat different story line to make sense of their materials. And so, a more complicated picture of the making of modern science began to emerge. "It may be illuminating," Yates wrote in 1964,

to view the scientific revolution as in two phases, the first phase consisting of an animistic universe operated by magic, the second phase of a mathematical universe operated by mechanics. An enquiry into both phases, and their interactions may be a more fruitful line of historical approach to the problems raised by the science of today than the line which concentrates only on the seventeenth-century triumph. (Yates 1964, 452)

Although the "Yates thesis," as it has come to be called, with its (over)emphasis on the roles that magic and mysticism played in the making of modern science, has since been questioned, there can be little doubt that many of the processes of appropriation that took place in the sixteenth century were quite different from those that occurred in the seventeenth century. And it can be useful, at least as a heuristic device, to think of them as different phases in relation to more general processes of cultural appropriation.

In the late fifteenth and early sixteenth centuries, even before Martin Luther nailed his theses on the church in Wittenberg, there was, among humanists and religious reformers, an identifiable social and political movement—*devotio moderno*—that represented a deep-seated challenge to traditional ways of thought in social and religious life (Mandrou 1973/1978). The British archbishop Thomas More, who coined the term *Utopia* and who battled with his king over the relations between church and state, and Erasmus of Rotterdam, who was among the first to develop forms of scholarship that broke with religious authority, are probably the most famous names from that movement. But throughout Europe, there were, in the period of the late Renaissance, a number of organized challenges to the old social and cognitive orders from the learned and the landless, the noble and the poor. The Reformation, of course, was a mass movement of *protest* against the Christian Church and its imperial authority (which is why the members of the movement came to be called Protestants). It was a broad social and cultural movement that articulated and practiced alternative, or oppositional, forms of religion, politics, and learning as part of its political struggles. And there were, in addition to the different Protestant denominations that emerged, also new Catholic groups, such as the Jesuits, who created new sites, or places, for combining study of the natural world with religious and social activities of various kinds (Jacob 1997).

One of the most important of these transition figures in the early sixteenth century was the chemist and medical doctor Philippus Aureolus Theophrastus Bombastus von Hohenheim, better known as Paracelsus, who combined a questioning of established religious and political authority with an interest in scientific observation, mathematics, mechanics, and technical improvements (Grell 1998). Paracelsus was the son of a physician in Zurich, and he combined a practical experience in mining and metallurgy with a university education, in

Switzerland and Italy. He served as a physician and university lecturer in Basel, but he was continually in conflict with the authorities and often forced to flee into the countryside. He traveled in the mining regions, where he worked as a doctor and compiled his works of chemical philosophy, reforming the spiritual and mystical teachings of the alchemical tradition on the basis of his own experiences. He was among the very first to teach at a European university in the vernacular, and he invited practical people—apothecaries, metallurgists, miners, craftsmen—to his lectures. His approach to medicine combined the spiritual and the practical, and the theories he developed represented a kind of protochemistry, as he sought to provide general principles for the observed activities of metallurgists and miners, doctors and alchemists. In this sense, Paracelsus was a paradoxical figure. In his own time, he was a rebel, opposing the medical establishment with his chemical cures. Seen in retrospect, however, his approach to medicine helped establish what grew into a huge pharmaceutical industry, which has strongly opposed the attitudes to nature that Paracelsus represented.

Medicine, for Paracelsus, required an understanding of different substances and how they combined, in creating illness and in providing cures. And it was curing that most interested him, the practical work of medicine rather than the scholarly disputes over fundamental physical forces or the ambition to get rich by making gold from alchemical knowledge. F. Sherwood Taylor said, "Paracelsus is the first to turn his attention wholly in the direction of healing" (Taylor 1952, 149). As was the case with Bacon in the seventeenth century, Paracelsus inspired a movement in his name, the Paracelsians, who were especially active in the Lutheran regions of central Europe, conducting chemical and medical research, encouraging educational and public health initiatives, and practicing scientific observation and experimentation. As some of the movement's members won official recognition for their work, the broader links to social and educational reform—and to a vitalist philosophy of nature—gave way to a more professional form of knowledge production.

HYBRIDIZATION IN ACTION:
THE STORY OF TYCHO BRAHE

Tycho Brahe was one of those who had been inspired by the teachings of Paracelsus, when he studied in Germany in his youth. On Brahe's return to his native Denmark, the Danish king gave him the island of Hven in the straits that now separate Sweden and Denmark to establish one of the world's first scientific communities (Christianson 2000). For twenty years, Brahe carried out systematic observations of the heavenly bodies and alchemical experiments; when royal support was withdrawn in 1597, he moved on to Prague and met Johannes Kepler shortly before he died (Elzinga and Jamison 1984). Hven—or Venusia as Brahe called his scientific community—developed into a site where scholarship and craftsmanship were mixed into a combined set of values. Brahe was perhaps the most visible figure in sixteenth-century Europe to begin to fashion, in an explicit and coherent way, the modern scientific way of life. He rejected a professorial post at the classical and theologically oriented university in Copenhagen, and he neglected his traditional responsibilities as a feudal lord to accomplish something new. At Hven, visitors could behold some of the most advanced astronomical instruments imaginable; they could wander through gardens filled with exotic plants, buildings constructed with artistic ambitions, and laboratories designed for systematic pharmaceutical experimentation and learning; and they could even have a look at a printing press for publishing the scientific results.

On Brahe's island, science was given a public face, and as the years passed, hundreds of people from all over Europe spent time there. Hven became something of a tourist attraction, marked off on maps and praised inside and outside of Denmark. It was also, of course, a training center for a large number of students and colleagues, who worked with Brahe on his many and varied projects. It is important to recognize that Brahe created a place where people from an aristocratic background, many of whom would perhaps have become traditional scholars, public servants, or priests, could work together with poorer people whom they normally would never have had the opportunity to meet. Like Gresham College in London, Venusia was a temporary site for hybrid identity formation. At Gresham, craftsmen could learn mathematics and a kind of scholarly distance to reality, and, as Christopher Hill (1965) suggested, Gresham thus served to provide some of the intellectual origins of the revolutions of the seventeenth century. A Gresham graduate was no longer merely an artisan; he was also imbued with what might be termed the gift of scientific hubris, that attitude of superiority that is central to almost all acts of knowing.

The personality of Brahe was certainly filled with an unusually large amount of hubris. Not born a king, he definitely tried to live like one throughout his life. He had no taste for politics or economics, the typical basis of royal authority; instead, he saw in his diligence and in the clarity of his thinking a path toward earthly power. He was one of the very first Europeans to see the value of science for achieving

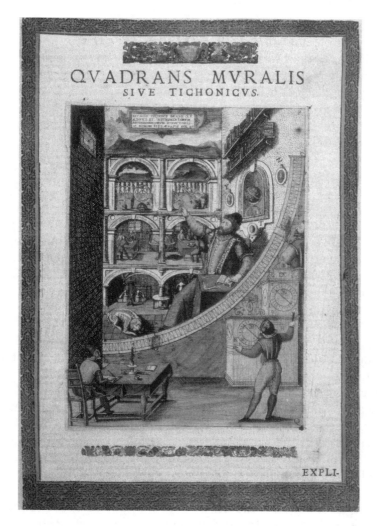

Figure 1. The astronomer Tycho Brahe among his astronomical instruments. From *Tychonis Brahe Astronomiae instauratae mechanica*, 1598. Reprinted by permission of Gettyimages, Munich, Germany.

personal success. What Bacon later categorized as "useful knowledge," Brahe had produced all his life—from the horoscopes he derived from his observations of the heavens to the medicaments he made in his alchemical laboratories. By combining separate skills and interests and by bringing them together in one place, Brahe was one of the main contributors to a widespread reformation of science and technology in sixteenth-century Europe. In one sense, it was a kind of attempt at institutionalization, but it was short-lived and all too personal: Brahe alienated as many people as he excited. The tenants on Hven, whom he exploited, and the young king, whom he disappointed by neglecting the duties to which he had been assigned, eventually put a stop to his regime. But even though it was destroyed soon after his departure, Brahe's scientific community served as a source of inspiration—a scientist's Garden of Eden—for all the ensuing reformation activities.

The first attempts to create scientific academies, for example, where scientists such as Galileo could present their controversial new theories, were, like Brahe's community on Hven, short-lived and often curtailed by social and cultural barriers. While Brahe had tangled with the king, Galileo tangled with the Pope and his cardinals. While both men survived with relatively little personal discomfort, there were others who gave their lives to the emergent scientific identity. In Italy, Giordano Bruno was burned at the stake for professing heretical scientific theories, and Tomaso Campanella was killed when his attempts to combine a political reform with a scientific reform were defeated. Many of the early institutions were outside of the established, aristocratic circles, and they were also, in certain respects, not sufficiently narrow to win political acceptance and support. Brahe, for example, remained an astrologer until the end of his life, and Galileo, along with Bruno and Campanella, was not one to keep his controversial opinions confined to the movements of the heavens.

There were others who suffered as well so that Brahe and Galileo could reform the scientific understanding of reality. The story of Galileo's daughter has reminded us of the human sacrifices that were also a part of the scientific reformation. Despite her intelligence, her skill as an apothecary, and her abilities as a confidante and supporter for her father, Suor Maria Celeste lived her short adult life in a nunnery, and, because of the conditions there, she died at the age of thirty-three, while Galileo lived on to the age of seventy-eight (Sobel 1999). There was no place in the scientific reformation for women; indeed, it is not merely coincidence that Galileo's writings were published at the same time that witches were being hunted throughout Europe in what has been referred to as a craze (Briggs 1996). The mechanical ideas that were being developed by Galileo and Descartes were at variance with the ideas of animism and natural magic that led many of those accused of witchcraft to be hunted down and burned.

THE MAKING OF AN ACADEMIC CULTURE

In the seventeenth century, the discourses, institutions, and practices that continue to characterize technology and science today gradually took form. There was, on one hand, the elucidation of a new kind of rationality that has proved to be remarkably robust. Although each of the different components, or elements, of the discourse had developed somewhat separately from one another, by the seventeenth century, the different elements had come to be shared by a growing number of ideologues and philosophers. The discourse has since provided a common way of talking about science as more than a unified theory or universal methodology, and different writers have identified different aspects as being the most significant. At a discursive level, modern science is a set of worldview assumptions, or beliefs, that came to be consolidated in the seventeenth century and that can be depicted schematically as a particular form of knowledge that has been characterized in different terms by different authors (see Table 3).

The scientific reformation, however, was not merely conceptual and theoretical. The new form of rationality that emerged, the discursive frameworks of experimental philosophy, needed to be put into practice and institutionalized. It is at the institutional and practical levels that the different phases of reformation become more clearly apparent, with a turning point in the second half of the seventeenth century after the founding of the Royal Society in London and the *Académie des Sciences* in Paris. In other parts of Europe, there were somewhat different key events, and, as in all processes of appropriation, it is important to remember the national variations, or styles (Porter and Teich 1992).

In sketching the historical development of the scientific role, the sociologist Joseph Ben-David (1971) contrasted a "scientistic movement" in the late sixteenth and early seventeenth centuries with the institutionalization process of academy building that took place in

TABLE 3. Modern Science as a Form of Knowledge

Instrumental	"rationality of means" (Weber)
Experimental	"logic of discovery" (Popper)
Systematic	"order of things" (Foucault)
Reductionist	"one-dimensional thought" (Marcuse)
Objectifying	"the death of nature" (Merchant)
Futuristic	"myth of progress" (von Wright)
Quantitative	"the measure of reality" (Crosby)

the late seventeenth and early eighteenth centuries. Bacon had been the prophet of the movement phase, with his proposals for new methods of scientific investigation that broke with the "idols of the past." With Bacon, the project remained programmatic, visionary, and prophetic. In the revolutionary period from 1640 to 1660, his writings formed part of what has been termed the "great instauration," when dissenting groups and other movement organizations carried out experiments in agriculture and medicine and produced a vast amount of popular scientific and technical literature in their pamphlets and informal treatises (Webster 1975).

We have already mentioned the Diggers, who planted crops together and developed a "law of freedom" according to which no one person could own the earth. The institutions of science grew from seeds planted by such puritan activists, who were driven by a millenarian worldview to create a new kingdom of God and to share the earth collectively. It was shortly thereafter that science began to find its characteristic institutional form, and its adherents vowed not to meddle "with Divinity, Metaphysics, Moralls, Politicks, Grammar, Rhetorick or Logick," as it was expressed in the charter for the Royal Society.

It was a particular form of knowledge making, or "logic of scientific discovery" (Popper 1959), that came to be institutionalized. A way of knowing reality was constituted that was mediated through technology (Böhme et al. 1978). This was accomplished through the use of scientific instruments and experimental rituals and through the mutual interaction between scientific inquiry and technical improvement, such as took place in the development of steam power, shipbuilding, and navigational techniques. The hybrid entities that were being constructed called for the formation of hybrid identities on the part of those who were doing the constructing. As the telescope and microscope literally disclosed new dimensions of reality, the clock and the compass provided scientists and merchants with images and metaphors that—through a kind of incorporation process—enabled them to recognize the natural world.

What eventually came to be characterized as modern science represented a form of knowledge production that drew much of its inspiration from earlier and much broader social and political struggles. The historical project of modernity, we might say, did not begin as a new scientific method, or a new mechanical worldview, or, for that matter, as a new kind of state support for experimental philosophy in the form of scientific academies. It was rather a more all-encompassing project, to "turn the world upside down" as one pamphleteer of the English civil war put it: "to set that in the bottom which others make the top of the building, and to set that upon the roof which others lay for a foundation" (quoted in Hill 1975, 13).

Gerrard Winstanley's ideal of knowledge, like that of Paracelsus in the sixteenth century, was eminently practical, but it was also moral and spiritual. To Bacon's notion of useful knowledge, Winstanley and the other puritan radicals added what might be termed a sense of accountability, or social responsibility, and a broader meaning for the pursuit of knowledge. Winstanley distinguished useful knowledge from the "idle, lazy contemplation the Scholars would call Knowledg," which was "no knowledg, but a shew of Knowledg, like a Parrat who speaks words, but he knows not what he saith" (Winstanley 1652/1973, 126). And he and the other movement intellectuals had fostered a democratic and informal kind of organization, rather than the formalized and professionalized practices and organizational forms that came in the period of Restoration.

As the broader movements gave way to more established institutions in the late seventeenth century, the political and social experiments, and the idea of pursuing science for the good of the "Common-wealth," came to be transformed into scientific experiments for the good of certain groups; the political and religious reformation, tinged with political radicalism and filled with mistrust of authority, was redefined and reconstituted. This was a kind of scientific counterrevolution. And a broader, open-ended movement of discovery and exploration came to be transformed into the institutions of modern knowledge making. Ingenuity was deflected into narrower trajectories, at the same time as the production of knowledge came to be supported by, and increasingly dependent on, the support of the powerful. In so doing, an approach to knowledge making was put in place that proved to be remarkably successful in applying the fruits of science to economic production, but rather less successful in sharing and distributing those fruits in a collective—and environmentally responsible—manner. As Charles Webster put it in the 1970s,

> Environmental circumstances have necessitated reference to an idea of the social accountability of science, analogous to the view which the Puritans more readily derived from their religious convictions. ... Although the Puritans looked forward to an unprecedented expansion in human knowledge, they realized that it would be necessary to exercise stringent discipline to prevent this knowledge resulting in moral corruption and social exploitation. (Webster 1975, 517–18)

The new institutions of modern science did not go unchallenged in their own time. The experimental philosophy was opposed by the upholders of traditional, religious knowledge and by the marginalized radicals and their descendants. In the late seventeenth and early eighteenth centuries, the scientific aristocracy that had emerged in London and Paris at the Royal Society and the *Académie des Sciences* was challenged by new kinds of dissenting groups and by representatives of the emerging middle classes. In this sense, the Enlightenment was also a kind of social movement, or broader-based cluster of social activity. Many of the radical dissenters fled from Europe to the colonies in North America, and some of them who stayed behind established scientific societies, often in provincial areas in opposition to the established science of the capital cities.

Many of the participants in the radical Enlightenment shared with the academicians and their royal patrons a belief in what Max Weber termed the Protestant ethic—that is, an interest in the value of hard work and the virtue of making profits on investments—and most had an interest in useful knowledge. But the new movements that developed in the Enlightenment and helped inspire the French—and American—revolutions objected to the limited ways in which the Royal Society and the Parisian academy had organized the scientific spirit and institutionalized the new methods and theories of the experimental philosophy (Jacob 1997, 99ff.). The Enlightenment, as we shall see, also led to a geographical diffusion of the scientific spirit and academic culture—to places such as Scandinavia and North America, where academies of science were created in the eighteenth century. It also led to new kinds of scientific disciplines, or what Michel Foucault termed a new "episteme," the discipline of ordering, naming, and classifying, which is epitomized in the works of Carl Linnaeus, who was also an important actor in the establishment of the Swedish Academy of Sciences (Frängsmyr 1989). The American Philosophical Society for the Promotion of Useful Knowledge, founded in Philadelphia in 1768, was a center of scientific and technical activity in the colonies and after independence. Under the leadership of Benjamin Franklin, it was a place where the particularly American form of republican science was fostered.

The various attempts to democratize scientific education in the wake of the French Revolution and to apply the mechanical philosophy to social processes—that is, to view society as a topic for scientific research and analysis—indicate how new forms of scientific practice and new institutions are inspired by broader movements (Hobsbawm 1962). The revolutionary government was the first to establish a science-based

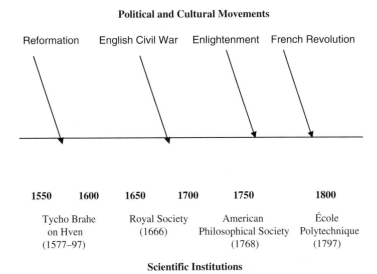

Figure 2. Political and cultural movements and scientific institutions.

institution of higher education, the *École Polytechnique,* and it was there that visions of a technocratic order developed in the writings of the count Saint Simon and his secretary August Comte. The institutionalization process included the articulation of new philosophies of science—positivism, in particular—and new disciplines, related to the emergent needs of an industrializing social order: statistics, geology, thermodynamics, political economy, and the sociology of Comte (Teich and Young 1973). Once again, out of social movements, there emerged new scientific institutions and disciplines, new forms of knowledge making. The Enlightenment too was filled with contradictions, and as with the general development of technology and science, it can be seen as a part of a cyclical pattern, a continuing dialectical process of movements and institutions in interaction.

2

THE INDUSTRIAL TRANSFORMATION

And did the Countenance Divine
Shine forth upon our clouded hills?
And was Jerusalem builded here
Among these dark Satanic Mills?

. . . .

I will not cease from Mental Fight,
Nor shall my sword sleep in my hand
Till we have built Jerusalem
In England's green & pleasant Land.

—William Blake, *Jerusalem* (1804–08)

FROM RESISTANCE TO APPROPRIATION

In the 1810s, when factories using new-fangled textile machinery had
been established throughout central England, there emerged a loosely
organized movement of resistance that came to be named after the
mythical leader Ned Ludd. On a regular basis, groups of craftsmen
and workers who had lost their jobs to the new machines organized
attacks on the dark Satanic mills, as the poet William Blake called them
a few years before. They moved quickly and made their forays at night,
making sure that there were no people in the buildings they attacked,
and selectively laid waste the specific machines, primarily for spinning
cotton yarn and for weaving cloth, that had made them redundant. In a

relatively short time, the Luddites managed to cause a good deal of physical damage and create a widespread sense of alarm and anxiety among the owners of the textile factories and their political supporters and financial sponsors. As Lord Byron put it in his maiden speech in the House of Lords in February 1812, "During the short time I recently passed in Nottinghamshire, not twelve hours elapsed without some fresh act of violence; and on the day I left the county I was informed that forty frames had been broken the preceding evening, as usual, without resistance and without detection" (quoted in Jennings 1985, 131). The Luddites fought so effectively, and managed to destroy so many machines, that certain factory towns were occupied for many months by soldiers from the British army. Like the Diggers a century and a half before, the Luddites had only a brief moment of visibility on the historical stage, but they nonetheless made their presence felt.

The Luddites had little in the way of a systematic philosophy; their attacks were motivated by rage and frustration, based on the experience of what Lord Byron called in his speech "circumstances of the most unparalleled distress." If there was an underlying logic or rationale behind their actions, it was an ambition to give the ongoing industrial transformation taking place in England a more appropriate direction. In Lord Byron's somewhat ironic words,

> In the foolishness of their hearts they imagined that the maintenance and well-doing of the industrious poor were objects of greater importance than the enrichment of a few individuals by any improvement, in the implements of trade, which threw the workmen out of employment, and rendered the labourer unworthy of his hire. (quoted in Jennings 1985, 132)

The Luddites have gone down in history as "machine-breakers" or "machine-stormers," and they are remembered, in the dominant narratives of industrialization, as naive people who tried to stand in the way of progress. In their efforts to block the use of machinery for the purposes of industrial development and economic growth, the Luddites have come to symbolize the futility of opposition.

The Luddites failed, more or less totally, in their efforts to stop progress or, for that matter, alter the direction of industrial development. In the course of the nineteenth century, industrialization and the use of machinery expanded and spread to literally all areas of social and economic life, and the industrial spirit, or mind-set, spread throughout the world as well, in some places by peaceful means, in many more by the armed force of colonial might. And yet, as with so many loosely organized movements of opposition before and since, even though the Luddites lost the specific battles they fought, they have continued to live on in the collective memory. One could even say that they did win out in the end—the factories they attacked have all been closed down by now and become part of an "industrial heritage." Their story continues to say something significant about the way in which the transition to an industrial society took place.

For those who benefited from industrialization, the Luddites have served as a warning example. The story of the machine-stormers, as, somewhat later, the resistance of the Native Americans to the occupation of their lands and destruction of their livelihoods by the white settlers, has been used to remind people of all that was wrong and backward with the preindustrial past. Only by looking forward can humanity make effective use of its technological innovations and scientific discoveries. The appropriate place for the past is in specially constructed sites—reservations, museums, history books, amusement parks and theme parks, and moving pictures and television programs—where older ways of life can serve as sources of entertainment and relaxation from the modern world of the present. For the emerging industrial culture, the past became a kind of mine, representing the darkness and depression from which science-based products offered light and emancipation.

For others, in particular those who organized opposition to the power elites of industrial society, the Luddites and the Native Americans became exemplars of moral protest and alternative ways of life. As the parties and organizations of the working class grew into influential social movements in the late nineteenth century, the Luddites were often portrayed sympathetically, as sources of inspiration rather than disapproval. And as environmental movements developed in the twentieth century, the legacy of the Native Americans was reinterpreted as part of the search for ecological ways of life, in terms of techniques and knowledge, practices and ideas. There have periodically been those who have tried to reawaken their spirits and encourage a principled resistance to technological development, in much the same way as the Luddites and the Native Americans performed their politics in their moments on the historical stage. One of the Luddites' later admirers, who has written a new history of their struggle, has called for a movement of neo-Luddism to oppose technologically based globalization. In an attempt to reinvent their tradition, Kirkpatrick Sale also extracted what he called lessons from the Luddites, one of which, he contended, is that "resistance to the industrial system, based on some grasp of moral principles and rooted in some sense of moral revulsion, is not only possible but necessary" (Sale 1995, 269).

The Luddites represented one kind of response to the coming of the machinery of industrial society. Their story reminds us that there have been losers and winners in each phase of technological and scientific change, and resistance has been a recurring theme in each wave of innovation. Whenever new technology is introduced, there are almost always those whose livelihoods are threatened, and sometimes their rejection of new technology gets destructive, as was the case with the Luddites. It is misleading to think of such resistance struggles as anti-technological, for the Luddites and the Native Americans had their own technologies of work and everyday life that they had not only mastered but based a good deal of their identities on. For them, resistance was a matter of survival, because they saw in the machines of the emerging industrial society—and the barbed wire fences around the white settlers' farms and ranches—a fundamental threat to the continued existence of their ways of life.

In this chapter, we focus on processes of synthesis and hybridization, by which negative and positive responses to industrialization—the tragic and the heroic stories, those of the winners and the losers—came to be combined into forms that were more widely acceptable. Cultural appropriation, or the making of an industrial culture, involved the bringing together of different ideas and concepts, institutions and organizations, practices and identities as the new technical and scientific opportunities were made to fit into human societies. In the process, social relationships and the relationships between people and their natural environments were transformed. As the traditional culture gave way to the industrial, the image of "society"—*Gesellschaft*—replaced that of "community"—*Gemeinschaft*—as the fundamental basis for the bonds of human solidarity (Tönnies 1887/2001). The customary way of life was transformed into the civilized, in terms of shaping everyday behavior and values.

As the primacy of direct contact with natural working materials was displaced by the organized business of industry, the word *industry* primarily came to connote a societal context rather than a personal trait. Artificial, humanly constructed environments—factories, department stores, city parks—replaced the natural environment as the basic sites for human interaction with nonhuman reality. And as the locales of learning moved from the places of work and everyday life to new public schools and technical colleges, the mathematical logic and experimental procedures of science replaced the relatively undifferentiated and informal processes of lived experience as the main sources of knowledge. At the same time, industrial technology was reformed and redesigned by new sorts of engineers and technicians with their hybrid

TABLE 4. The Industrial Transformation as Cultural Appropriation

At the Discursive Level
A semantics of invention
A grammar of technology and engineering
A language of development
At the Institutional Level
Systems of production and consumption
Formalization of education and training
State regulation and scientific administration
At the Level of Practice
Disciplinary scientific/engineering identities
Hybridization of everyday life
Research as vocation

skills and competencies, and the scientific ideas on which technology was increasingly based came to be reformulated into specialized disciplines with their own expert vocabularies and professional values (see Table 4).

INTERPRETING THE REVOLUTION

As with the scientific revolution of the seventeenth century, interpretations of the so-called industrial revolution of the eighteenth and nineteenth centuries have shifted over time (Cannadine 1984). It was in the late nineteenth century, as part of the consolidation of history as an academic discipline, that Arnold Toynbee attached the revolutionary label to the events that had taken place one hundred years before. As it began to be used, the term took on negative connotations, because the late 1800s was a period of active social reform, and economic and social historians played their part by investigating the social problems that had been associated with the transition to industrial society. It was only later, and especially during the boom years of the postwar period, that historians came to describe the industrial revolution in more positive terms, attempting to derive from the transformations that had taken place a more general understanding of the conditions of economic growth and science-based development.

At the center of these economic histories are the technical innovations and the technical innovators. Certain radical innovations, as Joseph Schumpeter (1942) called them, were seen to have served as motors for a general process of change. They were said to have come in clusters, or meaningful combinations, at particular points in time.

Crucially important in the early phase of industrialization were a number of machines and chemical techniques that were developed in the 1770s and 1780s and were rapidly applied to different areas of manufacturing: clothing and ceramics, in particular. At the same time, James Watt made fundamental technical improvements to the efficiency of the steam engine, which helped make it possible to develop production sites away from the rivers that had previously provided the main sources of power. Completing the cluster were the innovations that were made in relation to coal mining and exploitation, which effectively and substantially increased the supply of energy to the factories where the new machines were located. According to the economic, or innovation, story line, it was primarily the diffusion of this innovation cluster that propelled economic growth and the enormous increases in output and productivity that marked the first stage of industrialization.

The heroic tales are of the factory owners who applied the machinery to industrial purposes, and of the scientists and inventors who made the key creative breakthroughs. Like the innovations they made, the innovators also clustered around certain places—such as the "lunar

Figure 3. Young James Watt playing with steam. Reprinted by permission of Gettyimages, Munich, Germany.

men" around Birmingham: Josiah Wedgwood, James Watt, Samuel Boulton, Joseph Priestley, and Erasmus Darwin. Wedgwood was the innovator who brought chemistry and modern production techniques to the pottery and ceramics industry, whereas Watt and Boulton were the team that so successfully combined technical expertise with business acumen. Priestley was the tireless proponent of political and scientific progress, and one of the main contributors to the making of modern chemistry, and Darwin, a medical doctor, helped implant the new technological interests into the wider culture through his poetry and philosophizing, which later influenced the evolutionary theory of his famous grandson, Charles Darwin. Not least because of their personal interaction and their collaborative projects with one another, these scientists, engineers, and businessmen were the kind of individuals who "made the future," we are told, by putting mechanical instruments to industrial use (Uglow 2002).

Many of the important technological innovations of the first period of industrialization were developed in specific settings for specific purposes, but, as industrialization progressed, production and the process of innovation became more systematic and complex. The horizontal and vertical integration of the capital-goods industry, the standardization of parts—starting with the production of instruments of warfare—and the emergence of the machine-tool industry as a central branch were especially important in the expansion of industrialization across the European and American continents (Landes 1969). The development of new power sources and industrial materials—especially oil and steel—were also crucial components of the second wave, or cycle, of industrialization in the latter half of the nineteenth century. These innovations—along with railroad locomotives and telegraphic communication—provided the material conditions for the consolidation of what institutional economists have termed "national systems of innovation" by which inventiveness and creativity were transformed into economically significant activities (Nelson 1993). These systems involved a range of new institutions—educational, financial, legal, and technical and scientific—all of which were organized somewhat differently in each industrializing country.

The basic narrative of the economic story line focuses on the specific institutions of innovation and the more general institutions of capital accumulation—factories and joint-stock companies, banks and corporations, regulatory laws and state agencies—that brought about what we call the incorporation of technology and science into the pursuit of business. As the process grew more complex and multifaceted, the key individuals, the "system-builders" as historian Thomas Hughes (1983) called them, came to acquire ever more skills and develop a more scientific, or expert, competence. The factory owners of the late eighteenth century and the famous entrepreneurs were gradually replaced by the railroad tycoons, investment bankers, corporate managers, and, not least, scientific inventors of the late nineteenth and early twentieth centuries. And, as such, the stories of the so-called second industrial revolution, which took place in the late nineteenth century, have often been tales of corporate expansion, featuring the heroic sagas of the Carnegies and the Du Ponts, the Siemens and the Rockefellers, the Citroëns and the Wallenbergs, the Edisons and the Fords.

Regardless of how one judges the industrialization process, it is important to remember that it was controversial at the time in which it was taking place. What has been brought into focus by recent scholarship is the conflictual, or contested, nature of the industrial transformation. As Maxine Berg, one of the leading proponents of this new cultural history of industrialization, wrote,

> The machine was not an impersonal achievement to those living through the Industrial Revolution; it was an issue. The machinery question in early nineteenth-century Britain was the question of the sources of technical progress and the impact of the introduction of the new technology of the period on the total economy and society. (Berg 1980, 9)

From the perspective of the history of technology and science, one of the most important sources of debate and disagreement has been about the role that science played in the industrial transformation of the eighteenth and nineteenth centuries. To what extent was there a direct connection between the forms of knowledge making that had been constituted in the seventeenth century and the forms of economic activity that characterize the industrial revolution? What contribution did science and scientists actually make to industrialization?

More than any particular scientific theory or science-based idea, the idea of progress was central to the deep changes that began in the mid-eighteenth century (Liedman 1997). And in that change of attitude, science played a major role, directly and indirectly. Before the industrial transformation, most people lived on the land, and they obtained their livelihoods from agriculture, animal husbandry, fishing, and forestry. There were other people, of course—priests, doctors, craftsmen, merchants, soldiers—who were separated from the lifeworlds of primary production and who derived their social status from some kind of specialized skill or knowledge. But for the most part, the role of knowledge making in those preindustrial societies was directly related to everyday life experiences. People learned most of what they needed to know by observing their parents and neighbors and by trying to do the things that they did. Most of what they knew was not formalized or codified but informal and tacit, an experiential and highly situated form of cognition (Liedman 2001). Knowledge was customary, rather than scientific, and it was produced and communicated in informal settings rather than formal research and educational institutions.

The emergence of modern science in the seventeenth century challenged these traditional forms of knowledge and knowledge making (Scheler 1924/1980). For one thing, science provided ways of knowing—mathematical logic, systematic experimentation, mechanical models—that were different from the older forms. Scientific knowledge was abstract, but it could be communicated in writing and it could be applied to different tasks. By means of systematic experimentation, for instance, craftsmen—in cooperation with men of science and not seldom supported by the state—could make the traditional techniques of energy production, mining and metallurgy, and manufacturing and agriculture more efficient. With the help of mathematical reasoning, new kinds of regulation and management could be developed, and mechanical models could provide much greater degrees of precision and possibilities for control over normal processes of primary and secondary production. It was not until the mid-nineteenth century that such effort really began to pay off. More important in the early period than the particular scientific methods was the progressive project, the ambition to develop knowledge for the expressed purpose of improving things and creating things that did not yet exist (Landes 1969).

This utopian imagining, rather than any specific uses of scientific knowledge, was perhaps the most significant role that science played in relation to the early period of industrialization. Across Europe and North America, as science gained more adherents in the course of the eighteenth century, ever more people began to envision another kind of society, based on the applications of scientific-technological rationality. Science, we might say, helped to open up the realm of the imagination—sometimes to such a degree that it took on the character of hubris: the overextension and superhuman transgression that was characterized by Friedrich Nietzsche at the end of the nineteenth century as the *Übermensch*, or superman, driven by an excessive will to power. As Humphrey Jennings put it in his remarkable collection of documents tracing the "coming of the machine," the new realistic, scientific attitude, or what he called a "fundamental alteration of 'vision'" in the course of the eighteenth century, was "being achieved not merely as a *result* of changing means of production but *also* making them possible" (Jennings 1985, 38). And the dual revolution—the political revolutions that ushered in democracy and the technical and economic revolutions that ushered in industrialization—was the immediate outcome, we might say, of this altered vision.

WAVES OF APPROPRIATION

It can be helpful to think of the industrial revolution of the late eighteenth and early nineteenth centuries as the first in a recurrent series of cultural appropriation processes that correspond, in a cyclical way, to the development of technology and science. During the past two hundred years, waves of industrialization have been countered by phases of cultural critique: as technology and science have periodically been invented so have the social and cultural responses. Jenny Uglow aptly observed, "With each new wave of technological advance, the rhetoric of social possibility, and the reaction to it, resurfaces" (Uglow 1996, 8). But the critique has also advanced, as its articulators have reinvented the ideas and practices of previous phases and identified new problems, new consequences of technology and science. In this way, cultural appropriation can be thought of as the gradual acceptance and simultaneous transformation of the critique by the established society. On a discursive, institutional, and practical level, agents of appropriation transform the critical responses to a previous wave into constructive criteria for a new wave of industrialization.

In the 1930s, the economic historian Joseph Schumpeter delineated "long waves" of approximately fifty-year duration, which had characterized the pattern of development of the industrial economies up until that time. He drew on statistical investigations that had been conducted by the Russian economist Nicolai Kondratiev some years before, which had indicated that since the late eighteenth century, there had been three identifiable cycles of industrial expansion and decline (Freeman and Louçã 2001). The periods of expansion were characterized by rising rates of productivity and employment in the leading industrial countries, and roughly corresponded to the so-called boom periods of the original industrial revolution of 1780 to 1810 and the continental expansion of 1845 to 1870. Schumpeter also identified a third period of expansion, from 1890 to 1915, that had followed the downturn and recession of the 1870s and 1880s.

In his book *Capitalism, Socialism and Democracy*, which he published in 1942, Schumpeter used the term *creative destruction* to indicate that each wave, or phase, had not merely replaced the previous one but also eliminated or destroyed much of the material basis of the preceding period. By mobilizing radical innovations that had brought with them a range of new technical opportunities into the productive sphere—textile machines in the first wave, railroads and the telegraph in the second wave, and electricity in the third wave—entrepreneurs and engineers had been able to create new branches of industry and fundamentally different types of products in each of the waves. The first wave had been a wave of mechanization, the second a wave of transportation, and the third a wave of electrification. As such they had built on each other, but the actual goods and services that were produced, and the types of actors and institutions involved in their production, had been creatively destroyed or transformed from one wave to the next.

In the 1980s, Christopher Freeman and other innovation economists, responding to the declining productivity and employment in the industries that had fueled the economic expansion after the Second World War, developed these ideas into a more all-encompassing theory of so-called evolutionary economics (Nelson and Winter 1982). For Freeman, the long waves were characterized by different "techno-economic paradigms," and he and other economists in the 1980s looked to the emerging information technologies as the central core for a wave of industrial development (Freeman 1987). The techno-economic paradigms were seen as structuring devices for the economy as a whole, and they were related to different core technologies and supporting innovations, as well as involving different sorts of institutional frameworks. The waves were, in turn, related to geographical shifts as industrialization progressed, with technological leadership moving first, in the early twentieth century, from Europe to North America and then, in the late twentieth century, to Japan. The lessons he derived from history were framed within the language of institutional economics, which meant that the systemic linkages between actors and the rule systems and legal frameworks that had been put in place were given central attention.

What neither Schumpeter nor Freeman considered in any detail is the role that culture has played in these recurrent cyclical processes of industrial transformation. It is interesting to note, for example, that the periods in between the waves, the periods marked by economic stagnation and decline, happen to be periods that have been characterized by rather intense intellectual, cultural, and social activity. In the 1810s and 1820s, as well as in the 1860s and 1870s, there were new social movements of resistance and opposition, and influential intellectual responses to technological development, identifying problems but also pointing to new solutions (Baark and Jamison 1986). In the first period, romanticism and positivism emerged and, in many countries, cooperative movements developed, and in the second period, socialist, populist, and nationalist ideas and movements helped give meaning to the ensuing developments in technology and science. Similarly, in the 1910s and 1920s, and then again in the 1960s and 1970s, there were widespread public debates, and a range of new actors and movements emerged—fascism, communism, and national liberation in the earlier period and the so-called new social movements of anti-imperialism, environmentalism, and feminism in the latter (Eyerman and Jamison 1991). As we see in the following chapters, the debates and movements of the twentieth century drew inspiration from previous phases of cultural critique, but they also responded to the immediate experiences of the preceding wave (see Figure 4).

Cultural appropriation can be thought of as the ways in which the waves of industrialization and the phases of critique interact, the processes by which social and cultural critique is influenced by and, in turn, affects technological and scientific developments. By responding critically to one wave of industrialization, cultural spokespersons and social movements help to construct the next. In each of the long waves of appropriation, there has been a characteristic trajectory or life cycle, as opposition and cultural critique has gradually been transformed into more constructive discourses, institutions, and practices. The Luddites and the early romantic poets, for example, entered into the appropriation process as sources of inspiration for critical artists and writers throughout the nineteenth century, as many came to construct what has been termed a "spirit" of anti-industrialism (Wiener 1981). Even more significant, however, they helped stimulate what became more constructive strategies of appropriation.

Whereas the Luddites and the romantic poets tended to turn their backs on technology, other cultural critics sought to develop a more

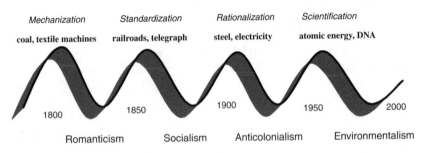

Figure 4. Waves of industrialization and cultural critique.

positive language with which to discuss the meanings of industrial technology. In the early 1840s, the young Friedrich Engels wrote of the "condition of the working class" in Manchester, and Karl Marx explored the material, rather than spiritual, basis of humanity's "species being" before the two of them combined forces, in 1848, to outline a new approach to history and a new political agenda in *The Communist Manifesto*. Out of this critique developed a new discursive framework that put traditional, idealist philosophy, as they put it, on its feet. The lifelong effort by Marx and Engels to identify the "iron laws" of capitalist development, and place what they termed the class struggle on a firm, scientific basis, was one of the more ambitious projects of cultural appropriation of technology and science in the nineteenth century. But there were other activities, individual and collective, that also represented the gradual shift from critical rejection into constructive reformation. In particular, institutions of social reform and public welfare were eventually established to deal with the consequences of industrialization against which the Luddites and Native Americans had reacted directly.

THE ROLE OF WAR

Ernest Mandel (1980) argued that wars have often served to provide direction for various transformation processes throughout history. The first wave of industrialization—in the late eighteenth century—was also a time of armed political conflicts in North America and France, and, partly as a result, in both places the appropriation processes took on a strongly military coloration. The need of the French army for uniforms helped create the basis for true mass production in the clothing industry. In the United States, technology and science were mobilized, from the outset, to the needs of war. The first technological university was the military academy at West Point, and the first state initiatives in relation to supporting technology and science were also related to the military (Maier et al. 2003). Later, the first developments in standardization of parts took place in the production of weapons and were then transferred to nonmilitary industries. The phenomenon of spin-off from the military in relation to computers, the Internet, and other information technologies that are so well-known today can trace their lineage back to the early nineteenth century at places such as Harper's Ferry Armory in West Virginia, where techniques that later were used for producing bicycles and automobiles were first applied to the making of muskets and artillery (Smith 1977).

In France, the Napoleonic wars helped shape the ways in which technology and science were appropriated in the early nineteenth century.

Strong state institutions and a comparatively centralized system of decision making and accountability characterized the French style of appropriation from the outset. As in the United States, research and education were given a strong military orientation, as technology and science were made to fit the interests of a modern state and modern industry often in conflict with its neighbors. This system had its roots in previous periods of state building, in the early modern period, when the nascent nation-state had sponsored projects in weapons productions, and during *l'ancien régime* that preceded the revolution, when the state had created the first national educational and research institutions primarily for military and infrastructural purposes (Gillispie 1980).

For Britain, the wars of the nineteenth century were largely related to the consolidation of the empire. Because of the distance and the fact that there was little actual armed conflict at home, the direct impact of the military on the national system of innovation tended to be weaker. Because of the colonization of the Indian subcontinent and other parts of Asia and Africa, the imperialist aspects of technology and science were formative for the discourses, institutions, and practices of what we might term the British appropriation style. Imperialism was motivated, however, more in terms of economic expansion and a civilizational mission than as an explicitly military conquest. The weapons were important, of course, and the development of weaponry had a certain economic significance, but the role of imperialism in the development of technology and science was probably more significant, at least in the British case, at the level of ideas and ideology than at the technical or practical level (Headrick 1981; Adas 1989).

For the United States, the Civil War was a hugely formative influence on the industrialization process, in practical and discursive terms. In many respects, the War between the States marks a central dividing line in the consolidation of an industrial culture. For one thing, the war led to the "creative destruction" of the Southern rural way of life, which had been based on agricultural production using slaves imported from Africa rather than machines built in factories. And for another, the war provided an enormous stimulus to the development of more effective instruments of warfare. The outcome owed a great deal to more advanced technology on the part of the Northern army—from the *Monitor* at sea to the Colt rifles on land. On a discursive level, the war helped to construct a particularly powerful ideology of industrial progress, which combined the moral righteousness that came from fighting for a just cause ("freeing the slaves") with a commercial and practical sensibility that made victory possible ("the war is good for business") with a religious faith that had been strengthened by the hardships and sacrifices of emigration from the old country ("God is on our side").

In the United States, the appropriation of technology and science was also shaped by the American Indian wars. The civilizational mission was, in many respects, similar to the one that motivated British imperialism, but unlike the situation with European colonialism, the victims were not overseas; the mission was not carried out at a distance. In moral terms, the Native Americans were not merely believers in another religious faith, as were many of the victims of European colonization. They were seen by many of the white majority as having no religion at all, as being savages rather than infidels. The brutality of the warfare and the religious fervor of the process were thus somewhat greater in North America than in many other parts of the world. American exceptionalism, in this context, meant an exceptionally strong sense of national identification with the military uses of technology and science. In the early twenty-first century, this remains the case.

In other industrializing countries, the experiences of war were somewhat less direct and influential. In Germany and Italy, for example, even more formative influences on the cultural appropriation of technology and science were the struggles for national unity and independence; on the discursive level, nationalism provided the main story lines, as was the case, as well, in many other European countries. In Sweden, Norway, the Netherlands, and Denmark, the appropriation of technology and science was filtered through broader political processes of national identity formation. In these countries that were relatively late to industrialize, large proportions of the population emigrated to the Americas in the course of the nineteenth century; for those who remained, it became essential to use images of past glory to mobilize support for the emerging industrial order. Some of these countries, most especially perhaps Sweden, as we see in chapter 4, mobilized images of their warlike, imperial past, which affected the industrialization process. Other countries, such as Norway, which had long been subjected to foreign domination, gave the industrialization process a kind of national mission, which affected its specific technical and scientific content, as well as its organizational form.

THE ROMANTIC REVOLT

The machines and steam engines that characterized the first wave of industrialization were rejected outright by many influential poets and writers. As we have seen, William Blake decried the "dark Satanic Mills" of the industrial cities, and he also scorned the narrowness, what he called the single vision, of Newton's mechanical philosophy, while William Wordsworth, John Keats, and other poets sought escape from the emerging mechanical world into a world of beauty and passion, countering the coming of the machine by inventing new forms of literary expression. Many were the romantics—in art and music, as well as in literature—who turned their backs on industrial society to gain inspiration from the wilderness or from the ideals of earlier, preindustrial epochs. Most significant in the long run was the book first published by Mary Shelley in 1818, in which the industrial or mechanical worldview was symbolized in the monster constructed by the crazed Doctor Frankenstein. Still of relevance in an era when human cloning has reached the level of practical possibility, Shelley's novel provided a profound questioning of the hubris that turned the medical doctor into a mad scientist. As her Frankenstein put it, "Learn from me, if not by my precepts, at least by my example, how dangerous is the acquirement of knowledge, and how much happier that man is who believes his native town to be the world, than he who aspires to become greater than his nature will allow" (Shelley 1818/1993, 35).

The romantic "revolt of the senses," as Alfred North Whitehead (1925) once called it—the personal, direct opposition that was manifested in a range of different forms in the first half of the nineteenth century—was a wide-ranging social and cultural movement, and, like many movements before and since, it included new forms of knowledge production. These movements differed from the Luddites' movement in that they did not aim to save or preserve the knowledge of the past but sought instead to combine industrial and preindustrial forms of knowledge in new combinations, in cooperation rather than conflict. Already in the 1810s, new sorts of constructive discourses, institutions, and practices began to emerge, first in England and then throughout the industrializing world. In 1817, industrialist Robert Owen started to develop his programs for factory and eventually social reform; in the 1820s, the mechanics' institutes began to be established to educate workers in the new kinds of skills and knowledge that industrialization required. A kind of cultural assessment of technology soon emerged among journalists and novelists, such as Charles Dickens and Elizabeth Gaskell, a literature that identified problems and concerns for the emerging industrial order to try to solve.

In the 1830s, Andrew Ure and Charles Babbage were among those who more systematically analyzed the underlying principles of industrial technology, and Babbage also conceived of the first machine for computation and calculation, his so-called analytic engine, which is generally considered the first computer design. William Whewell at

Cambridge not only coined the term *scientist* but also was instrumental in organizing the British Association for the Advancement of Science (BAAS), a professional society for the new kinds of natural philosophers who were finding places of employment in the emerging industrial society. In the United States, Jacob Bigelow in a series of lectures at Harvard in 1829 said, "There has probably never been an age in which the practical applications of science have employed so large a portion of talent and enterprise of the community, as in the present. To embody ... the various topics which belong to such an undertaking, I have adopted the general name of Technology" (quoted in Noble 1977, 3).

These diverse efforts of appropriation contributed to the science of economics, or political economy, as it was called at the time, and to more sophisticated methods of production in the ways that machinery came to be used and further developed. In Britain, among the followers of Owen, as well as in some other branches of the cooperative and Chartist movements, alternative forms of production and manufacture were developed. There was a kind of widespread amateur experimentation activity, which generated a literature about technology and appropriate applications of machines to agriculture, transportation, and communications (Kingston 1976). In Denmark, the priest and historian N. F. S. Grundtvig initiated a new form of education by proposing "people's high schools" in the countryside to provide an education for life, as he called it, rather than the dead, Latin education at the universities. At these schools Danish farmers could learn about new agricultural techniques and about new cooperative forms of organizing their food-processing business activities, which became the main source of Danish industrialization (Borish 1991).

In North America, one of the more influential romantics in relation to the appropriation of science and technology was Henry David Thoreau. Withdrawing in self-imposed isolation to a house that he built himself on the shores of Walden Pond in Massachusetts, Thoreau used the opportunity to reflect on the underlying meanings of the emerging industrial order. His book *Walden* was more or less unread in its own day, but, for later generations, it became an important part of what we might call the American discursive framework and its glorification of practicality and individuality.

Thoreau also tried to contribute to the development of science. He was a transition figure in his approach to knowledge, at first rejecting the cold truths of professional science for a more explicitly personal and poetic method. In 1842, he wrote in one of his first published articles,

The true man of science will know nature better by his finer organization; he will smell, taste, see, hear, feel better than other men. His will be a deeper and finer experience. We do not learn by inference and deduction, and the application of mathematics to philosophy, but by direct intercourse and sympathy. It is with science as with ethics—we cannot know truth by contrivance and method; the Baconian is as false as any other, and with all the helps of machinery and the arts, the most scientific will still be the healthiest and friendliest man, and possess a more perfect Indian wisdom. (quoted in Walls 1995, 41)

After his time at Walden Pond and the commercial failure of the book he had written about his experiences there, Thoreau gradually altered the tone of his writing. In the 1860s, he practiced a form of science that has only now, in our age of ecology, begun to be properly appreciated and understood. For one thing, he became much more like a professional scientist in his commitment to detailed observation and systematic empirical investigation. For another, he replaced the philosophical language and more literary style of presentation that had characterized his earlier writings with a more mainstream scientific vocabulary and writing style. He was influenced by Darwin's theory of evolution, and he tried to bring a more rigorous kind of reasoning into his own form of empathetic knowledge making. In the detailed nature journals and perhaps especially in the remarkable essay "The Dispersion of Seeds," which was published only in the late twentieth century, Thoreau had taken on what we might call a hybrid identity—the social critic and the scientist had been combined into an ecologist, even though he used the word *naturalist* (Walls 1995).

The forms of knowledge production and education that developed in the nineteenth century were often created in opposition to the professionalization of science and engineering that was taking place at the universities and the new technical colleges (Russell 1983). In many countries, there were significant conflicts over how the new universities and technical faculties were to be organized. For example, the founding of the Danish Polytechnic University in 1829 involved a dispute between a science-based educational ideal favored by university professors, led by physicist Hans Christian Ørsted, and a more practical approach favored by technical publicist G. F. Ursin (Wagner 1999). Ørsted, who discovered electromagnetism and was inspired by the romantic teachings of German *Naturphilosophie,* was a firm believer in the importance of science for industrial development. His public lectures at the Society for the Diffusion of Natural Knowledge were attended, among others, by J. J. Jacobsen, who later turned beer brewing into an industrial activity and set up a laboratory and the Carlsberg Foundation. In general terms, Ørsted played a major role in the cultural appropriation of technology and science in Denmark. He had little respect, however, for the approaches to science and technology that were promulgated by Grundtvig and Ursin.

The alternative technology movement of the early nineteenth century—a kind of artisanal polytechnical cognitive praxis, with links to cooperative forms of organization—was largely overtaken, or at least made problematic, by the course that technological development was to take. With the coming of the railroads and telegraph, it became ever more difficult to escape from, or oppose, the dominant industrial society. But some of the ideas of the movement did have impacts on the emerging industrial order and the professionalization of science that accompanied it.

On one hand, a form of romanticism, which Alvin Gouldner (1985) termed "popular materialism," became a part of scientific and broader cultural traditions. A romantic biology developed in the Germanic and Scandinavian countries, partly as an outgrowth of *Naturphiloso-phie*, and new kinds of science—cell biology, biochemistry, and eventually ecology—grew in the seeds planted by the romantic movement, by J. W. von Goethe in particular (who, in addition to writing *Faust* and other plays, developed alternative theories of color and optics). More generally, the very concept of culture and the various practices of cultural criticism—in journalism, the arts, and literature—can be seen as institutionalized forms of the romantic revolt (Williams 1958/1971). The turn to science and the development of an experimental natural science at the universities was, in many ways, an outgrowth of a romantic impulse, and the historical sciences of geology and archaeology and eventually evolutionary biology certainly owed something to the interest in the past that was so prominent in the romantic era (Hobsbawm 1962).

In the wake of the industrial revolution, the "machinery question" shook British society and heavily influenced the development of political economy. Authors have suggested that economics as an academic discipline, and the labor movement as a political force, were formed largely as social responses to mechanization (Berg 1980). But in responding to mechanization, the new institutions of social science and working-class organization also served to change the nature of the critique. From being a force of the devil and of mankind's darkest emotions, technology became a fundamental economic factor, or productive force, for scientific socialists such as Marx and Engels and a potential source for new forms of collective action for others, such as the craftsman revolutionary William Morris in Britain and the populist publicist Edward Bellamy in the United States.

THE CONSOLIDATION OF AN INDUSTRIAL CULTURE

A positive philosophy, or positivism, emerged in the wake of the French revolution at *École Polytechnique,* the first explicit university of science and technology in the world. As the revolutionaries had replaced *l'ancien régime* with a new political order, positivist philosophy sought to replace theology and metaphysics with a new cognitive order. Formulated in schematic form by Count Claude de Saint-Simon and, most influentially, in a series of writings by his secretary Auguste Comte, positivism imparted to technology and science a revelatory role in human history (Kolakowski 1972). Rapidly spreading across Europe and later throughout the world, not least to the American hemisphere, positivism helped legitimate the new roles that technology and science were playing in society.

For Comte, science marked a new stage in human development. As the results of science came to be put into industrial use, the superstitions of the past, with their religious beliefs and their unfounded metaphysical theories, could be replaced by the hard facts of objective scientific knowledge. The positivist philosophy provided an ideology and a common grammar for many in the emerging industrial world, and, in particular, for its new professional experts. It gave the scientists and engineers, the factory owners, and the new middle classes something to believe in. But it also offered a vocabulary, a way of talking about the new society and especially about its sciences and technologies. Comte coined many terms, perhaps the most important of which is the word *sociology.*

Of all the people who contributed to the fashioning of the central discourses about industrial society, perhaps no single person was more important than Karl Marx. He was far from alone in providing industrial technology, and industrializing society more generally, with a historic sense, assigning to industrialization and to technology and science a revolutionary role in human history. Although disagreeing with many of their conclusions, Marx drew on the writings of political economists, idealist and positivist philosophers, and not least those he called "utopian socialists," such as Robert Owen in England and Charles Fourier in France, to develop a powerful intellectual synthesis that provided a narrative of science-based progress that many different types of people could share. Not all of them can be called Marxists, although an explicitly Marxist ideology was an important part of the belief system in the socialist and broader working-class movements that took shape in the 1880s and 1890s. The positivist message, and, in particular, its enthusiasm for technology and science when put to industrial use, was never formulated as eloquently and rigorously as it was by Marx in his book *Capital* (*Das Kapital*), the first volume of which was published in 1867.

Unifying liberals and Marxists was the shared belief in science as a positive and inherently beneficial force. Science was seen as a fundamental element in the continuous improvement of the human condition and, more specifically, in the continuous expansion of human powers and control over the natural environment. New artifacts such as steam engines and railroads, as well as sciences such as geology and organic chemistry, became the embodiments of a social philosophy, and the machines that spread into working life and everyday life became the exemplary instruments of an industrial rationality, a techno-logic. Technology became, in the writings of many a positivist, a new kind of religious icon, symbolizing the power of rational thought and the progressive value of scientific reason and methods.

Building on this tradition, Marx and the political economists he criticized provided a heroic terminology of productive forces driving history, translating the concepts of physics and mechanical engineering—motors and engines, machines and forces—into social and political terms. As such, they served to fit the new machines into discursive frameworks that could be understood and embraced by many different actors on the stage of history. The story line was one of progress and transcendence, of conquering the frontier, as it was characterized in the United States, and of eliminating superstition and ignorance, as it was thought of everywhere. In an almost eschatological manner, science came to represent the future, and those who did not share the belief in science came to be seen as part of the problem. Philosophers and humanists who questioned the values underlying science-based progress became the institutionalized critics, or pessimists, leading to the characterization in the twentieth century of two opposed intellectual cultures.

In the 1870s, it was the historian Arnold Toynbee who brought the term *industrial revolution* into the vernacular, but in doing so, he gave voice to a position that had come to dominate the discursive terrain (Cannadine 1984). Something fundamental had happened in the late eighteenth century with the coming of machine-based factory production. By calling it a revolution and implanting the idea of an industrial revolution in the public consciousness—at least in the political realm—the experience of industrialization was made more acceptable. The cataclysmic transformations that had taken place were given a deeper meaning and could make sense for all sides, the winners and the losers, the capitalists and the workers. Like eschatological ideas in the religious realm, a positivist worldview made it easier for those who were prevented access to the riches of the present to nourish hopes of a better future.

An important source of the Marxian synthesis—and the consolidation of an industrial culture—was the theory of natural evolution that Charles Darwin presented in his book *On the Origin of Species,* published in 1859. Where Darwin had tried to derive fundamental laws of evolution from his many observations of natural phenomena, Marx saw himself as propounding laws of social evolution. Both men were enormously influential in framing the scientific theories of the twentieth century—Darwin in the natural realm and Marx and other social Darwinists in the human realm. They shared, and contributed to, the ideas about progress and the inevitability of change that were central to the industrial transformation and to the ways in which technology and science were put to use (Bowler 1984/2003).

Marx believed passionately in the power of science and technology to transform human society, and the unleashing of human creativity and ingenuity was seen as one of the defining features of the industrial society:

Modern industry never views or treats the existing form of a production process as the definitive one. By means of machinery, chemical processes and other methods, it is continually transforming not only the technical basis of production but also the functions of the worker and the social combinations of the labour process. (Marx 1867/1976, 617)

Marx placed changes in what he termed "productive forces" as the foundational base for all other changes in society. It was technology—the "means of production"—that formed the basis for changes in work organization, social relations, and even in the "superstructural" realm of art and science: "Technology reveals the active relation of man to nature, the direct process of the production of his life, and thereby it also lays bare the process of the production of the social relations of his life, and of the mental conceptions that flow from those relations" (Marx 1867/1976, 493).

Marx's ideas were challenged by anarchists, such as Mikhail Bakunin and Petr Kropotkin, who criticized Marx for his overly positive attitude toward capitalist science and technology and viewed the ideas propounded by Marx and later Marxists as the ideology of a new elite within the working classes. As a socially minded geographer, Kropotkin corrected Darwin and Marx, emphasizing in his *Mutual Aid* the cooperation that was also a central feature of natural life and in his *Factories, Fields and Workshops* an alternative, decentralized, and not least rurally based form of technological development. In this respect, the anarchist perspective resembled some of the ideas expressed by William Morris in England, which proved to be influential, as we see in chapter 7, within the worlds of art and design, where he was active for many years, but also in the environmental movements that emerged in the twentieth century.

Marxism became the dominant ideology of the social democratic parties and organizations that were established to represent the working classes throughout Europe. In the 1890s, the so-called revisionists of the German Social Democratic Party, notably Eduard Bernstein, modified Marxism and, in particular, toned down many of its more deterministic elements and a good deal of its revolutionary program. But at much the same time, a more militant and dogmatic variety was articulated in Russia, and those in the socialist movement eventually split into reformist social democrats and revolutionary communists, as they called themselves after the Russian Revolution of 1917. On the institutional level—especially, in relation to the creation of state or public institutions, for the regulation, administration, and eventually financial support to technology and science—social democratic and communist governments played a pioneering role.

The critical social movements that emerged in the United States in the late nineteenth century were less directly associated with socialism than were those in most European countries. Instead, particularly in rural areas of the country where small farmers and businessmen were struggling to survive, a populist movement—often with a religious flavor—developed to oppose the eastern trusts and railway tycoons and propose alternative approaches to technology and science (Kazin 1995). The populist sensibility was not opposed to industrialization as such but wanted the fruits of science and technology to be of benefit to the people rather than to the elites and experts "back East." The populist influence on technology was significant—in terms of fostering new uses for technical innovations and in opening educational and scientific opportunities for the rural population. In the United States, the land-grant state universities and the smaller private colleges were influenced by the ambition to make knowledge making and technological development popular and accessible to the entire population. The strong social orientation of many scientific and engineering projects at the turn of the century—from the geological surveys to the urban sociology that developed in Chicago—owed much to the populist movement, as it exercised influence over the Democratic Party and many local and state governments.

Somewhat different forms of populism emerged in other parts of the world. In Denmark, for example, cooperative forms of production became institutionalized in the late nineteenth century. In Denmark, the farmers' movement, as it has been called, was an important site for technical development, in relation to agricultural machinery but also to wind energy and food-processing technology. In a similar way, the land-grant colleges and engineering schools that were established throughout the western United States also served to institutionalize industrial technology and science in ways that were appropriate for rural populations and agriculturally based economies. As in Denmark, where a system of state-supported technical consultancy was set up, along with the spreading of people's high schools in the countryside, the land-grant colleges—and the technical and scientific extension services that they provided to farmers and small businesses—represented a transformation of the populist critique of the power of the urban elites into more constructive institutions and practices.

Marxism served as a point of departure for many of those who developed new social and historical sciences in the late nineteenth and early twentieth centuries. Max Weber in Germany and Émile Durkheim in France developed much of their own social theories in a kind of explicit debate with Marxism, and in economics and economic history, writers such as Arnold Toynbee in Britain and Thorstein Veblen in the United States were inspired by Marx to focus on the role of technology and science in economic development. In the United States, Marxism played a role in history and economics, and, more indirectly, was a contributor to the various political programs of the so-called progressive era.

The consolidation of an industrial culture included a range of social, or institutional, innovations, from technological universities, engineering societies, world fairs, and industrial expositions to geographical surveys, metric and ordinance systems, and science and technology museums. As we discuss further in the following chapter, scientific and technological research became increasingly institutionalized—by means of industrial laboratories and institutes and by professionalizing and systematizing invention in new sites or locations. From the workshop in Menlo Park, New Jersey, set up by Thomas A. Edison, where he tirelessly searched for the appropriate way to produce electric light, to the bicycle shop where the Wright brothers built their machines that could fly, science became a business, a vocation. The institutions of industrialization included also the establishment of a range of new systems—the metric system to standardize the terms of calculation and measurement, the patent system to legalize the financial transactions associated with invention, the regulatory system to deal with the inevitable cheating and corruption that the new opportunities entailed, and a power system to provide energy to fuel the wheels and motors of industry. Each system entailed the creation of new experts who could operate the systems and of new places to educate and train the new professionals.

The industrial transformation did not end, of course, with the turn of the century. In many respects, its discourses, institutions, and practices are still very much alive in the early twenty-first century. On the discursive level, the language of science-based progress still dominates contemporary thought, embedded as it is in ideologies and philosophies and even most religious belief systems. Institutionally, systems of innovation—now transnational and corporate controlled—continue to structure the operational procedures for the organization, administration, and regulation of technology and science. On the practical level, as we discuss in more detail in part 3, the types of action and behavior that have been influenced by technology and science are still structured, to a large extent, by the industrial transformation. Our means of transportation, communication, information processing, and patterns of production and consumption can still be characterized in industrial terms. We are embedded in an industrial way of life that was consolidated in the nineteenth century.

3

THE SITES OF ENLIGHTENMENT AND INNOVATION

Whereas John Thorold and Martin Triewald, at the Desire and Invitation of some Gentlemen of this City [*To come from* England *to Perform a* COURSE *of* NATURAL *and* EXPERIMENTAL PHILOSOPHY *at Edinburgh*] came hither, and issued out their *Proposals*, setting forth, "That their COURSE was to commence in *December* last, consisting of 28 LECTURES, to be read three Times a-week, namely on *Monday, Wednesday,* and *Friday,* and to begin at Five a-clock in the Evening; ... The whole COURSE will be found to be very Useful and Instructive, not only to those who have studied the *Mathematicks,* but even to such as are not acquainted with that Science.

—*Caledonian Mercury,* **March 25, 1725**
(quoted in Lindqvist 1984, 209)

ATHENS OF THE NORTH

In 1790 Frederik Sneedorff, a Danish professor of history, visited the small town of Trondheim in the middle of Norway, a fortnight's journey away from Copenhagen. His hosts were eager to introduce him to the local master printer, take him to see some of the well-equipped private libraries, and guide him through the two local schools—the traditionally oriented Cathedral School and the newly founded Public School. The members of the Royal Norwegian Society of Science organized a special session in Professor Sneedorff's honor, and were more than happy to show him their natural-history collection. On several occasions the guest was invited to private dinner parties where food and drink were combined with learned discussions. Noticeably overwhelmed by the hospitality and the surprising richness of the town's cultural life, the professor wrote home that Trondheim, this "Athens of the North," was "the most beautiful Norwegian town I have ever seen" (quoted in Lysaker 1988, 126, 131).

Other observers were less impressed. When Leopold von Buch, a member of the Berlin Academy of Science, visited Trondheim almost twenty years later, he was also invited to the Society of Science. His verdict of his hosts was harsh: "The people in the Society at present are limited to a few barely glowing sparks" (Buch 1810/1814, 92). By this time, *Videnskabsselskabet* had degenerated into a kind of agricultural society that issued prizes for persons who were willing to try out exotic crops and cultivate new land. Obviously, decline had set in—a decline that would have upset its founding father, Bishop Johan Ernst Gunnerus, had he not passed away some thirty years earlier. The network that he had mobilized in the 1760s turned out to be fragile, and the ten thousand citizens of this ecclesiastical and commercial town had found other activities more important than dissecting animals, classifying plants, and arranging public lectures on scientific topics.

The pioneering phase in the mid-eighteenth century had been different. When Gunnerus had arrived in Trondheim in 1758 to take on his duties as bishop, he brought a kind of scientific spirit along with him (Aase and Hård 1998). He had studied and taught for more than a decade in Germany where he was exposed to enlightened philosophy, but after his move to Norway he decided to devote most of his time to the modern sciences. Gunnerus's chief interests came to concern those areas of natural history that we today call botany and zoology. During long excursions in his huge diocese he collected all kinds of plants and animals, in addition to objects of geological and historical interest. The local medical doctor helped Gunnerus dissect, preserve, and classify the material and compare it with other items that the bishop's subordinates more or less willingly gathered for him. Out of this activity emerged a unique collection, and the first comprehensive book on Norwegian plants, *Flora norvegica,* published in 1766 and celebrated by no one less than Carolus Linnaeus, the famous Swedish botanist and founder of the modern system of biological classification.

What interests us in this chapter are not primarily such contributions to the science of botany. We focus rather on the networks and institutions of science that Gunnerus and other intellectuals were instrumental in setting up in the periods that we call the scientific reformation and the industrial transformation. To analyze these changes we develop a kind of "cultural geography of science and technology" (Orange 1983, 205), an approach to the production and appropriation of knowledge that highlights the spaces and the arenas where these processes take place. Because these have always been collective processes, it is of essential importance that we develop an understanding of the sites where scientists and engineers meet, where they exchange ideas, quarrel over the latest findings, or simply socialize. Throughout the chapter we observe a tension between exclusiveness and openness, between private and public. Research activities have for the most part been carried out in individual homes or at corporate premises, but they have also taken place in more public settings where the ordinary citizen has been able to question or confront the makers of knowledge—and at times even been allowed to participate (Burke 2000).

THE CENTER OF THE ENLIGHTENMENT

Urban spaces play a paramount role in the literature that forms the basis for a cultural geography of knowledge (Heßler 2003). Cities that are often mentioned in this regard include Paris in the eighteenth century, Manchester in the nineteenth century, and Vienna in the early twentieth century. As a contemporary Swedish observer wrote about the French capital in the late 1700s,

The capital of all of Europe, a meeting place for people of all nations, for every craziness, for every vanity, for every possible amusement, for sciences, for stupidity, for knowledge, for ignorance, for virtue, for the most decadent behavior, for free-thinking, for superstition, for wealth, for the greatest poverty, for freedom, for slavery, and so on. (Johan H. Lidén, quoted in Ambjörnsson et al. 1986, 108)

In fact, already in the Middle Ages Paris had attracted students and intellectuals from all over Europe, and toward the end of the 1800s it became a mecca for artists and writers. In the decades before the French Revolution, Paris exerted a powerful attraction on persons from near and far—the famous scientist and politician Benjamin Franklin among them. The activities that flourished under the Old Regime sometimes tend to be forgotten amidst the turmoil and terror of the post-1789 era. Despite censorship, publishing thrived, and booksellers on the banks of the Seine river were able to make a reasonably good living. Printing became an industry in its own right, and channels of communication opened up for the established and nonestablished. Although they faced police repression, scholars found ways to circulate their ideas, not only in written form but also in various social institutions. As such, scientific theories were able to make their way through society, in spite of *l'ancien régime*'s having created a highly centralized system of education and research (Gillispie 1980).

One of the informal institutions where Swedish observer and scholar Johan H. Lidén was exposed to freethinkers and lunatics was the Parisian café. A visit to some of the 1,800 cafés was a must for any newcomer who wanted to get an idea of what people thought. Like the British coffeehouses, which had begun to mushroom around the time of the Glorious Revolution in 1688, the French premises could be said to represent the coming of a new kind of discursive space. They provided an opportunity for those who did not belong to the establishment to present and discuss alternative ideas and philosophies. The spread of newspapers and magazines was of paramount importance to this emerging *bürgerliche Öffentlichkeit,* the public sphere that the middle classes carved out in the eighteenth century (Habermas 1962/1989). If the printed word had originally served the Church and the State, it was now increasingly being appropriated by new groups for their own purposes. In the 1720s eighteen newspapers were reportedly being published in the British capital, and most of them were available to readers in the city's roughly five hundred coffeehouses. The papers and cafés came to play an important role for the rapid dissemination of new ideas and visions. Or, as the *Grub Street Journal* wrote in 1732, "True information about the politics of the government or about religious questions is best acquired in the coffee-houses" (quoted in Ambjörnsson et al. 1986, 102).

In eighteenth-century Paris another institution had developed that was essential for the cultural appropriation of radical ideas in the decades preceding the revolution. We are thinking here of the salon, where members of the nobility and aspiring young men of other classes met to converse and consume, discuss and debate. The salons were mostly run by wealthy women who found a calling in organizing intellectual and artistic events, where intellectual discussions were combined with gourmet dinners and musical entertainment (Outram 1995). Although the secret police often managed to infiltrate them, these

Figure 5. An early London coffeehouse, c. 1705. Reprinted by permission of Gettyimages, Munich, Germany.

private circles provided nonconformist thinkers and artists with a place where they could display their latest works and discuss new ideas. Unlike the cafés, these were not public spaces; admission was by invitation only.

Perhaps the most famous mid-eighteenth-century salon was that of Marie Thérèse Geoffrin, the widow of a rich Parisian merchant. Her sessions became legendary. A contemporary painting that depicts one of these events is a true French hall of intellectual fame. Basically, all of the people whom we associate with the movement called the French Enlightenment are present: the philosopher d'Alembert, the biologist Buffon, the writer Diderot, the economist Quesnay, the educator Condorcet, the *enfant terrible* Rousseau, and the materialist thinker de la Mettrie, to mention just a few (see Ambjörnsson et al. 1986, 115). It is easy to imagine the intensity of the debates that took place under Mme. Geoffrin's auspices. Like Tycho Brahe's Hven, her salon was a site that attracted the best brains of the age, and, like the sessions of the Lunar Society in Birmingham, it provided an opportunity for intellectuals and scientists from different walks of life to exchange ideas in a congenial atmosphere.

The salons point to the crucial role played by informal social institutions in the assimilation and dissemination of knowledge. Of course, books and journals have been essential in these processes, as have formal institutions such as universities and scientific societies. But, as stories from private dinner parties, Viennese *Kaffeehäuser*, and restaurants and bars of Silicon Valley indicate, creative communication is not limited to formal establishments. Without the existence of informal meeting points, the leading enlightened thinkers, the so-called *philosophes*, would never have been able to turn their individually held ideas into a collective project, such as the *Encyclopédie*, a thirty-five-volume collection of human knowledge and skills. This work was edited by Denis Diderot and Jean Le Rond d'Alembert and included articles written by some two hundred authors, the most active ones being among Mme. Geoffrin's regular guests. Their epistemological and political goal, in the words of their contemporary, the German philosopher Immanuel Kant (1785/1913, 169), was "the emancipation of man from a state of self-imposed tutelage," and to this end articles on education, natural law, and the sciences were solicited. On a more practical level, the *Encyclopédie* documented an array of craft techniques and production methods. By means of detailed descriptions and exact drawings, produced in close collaboration with artisan craftsmen, an attempt was made to turn technical skills into broadly accessible knowledge.

FROM THE AGORA TO THE ACADEMY

The salon was but one of several sites that emerged in the modern period to allow collective creativity to unfold in more or less organized forms. For a geography of technology and science, the societies and academies that were created in the seventeenth century are important, as are the laboratories and seminar rooms that emerged in the nineteenth and twentieth centuries (see Table 5). Whereas all of these institutions were comparatively exclusive, other sites were accessible to larger segments of the population. Libraries and lecture halls enabled people across class and gender lines to keep apace with the latest

TABLE 5. Key Sites of Appropriation

Analytical Level	Processes	Representative Sites
Discursive	Communication and assimilation	The agora, salons, cafés, journals, informal networks, chat rooms, Internet cafés
Institutional	Organization and dissemination	Libraries, academies, scientific societies, lecture halls, museums, conferences
Practical	Internalization and habituation	Anatomical theaters, botanical gardens, laboratories, seminars

developments, and the anatomical theaters and botanical gardens were, at least occasionally, open to the public (Pyenson and Sheets-Pyenson 1999). Ideas certainly emerge in the minds of individual human beings, but these beings never work in a social vacuum. Scientists try their theories out at seminars or present their findings in journals and at conferences. More recently, Internet cafés and electronic chat rooms have been developed to serve similar functions. Engineers communicate their ideas with colleagues at informal forums or in work teams. If they fail to do so, then their contributions will usually not be accepted by their peers.

For Socrates in the fourth century BC, wisdom was conceived as something created not by isolated individuals in the countryside but by the collective participation of free, male citizens. The perfect site for such interaction was the agora, the open marketplace in the center of Athens that still today serves as an ideal for some philosophers and sociologists of science (Nowotny, Scott, and Gibbons 2001). According to Socrates, the development of knowledge can take place only in dialogue, and the best place for such dialogue is in the midst of the city center. Perhaps needless to say, Socrates never problematized the fact that the majority of humankind—women and slaves in particular—remained excluded from the agora.

It did not take long, however, before science left the Socratic ideal public space behind. Already Plato, Socrates' own pupil, turned his back on Athens and opened up his *Academia* outside of the town. Here, only those who could afford to pay a fee were welcome. Similarly, Aristotle founded his *Lyceum* for the collective investigation of natural phenomena and human endeavors. With these moves, the scientific spirit was for more than a millennium taken out of public space and confined to secluded institutions, and its unfolding became defined as an elitist activity. Well in accordance with this tradition of seclusion and exclusion, the *Museion* in the Hellenistic center of Alexandria was not open to the public. Similarly, the scientifically creative sites of the Islamic world, with Baghdad as its long-standing center, were controlled by the Caliph and were accessible only to a privileged few. But all the same, and this seems to be important to stress in the early twenty-first century, these chosen scholars enjoyed freedom of thought and an abundance of resources. The outcome was impressive. By preserving important parts of the Greek intellectual heritage, Islamic culture served as a bridge between Antiquity and the Middle Ages, and by fostering new areas of knowledge, it gave European technicians and scholars important impulses. As is still apparent from concepts such as *algebra* and *algorithm*, not to mention our Arab numerals, new forms of mathematical knowledge developed in Muslim culture. Advances were also made in alchemy and philosophy, astronomy and architecture, water irrigation and philology (Huff 2003).

In Europe a more open kind of intellectual inquiry was reestablished only in the twelfth century, as some cathedral schools were transformed into universities. In sharp contrast to the seclusion practiced by monastic orders, universities were characterized by a striking openness. Students came from near and far to listen to famous teachers who, because lecture halls were scarce, often addressed their audience in the streets. Salamanca, Bologna, and Padua turned into crowded student towns, a development that was not to everyone's liking. In Paris, for instance, fights between students and tavern owners and landlords were frequent occurrences. To support the universities, kings and princes granted them certain economic privileges, and when there were conflicts—occasionally with lethal consequences—the local citizens were often at a disadvantage. Once a number of Parisian religious schools had been given a university-like structure and the news about their quality had begun to spread across the continent, the French king was very keen to retain it at all costs. A contemporary observer wrote,

> With such kind favor did [Louis VII] promote clerics that in his time they flocked to Paris from all quarters of Christendom and, nourished and protected under the shadow of his wings, have continued in the schools unto this day. (Walter Map [1190s], quoted in Ferruolo 1988, 29f.)

Discussing the reasons that Louis VII and his followers had to protect the schools and, later, the university, historian Stephen Ferruolo (1988) argued that these institutes of learning gave the royalty status and recognition. Perhaps unexpectedly, the main reason was neither pecuniary nor practical. For sure, some three thousand or so students and teachers contributed to the economic prosperity of the capital, and the king also exhibited an interest in appointing some of them in his administration, but, more important, the schools guaranteed Paris a place in the history of civilization. Thus a royal chronicler proudly noted in 1210, "Neither Athens nor Egypt ever had as many scholars as Paris now does" (quoted in Ferruolo 1988, 33).

In Paris and elsewhere, universities were breeding grounds for priests and medical doctors, and they provided earthly powers with legally trained civil servants, but they also gave their promoters a kind of "cultural capital" (Bourdieu 1979/1984). To house a university where famous teachers debated the burning theological or legal issues of the day gave a ruler prestige. Much later, starting in the seventeenth century, German princes sought to attract the best scholars and the most famous scientists to their local universities.

In other instances, princes had a directly utilitarian interest in fostering formal sites of knowledge production, and they often tied scholars and scientists directly to their courts. The *Accademia del cimento* in Florence is a case in point. Prince Leopold of Tuscany not only took the initiative to found this "Academy of the Experiment" in 1657 but also took a very active part in its operation (Middleton 1971). Topics ranged from astronomy to meteorology and heat theory to chemistry. To make sure that the experimental philosophers and engineers whom he had appointed remained devoted to their tasks, he insisted that experiments be carried out at the court, which, in other words, became an unlikely site of knowledge production. Throughout the brief life of his academy, the prince stayed in close contact, sometimes on a daily basis, with the secretary of the academy, Vincenzo Vivani. As a construction engineer and, simultaneously, a teacher at the University of Florence, Vivani had internalized a kind of hybrid identity on the borderline between technology and science, between academic scholarship and government tasks (he was responsible for the control of river flows in Tuscany), between the university and the court.

Not all academies enjoyed state support, and they did not always make their results known to the public. In contrast to the Florentine academy and the Parisian *Académie des Sciences*, several of these societies were private undertakings. When the first academies were founded, their members often deliberately met in private to avoid publicity. Typical are the Italian names of some of these: *incognito, segreti,* and *affidati;* that is, "unknown," "secret," and "faithful," respectively. In fact, the academy model as such implied a high degree of exclusivity, and in this respect it shares certain characteristics with freemasonry. Meetings were often closed to the public, and internal discussions were not always recorded. New members were usually recruited among friends and peers. Wealthy and famous persons were invited to join, especially if a society was in need of additional funds and public support. Even today, to be invited to become a Fellow of the Royal Society in London is one of the highest honors in British scientific and engineering circles.

THE ENLIGHTENMENT AS A MOVEMENT

For a limited period of time, Mme. Geoffrin's salon provided an informal social space for the chief propagators of enlightened thought.

Despite editorial headaches and the financial risk involved, the collective book project was ultimately completed. Diderot and d'Alembert had faced problems with the French censor and were forced to print the last volumes of the *Encyclopédie* abroad. But finally, the propagators of Enlightenment philosophy had a concrete product that summarized their thinking and facilitated the further dissemination of their ideas. At the core of this philosophy was a progressive, or positive, view of the individual as open and capable of limitless development and improvement. As is well-known, these ideals came to be transformed during the French Revolution into the powerful parable "freedom, equality, brotherhood." For the areas of technology and science, "utility" and "rationality" were of similar importance. Economically and technologically useful knowledge was central to enlightened thinking, as was the corresponding idea that such knowledge ought to be disseminated throughout the population.

French philosophers were not the only ones who contributed to the project of Enlightenment. Famous are those persons who made up what has come to be called the Scottish and German Enlightenment: Joseph Black, Adam Smith, and David Hume in Edinburgh; Christian Wolff in Halle; and Immanuel Kant in Konigsberg. Not least because of the politically liberal atmosphere of the Low Countries, the Dutch city of Leiden became a center for rationalist philosophy and modern science. And, in the young Americas, facing revolutionary turmoil, the city of Philadelphia emerged as a site where modern philosophy was developed and practiced. From midcentury onward we even find outposts of enlightened thinking in countries such as Sweden and Denmark-Norway. (Norway was under Danish rule until the nineteenth century.)

The Enlightenment that unfolded in the 1700s was a kind of cultural movement. Although active at different sites, philosophers and scientists were held together by means of correspondence and personal contacts. The distribution of pamphlets and books occurred through networks that thus facilitated the institutionalization of Enlightenment thought. Of course, these means were closely linked to the intensification of trade and the dramatic increase in book production. What Dorinda Outram (1995, 22, 29) called the "commodification" and "commercialization" of the written word had direct connections to the emergence of an internationally close-knit "republic of letters." A decrease in illiteracy, especially in towns, and an increased demand for books and magazines made it easier for intellectuals to reach a larger audience, and for some individuals even to live off their writings (Darnton 1982).

In various ways, these technologies and processes were paramount for the Scottish Enlightenment. The liberal ideas that developed in Edinburgh and Glasgow can, on one hand, be interpreted as an effect of the growing power of a middle class in search of a worldview and of systems of thought that differed from traditional, theologically oriented ways of philosophizing. But, on the other hand, they can be seen as a logical outcome of the relatively intense contacts that members of this class upheld with the European continent. Already in the late seventeenth century it was common for tradesmen, lawyers, and doctors to send their sons to Leiden, where the young men had been exposed to the classics and to civil law and modern medicine. Not surprisingly, then, the men responsible for subsequent college reforms in Edinburgh quite explicitly used the Dutch university as a model (Phillipson 1988). Toward the mid-1700s, keen youngsters could enjoy an exciting, strikingly modern mixture of civil law and clinical medicine, history and natural science that attracted students even from outside Britain.

As an intellectual site, Edinburgh is of interest not only because of its university and its many freelancing teachers. In the eighteenth century the city boasted a handful of scientific and scholarly societies that provided spaces for mutual discussion and collective investigation. Most famous, perhaps, was the Rankenian Club, which was described at the time as

highly instrumental in disseminating through Scotland, freedom of thought, boldness of disquisition, liberality of sentiment, accuracy of reasoning, correctness of taste, and attention to composition. (*Scots Magazine* 1771, quoted in Phillipson 1988, 107)

Among the other societies were the Medical Society and the Physiological Library—which counted the philosopher David Hume among its members. As is bluntly indicated by the name of a third one, the Select Society, these associations were not public institutions but rather organized as private clubs. Unlike coffeehouses, which catered to a larger audience, only members of the establishment had access to the learned lectures and were allowed to take part in the discussions that the societies arranged. For the spread of scientific knowledge, philosophical insights, and polite manners, these societies were essential in that they provided a meeting place for established scholars, reformist clerics, and various gentlemen—be they medical doctors, lawyers, or civil servants.

As we indicated earlier, the Enlightenment project was much more vulnerable in smaller towns on the European periphery. In addition to the philosopher-turned-bishop, the leading personalities in Trondheim included not only the rector of the cathedral school, the town doctor, local priests, and various civil servants but also such unlikely persons as the head of the local fire brigade. The following groups were welcome to the meetings of the Royal Norwegian Society of Science: "all civilized, profane and clerical persons, as well as the town's most honorable citizens and ... students" (*Adresseavisen*, 2 [1768], No. 4, quoted in Aase and Hård 1998, 50). Although the society had received royal privileges in 1767, it remained very much a private institution. Women were not accepted as members, but they were welcome to attend public lectures and, perhaps more important, donate money to the society. For more than twenty years the society held its meetings in the home of its secretary, and Gunnerus orchestrated most of its work.

Gunnerus was a true hybrid who did not draw a line between his duties as a bishop and civil servant, his activities as a scientist and chairman of the Society of Science, and his private life. In contrast to several continental academies, the semiprivate character of the society should, however, not be taken to mean that its activities did not receive public attention. Its proceedings were published on a regular basis, as were several of the speeches that were held at the annual meetings. The local Trondheim newspaper reported from the public lectures being organized by the society, and it also allowed the bishop to run a regular column on "learned news." A survey of the paper reveals a striking openness for Enlightenment thinking in general and scientific issues in particular. Excerpts from Montesquieu's writings on human rights were reprinted, and there were articles on "the usefulness of mathematics" and on various aspects of the history of technology and science.

IN THE NAME OF UTILITY

The emphasis on usefulness, or utility, reflects changes that can be observed in other countries. The tasks of the Berlin Academy of Science also lay within the area of agriculture and horticulture. The number of agricultural societies grew throughout the eighteenth century, reflecting the growing importance of physiocratic thinking. In Sweden *utilism* was launched as an ideology in its own right. When the Royal Swedish Academy of Sciences was set up in Stockholm in 1739 its purpose was explicitly utilitarian and patriotic (Frängsmyr 1989). Linnaeus, the most famous of the academy's founding fathers, effectively used this institution to solicit state support for extensive surveys of the natural resources of this enormous country—at the time larger even than France. Parliament financed his trips in the search not only for rare plants but also for potentially profitable minerals, and not least technical skills.

When Linnaeus was not on the road in Lapland or Scania, he could usually be found at one of three interconnected but distinctly different scientific sites. He earned his bread and butter as a professor at the University of Uppsala, and in this town he also set up a botanical garden. Like the *Jardin des Plantes* in Paris, Linnaeus's garden served different purposes: education, experimentation, and popularization. Here, students learned firsthand how to apply the revolutionary classificatory system that Linnaeus had developed, and the professor and his assistants were able to test the natural basis of his *Systema Naturae* by trying to crossbreed various plants. To find the peace of mind necessary for reflection and writing, Linnaeus withdrew to his own private estate, Hammarby, outside of Uppsala. As was common among gentleman scientists in those days, Linnaeus was able to carry out a large part of his research at home.

As we indicated earlier, the third site, Stockholm, was essential for the securing of the funds that Linnaeus needed for his type of "big science." By means of public lectures and active lobbying, he tried to convince members of the higher echelons that science was worth supporting. Indeed, in the decades that have gone down in Swedish history as the Age of Freedom—abruptly ending with King Gustav III's coup in 1783—the city became a center for a variety of scientific activities. The story of the young, aspiring engineer Morten Triewald is a case in point. After having failed to install the first steam engine in a mining district some one hundred miles north of Stockholm in the mid-1730s, Triewald put all his efforts into establishing himself as an experimental philosopher in the capital (Lindqvist 1984). During a sojourn in Britain in the previous decade, he had given public lectures on physical topics, and he continued in this vein by offering lectures and demonstrations in the highly prestigious House of Knights in the heart of Stockholm.

Triewald, the son of an immigrant mechanic from Germany and a member of the striving middle class, belonged to the founding fathers of the Stockholm academy. It was definitely a stroke of genius by Triewald, Linnaeus (who came from even poorer conditions in the provinces), and their partners to try to make *Vetenskapsakademien* a royal institution and to place it in the capital. This double strategy enabled them to distance themselves from the classical forms of scholarship at the University of Uppsala and to place modern, utilitarian science and technology close to the center of power. In a very concerted act of cultural appropriation, the proponents of what Christopher Polhem, the grand old man of Swedish engineering, called *mechanica* and *mathesis* inserted new types of knowledge into familiar, traditional settings (Hård 1986).

Apart from Sweden, utilitarian thinking might have been strongest in Britain. As we show in chapter 1, this country had bred a fascination for useful knowledge since the days of Bacon and the founding of the Royal Society. Not surprisingly, the industrial cities of Manchester and Birmingham followed the pattern. Not only did they foster an entrepreneurial spirit that resulted in the foundation of numerous factories and other production sites, but by lacking many of the orthodox, obstructive institutions that one could find in Oxford and Cambridge, they also offered conditions more conducive to scientific creativity. Consequently, we find in these Midland cities an array of the individuals who appear in any work on the history of British engineering and science, from John Dalton to James Watt.

Truly creative milieus allow the unexpected to happen. Innovation requires freedom and flexibility. As we indicated earlier, certain sites were particularly supportive of the investigative mind throughout history. In the industrious circles of Birmingham the private home was such a site. Because the town did not have a university, laboratories and libraries were, in the first instance, private institutions. But the private home was also important as a meeting place, where individuals of different disciplinary and industrial backgrounds could convene. In this regard, Matthew Boulton's home, Soho House, stands out. Here, the famous Lunar Society met for the first time in 1775, and on a regular basis this beautiful mansion housed sessions during which "metaphysical, mechanical and pyrotecnical" demonstrations were carried out and political and economic topics were discussed (Erasmus Darwin 1778, quoted in Uglow 2002, 265). Admission was limited. In fact, historian Jenny Uglow (2002, 353) went so far as to say that "the Lunar Society was rather a tight, exclusive circle." Not all local industrialists and philosophers were welcome, and "there were certainly no women."

The Lunar Society was a truly hybrid forum, as were most of the other institutions that we have met so far in this chapter. At its meetings chemists exchanged experiences and reflections with businessmen, and medical doctors discussed ethical and social issues with industrialists. The members also had hybrid identities. Josiah Wedgwood, the famous manufacturer who transformed pottery making into an industry, carried out scientific experiments on the nature of heat. And Joseph Priestley, one of the discoverers of oxygen, who moved to Birmingham in 1780, developed his research agenda in close collaboration with representatives of industry.

We find a similar kind of intermingling of identities in Manchester. In the first decades of the nineteenth century, the city counted more than ten societies with a technological or scientific orientation. Among the more distinctly utilitarian institutions were the Agricultural Society and the Royal Victoria Gallery of Practical Science, but best known is the Literary and Philosophical Society, to which no subject was foreign. Physicians had been most active in its first years, but, increasingly, natural scientists, engineers, and manufacturers were enrolled. As elsewhere, many persons were attracted by practical topics. However, the cultural capital and social status that one could gain by joining also played an important role (Thackray 1974).

The salons, the scientific academies, and the learned societies thus contributed to making technology and science an integral part of industrial society and modern culture. The processes by which modernizing societies began to appropriate these activities were never solely economic or instrumental but always had distinctive cultural components. When, in the 1980s, the Royal Society set up a campaign to improve the "Public Understanding of Science," it acted in line with a well-established tradition.

BETWEEN THE LECTURE HALL AND THE LABORATORY

The university and the institute of technology are two other institutions that have contributed to society's appropriation of technology and science during the past two centuries. The university's roots go back much further in time, but in the nineteenth century it went through fundamental changes. Also, technical education took a new start in that it was academized and modeled on the university (Layton 1971). In the process, new sites of learning, training, and research were formed at both types of institutions.

The main task of universities was originally professional instruction, but after 1800 another kind of mission was formulated. These changes started out in Prussia and were inspired by idealist philosophers who attacked the universities' narrow orientation toward educating young men for clerical and civil service. In his lectures *On University Studies* (1802/1966, 6, 7), Schelling stated another goal: the "higher purpose of learning ... is to ennoble one's mind though knowledge." Instead of, or at least in addition to, educating priests, lawyers, and physicians, the modern university should contribute to the development of the personality. Instead of communicating highly specialized knowledge, students should try to inform themselves as broadly as possible: "Knowledge of the organic whole of the sciences must precede special training for a particular profession." Central in this program was the German concept of *Bildung*, usually translated as "cultivation." The active search for knowledge was to be a prerogative in university studies, and to this end students would also have to learn how to search for new knowledge on their own.

The idea of cultivation had two important consequences for those institutes of higher learning that followed the German model. First, it implied that teachers and students should advance the frontier of knowledge through research, and, second, it involved the intertwining of research and teaching. To carry out research became, as R. Steven Turner (1980) put it, an "imperative," as did the propagation of the results of this research. The outcome was the creation of a number of sites within the walls of the university that were conducive to following this command. In experimental philosophy, and somewhat later in the engineering sciences, the laboratory became such a site. Together with the seminar, the laboratory was now integrated into university education. Both institutions became places for training and the collective pursuit of knowledge, and they soon proved to have powerful impacts on social and economic life.

The seminar was a nineteenth-century invention, and it was to be found in the natural sciences and the humanities. Friedrich Neumann's seminar for theoretical physics and Leopold von Ranke's seminar in history are legendary. Here, advanced students presented preliminary results of their own research and were given the opportunity to discuss them with their peers and the professor. Various intellectual problems were tackled together. In the history seminar, for instance, the deciphering and interpretation of original manuscripts became a collective activity.

If we view the pursuit of science as a social process, then the introduction of the laboratory and the seminar into the university were crucial innovations. Unlike the lecture hall, the laboratory and the seminar were exclusive sites that guaranteed that only a selected few participated in knowledge production. Whereas at most universities the interested public had access to the lecture hall, the two other institutions were closed to the *Öffentlichkeit*. As the importance of the philosophical faculty—to which the natural sciences and the humanities belonged—grew in the nineteenth century, public lectures attracted increasingly larger audiences. Here, the history professor presented the results of the seminar work in an accessible manner, and the chemist carried out exciting experiments to demonstrate the latest findings.

From a gender point of view, it is essential not to forget that the lecture hall was usually open to both genders, whereas the laboratory and the seminar became a virtually exclusively male domain (B. Smith 1995). When women began to make their way into the institutions of higher learning toward the end of the century, they faced the heaviest resistance at the seminar and laboratory doors. So-called benevolent opponents argued that laboratories were too dangerous for women and that female attire was inappropriate for lab work. By means of overt exclusion mechanisms, the advanced search for knowledge continued to be restricted to just one of the genders.

By focusing on collective research tasks, the laboratory and the seminar became central vehicles for a process that has, in the positivist discourse, been called the advancement of science. They were unprecedented as training sites. Particularly famous is Justus von Liebig's laboratory at the University of Giessen, which produced not only significant results in the area of organic chemistry but also a herd of young chemists who made their way into academia and industry—in Germany and abroad. Liebig's success was so great that students traveled all the way from the United States to this small town in Hesse to study. There, they met well-equipped laboratories and a style of instruction that stressed individual initiative and collective critique. Under this system the professor was not primarily a teacher but rather a mentor or a coach who set up a research agenda and discussed procedures and results with his students. Giessen came to serve as a direct model for U.S. chemistry departments. In Britain, several of Liebig's students became instrumental in the foundation of the modern, research-based chemical industry. The investigative methods that Liebig had propagated turned out to be highly useful for the analysis of coal tar and for the subsequent production on a large scale of artificial dyestuffs for the textile industry.

Developments were somewhat different in regard to technical education. Following the *École Polytechnique,* a product of the French Revolution, technical education stressed the methodological unity of various fields of engineering and their common basis in mathematics and natural science. This so-called polytechnic ideal had spread to Germany, from where it made its way into other countries. In this tradition the drawing room played a role similar to that of the university laboratory, and students of engineering had to spend hour after hour practicing technical drawing. Gaspard Monge, a French engineer, developed descriptive geometry into a visual lingua franca, by means of which one could transfer three-dimensional objects onto paper. The importance of this technique for industry and the engineering sciences can hardly be exaggerated. It enabled designers to present their ideas in such a way that mechanics and manufacturers could understand them, and it remained central to engineering education until computer-aided design made its inroads in the 1970s and 1980s.

The first laboratories of mechanical engineering appeared in the last quarter of the nineteenth century. Before that, the most important instruction site for aspiring mechanical engineers had been the machine shop, equipped with lathes, mills, drilling machines, and various workbenches. In addition to learning how to operate such machines, students became acquainted with different metals and made their first attempts at dismantling and reassembling various types of engines. This shop culture remained particularly strong in British engineering education, where it had been developed to serve the needs of the textile industry, the manufacturers of agricultural machinery, and the energy sector. By contrast, the machine laboratory became an integral part of a more academically oriented school culture that emphasized systematic parameter variation and exact methods of investigation (Calvert 1967). The primary goal of this tradition, the roots of which are found in France and Germany, was not to handle specific machines but to be able to analyze and calculate various processes. With the laboratory also entered the research imperative. As in the natural sciences, the engineering laboratory became a place where students tried out, by means of a kind of "learning by doing" process, what they had heard in the lecture hall.

BETWEEN ACADEMIA AND INDUSTRY

One of the pioneers of an academic approach to engineering was Carl von Linde, a professor of mechanical engineering at the Munich Institute of Technology. His specialty was technical thermodynamics, the main goal of which was to apply the mechanical theory of heat to the analysis and the ultimate improvement of heat engines. His central object of investigation was the steam engine, and a number of such engines were mounted at the heart of the laboratory of mechanical engineering that Linde inaugurated in 1875. Only matriculated students and employed machinists had access to this room. The purpose was to examine the way the steam engine worked under various conditions, not in the first place to learn how to maintain and repair it. To this end the consumption of coal was measured, and the so-called indicator diagram was employed, a visual aid for the analysis of the relationships between pressure, heat, and volume.

Linde was a person with a hybrid identity, and at least in the beginning of his career he had been driven by a form of hubris. In both respects he was similar to his most well-known student Rudolf Diesel, the inventor of the heat engine that carries his name. Both men mixed engineering and science, always hunting for higher degrees of efficiency and striving to design theoretically optimal, ideal engines but at the same time applying concepts and worldviews from the natural sciences. They argued that the engineer could understand the nature of machines only by moving between academia and industry and by translating scientific insights into machinery that worked.

The rise and fall of Diesel is well documented (Thomas 1987). In the early 1890s this young engineer had envisioned a "rational heat engine" that would surpass all existing prime movers in terms of fuel efficiency. Diesel was so convinced of the power of his ideas that he chose to go public before he had had time to test them in a laboratory. He presented his design principles at a meeting of the Society of German Engineers, one of the most prestigious official sites in the German engineering culture, and simultaneously he published a book to guarantee that the word about the new engine—which existed only on paper—spread among engineers and industrialists. After experiments had started in the workshops of the *Maschinenfabrik Augsburg*, the impracticality of his theoretical deliberations became obvious. Substantial changes had to be made to his original design, and in the end several of his patents were not upheld. Diesel ended up committing suicide.

Diesel's teacher was more successful. In the early 1870s Linde, still in his twenties, had described an ideal refrigeration system, thus laying the foundation for a new area of technical thermodynamics (Hård 1994). He had a large teaching load, and he began to try out his ideas in practice only when approached by representatives of industry. Perhaps surprisingly, these men came not from machine building but from beer brewing. The production of lager beer requires fairly low temperatures, and several mild winters had taught brewery owners that natural ice was often a rare and unreliable resource. Eager to find an alternative to natural ice, they provided Linde with an experimental laboratory at the Spaten Brewery in Munich. Soon, patent applications were filed, and a first prototype could be built.

Spurred by this success, Linde began to commute between different sites of research and development in academia and industry. In addition to his college laboratory and various machine shops, he was also active at the drawing board and at a testing station that he founded to compare different brands of refrigeration machinery. In the lab the focus was on analysis rather than design, and at the testing station the focus was on measurement rather than improvement.

The interest on the part of the brewing industry in Linde's ideas is, at least at first sight, surprising. Why would two brewery directors want to support the experiments of a young professor who had published only two scientific articles and not been even close to constructing a refrigeration machine? Brewing is a sensitive undertaking, and brewers have always been afraid that the process could get out of control, resulting in whole batches having to be discarded. In the nineteenth century the search for pure yeast became a primary concern, and to solve this task brewers enrolled renowned scientists, and some of the first industrial laboratories were set up. Louis Pasteur wrote a book on yeast cultivation and did important research for the brewing industry, and the Danish Carlsberg Brewery set up a biochemical laboratory. Experience from yeast cultivation and chemical quality control had taught brewers the potential value of a scientific approach to the solution of industrial problems.

TRANSPLANTING THE LABORATORY INTO INDUSTRY

In other branches of industry, scientists were employed to control the production process and to guarantee that products met certain quality criteria. Chemists began to enter industry in the middle of the nineteenth century, and physicists soon followed suit. After the First World War, even social scientists were hired—in this instance to make sure that companies were able to get the most out of their workforce without the quality of their products being threatened. To move from the safe haven of a university laboratory to the hectic, but often more remunerative, environment of a private company did not suit all individuals and required that the scientist take on a kind of hybrid identity. As J. J. Carty, chief engineer at the American Telephone and Telegraph Company (AT&T), declared, "The distinction between pure scientific research and industrial research is one of motive" (quoted in Noble 1977, 112).

The notion that scientists could be employed for other purposes than control, regulation, and analysis slowly but surely spread throughout the industrial world, in particular to the chemical, electric, and pharmaceutical industries (Fox and Guagnini 1999). By assigning chemists and physicists specific tasks in the areas that were later called "research and development," companies hoped to gain competitive advantages in the marketplace. Pioneering in this process were a number of British and German companies that belonged to the coal-tar-based dying industry mentioned previously. After the first lab-produced color had taken the world by storm in the mid-1800s, demand soared. "Aniline purple," as the new man-made color was called, was developed by William H. Perkin, a university-trained chemist who, against the advice of his teacher, had decided to leave the academy for business. For manufacturers these products had obvious advantages in comparison with natural dyes. As historian John J. Beer (1959, 5) explained, artificial colors

> not only came to surpass the old dyes in fastness, clarity, and variety, but they were perfectly standardized so that the exact color could be reproduced repeatedly with absolute certainty. They were far easier and quicker to apply and very much cheaper.

To profit from these advantages, laboratory-based companies began to mushroom on both sides of the Channel, and some of them are still going strong: Agfa, Bayer, and the Badische Anilin-und Soda-Fabrik (BASF), among them. To be able to survive growing competition, companies needed a well-equipped laboratory.

The success of the laboratory as a site of knowledge production and dissemination was not only measurable in economic terms. From this time on, the lab took on almost mystical dimensions in the public imagination. The bearded man in a white robe became either a godlike figure who would save the world from germs and other dangers or, according to a story line that has been reproduced over and over again by novelists and moviemakers, a satanic madman driven by an indefatigable passion to rule the world. In France Louis Pasteur became the prototypical scientist who used his laboratory at the *École normale supérieure* to save the world from dangerous diseases. And in the United States at about the same time, Thomas Alva Edison, "the wizard of Menlo Park," churned out inventions on a regular basis. The site of knowledge production in this heroic story line is the laboratory, a strange place that is difficult to understand, but a place from which new discoveries and inventions emerge that contribute to the progress of mankind. Or, as Ronald Reagan used to say in television commercials for General Electric well before he launched the political career that landed him in the White House, "Progress is our most important product!"

The appropriation of science—not only in a figurative but also in the very legal sense of the term—by the captains of industry became normalized in the opening decades of the twentieth century. Among the leading companies in this process were American firms such as DuPont, General Electric, and AT&T, the latter being best known in the area of research and development for its subsidiary Bell Labs. Revolutionary chemicals and drugs, household products and appliances, and new communication gadgets guaranteed growing market shares. Perhaps more important than individual product innovations was the system as a whole, the organizational innovation of the research and development laboratory as an integral part of business. As historian David Noble (1977, 118) nicely put it, "In the nineteenth century, scientific ideas had given rise to industrial manufacture; now the industrial corporations undertook to manufacture scientific ideas." If there had ever been such a thing as pure, disinterested research, it was now definitely a thing of the past.

The establishment of industrial research laboratories was accompanied by a process of growing anonymity. As we already mentioned, the private home used to be the main site for experimental work. Only after the natural and engineering sciences found a permanent sanctuary in the academic world in the nineteenth century did it become conceivable to build university laboratories. Even Liebig initially had to fight to get a properly equipped laboratory erected in Giessen. In the late 1800s, the development of technology and science could still, to a large extent, be directed and overseen by one person. As a result of growing complexity and the need for ever-larger investments, however, it became increasingly difficult for any one individual to try out new ideas and develop new products on his or her own. The fate of Edison and his companies proves this point. In the 1870s and 1880s, Edison was able to take an active part in the development of products such as the electric light, the phonograph, and the kinetoscope. But as research and development grew in cost and scale, the process of invention and innovation became an increasingly collective effort. By the time General Electric opened up its first research laboratory in the year 1900, research and development had been transformed into teamwork, and the research process had been transformed into a project-oriented activity led by managers (Reich 1985). The road toward bureaucratized big science had begun.

EXTENDING THE BOUNDARIES OF THE LAB

After the emergence of the industrial research laboratory, it became something of an anachronism to discuss research in terms of *Bildung*. Rather than cultivation, it was processes of industrialization, militarization, and commercialization that accompanied research and development into the twentieth century. One contemporary observer who understood where the world was heading was Max Weber, the grand old man of German sociology. In his famous speech to the student body in Munich, Weber in 1918 discussed the conditions for research and teaching. According to Weber, there could be no going back to the days when research had been carried out for the sake of individual development. To do research was still an imperative, but it now was carried out in other settings, for other reasons, and was under the control of other masters. Under the modern system, research and teaching were specialized and bureaucratized, and in many contexts it was impossible to uphold a close connection between them. Scientific activity had become a "vocation" or, perhaps more fittingly, a profession (Weber 1919/1958).

Weber saw the professionalization of science as part of the general process of rationalization of the Western world. Among other things, this meant that science began to expand into ever more areas of society. The following example from the area of mechanical engineering illustrates two important points about scientific research in the modern age. It shows that research no longer is limited to the lab but also takes place at a number of other sites in society, but it also indicates that the investigations that take place behind the doors of a laboratory are often—despite its allegedly scientific character—quite mundane and pedestrian.

Let us pay a quick visit to the so-called laboratory of the company Ricardo Consulting Engineers Ltd., situated in Shoreham-by-Sea on the English southern coast. It was created in the early 1920s by Harry R. Ricardo, a typical hybrid figure who has been given the epithet "the high priest of the internal combustion engine" (French 1995). On one hand, Ricardo was a commercially successful engineer whose consulting firm was a pioneer in the areas of gasoline and diesel engine design. On the other hand, he had taken the tripos at Cambridge and worked there a couple of years as a research assistant in the mechanical sciences before entering the world of business. As a practicing engineer, he not only designed engines and took out patents but also published his results in renowned engineering journals and traveled around the world giving lectures about the theory and practice of internal combustion engineering. At the age of forty-four, he was elected a Fellow of the Royal Society, and after the war, he was even knighted, an accolade that is seldom given to mechanical engineers. Thus, in public, Ricardo represented not the dirty world of machinery but the higher echelons of science. Unlike Thomas Alva Edison, he was regarded not as a wizard but as a rational scientist.

A closer look at Ricardo's laboratory reveals a different picture. The kind of work that was carried out under the heading of "applied research," as Ricardo (1945, 143) called the core activities at his company, was neither abstract nor pure, and it was certainly very far from the image that scientists like to give of their work. On the premises was an office building, including one room where designers sat bent over their drawing boards; a joiner's shop, where carpenters were busily building engine models; a craftsmen's area, where millwrights, copper-smiths, and blacksmiths reigned; and one room where the characteristics of various lubricating oils were tested; in addition to a machine shop equipped with a number of general purpose machine tools and a test shop with thirty-two test beds where technicians and engineers examined the performance of various engines.

Even bus drivers were among the people who took part in "the practice of research," as two of Ricardo's assistants called the core activities of the company (Alcock and Glyde 1930). Ricardo's engineers at strategic moments had to leave Shoreham and take their laboratory to garages and on the road. Experiments on the road served the purpose of testing engine performance and fuel consumption. To "imitate service conditions" as closely as possible, the engineers needed to have a technological, geographical, and chronological setup that was reasonably close to real-life conditions. It was also important to have drivers on hand that treated the engine as it would be treated in ordinary traffic. Many things could happen to an experimental engine, and in such cases it was an advantage to have an experienced person behind the wheel. A good test driver could use his senses to register problems, his imagination to make a diagnosis, and his experience to make minor repairs.

Engineers at the Ricardo company moved more or less effortlessly not only between the desk, the drawing board, and the test bench but also between the laboratory and the production site. Already Pasteur had been aware that success required that he at times left his well-organized and tidy lab and transplanted parts of his laboratory to the outside world. Only by carrying out experiments with the anthrax bacillus at farms in the French countryside was Pasteur able to convince farmers that the lab-produced vaccine would protect their cattle (Latour 1984/1988). In the course of the ensuing century, engineers and scientists came to be increasingly interested in extending the boundaries of their laboratories to encompass all of society. The most ambitious of their kind from the 1930s onward began to claim the right to turn, literally, all of society into their own playground. The Soviet Five-Year Plan, the U.S. New Deal, and not least the German Third Reich provided engineers and natural and social scientists with experimental sites of formerly unheard of dimensions. The seeds that French *philosophes* and Swedish utilitarians had sown in the 1700s had begun to come to fruition in the hubris of social engineering.

Part 2
The Machine in the Mind

4

TECHNOCRATS AND THEIR CRITICS

We would not destroy the rigorous method of science or the resourceful technology of the engineer. We would merely limit their application to intelligible and humane purposes. Nor would we remove altogether the mechanical world-picture, with its austere symbolism; we would rather expand it and supplement it with a vision of life which drew upon other needs of the personality than the crude will-to-power.

—Lewis Mumford (quoted in Pells 1973, 31)

AN AGE OF HUBRIS

On December 17, 1903, two American brothers succeeded in flying, and successfully landing, an air machine on a North Carolina beach. Orville and Wilbur Wright worked in a bicycle shop and were largely self-educated in matters of technology and science. They were, however, dedicated experimenters, and they showed themselves to be extremely adept in the arts of problem solving. They had the "considerable perspicacity," as Thomas Hughes put it, to determine that "maintaining equilibrium in flight was the critical and unsolved problem, the stumbling block for the earlier inventors and experimenters" (Hughes 1989, 58). With the help of wind tunnels, and expert advice from scientists in Washington about aerodynamic principles, the Wright brothers were the ones who won the race to achieve manned flight. It was one of the oldest forms of hubris, and by the end of the nineteenth century, it was only a matter of time before someone would break the jinx of Icarus and show that man was indeed meant to fly like a bird. The quest of the Wright brothers and their many rivals was fueled by the promise of fame and fortune. But it was also inspired by all the other momentous inventions that had recently been made—the electric light, the telephone, moving pictures, the horseless carriage—by which human capacities were being transformed so fundamentally. It was indeed an age of hubris, and nothing seemed to be able to hold back the powers of human ingenuity. It had been a competition for many years to achieve manned flight, as was the case with other inventions of the time, and the Wright brothers were the ones who made the key technical breakthroughs.

Earlier that same year, a German medical doctor named Wilhelm Schallmayer won a very different kind of competition, a large cash prize for writing a book titled *Heredity and Selection in the Life Process of Nations* (*Vererbung und Auslese im Lebenslauf der Völker*). His book was judged to be the best answer to the question of how the theory of evolution could be relevant for "internal political development" (Weiss 1987). The competition was the brainchild of Friedrich Krupp, the son of Alfred Krupp, who had made a fortune in the weapons business

Figure 6. Orville Wright's flight show on Tempelhof Field near Berlin 1908, organized by the newspaper *Berliner Lokal-Anzeiger.* Reprinted by permission of Deutsches Museum, Munich, Germany.

(as had, of course, Alfred Nobel, whose prizes for achievements in science, literature, and peace had begun to be awarded two years before).

Schallmayer was one of many biologists and doctors at the turn of the century who were attracted to the ideas of eugenics. Ever since Francis Galton, Charles Darwin's cousin, had coined the term in 1883, scientists had been trying to apply Darwin's theories of natural selection to improving the inborn qualities of humans (as Galton had characterized the task of his science). The ideas of eugenics fit well with the so-called civilizing mission that Britain had taken on in relation to its far-flung empire, on which the sun never set. As eugenics ideas spread across Europe and North America, they took on different forms and meanings, as Galton's ideas were integrated into various social and cultural movements. In the United States, eugenics appealed to those who were distressed by the large numbers of immigrants coming into the country, and it fed into movements of social reform in the so-called progressive era (Kevles 1985). In Germany eugenics became a part of the broader discourse of "life reform" and cultural revival that were so widespread before and after the First World War, before becoming so disastrously integrated into the "final solution" to the problems of ethnic variation that the Nazis imposed on the European population. In other countries, such as Sweden, eugenics became a component part of the political programs of social engineering and led to the forced sterilization of thousands of people under the social-democratic governments of the 1930s and 1940s (Broberg and Tydén 1996).

Eugenics became socially accepted in the early years of the twentieth century, and academic departments and scientific societies were established throughout the world to diffuse the ideas further. Across the political spectrum, from conservatives and liberals to social democrats, "racial hygiene" was seen as an effective way to select which people were most fit to reproduce. As Schallmayer put it in his book, "The twentieth century is called upon to apply the theory of descent to everyday life" (quoted in Weiss 1987, 205). In the first decades of the century, eugenics was considered to be a highly legitimate scientific activity and, in its applied forms, such as the sterilization programs that developed in Sweden, it was seen as an appropriate part of public policy making.

The invention of the flying machine by the Wright brothers and the promulgation of racial science by the eugenicists are familiar topics in the historical literature—the heroic sagas of manned flight in the name of technological progress, and the tragic tales of mass murder in the name of science. We are aware of the details of many such stories in the history of technology and science, but the specific stories are seldom related to the story lines that help give the details a deeper historical meaning, the underlying processes of cultural appropriation that made the particular cases possible.

The manifestation of manned flight was part of a much broader journey of the collective imagination. And the hubris of racial hygiene was part of a much deeper reaction to cultural trauma. What were the patterns of thought that shaped and justified these feats of daring and dementia? What were the states of mind that could encourage these expressions of hubris—the exciting new opportunities for experiencing reality on one hand, and the frightening new methods of control and oppression on the other? Since Genesis no one had dared try to modify human nature, the very crown of God's creation, and since Icarus no one had dared to fly a vehicle heavier than air and risk all of the dangers and consequences that would inevitably ensue. These steps were only possible, we suggest, in an age in which God had been declared dead, at least among influential portions of the intellectual elite, and a new deity, or belief system, had begun to take his place, a religion of technology and science (Noble 1997).

In this chapter, we explore the roles that this surrogate religion played within the mind-sets of modernity. Technology and science became part and parcel of modern societies not merely as artifacts and facts, as institutions and innovations. They were also appropriated as ideas and values and articulated in the form of discourse, in a multifaceted debate between the promoters of technology and science and their various cultural critics (Hård and Jamison 1998). In the first half of the twentieth century, self-proclaimed technocrats vied with a diverse array of humanists over the meanings of modernity, and the results of those encounters are still with us today. In the process, a number of hybrid intellectuals emerged from both sides of the often polarized field of debate, mediators who tried to achieve a more balanced assessment of the pros and cons of the new facts and artifacts and evaluate the promise and problematic implications of technology and science.

FROM MOVEMENT TO DISCOURSE

We saw in chapter 2 how various movements of the nineteenth century—the cooperative and romantic movements of the early part of the century and the socialist and populist movements of the latter part—provided sites for the mixing of ideas and the articulation of new social and cultural visions. In the subsequent processes of consolidation, which corresponded in time to the long waves of technological and economic development, the visions tended to be deconstructed and reformulated by intellectuals linked to separate organizations and political projects. In the first half of the century, the visionary, utopian ideas gave way to liberalism, political economy and what we have termed the positivist discourse. And in the latter part of the century, the movement visions were transformed into the ideologies of communism and conservatism, the disciplines of political and social science, and the broader discourses of nationalism and imperialism.

From such a perspective, the 1910s and 1920s also marked a period of social and cultural movements, which provided the cultural seedbeds for the regimes that came to power in the 1930s—the New Deal order in the United States, Communism in Russia, Nazism in Germany, Keynesian welfare states throughout Europe. In the United States, there were movements promulgating ideas of urban planning, regional revival, and social reform, while in Europe there emerged movements that articulated visions of economic planning, cultural revitalization, and life reform (Rodgers 1998). They differed in many ways, but what the diverse movements shared, at least at the outset, was a critical attitude toward the cultural chaos and social inequalities that resulted from unfettered industrial expansion. From our perspective, they all had a core interest in contemplating the values that were appropriate to an age that was, at one and the same time, fascinated and fearful in regard to the scientific and technological hubris that filled the air.

Some of the movements were avowedly futuristic, whereas others were passionately opposed to the new modernist faith. Progressives, pragmatists, and technocrats were countered by conservationists, regionalists, and mystics. The visions that were articulated in those movements, and the interpretations that were given of the modern condition, were formative for the ways in which people thought about technology and science throughout the twentieth century, and they continue to be influential in the twenty-first century. In this chapter we focus especially on these processes as they unfolded in the United States, Germany, and Sweden; in the following chapter, we journey to the East and examine some of the underlying cultural contradictions involved in the appropriation of technology and science in Asia.

In the United States, Henry Ford's methods of mass production and Frederick Winslow Taylor's techniques of scientific management heralded the coming of an age in which technology and science were directly integrated into economic life. Ford's conveyor belts and other organizational inventions provided a centralized approach to the production process and, not least, to the distribution and marketing of products. Taylor's time and motion studies and more general program of scientific management provided a systematic approach to the use of so-called human resources and thereby the possibility of a much more ambitious rationalization of production than had previously been attempted. At the same time, Thomas Edison's invention of the research company provided an organized approach to invention that turned technical and scientific ingenuity into a new form of business.

This "American system of production" was not confined to Ford's, Taylor's, and Edison's innovations (Hounshell 1984). It also included the widespread use of interchangeable parts across the industrial landscape and the spread of new manufacturing and building materials, such as steel and other alloys, and new sources of energy, such as oil and electricity. Mass production also engendered mass consumption, and at the turn of the century, new forms of advertising and marketing became important features of contemporary life.

These social innovations spread quickly around the world as the exemplary models of modernity, even to the new Soviet Union. In a survey of American technological history, Thomas Hughes noted, "The United States had never enjoyed greater respect, or been more envied, than after World War I. Many foreign liberals and radicals perceived its examples as opening for their nations a path to the future" (Hughes 1989, 249). It was particularly the new production technologies and organizational techniques that inspired admiration; the cultural ideals associated with the new technologies were often seen more critically. Indeed, there was concern that the U.S.-dominated Western civilization would involve a general decline in cultural values. As Max Weber wrote in 1918, in his famous lecture on "Science as a Vocation,"

The American boy learns unspeakably less than the German boy. ... The young American has no respect for anything or anybody, for tradition or for public office—unless it is for the personal achievement of individual men. This is what the American calls "democracy." This is the meaning of democracy, however distorted its intent may in reality be, and this intent is what matters here. The American's conception of the teacher who faces him is: he sells me his knowledge and his methods for my father's money, just as the greengrocer sells my mother cabbage. ... No young American would think of having his teacher sell him a *Weltanschauung* or a code of conduct. (Weber 1919/1958, 149–50)

Weber's response to Americanization was representative of the attitudes of many older "mandarin" scholars; Weber emphasized what was lost, or left behind, in the promulgation of modern instrumental values.

The technological civilization that developed in the wake of the Second World War was to be quintessentially American, and it is therefore important to understand how it got to be that way. In Germany, another vision of a technological civilization had been articulated, a peculiar mixture of the reactionary and the modern, the backward looking and the forward looking. Like their U.S. counterparts, German interwar intellectuals can be divided into technocrats and humanists in their attitudes to technology and science, but the national discursive frameworks were fundamentally different. Whereas Americans generally welcomed modern civilization, Germans tended to bemoan the loss of what they termed *Kultur* and the values associated with the past. And whereas American intellectuals tended to operate within a transcendental mind-set, often finding a kind of religious meaning in their facts and artifacts, German intellectuals tended to think in more organic, or natural, terms. The outcome was an American civilization where the instruments eventually came to take on a life of their own, and a German culture that went down to defeat trying to impose its values on the rest of the world.

The Swedish experience provides an interesting contrast to the American and German appropriation processes. In Sweden, the debate between technocrats and humanists led neither to technocratic victory, as in the United States, nor to humanist defeat, as in Germany. Rather, the country's intellectuals and politicians were able to shape a "middle way" (Childs 1936) between the two extremes, within a thought-figure of national unity and paternalist social welfare, the "people's home." The Swedish model gave ample place to science and technology for purposes of economic and social development while retaining a sense of solidarity between the rich and the poor and, for that matter, the future and the past. In the United States and Germany, the First World War was a decisive turning point in the appropriation of technology and science. In Germany, the experiences of the war served to mobilize thoughts of reaction and regulation, whereas in the United States, the dominant thoughts were of rationalization, on one hand, and reassessment, on the other. In Sweden, the central thoughts were those of remembrance and reconstruction of the great power that the country once had been. And, as we shall see, it was more the loss of Norway in 1905 that marked the turning point in the process of discursive appropriation than the war that Sweden managed to keep at a healthy distance.

THE MAKING OF A HYBRID INTELLECTUAL

Lewis Mumford was born in New York City in 1895, in what has later come to be called the progressive era. It was a time when the United States was beginning to assert its global supremacy and take over responsibility for extending—and defending—Western civilization. Technology and science were to become central to these tasks by providing instruments of military conquest and economic growth and by providing tools for intellectual expression and popular entertainment. When Mumford was three years old, in 1898, the Philippines were conquered in the Spanish–American War, and he came of age during the Great War, when the European empires began to decompose and a new vision of the United States's role in the world was articulated by President Wilson. The international "civilizing mission" that European powers had been exercising over the rest of the world for four hundred years was passing on to the United States.

The early years of the century was a time of social reform in the United States, with many young intellectuals-to-be following in the footsteps of the philosopher John Dewey and the social worker Jane Addams to try to do something about the myriad deficiencies in the emerging American civilization. Economic expansion and the assumption of international power had come quickly, fueled, to a large extent, by the growth of business firms in the new electrical and chemical industries. The cities of the northeast—Boston, Philadelphia, and New York but also Cleveland, Chicago, and Detroit—had grown rapidly at the end of the nineteenth century as waves of immigrants came from Europe in search of work and outlets for their creativity and ingenuity.

Like many American boys before and since, the young Mumford was fascinated by technology. From an early age he enjoyed tinkering with his home radio set, but he also loved to draw, and many of his artistic efforts were devoted to machines and buildings—above all else the Brooklyn Bridge, which he regarded as one of the most beautiful things he had ever laid eyes on (Mumford 1982). The links between, and the need to combine in creative balance, the worlds of technics and civilization was one of the recurrent themes in his writings. His city, with its skyscrapers and factories, its boundless energies and endless enthusiasms, its mix of local neighborhoods and ethnic identities, and not least its sites of cultural appropriation—its museums, libraries, and parks—became his school. And its reform-minded public sphere of the 1910s and 1920s became his workplace, the site for his particular form of hybrid identity formation. In his teens he started writing for the *Dial* (where Thorstein Veblen, Randolph Bourne, and John Dewey were among the main contributors), and in the 1920s he took active part in envisioning another, more humanly appropriate kind of American civilization, serving as secretary of the Regional Planning Association of America and beginning his long series of books dealing with the interconnections between technology, cities, art, and literature (Hughes and Hughes 1990).

Like the movement intellectuals of the nineteenth century, whom we discussed in chapter 3, Mumford formed his identity within the social and cultural movements of his time. Like many movements before and since, the movements of his youth had their own distinctive form of cognitive praxis by which visionary ideas and scientific-technical activities were mixed together in intriguing new combinations (Eyerman and Jamison 1991). The task that these movement intellectuals set for themselves was to define goals for the mechanical civilization derived from the traditions of the American past.

On one side were the technocrats for whom the economist Thorstein Veblen served as spokesperson (Jamison 1989). His books from the early 1920s, *The Engineers and the Price System* (1921) and *Absentee Ownership and Business Enterprise in Recent Times* (1923), included a view of technology that sought to give engineers a central role in society. His writings provided a kind of theoretical underpinning for the various efforts taken during the 1920s by politically and socially minded engineers, from scientific management and industrial research to urban reform and political propaganda for social engineering, eugenic measures included.

Veblen's emphasis on the important role that engineers had to play in the industrial economy of the early twentieth century was not unique; many of his fellow progressive intellectuals recognized the new technical potentialities that had been unleashed by the linking of science with technology and by the infusion of systematic research into the production process (Tichi 1987). But no one singled out engineering as the decisive force of social transformation to the same extent that Veblen did. At the outset of his most ambitious philosophical work *The Instinct of Workmanship*, he boldly stated,

> It is assumed that in the growth of culture, as in its current maintenance, the facts of technological use and wont are fundamental and definitive, in the sense that they underlie and condition the scope and method of civilization in other than the technological respect, but not in such a sense as to preclude or overlook the degree in which these other conventions of any given civilization in their turn react on the state of the industrial arts. (Veblen 1914, 1)

In *Absentee Ownership*, Veblen contrasted the habits and customs of American culture with the requirements of the new order of mechanization and science-based industry. For Veblen, the quintessential American value was trade and business, and throughout his life he castigated the businessmen and their vested interests for holding back the flow of mechanical innovations and technological progress.

As David Noble has shown, the 1920s were a time when many engineers tried to design the United States in their image, and their achievements are still with us (Noble 1977). This technocratic pole in the technology debate attracted many of the founders of management science and the corporate research managers and production consultants. In the postwar era, those ideas came to be embedded in what John Kenneth Galbraith (1968) called the "technostructure" of a new industrial state. In the United States, the iconoclastic Veblen served as theorist, whereas President Hoover came to embody the engineer as politician and state bureaucrat. In his activities at the Department of Commerce during the 1920s, Hoover sought to bring a technological logic into the center of state economic policy.

The humanist critique that was so widespread in Europe tended to be marginal in the United States. Many American writers, such as T. S. Eliot and Gertrude Stein, fled to Europe. Eliot mounted a traditionalist defense of classical values against the cultural wasteland that he felt his homeland had become. Only a few of those who stayed behind dared to take on the technocrats and the general enthusiasm over modern science and technology. Joseph Wood Krutch, a drama critic and professor of literature at Columbia University, produced perhaps the most influential humanist critique in his book *The Modern Temper*, published in 1929. In it, he sought to diagnose the mood of the times and address directly what he termed the "disillusion with the laboratory" that was driving so many people away from civilization:

We went to science in search of light, not merely upon the nature of matter, but upon the nature of man as well, and though that which we have received may be light of a sort, it is not adapted to our eyes and is not anything by which we can see. … We are disillusioned with the laboratory, not because we have lost faith in the truth of its findings but because we have lost faith in the power of those findings to help us generally as we once hoped they might help. (Krutch 1929, 47, 53)

After the war, Krutch left New York for the southwestern desert and wrote a biography of Thoreau and took part in the awakening of an environmental consciousness in the postwar United States. In the depth of his critique of the technological civilization, he had few emulators in the interwar years.

Mumford accepted neither the technocratic position nor the disenchantment of the humanists. In his hybrid identity, he combined ecology and history, geography and sociology, and an interest in the past and the future to provide what might be termed a cultural assessment of technology. Mumford's perspective resembled that of the academic field of human ecology, which developed in different guises in the interwar years: among sociologists at the University of Chicago, who had been inspired by the progressive social work of Jane Addams, and among the "southern regionalists" such as Howard Odum at the University of North Carolina. For Mumford, technocratic thought represented primarily a failure of imagination. In glorifying the machine, the utopian side of man had developed into a sort of hubris, and with it there was an urgent need for a cultural evaluation of the contemporary technological civilization. As he put it in 1926,

> The whole industrial world—and instrumentalism is only its highest conscious expression—has taken values for granted. ... An instrumental philosophy which was oriented toward a whole life would begin ... by a criticism of this one-sided idealization of practical contrivance. (Mumford 1926, 137–38)

In *Technics and Civilization* (1934), Mumford drew on his technical interests and his artistic inclinations to fashion a synthetic interpretation of technology and science. He described the rise of the machine as part of a cyclical process and showed how the development of technology was a product of culture—and of cultural criticism. His aim was to humanize technology, to give "the machine" a life, from its infancy in the Middle Ages, through its wild aggressive youth of the nineteenth century, to its potential maturity of the twentieth century. But he also sought to give the science-based technologies a meaning beyond the purely instrumental. He tried to invent a philosophy of "neotechnics" that could supersede the mechanical philosophy of the eighteenth and nineteenth centuries. The Wright brothers, for example, succeeded where others had failed because they had closely observed nature:

> The final touch, necessary for stable flight, came when two bicycle mechanics, Orville and Wilbur Wright, studied the flight of birds, like the gull and the hawk, and discovered the function of warping the tips of the wings to achieve lateral stability. Further

improvements in the design of airplanes have been associated, not merely with the mechanical perfection of the wings and the motors, but with the study of the flight of other types of bird, like the duck, and the movement of fish in water. (Mumford 1934, 251)

Technics and Civilization marks, in many respects, a turning point in the intellectual discourses about technology and science in the twentieth century. Where previous writers had tended to either glorify or denigrate the facts and artifacts of science and technology, Mumford sought to provide a more comprehensive mode of appropriation. He wanted to encompass the positive and negative features and develop what later came to be termed technology assessment. As the 1930s progressed, such technology assessment became an integral part of the New Deal era, with its programs of regional development, such as the Tennessee Valley Authority, and various activities sponsored by the Department of Commerce (Pursell 1979).

WESTERN CIVILIZATION VERSUS GERMAN CULTURE

Many of the social and cultural movements that developed in Germany in the early part of the twentieth century were less concerned with a reform of society than with a reform of life (*Lebensreform*). They emerged in protest against a society that had been increasingly affected by impersonal relations, materialist ideals, and rational, scientific thought. Or, in the words of Adolf Just, one of the proponents of moving "back to nature":

The misery, the alienation, and the mendacity of the human being ... are largely the outcome of the development of the scientific spirit, of inventions and technologies that transferred manual labor onto the machine, thus evoking a similar kind of mechanization in all areas of life. (quoted in Krabbe 1974, 14)

Vegetarians rejected animal farms and meat production on ethical grounds. Followers of the philosopher Rudolf Steiner founded schools based on organic, or holistic, pedagogical principles. Critics of scientific medicine developed a range of alternative treatments and healing cures such as homeopathy. Young people turned their backs on urban life and found a sanctuary in the more or less untouched wilderness—romantics and naturalists in the so-called migratory bird and working-class youngsters in the "nature-friends" movement. Whereas most of these movements originated in cities and exhibited a critical stance toward modern urban life, rural groups tried to protect their local environment from being drawn into the maelstrom of industrial exploitation and mass tourism (Sieferle 1984).

These movements developed alternative practices and oppositional routines, some of which have survived into our own time. Health food stores, their roots going back well into the 1880s, are still to be found in most German towns. Nudism, a particularly visible protest against the artificiality of modern life, was strong even in the otherwise not particularly wild German Democratic Republic. In the 1970s the tradition of withdrawing from the city and forming collectively owned communes in the countryside was revived.

The life-reform groups formulated their own philosophical and ethical ideas. In many instances they received support from various intellectuals or found inspiration in their works. We have already mentioned Steiner. In a comprehensive book fittingly titled *Another Modernity?* historian Thomas Rohkrämer (1999) analyzed "movement intellectuals" and their relationship to some of the groups mentioned previously. The philosopher Ludwig Klages, for example, upheld close connections to the life-reform movements. He had been a member of esoteric—today we would say "new-age"—sects in his youth, and he joined various environmental and nature groups later on. His writings, most notably his essay "Man and Earth," were very favorably received in these circles. Here Klages attacked modern science for exploiting rather than trying to understand nature, and modern technology for ruining rather than trying to save Mother Earth. Still, it was not the case that Klages turned his back on all technological achievements. He was fascinated by Count von Zeppelin's dirigible airship, recognized the educational potential of motion pictures, and argued in favor of technological solutions that helped protect nature. It is of particular interest to note that Klages's main target was what we call the hubris of modern science and engineering. In several pamphlets he vehemently criticized the "unholy curiosity" of our age, a kind of investigative sensibility run amok. Civilization has forgotten what restriction and caution mean, and entered into a vicious circle of expansion, subjection, and control.

Key elements in the German discursive framework were the interrelated terms *Bildung* and *Kultur,* sometimes translated as "cultivation" and "culture," respectively (Bollenbeck 1994). *Bildung* implied personal development through, in the first instance, classical education. Latin and Greek, being taught at the humanistic Gymnasium, were the formative subjects in this tradition. Although increasingly anachronistic, this ideal was repeatedly invoked in instances when educational reform was on the agenda. Similarly, the concept of *Kultur* was mobilized in debates where not only these classic ideals but also allegedly German values seemed to be at stake. As long as they managed to adhere to the principles of cultivation, the Germans could fulfill their mission as a "cultural nation" (*Kulturvolk*).

Inherent in this notion of culture was the idea that a truly cultivated nation develops along harmonious lines and that it, in this process, unfolds its truly authentic character. By contrast, *Zivilisation* came to denote nations that have sold out to the values of materialism and liberalism. The French- and English-speaking countries were regarded as the main carriers of these barbaric ideas. In the seventeenth and eighteenth centuries, rational philosophy and a materialistic worldview had emerged in these countries, along with a laissez-faire economic system and widespread individualism. By default, French and Anglo-Saxon technology and science had become permeated by what Max Horkheimer (1947) later called "instrumental rationality" and narrowly oriented toward commercial interests.

In the first instance, the problem that bothered German intellectuals at the turn of the twentieth century was perhaps not the instrumental character of technology and science. What troubled humanists and other classically educated so-called mandarins was rather the tendency of modern societies in toto to become affected by soulless reason and cold calculability (Ringer 1969). It might be acceptable that an industrial enterprise is run in accordance with capitalist principles, but it is highly problematic to transfer these principles to other areas of society, such as politics, art, or family life.

"The struggle about technology," as the contemporary x-ray engineer and self-taught philosopher Friedrich Dessauer (1956) called the debate between humanists and engineers in the first decades of the twentieth century, did not primarily have to do with the advantages or disadvantages of technical products. The struggle rather concerned the whole of modern society, its fundamental values and basic principles. Instead of exploiting workers and nature, society's means of production ought to allow the development and unfolding—the cultivation—of individual personalities. In a similar vein, the best-selling doomsday prophet Oswald Spengler criticized the capitalist and theoretical orientation of modern engineering. Under Anglo-Saxon, French, and possibly Jewish influence, profit-seeking and mathematical abstraction had come to dominate what used to be an honorable activity. In the closing chapters of his monumental *Decline of the West* (1918/1922), Spengler argued in favor of a kind of engineering that is based on immediate observation and concrete experience, and a technology that is well integrated into established culture.

The struggle about technology was not just a verbal fight about principles. It was also about power, influence, and recognition, particularly for the new actors of industrial society, especially engineers. Beginning during the so-called founding years (*Gründerjahre*) in the early 1870s, Germany transformed rapidly into an industrial country. Entrepreneurs, engineers, and natural scientists became in many circles the heroes of the day. Inevitably, these changes meant harder times for men of letters, classically educated scholars, and legally educated professionals. Facing concrete demands for influence, public posts, and educational reform, the members of the intellectual elite had to protect old privileges and defend established positions. To speak with the French anthropologist Pierre Bourdieu (1979/1984), we could say that the "cultural capital" of the old elite was threatened by the economic capital of the new. As the importance of the industrial classes grew, so did their demand for influence.

Members of the engineering profession fought on many fronts. They founded societies to take care of their interests, tried to break the lawyers' near monopoly on positions in the public service, and argued for equality between technical colleges and the classic universities. When the Prussian government in 1899 decided to grant the institutes of technology the right to issue doctoral degrees, engineers considered it a symbolic victory. The breakthrough was to a large extent an outcome of the ambitions for making engineering work more theoretical and scientific. The fight for public acceptance went further, however, and after the turn of the century it continued on the home turf, so to speak, of their classically educated opponents. Not only Dessauer but also a number of other engineers began to develop a kind of philosophy of technology, in which *Kultur* and *Bildung* played central roles. Classical humanism and art in modern society could not be regarded the sole components of culture. Knowledge of Greek and Latin or artistic expression could no longer be the sole signs of cultivation. Engineers picked up the positively charged notions of personal growth and creative development and argued that innovative engineering work should also be considered cultural. Although its ultimate outcome might be material, its character is spiritual. An engineer works not only with his hands but first and foremost with his brain. Technology's "social and spiritual relations" had been overlooked for centuries, and finally the time had come—so the argument went—to recognize them as a kind of "cultural power" (Wendt 1906).

In their endeavor to prove the cultural potential of technology, engineers also turned to history. One of these engineers was the indefatigable Oskar von Miller, the founder and champion of the "German Museum of Scientific and Technological Masterpieces" in Munich. Generally known as the *Deutsches Musuem,* this collection must be considered a highly successful attempt to propagate the greatness of modern technology and science to the public. When the museum moved into a completely new, impressive building in 1925, visitors were intrigued, and they applauded Miller's strategy to focus on prominent individuals and impressive artifacts. There were critics, of course, and most of them bemoaned the, mildly speaking, loose connections that were made between technology and science on one hand and social, cultural, and economic change on the other hand (Osietzki 1985). Without the help of social historians, sociologists, or those who we nowadays call historical anthropologists, it was difficult to transform the official culturalist rhetoric into a manageable exhibition concept.

THE STATE AS SAVIOR

Rather than contributing to the integration of technology and science into culture, the *Deutsches Museum* and similar institutions tended to glorify scientists and engineers and their achievements. The public was caught by means of fascination and enchantment, and—it was hoped—young men were stimulated to take on a career in these fields. One man, who had certainly been thrilled by the intricacies of engineering in his youth, was Ulrich, the "man without qualities" in Robert Musil's famous novel of that name:

> From the moment Ulrich set foot in engineering school, he was feverishly partisan. Who still needed Apollo Belvedere, when he had the new forms of a turbodynamo or the rhythmic movements of a steam engine's pistons before his eyes! Who could still be captivated by the thousand years of chatter about the meaning of good and evil when it turns out that they are not constants at all but functional values, so that the goodness of works depends on the psychotechnical skills with which people's qualities are exploited? Looked at from a technical point of view, the world is simply ridiculous: impractical in all that concerns human relations, and extremely uneconomic and imprecise in its methods. (Musil 1930/1995, 33)

Obvious to anyone, Musil's Ulrich was no one less than Walther Rathenau, the son of Emil Rathenau, who had founded the German

Edison Company (later AEG). As with so many other young men of his age, Rathenau had been attracted by the intricacies of engineering and science, but, unlike many, he later left this world and turned to philosophy and politics. During the First World War, he was responsible for organizing the provision and distribution of raw materials and other resources for the German war effort, and after the war he became a member of several governments—only to be murdered by right-wing terrorists in 1922.

Although Rathenau did not work for long as an active engineer, he never forgot the basic principles of engineering. The second half of the quotation from Musil describes well the technocratic attitude that Rathenau brought with him from the world of technology into public administration and politics. Practicality, efficiency, and exactness ought to be guiding all state affairs. During his years in industry, Rathenau had come to the conclusion that free competition was often disadvantageous, sometimes even ruinous for the economy as a whole.

Rathenau became director of an electrochemical company at the age of twenty-seven, only to face severe losses of market shares. As a board member of the AEG he argued unsuccessfully in favor of cartel agreements. Marked by these difficulties, he later in life developed a political-economic ideology that foresaw a combination of private ownership and strong state supervision. In several pamphlets and books, most of them published during and shortly after the war, he formulated a kind of neomercantilist position, according to which the state was given a decisive say on economic matters.

In Rathenau's thinking the righteous distribution of goods and services, one of the main tasks of any government, requires precise calculation and central planning. And not only that: even the development and production of material goods, and thereby also technology, has to be subjected to central control. To some extent, Rathenau's urge for central planning was a part of the contemporary *Zeitgeist*, the spirit of the times. It did not take long until the first five-year plan was set up in the Soviet Union, and not much longer until the New Deal was launched in the United States. But still, it can be argued that Rathenau's program had a typical German slant to it.

Take his concept of *Euplutism*. More or less opposed to "individualism," it meant something like "the well-being of the many." Rathenau gave this term a kind of story-line character in his works, and he applied it over and over again to convince his readers that a collectively oriented society based on solidarity was preferred to an atomistic, individualist society based on egotism (Rathenau 1912). In Rathenau's ideal society not even the economy would be a private matter.

Although the term *Euplutism* was novel, its meaning was immediately recognized by his fellow Germans. The communal ideal, according to which the members of a certain society are mutually responsible and do not follow only their own narrow interests, had held a strong position in the German debate at least since the times of the romantics at the early nineteenth century.

If Britain had its Adam Smith, the first and foremost spokesperson of economic liberalism, then Germany had its Adam Müller. Müller had been a firm defender of the old estate society, which he, in a text originally published in 1819, called the "really natural order" (quoted in Sieferle 1984, 52). This order had grown in a harmonious way, and it had developed into a kind of organism, where each member had his or her rights and duties. As we have seen, this idea—freed of its reactionary overtones—was later reformulated by Ferdinand Tönnies, who, in a very German manner, opposed the traditional community (*Gemeinschaft*) to modern society (*Gesellschaft*). What Rathenau envisioned with his term *Euplutism* was a social body that took it upon itself to regulate economic matters and technical developments to the benefit of all, rather than to the benefit of a few.

The second reason for our calling Rathenau's position distinctly German is his statism. As we have seen earlier, this capitalist—he was a member of innumerous corporate boards, and after 1915 he was given the director's title by the AEG—put a remarkably strong faith in the state. Rathenau's state does not serve the interests of a few but has the task of taking care of the needs of all citizens. Because its dealings are based on objective matter-of-factness rather than subjective economic interests, the state is the only body that can properly coordinate economic life.

Historian Otto Dann (1993) showed that this glorification of the state is a story line with a long-standing tradition in Germany, going back well before the 1860s, when Bismarck unified Prussia and a number of smaller states into one German Reich. Müller's thinking is emblematic also in this case. Terrified by the events in France during and after the French Revolution, Müller argued vehemently in favor of the old order. To him, *l'ancien régime* had represented stability and continuity, and history had shown that its overthrow would inevitably lead to chaos and terror. Only an intact, slowly and gradually changing state is able to provide its citizens with a harmonious life. This strong belief in the state had hardly lost its power in Rathenau's time. When Rathenau called on the state to coordinate technical developments and industrial production, he made effective use of an established conception in the German discursive framework and adopted it for his particular purposes.

The same can be said about the economist Werner Sombart, who wrote frequently about technology and society. Throughout his long academic career, he remained faithful to the idea of a strong state. At times he saw the state as an unselfish mediator between different social groups, at times as a representative of a kind of higher, objective reason. Toward the end of his active life he also adopted this idea to the area of technology. In an infamous book called *German Socialism,* published in 1934 as a largely unsuccessful attempt to appease the new National Socialist rulers, Sombart had a go at the excessive manifold-ness of goods in modern society (Sombart 1934). Most inventions are senseless, and most products that leave the factory gates are unnecessary. To handle this situation the state ought to set up a so-called cultural council, whose task it should be to decide what innovations should be accepted, rejected, or perhaps modified. This council should be a kind of gatekeeper in the world of engineering, and the state should guarantee its power base. Because Sombart discussed its purpose in terms such as "the taming of technology" (*die Zähmung der Technik*), it lies close at hand to interpret his program along appropriation lines. Only those technologies that had a chance of being assimilated into the existing culture—domesticated—should be accepted. To ensure that new technologies do not become juggernauts, philosophers and other nontechnical experts should be involved in their development. Sombart even went so far as to talk about "planned research" in this connection, and he explicitly denied scientists and engineers a decisive influence on the decisions of the cultural council.

A MIDDLE WAY: THE SWEDISH CASE

In the middle of the Great Depression, an American journalist named Marquis Childs paid a visit to Sweden. The recently elected Social Democratic government, Childs contended, seemed to be providing a new sort of model for modern societies to follow that was neither purely capitalist nor purely socialist. With a highly influential and institutionalized labor movement, and a number of cooperative organizations in retail trade and many public services, Sweden was carving out an exemplary path to modernity. The land of lakes and forests at the northern periphery of Europe provided a middle way between the polarized, ideological extremes that were propelling the world into a new global conflict (Childs 1936).

Together with the mass emigration to North America in the late nineteenth century, it was the dissolution of the union with Norway in 1905 that served to set in motion a Swedish discussion about modern industry and its social implications. In reacting to Norwegian independence—and to the long-term decline of their country's status in the world—Swedish movements and their intellectuals mobilized a range of cultural resources to try to bring their country back to life. In the land of Carolus Linnaeus, the technology debates had a decidedly pastoral air about them, and there was a comparatively strong interest in conservation and an efficient use of natural resources. Indeed, the enormous forests and substantial mineral resources were seen by many commentators as providing the basis for a Swedish industrialization that could bring back to the country something of its lost prominence in the world. Norrland, the vast and largely uninhabited northern part of the country, was to be the great frontier for expansion and development that the western territories had been in the United States (Sörlin 1988). Such was not the case—the northern region never inspired much of an inner colonization, even though the forests did provide the raw materials for much of the industrial progress that the country experienced. But geographical and natural resources nonetheless contributed to the formation of a rural awareness, especially on the conservative side of the political spectrum, as intellectuals sought to integrate machine technology into the natural landscape by giving it new kinds of meanings in theory and practice.

There never developed an influential conservative critique of modernity in Sweden, unlike in many other countries. Neither side of the field of debate ever pushed to an openly confrontational politics but preferred to retain, and indeed even strengthen, the paternalist consensus ideal that was part of the Swedish political heritage. It is, above all else, the rationalist mode of negotiation and consensus building that is characteristic of the Swedish style of debate, and it remains so even today. In trying to explain this, we refer to several deeply ingrained features of Swedish history.

First of all, the distinctively bureaucratic mode of governance derives from the imperial culture of the great power era in the sixteenth and seventeenth centuries, when absolute monarchs created a multifaceted state apparatus that unified the interests of aristocrat and peasant in a common project of expansion. Already at that time, Sweden's kings had understood that the state would have to create sites for technical development and places for higher learning (Jamison 1982). State companies were established, and to ensure that the new great power could hold together, the state founded universities in the conquered provinces. This policy continued into the eighteenth century as the state established laboratories for chemistry and mechanics and supported Christopher Polhem's experiments with mechanical improvements that were to be used in Swedish mining and metallurgy.

A second feature is the archetypical rural mining community—the *bruk*—out of which Swedish economic development first emerged in the early modern period, laying the groundwork for the short-lived imperial expansion (Ruth 1984). These protoindustrial enclaves, which combined the extraction of silver, copper, and high-quality iron ore with metallurgical and munitions workshops, were overseen by the aristocrats and served as conduits for the importation of foreign technical expertise (especially the Walloons from the low countries). The *bruk* was a factory village of a semifeudal nature, where a paternalistic way of life with housing, medical care, education, and other amenities unknown to society at large were provided to the workforce in exchange for labor. In the nineteenth century this pattern of integrated rural economic development was given a new impetus from British civil engineers, who helped develop canals and railways and contributed to the establishment of manufacturing and modern weapons production in machine shops, textile mills, and other factory sites often located outside the large cities.

A third feature of Swedish society is the systematic and long-standing incorporation of expertise into the established social order, which affected the ways in which intellectual life has been organized and institutionalized (Elzinga 1993). For ages, the intellectual in Sweden has been structurally, even symbiotically, attached to the activities of the state and big business and, in our day, mass media. Institutions of higher learning also have been a part of a unitary national system under central authority. As a result, the comparatively few oppositional intellectuals—from the writer August Strindberg to the filmmaker Ingmar Bergman—are found almost exclusively in artistic and literary circles. For their part, academics are first and foremost civil servants and subjects of the state, often drawn on as experts by the multitudinous investigative commissions that are established by central government to address new challenges. Again the pattern was set early on, during the great power era: when the Swedes conquered the county of Scania from Denmark in the mid-seventeenth century, one of the first acts was to establish a university in the old cathedral town of Lund.

In 1866 the political tradition of interest harmonization and state-guided technocracy was strengthened by a parliamentary reform that introduced a bicameral legislative system that served to reinforce the political hegemony of conservative coalitions of landed aristocracy, well-to-do farmers, urban nationalists, and monarchist forces, including the central bureaucracy, which, toward the close of the century, was challenged by a growing labor movement and a modernizing liberal bourgeoisie. This emerging tension among intellectuals between traditionalists and modernists came to color the twentieth-century debates about technology. But despite differences of emphasis, all sides shared a common discursive framework, which assumed two basic postulates: the inviability of the consensual mode of governance and the desirability of reconstructing Sweden as a major power, this time with technological and industrial attributes. Out of this framework grew the paternalistic idea of the "people's home" (*folkhem*), first introduced with a conservative connotation but later, especially after the onset of the depression, given a social-democratic interpretation as the model for a modern welfare state.

Vitalis Norström, a philosophy professor at Gothenburg College, was one of the few Swedish intellectuals to warn of the dangers of industrialization, or what he termed excessive, or supercivilization (*övercivilisation*). His writings served to inspire a group of young conservative intellectuals that included the economist Nils Wohlin, the publicist Adrian Molin, and the political scientist Rudolf Kjellén, to whom the notion of a people's home has been attributed. Kjellén developed a concept of geopolitics in which industrialization played an important role. In his view, countries with rich natural resources and the capability to exploit them with modern methods had a comparative advantage in the international competition among nations. As he wrote in one of his programmatic texts,

We great power Swedes dream of a Great Sweden within our own national boundaries, a new national greatness, but now based on the solid ground of material production, with enormous markets to the east, the old route of Swedish greatness. (quoted in Sörlin 1988, 197)

It was especially Molin who spread these ideas by writing in newspapers and by establishing a journal, *The New Sweden* (*Det Nya Sverige*), that provided a forum for debate for the young conservative movement. In the course of the 1920s, the idea of an economically strong Sweden, making use of advanced technology for the productive exploitation of the mines and forests, was appropriated by liberals and social-democratic intellectuals, such as Alva and Gunnar Myrdal.

Mechanization as such had few opponents in Sweden: the country has experienced few, if any, Luddite revolts. The controversies then and now have more concerned the consequences of technological development and its capitalist power relations than the actual content of modern production. The traditionalist rejection of technological civilization that was found in other European countries has been quite weak in Sweden. The positions that proved to be influential for the social-democratic synthesis of the 1930s were those that were more unabashedly positive toward technological development.

An influential technocratic publicist was Ludvig Nordström, who toured the country in the 1920s and 1930s and wrote books of reportage that, perhaps more than any other single contribution, paved the way for the welfare state and the Swedish model. In the style of an investigative, muckraking reporter, Nordström attacked the dirt and ugliness of Swedish society and called for a regime of social engineers. Everything that was old and traditional had to be eliminated. The architects and designers who sounded the call, in 1930, to accept modern technology, in a famous pamphlet issued at the time of the Stockholm Industrial Exhibition, were, in many ways, the true Swedish technocrats. It was largely under their inspiration that the Social Democratic Party when it came to power in 1932 explicitly sought to constitute the "first modern nation" (Ruth 1984).

When it comes to technology development, Ernst Wigforss, the long-time Social Democratic minister of finance, or secretary of the treasury, played a central role. For Wigforss, who had spent his student days as a Marxist, technology and scientific-technical expertise were seen as central ingredients in modern, democratic society; the important thing was for each kind of scientist or expert intellectual to contribute to the collective project of social development. In a speech to students at Lund in 1937, Wigforss put it the following way:

> Engineers for material production, architects and planners for construction work, social scientists to fulfill the tasks of social engineering, and scientists in general will be not less but more in demand if we consciously direct our efforts to strengthen the basis of civilization and culture. (Wigforss 1941, 181)

Science and technology figured centrally in the pact between politicians and industrialists that was fundamental to constructing the social machinery of the welfare state. As Wigforss put it, "If natural resources are one of the building blocks on which people build their welfare, discoveries, technical and organizational innovations are the other."

It was such a mind-set that made possible the widespread use of sterilization and gave financial and political support to the promulgation of racial science. The practical applications of eugenics were directed primarily toward social outcasts and the mentally retarded, and they fit well into a society that was governed by paternalistic structures and organized around programs of social reform and social engineering. The extent of forced sterilization was much greater in Sweden than most other countries outside of the Third Reich, and certainly more extensive than in the other Nordic countries. The practical application of eugenics continued into the 1970s before it was finally put to an end. A mixture of racial superiority and pragmatic planning doctrines—not least in relation to population control and family planning—made possible a tragic application of pseudoscience within the epitome of the modern nation, the Swedish welfare state.

The Swedish model that was articulated in the 1930s did not really come into being until the 1940s, and it benefited from the neutral position that Sweden had taken during the war. Sweden's productive capacities did not diminish as a result of the war—on the contrary; while most of the rest of Europe had to rebuild their industries, Sweden's industries continued full speed ahead. The special hybrid combination of great power conservatism and Social Democratic technocracy could thus emerge relatively unscathed, and continue to serve as a middle way between the polarized extremes of culture and civilization on one hand and capitalism and communism on the other. Although the exigencies of war would strongly affect U.S. populist pragmatism and German reactionary modernism—burdening the one with the responsibilities of an imperial superpower and subjecting the other to the trauma of defeat and occupation—the Swedish model lived on as a kind of third path to modernity.

5

EASTERN MINDS TAKE ON THE WESTERN JUGGERNAUT

What I object to is the artificial arrangement by which the foreign education tends to occupy all the space of our national mind and thus kills, or hampers, the great opportunity for the creation of new thought by a new combination of truths. It is this which makes me urge that all the elements in our own culture have to be strengthened; not to resist the culture of the West, but to accept and assimilate it. It must become for us nourishment and not a burden.

—**Rabindranath Tagore (quoted in Dutta and Robinson 1995, 222)**

FROM SILENT VALLEY TO THE THREE GORGES

In the mid-1970s, the Kerala State Electricity Board announced plans to build a hydroelectric dam in a forested area known as Silent Valley in the Ghat Mountains of southern India. Hydroelectric dams had been an important part of the Indian government's efforts to modernize the country after achieving independence from the British in 1947. Jawaharlal Nehru, the country's first prime minister, had referred to dams as the "temples of modern India," and they had generally been seen as a fairly benign form of technology, providing electricity that could be used for a wide range of industrial and domestic purposes

(Centre for Science and Environment 1982). In the 1970s, however, it was no longer clear for at least some members of the Indian population that hydroelectric dams ought to be built in places such as Silent Valley. The dam had originally been welcomed by the group of local scientists and schoolteachers, who in 1962 had formed the KSSP, or Kerala Sastra Sahitya Parishat. It was an organization that primarily carried out campaigns of scientific popularization, translating foreign texts into the local Mayalam language, rephrasing scientific ideas in more accessible terms. Like similar organizations in other parts of the country, the KSSP had seen its mission as seeking to inculcate scientific and technical knowledge as deeply as possible into the broader culture. It had agreed with Nehru that India needed to foster what he had termed a "scientific temper" so that the long colonial legacy and the continuing tragedy of rural poverty could be overcome. Hydroelectric dams had thus been seen positively, as one component of a more general strategy of applying technology and science to socioeconomic development. In line with the language of the United Nations and international development assistance agencies, science and technology were to be used in the newly independent nations to satisfy "basic human needs" (Wad 1988).

The KSSP, along with other self-proclaimed "people's science movements" that emerged in the 1960s and 1970s, began to question, however, whether it was appropriate to meet those needs by means of large-scale projects that had often shown themselves to be inefficient and costly, misusing financial, human, and natural resources. They were usually too big and ambitious, and, in most cases of such "technology transfer," the artifacts were not designed with the needs and knowledge of the particular people they were supposed to assist in mind. Many such development projects thus became ugly blights on the landscape rather than constructive contributions to human development, an often counterproductive reflection of scientific-technological hubris.

An "appropriate technology," as the term began to be used at the time, would most likely be small in scale and be designed in such a way that it fit into the cultural, social, and natural surroundings in which it was to be used. It would be a hybrid combination of the modern and the traditional: an "intermediate technology" in the words of E. F. Schumacher. Schumacher had taken part in many development projects while working for the British Coal Board in India, and when he wrote his book *Small Is Beautiful* his argument was that the use of technology and science for development had to be redesigned "as if people mattered" (Schumacher 1973).

In relation to Silent Valley, the KSSP contended that there were alternative means of producing energy that were more suitable for the local conditions, in that they did not ultimately destroy valuable natural resources. The needs of nature had, by the mid-1970s, become a factor to be reckoned with in the discourse of development. Silent Valley, it seemed, was not just any forest but a virgin *shola* forest, and largely because there had been no human habitation for many centuries, there was flora and fauna that were unique and would disappear if the area were placed under water. The human need for energy was thus in conflict with what was starting to be called concern for the environment (Parameswaran 1979).

Like other similar groups, the KSSP had begun to appropriate one result of modern science—the science of ecology—to oppose the (mis)appropriation of another; namely, hydroelectric engineering. And like their counterparts elsewhere in the emerging environmental movement, the KSSP members began to partake of the methods of persuasion that have since become common in the world of environmental politics: lobbying government officials, carrying out independent research investigations, communicating with the media, and generally trying to mobilize the amorphous public to participate in making the use of technology and science more appropriate.

At the outset, many of the people in the surrounding area were reluctant to support the protest—after all, they could be expected to derive economic and social benefit from using the electricity that would be produced. But the KSSP members held a series of meetings, as they conducted so-called marathon walks across the countryside, where they discussed their concerns with the people they met along the way. Among other things, they contended that, according to the plans, the electricity from the dam would primarily benefit the industries in the surrounding cities rather than the rural population. They also showed that small-scale biogas plants and wind-power plants were far more effective ways of producing energy in rural areas. Gradually, after hearing such arguments, many local people joined in the opposition, which became a widely reported case of emerging environmental politics in India.

The protests fell on sympathetic ears, as the prime minister Indira Gandhi, Nehru's daughter, had recently started to take an interest in environmental issues. She appointed a commission to evaluate the electricity board's plans and the KSSP arguments, and eventually the commission came to the conclusion that the dam should not be built. In 1985 the area was made into a national park, even though the state government has occasionally tried to revive its plans for building a dam.

In 2002, at the World Summit on Sustainable Development in South Africa, the Silent Valley protests were presented by the national government as one of the important "stories from India" in the long journey toward sustainability. A few years before, in 1995, the KSSP had been given one of the annual Right Livelihood Awards, the so-called alternative Nobel Prizes.

The conflict at Silent Valley was not just about the pros and cons of a hydroelectric dam; as with other protests in India in the 1970s, such as the Chipko and Appiko tree huggers in the north who opposed large-scale projects of social forestry, it was the underlying assumptions about development that were questioned. Not all the protests were as successful as at Silent Valley, and certainly the subsequent path of development in India has not followed the overall perspective of the people's science movements. As with groups in China, where an aging Mao Tse-tung unleashed the Great Proletarian Cultural Revolution in the late 1960s, the KSSP was searching for alternative ways to develop technology and science from those that had characterized the first two decades of independence (Jamison 1994). And although the alternatives in both countries have not been pursued in anything more than a marginal fashion, they did play a role in changing the ways in which modern technoscience was thought about in China and India.

In China, the quest for an alternative approach to development became an extremely ugly business. Universities and schools were closed for several years, and scientists and engineers were forcibly sent to the countryside to reeducate themselves, whereas uneducated "barefoot scientists" were given responsibility over research in the so-called people's communes. The Red Guards, the radical students who took effective power at the time, as Mao disavowed the Communist Party he had helped establish, attacked the professional scientists and engineers, and proclaimed with Mao that they, like everyone else, must "serve the people." The extremism and dogmatism that characterized the cultural revolutionaries shows that alternative visions also can be affected by hubris, leaving reality behind on behalf of a transcendent, totalitarian ideology.

When Mao passed away in 1976, the Cultural Revolution had already died a few years before, and soon China was headed on a new path to development—the four modernizations that were associated with the new strong man, Deng Xiaoping. Many of the country's scientists and engineers, and large numbers of students, were sent abroad to immerse themselves in the technology and science that Mao had so pointedly rejected. Within two decades Chinese firms began to compete with Western companies in many technological branches, as the Japanese had done earlier.

For all the modernization that has taken place in China, there have nonetheless remained, as Mao would have put it, "contradictions" among the people. In China and India, the benefits of economic prosperity have been highly skewed, channeled only to a minority of the population, whereas hundreds of millions of people continue to lag behind. As John Gittings put it in opening his 1996 book-length report *Real China,*

There are two Chinas in the 1990s. One is the China of the expanding cities, the coastal boom, and the entrepreneurial ethic promoted by Mao Zedong's successor and veteran political survivor Deng Xioaping. ... The second China lies further inland, in the provinces away from the coast, and within each province in the more remote rural areas away from the towns. Here millions of Chinese peasants continue to live at the mercy of their traditional enemies: flood, drought and official corruption which has returned recently to plague them. (Gittings 1996, 1)

The plans to dam the Yangzi River at the area known as the Three Gorges above Yichang was a gigantic project that would change forever the natural landscape and lead to the forced migration of millions of people. Chinese critics mobilized support among scientists and nature lovers around the world. But unlike the protesters in India—nongovernmental organizations, such as the KSSP—who can operate freely and develop their arguments in public, the protesters in China had no such opportunities. It was only in the short-lived democracy movement of the late 1980s that the protests against the Three Gorges dam received widespread public debate and some response by party officials. But after the massacre at Tiananmen Square in 1989, the protests came to an end, and the project went ahead.

In both cases, the arguments for and against the hydroelectric dams were much the same: the officials argued that the dams were needed to provide electricity for economic development, whereas the critics argued that the price to be paid was too high and that the natural environment had qualities of its own—aesthetic, scientific, recreational—that were worth preserving. In China, there was also an enormous human price to pay, as millions of inhabitants would have to leave their homes and move to other parts of the country. In India, the critics were heard and, at least in the case of Silent Valley, they had an effect on official policy making. Even in the age of neoliberalism, there continues to be opportunity for public debate, not merely over dams but over the direction of scientific and technological development in

Figure 7. Construction site for the Three Gorges Dam, China, Hubei Province, c. 1990. Reprinted by permission of Gettyimages, Munich, Germany.

general, whereas in China there is no such opportunity for public debate, and according to many observers, the environmental and social consequences of the four modernizations are growing ever more serious.

The different opportunities for debate in China and India indicate that, in this as in so many other areas, the large Asian nations have not followed the same paths to modernity. For internal and external reasons, the hubris of Western technology and science has been met by different kinds of appropriation strategies. In this chapter we contrast the ways in which Japan, in addition to China and India, has sought to indigenize Western technology and science and tried to make them fit into non-Western ways of life.

THE MEETING OF EAST AND WEST

All human societies have developed technical artifacts, but only in the West, or, more specifically, in a few places in early modern Europe, did the development of technical artifacts become intrinsically linked to the production of scientific knowledge. What remained separate in other places—the lifeworlds of the scholar and the craftsman—were combined in the hybrid identity of the experimental philosopher. The cultural transformations that took place in Europe—the discourses, institutions, and practices of what we have termed the "scientific reformation"—did not take place in Asia, and many have been the attempts to explain why. Some have argued that, because the mind-sets, or mentalities, were so different, the forms of science that emerged in the West were simply not able to develop in Asia. There was not the same intellectual predisposition, no supernatural God, for one thing, encouraging the will to power, and no strict distinction between the thought categories of "nature" and "society" for another. In Asia, nature was not as actively stripped of its life and mystery as had been so characteristically the case in the West. On the contrary, many influential Asian philosophies have continued to emphasize the connections between the human and the nonhuman spheres of reality, and they see in both an underlying dynamic process of emergence. The conceptions of law and social order, as well as of science and technology, were derived from a different set of discursive frameworks, and so the particular emphases that took on hegemonic importance in Europe—mechanism, utility, quantification, natural law—did not develop indigenously in Asia (Huff 2003).

As Francesca Bray (1986) has convincingly shown, the productive practices of Asian rice-based civilizations differ in fundamental ways from those of the West, not least in terms of the technical requirements associated with the organization of irrigation and distribution. Also significant is that in the administration of Asian societies there was a combination of political, economic, and social authority (Pye 1985). In China and Japan, as well as across the Indian subcontinent, there had developed elaborate structures of governance, with intricate codes of conduct and rituals of behavior, and, with them, sophisticated procedures for producing knowledge and making technical improvements. Elites in each of the Asian civilizations—mandarins in China,

Brahmins in India, and Samurai in Japan—combined scientific and technical expertise with authority and exercised power in the public and private spheres.

While Europe was in the throes of fragmentation and a drawn out, contested process of rebirth in the millennium between the "fall of Rome" and the Renaissance, the Asian structures of authority were periodically being consolidated in the face of external and internal pressures. When Europe began to reinvent—and reassert—itself in the early modern period, not least with the help of a reformed technology and science, the Asian civilizations were thus in a very different stage, or cycle, of development. The confrontations with the West were therefore difficult, not to say traumatic, experiences that had deep repercussions.

In an ambitious account written in 1946, the legal philosopher F. S. C. Northrop made an attempt to contribute to what he hoped would be a "meeting of East and West" after the disasters that had unfolded during the war. Like many others before and since, Northrop sought to grasp the basic difference between the civilizations of Europe and Asia so that the world might be spared another round of global warfare. At the core of the East–West divide, he claimed, was a fundamental dichotomy in "patterns of thought." He distinguished between what he termed theoretic and aesthetic patterns and claimed that the one was endemic to the West and the other to the East. Whereas the science of the West was formulated in symbols and dealt primarily with lifeless objects, the knowledge of the East was more subjective and sensual. It was no easy matter to reconcile the two underlying patterns of thought, but it was essential, Northrop contended, to see them as complementary rather than incommensurable. "Each has something unique to contribute to an adequate philosophy and its attendant adequate cultural ideal for the contemporary world," he wrote. "The East and the West, when analyzed to determine their basic scientific and philosophical foundations, are found to be saying ... two different yet complementary things" (Northrop 1946, 375–76).

As Asian countries struggled to free themselves from dependence on the West in the ensuing decades, the need to use technology and science for purposes of development took on increasing importance. The strategies of appropriation that had emerged in the late nineteenth century, by which the so-called modernizers had aimed to keep the facts and artifacts of the West from destroying underlying cultural values and traditions, provided central discursive frameworks for these efforts. The challenge then had been to mix together the best features of both worlds while retaining the difference; as the Chinese court official Zhang Zhidong famously put it, "Chinese learning should remain the essence, but Western learning be used for practical development" (quoted in Spence 1990, 225).

The varying degrees of success that the three largest Asian civilizations have had in appropriating Western science and technology can perhaps be explained by the somewhat different points of departure. Japan could arguably make use of its traditions in a more active way than China and India because there was more that remained of the traditional society: it did not need to be invented to the same extent as India and China (Hobsbawm and Ranger 1983). The less that had been destroyed the less need there was to invent, or resurrect, a traditional past. China was not directly colonized as India, the pearl of the British Empire, had been, but its imperial order had been fundamentally undermined by the advances of Western technology and science. The West came with its guns and ships and, not least, its opium, and forced itself on China, contributing eventually to the withering away of the Chinese Empire.

Although the Japanese could thus more easily pick and choose what to retain as the essence and what to graft on and take over, the Chinese and Indians were thrust into a much more severe identity crisis. Perhaps therefore the results have been so much more mixed in China and India than in Japan, as modernization has produced bifurcated, dual societies rather than the arguably more syncretic forms of hybridization that have emerged in Japan. Let us start then our Asian journey in Japan, as we explore the processes by which the great Asian civilizations have sought to make technology and science their own.

WESTERN TECHNOLOGY AND SCIENCE IN JAPANESE CLOTHING

In his book *Zen and Japanese Culture*, D. T. Suzuki put the matter succinctly:

We admire a machine most exquisitely and most delicately balanced and most efficiently working, but we have no feeling of going toward it; it is a thing altogether distinct from us, which stands here ready to obey our commands. Not only that, we know every part of it mechanically and the purpose for which it is to work; there is no mystery as it were in the whole constitution of it; there are no secrets, there is no continuous creativeness here; everything is thoroughly explainable. (Suzuki 1938/1970, 376–77)

This immediate and highly pragmatic approach to technology—take it for what it is, and nothing more—is a recurrent theme in the Japanese discourse on technology, science, and modernity.

In an essay published in the early 1930s, the author Tanizaki Jun'ichirō reflected on the problems he had in attempting to combine modern, Western technologies with traditional building ideals and materials as he tried to design a new house for himself and his family. He had developed severe headaches, and he wondered why. "It was not that I objected to the conveniences of modern civilization, whether electric lights or heating or toilets," he wrote, "but I did wonder at the time why they could not be designed with a bit more consideration for our own habits and tastes" (Tanizaki 1933/1977, 6).

The problem that haunted the author was how to domesticate foreign technology, how to make it compatible with traditional cultural values. Electric light was easiest to tackle. Tanizaki did not shun having lightbulbs mounted onto old, antique lamps and lanterns. As long as the bulbs did not have too much candlepower, this solution was perfectly in accordance with good taste. The drawback of electric light was not so much the bulbs or the cords but rather the trend toward increasing brightness that came with the adoption of this technology. Traditionally, Japanese houses were sparsely lit, and Tanizaki argued that the introduction of electric light contributed to making homes much brighter and the indoor environment consequently much colder and harder. In opposition to the allegedly Western predilection for high intensities of light and of bright, polished surfaces, the author argued in favor of an interior design that was based on dimness as an ideal and that made use of dull materials. Consequently, his somewhat nostalgic essay is called *In Praise of Shadows*.

It had proved particularly difficult to design the bathroom. Tanizaki had to agree that tiles have certain advantages over wood and straw mats in that they are water repellent and easier to clean. Their smoothness and glossiness, however, make them quite inappropriate in connection with the raw surface of traditional, Japanese building materials. To create a harmonious relationship between tiles and dark wood turned out to be a daunting task indeed. It also proved prohibitively expensive to find a craftsman who could build a water closet made out of lacquered wood. So, in the case of the toilet, the author unwillingly had to make some concessions:

It turns out to be more hygienic and efficient to install modern sanitary facilities—tile and a flush toilet—though at the price of destroying all affinity with "good taste" and the "beauties of nature." (Tanizaki 1933/1977, 5)

Aestheticism had given way to practicality.

Tanizaki's agonizing attempt to assimilate foreign technologies, rituals, and modes of thinking reflects an age-old problem in Japanese history—a problem that has occupied not merely a few authors and philosophers but virtually the whole of Japanese society. Already in the first millennium AD Japanese agriculture had gone through a kind of revolution based on new rice-production methods from the Asian continent. In the following centuries, a range of cultural elements—including writing techniques, cooking methods, and religious ideas and practices—had been imported, primarily from China. On the intellectual level, the Chinese influence was met by a concerted appropriation strategy. In their inimitable, minimalistic manner, the Japanese described this kind of assimilation with the words *wakon kansai*, "Japanese spirit and Chinese scholarship," a phrase that is attributed to the ninth-century philosopher Michizane Sugawara (Takezawa 1986, 97). On one hand, there was openness toward foreign ideas, and, on the other hand, a strong sense of self-esteem and national pride.

Western influence set in only in the sixteenth century. After the first Portuguese and Dutch ships were sighted off the Japanese coast, a period of interchange of goods and ideas began. Missionaries managed to introduce the Christian faith in some communities, and merchants established profitable business contacts. In the history of technology and science, the interest on part of the Samurai class in Western muskets and the fascination on part of Japanese medical doctors in Western medicine are well-known. Although it by and large favored an isolationist policy, the shôgun government realized the potentials of foreign knowledge and even set up an office for the translation of central texts of the so-called Dutch sciences. Commentators have often discussed the Japanese interest in and ability to rapidly appropriate certain elements of European technology and science; for instance, Japanese artisans learned how to manufacture their own rifles within a remarkably short time. Western and Japanese commentators have had a tendency to interpret this ability favorably. Interestingly enough, the political scientist Takezawa Shinichi even employed the concept of "appropriation" when discussing how his fellow citizens have learned how to adopt and modify techniques from the West to suit Japanese needs and skills (Takezawa 1986, 98). Similarly, Iida Kenichi, a specialist on the history of Japanese iron making, claimed that already "in the eighteenth century the foreign technical culture was not simply copied, but modified in such a creative way that it squared with Japanese preconditions" (Iida 1986, 168–70).

It is wrong to characterize the early period of Japanese–Western contacts in terms of dependency. Direct contacts were rare, and the Japanese made use of Western knowledge in a very selective and rather instrumental manner. Western merchants had to largely restrict their activities to the harbor of Nagasaki, and they remained dependent on the goodwill of the shôgun. The relationship between Japan and the Occident began to take on an asymmetric form only after the mid-nineteenth century. However, this should not be taken to mean that the Japanese thereby lost their ability to adopt foreign technologies to their own conditions. In the second half of that century, Japanese engineers were, for instance, able to depart from the British standard method of blast-furnace iron production by using charcoal instead of coke.

As a result of intense pressure from, in the first instance, the United States, more Japanese harbors were opened up for foreign trade in 1854, and fourteen years later the so-called Meiji restoration paved the way for a rapid modernization of administrative, economic, technological, and political structures. Picking up ideas from Prussia and other Western countries, the Japanese modernized their army and police force, created a postal system, largely abandoned feudalism, and introduced a Western-like parliamentary system. Under state supervision, model factories were erected, railroad lines were constructed, foreign experts were hired, and Japanese specialists were sent on study tours abroad. Although by no means uncontested, these changes were to some extent carried by a kind of "pro-Western euphoria" (Schwentker 1997, 103).

After the turn of the twentieth century, this euphoria was slowly replaced by a more self-conscious attitude on the part of Japanese intellectuals. Having proved its greatness through a number of military victories, Japan now seemed mature enough to set its own stamp on the world. Discursively, this conviction involved a revival of a mode of thinking that had been formulated by the philosopher Sakuma Shôzan in the mid-nineteenth century. In his book *Reflections on My Mistakes,* Sakuma maintained that Japanese society would profit immensely if it managed to combine Eastern ethics and cultural principles with Western arts and science in a balanced manner (Chang 1970). As long as it remained true to its national characteristics, Japan should not shun adopting the material accomplishments of Western civilization. To implement his ideas, Sakuma founded a kind of technical college, where such applied fields as weapon technology, agriculture, and glass-blowing were taught. For Sakuma and many later intellectuals, the task that the Japanese people faced was not to reject but to domesticate

Western technology and science, to make it appropriate from the point of view of traditional customs and institutions.

Reformulated as *wakon jōsai,* "Japanese spirit and Western knowledge," Sakuma's way of phrasing the problem and formulating an appropriate solution became, as it were, a kind of discursive framework within which thinkers positioned themselves. Tanizaki is but one of several examples. More famous is his contemporary Nishida Kitarō, one of the grand old men of twentieth-century Japanese philosophy. Throughout his life Nishida struggled to find a place for Japanese thought and culture in an increasingly Westernized world (Feenberg 1995). To him the choice was not between introvert revival of original Japanese values and an uncritical acceptance of Occidental civilization. Instead, there had to be a third path between isolationism and what we nowadays call globalization.

Nishida noted the formidable ability of Japanese culture to assimilate foreign philosophies and technologies without losing its own specific character, and he claimed on this score that the Japanese people could serve as a role model for other nations. Because it has always followed the unifying principle of "identity of contradictions," Japanese culture has been able to appropriate different cultural elements, first from China and later from the West. Through a concerted act of discursive transformation, Nishida tried to reinterpret the age-old credo *hakko ichiu,* "Eight corners of the world under one roof" (quoted in Feenberg 1995, 184, 187). Instead of its original imperialist connotation, it was now—in the midst of the Second World War—given a strictly internal meaning. Facing the possibility of defeat, so it seems, Nishida realized that Japan could no longer rule the world but had to try to find an appropriate place for itself in an increasingly global world. A policy of appropriation superseded the policy of expansionism.

This discursive strategy, to redefine a well-known concept within the limits posed by an established framework, has a long tradition in the history of political ideas and philosophy. In his fascinating study of Machiavelli, the British philosopher Quentin Skinner (1981) analyzed how this sixteenth-century Italian ideologue managed to cast radical political ideas in a traditional mould. Machiavelli wrote *The Prince* in an effort to free Northern Italy from French and Spanish military forces and to join it under the rule of the house of Medici. His (in)famous book was written in a language and given a form that was familiar to his contemporaries. For instance, the concept of "virtue" played a pivotal role in *The Prince,* just as in other pamphlets of this kind. In Skinner's interpretation, Machiavelli's success cannot be explained without reference to his ability to combine innovation on the conceptual level with tradition on the stylistic level. Instead of denouncing virtue as an anachronistic moral imperative, Machiavelli redefined it to serve his own purposes.

Nishida and his followers were no less innovative. At several seminars and in a number of texts some of them developed an argument in favor of a particular Japanese road toward modernity. The task that they set was not to oppose modern technology and science but—as they put it—to "overcome [European] modernity" (Feenberg 1995, 170). Like Machiavelli did with the concept of virtue, Nishida and his students did not discard the concept of modernity but tried to give it a new meaning. They argued, in opposition to the traditional Western discourse, that modernization should not be understood as a universally homogeneous process always following developments in Europe and the United States. To them it should be possible for each people or nation to develop its own kind of modernity, thus contributing to a differentiation of the modernization process. As a consequence, it would not be a contradiction in terms to try to incorporate Western technology and science into traditional Japanese culture.

Much of the development of Japan in the postwar period can be thought of in these terms. After the U.S. occupation, a uniquely national system of innovation, with strong institutionalized links between the state and the private sector, was established. A powerful Ministry of Trade and Industry was created to foster such hybrid institutions, to connect technoscience to business far more explicitly than anywhere else in the world. Nakayama Shigeru (1991, 85–86) pointed to the Samurai origins of this Japanese form of technocracy. In the nineteenth century, after losing much of their power when the state took over their hereditary sources of income, the Samurai "were forced to find an entirely new means of living. … The Samurai were naturally attracted by government-sponsored careers in science and technology." And they took their rituals and codes of conduct with them.

Beginning with manufacturing industries and moving into more science-based information technologies, Japanese technologists and scientists developed styles of management and production that suited their talents and fit their cultural predispositions. Much of the organizational culture of the Japanese system of innovation draws on a kind of Samurai ethic, especially in matters of discipline and loyalty. In relation to product design and process engineering, other aspects of Japanese culture have been mobilized. As the U.S. anthropologist Ruth Benedict (1946) once put it, the Japanese path to modernity mixed the chrysanthemum with the sword.

By combining the aesthetic (the chrysanthemum) with the instrumental (the sword), the Japanese have been able to make distinctive contributions to the global economy and the arts of cultural expression. After the war, it was the creative recombination, or reverse engineering of products, that had been developed in the West—from automobiles to radios, from television to computers—that made it possible in some thirty years for Japan to catch up with the most advanced Western countries in many fields of technology and science. Indeed, some of the central breakthroughs in modern technological development, such as videotape recorders and mobile forms of communication and entertainment, are, to a large extent, Japanese innovations (Gay 1997). From the 1970s onward, Japanese firms have been among the world leaders in devising new hybrid combinations of culture and economics, information and gaming. In the food we eat, the physical exercises we perform, the musical expression we enjoy, and, not least, the communication that we conduct with one another, the whole world has taken part in the Japanese appropriation of technology and science. Our lives would lose a good deal of their meaning without our sushi, karate, karaoke, and, not least perhaps, our Sony walkmans and cell phones—not to mention those small, safe cars that are so appropriate for the contemporary world.

WALKING ON TWO LEGS: TECHNOLOGY AND SCIENCE IN CHINA

Through long stretches of human history, China was the dominant producer of technology and science in the world. In medicine and astronomy, chemistry and mechanics, geography and biology, and philosophy and art there has been continuous Chinese activity for thousands of years. As the many volumes of *Science and Civilization in China* by Joseph Needham and his collaborators amply demonstrated, the Chinese were also technologically active in mining, manufacturing, and construction, as well as in hydraulic engineering and agriculture. Their ships and weapons allowed them to trade with and, at times, conquer and colonize much of the rest of Asia. By the time various Europeans, in their desire to sell products and save souls, began to find their way to the Middle Kingdom, many fields of Chinese technology and science had reached a certain impasse, however. What Karl Marx called the "Asiatic mode of production" had become so stabilized, and the mode of governance had become so set in its ways, that creativity and innovation were neither encouraged nor fostered by the authorities (Needham 1981).

Chinese civilization rested on a hydraulic base, with irrigation works and water management systems making possible an effective control and coordination of a vast area, whereas the predominantly peasant population worked the land. Overseeing it all was a multilayered imperial bureaucracy with its own system of knowledge production and education, where mandarin scholars exercised power in ways that were fundamentally different from those forms of government that existed elsewhere. As the sinologist Etienne Balazs put it,

> Without strict fulfillment of its coordinating function by the mandarinate, China with its mixture of races and tribes would quickly have disintegrated and fallen prey to the dissensions of particularism. It was only constant supervision and harmonization of individual efforts that prevented the system of communications from becoming disorganized, the vital tasks of water conservation and utilization from being neglected, and road, canals, dikes, and dams from falling into a state of disrepair. The calendar, too, depended upon the mandarinate, and without it all the agricultural tasks of the peasantry would have fallen into indescribable chaos. But the Chinese people had to pay an exorbitant price for all this. (Balazs 1964, 155)

Although securing stability, such a society was unable to provide the predispositions that led, in the West, to the making of modern technology and science. In China there was little incentive and even less opportunity for scientific-technical hubris to become socially significant; it was neither sufficiently necessary nor sufficiently desirable, for enterprising and creative people to take the risks involved in pursuing life projects that had to do with technological and scientific development.

The Europeans and Americans who came in ever-increasing numbers in the course of the eighteenth and nineteenth centuries were seen by most Chinese—and certainly by the mandarinate—as uncivilized barbarians. Well into the nineteenth century, little attempt was made to understand the underlying logic that had been materialized in the tools of the barbarians. Their artifacts were sometimes beautiful to look at, amusing to play with, and, not least, effective in warfare, but they were not seen to represent a challenge in any more fundamental sense to the values that had governed Chinese civilization since the time of Confucius. As the scholar and military advisor Feng Guifen put it in 1860, when he wrote a series of essays urging China to "strengthen itself," what was to be learned from the "barbarians is only one thing, solid ships and effective guns" (quoted in Spence 1990, 197).

A more systematic interest in understanding Western technology and science began to develop only slowly, among a few imperial officials who were charged with foreign affairs, and, in particular, with military strategy and policy. In the Opium War (1839–42), British ships powered by steam helped the barbarians win increased trading privileges in the treaty ports of Canton and Shanghai and occupy "for all perpetuity" the island of Hong Kong. In the Taiping rebellion (1850–64), the teachings of Christian missionaries fueled an indigenous revolt against central authority. The challenge from the West came to be seen for a perceptive few to shake the very foundations of Chinese civilization.

The *yangwu* modernizers, as they have come to be called, understood that it was necessary to learn much more about Western technology and science in order to defend the empire and to revitalize the economy. Some of them established technical schools, and others encouraged the imperial officials to send Chinese students abroad. By the late nineteenth century, the modernization process had brought a certain amount of technological development—in the form of railways, telegraph lines, and a so-called New Army—but little in the way of political and social change (Baark 1997).

In the first years of the new century, a Revolutionary Alliance was formed, with Sun Yat-sen as the titular leader. Unlike the modernizers of the nineteenth century, who were primarily imperial officials or what we might call "dissident" scholars, Sun came from a poor family and had lived for many years among the Chinese emigrants in Hawaii and North America before attending medical school in Hong Kong. He was a "cultural hybrid with great ambitions and a deep sense of alarm over China's impending fate," as Jonathan Spence (1990, 227) wrote. Like many of his fellow nationalists, Sun was inspired by American "republican values," and the movement he led sought to combine science with democracy, both economic and political modernization. But like many such movements before and since, it proved to be a rather combustible mixture of people and ideas. When the dynasty fell in 1911, and a nationalist government came into power, China rapidly deteriorated into a state of chaos, as the different political groupings vied for control along with the infamous regional warlords.

Soon there would be other influences on the young republic, most notably the Bolshevik revolution in Russia, and in 1919, there was a kind of mass popular uprising that began among university students in Peking but soon spread across the country—something like what happened in 1989. It has come to be called the May Fourth Movement, and it took the form of strikes and protest meetings opposing the peace settlement that had been reached at Versailles with its negative impact on China's territory and sovereignty.

The May Fourth Movement was a kind of great debate about the future, conducted in the streets and in a wide array of newspapers and periodicals as well as in meetings of various kinds. Many of the participants, especially the students and faculty at the university in Peking where the movement was most active, were inspired by the American pragmatic philosophy of John Dewey, who lived in China in 1919 and 1920. Lecture tours by Bertrand Russell, Margaret Sanger, Albert Einstein, Rabindranath Tagore, and others—as well as the dramas of Henrik Ibsen and other modernist writers—were of catalytic importance.

But the new national government and the cultural revitalization process did not bring an end to the endemic violence that seemed to have overtaken China. By the 1930s, the country was embroiled in a civil war, and soon the Japanese occupied large parts of the country. Through the many years of warfare, the eventually victorious Communist Party, led by Mao Tse-tung, had come to develop a far different vision of modern China than their adversaries in the nationalist government, led by Chiang Kai-shek. It was in many ways a conflict between a primarily urban vision of an industrial China, based in the port cities and infused with Western technology and science, and a primarily rural vision of a communist or "people's republic" of China, where technology and science drew on indigenous, local traditions. It is that conflict and those competing visions of China that have carried over into the decades of independence, following the communist victory in 1949 and the flight of the nationalists to Taiwan.

What was most distinctive about "Mao Tse-tung thought," as it came to be canonized in the 1950s and 1960s, and imposed on Chinese development strategy, was the combination of traditional ideas and beliefs with a kind of homespun version of Marxist theory. In this extremely influential process of hybridization, Mao developed a particular method, as he put it in one of the "constantly read essays" of the Cultural Revolution, for identifying contradictions among the people. It was a form of social science that, in many respects, was quite appropriate for a vast, underdeveloped country such as China, simple and down to earth and drawing on ancient proverbial wisdom. It was a method that he used in most of his writings and that represented a combination of the imperial rituals and codes with the dialectical philosophy of Hegel and Marx. When applied to society, it provided a framework for assessing what might be termed policy options. But in practice, the method led to madness because it was applied dictatorially in ruthless, dogmatic fashion. The Maoist ideological concoction was imposed as a set of commandments rather than debated in anything approaching reasoned deliberation.

When applied to nature, Mao's thought combined certain features of traditional Taoism with ideas about agriculture and geography that had been developed in the West. Particularly in the 1970s, when delegations of foreign scientists visited China and observed science "walking on two legs" in the people's communes, many were struck by the resemblance of communal activity to the so-called environmentally friendly practices that were emerging in the West—in animal husbandry, in recycling waste products, in mobilizing traditional construction and design techniques, and in managing water use and treatment (Kapp 1974; Science for the People 1974). But without any opportunity for critical debate and interpretation, the lessons of the communes were lost to posterity when the cultural revolutionaries were disbanded and lost power.

The potentially alternative process of appropriation became a disastrous interlude in the modernization of China and did not survive the death of Mao. Instead, the last two decades of the twentieth century marked a time of rampant Westernization. Outside of the democracy movement of the 1980s, there has been an almost total neglect of environmental concern and a systematic rejection of traditional Chinese technology and science in Taiwan and the mainland and not least perhaps in that last bastion of British imperialism, the former colony of Hong Kong.

ANOTHER REASON: EXPLORING INDIAN HYBRIDITIES

One could argue that India's struggle for independence from British colonization was, to a greater extent than elsewhere, also a cultural struggle. In India, traditional techniques and non-Western beliefs and customs were mobilized in the political struggle for nationhood much more explicitly than elsewhere. In the long process of living under, confronting, and replacing British imperialism, Indian identities and institutions took on many hybrid forms in producing what Gyan Prakash (1999) termed "another reason."

Under the inspiration of Mohandas, later the Mahatma, Gandhi the peoples of the Indian subcontinent were encouraged to revive traditional technical practices and even managed to put aside, for a brief period of time, some of their religious antagonisms to achieve independence. Gandhi was Western trained and had learned about

Western science while studying law in Britain. Even more significant perhaps, he had become acquainted with Western traditions of cultural criticism, associated with such names as John Ruskin, Leo Tolstoy, and Henry David Thoreau. The "experiments with truth" (as he came to characterize his life's work) were, in large measure, a conscious effort to combine critical Western ideas with a very personal interpretation of Indian traditions (Gandhi 1927). The idea of nonviolent civil disobedience came primarily from Thoreau, but he appropriated the idea within discursive frameworks provided by Indian tradition. As such, Gandhi embodied an alternative approach to technology and science in his very person—indeed, in the preface to his autobiography he presents himself as an experimental scientist.

Gandhi was not alone in his attempts to develop alternative approaches to science and technology in colonial India. It is customary to distinguish his strategy of appropriation from the pro-Western nationalist leaders, such as Nehru, and from more traditional-minded intellectuals, such as the Nobel Prize–winning writer and artist Rabindranath Tagore, the first Asian to win the Nobel Prize. Gandhi's lifelong debate with Tagore over the value of Western technology and science, and, more specifically, over the value of spinning one's own cloth, is one of the defining discursive tensions of modern India. For Tagore, Gandhi's political genius, and not least his great skills in mobilizing popular support, were of questionable value when applied to matters of education and science.

If Gandhi was too traditional for Tagore, he was not traditional enough for Ananda Coomaraswamy and many of the other independence leaders. Ashis Nandy contrasted Gandhi's "critical traditionalism" to the more absolute glorification of tradition represented by the art historian and Buddhist scholar Coomaraswamy, who served as curator at the Boston Museum of Fine Arts after taking part in the independence movement in Ceylon, now Sri Lanka. Where Gandhi made use of Indian traditions in an open-ended, reflective way, Coomaraswamy's

> tradition remains homogeneous and undifferentiated from the point of view of man-made suffering. … Today, with the renewed interest in cultural visions, one has to be aware that commitment to traditions, too, can objectify by drawing a line between a culture and those who live by that culture, by setting up some as the true interpreters of a culture and the others as falsifiers, and by trying to defend the core of a culture from its periphery. (Nandy 1987, 121, 122)

Although Gandhi was critical of Western technology and science, he was also highly critical of Indian traditions and, in particular, of the religious warfare that was so endemic to the subcontinent. It was the lack of morality, the lack of idealism in Western and non-Western civilization that Gandhi objected to, and his own hybrid identity was a unique, not to say idiosyncratic, mixture of the West and the East.

The double nature of Gandhi's critique is important in understanding the subsequent dilemmas of Indian development. Unlike the leaders of most other independence movements in non-Western societies, Gandhi sought to combine independence with truth and love; that is, *swaraj* (self-rule) with what he called *satyagraha,* a word he made up by combining the Sanskrit words *satya* (truth) and *agraha* (holding firmly) in a new hybrid concept (Dalton 1993, 9). His technology and science involved not merely alternative practical applications but also an alternative theory of knowledge.

India did not follow Gandhi's lead in the first two decades after independence. Instead, under the leadership of Nehru, ambitious efforts were made to implant technology and science in Indian society. His scientism, and that of his leading scientific and political advisors, was deep and unambiguous. For Nehru, Indian civilization, with its superstitions and religious strife, was in need of radical change, and his governments did their utmost to develop scientific institutions and a popular understanding and appreciation for science. From the late 1940s, scientific and technological research was organized roughly along the lines of the Soviet model, with central planning and strong state control over priorities and orientation.

It is an oversimplification to say that Nehru's death in 1964 led to a revival of Gandhian thought. But as the 1960s progressed, a number of challenges emerged to the developmental strategies and emphases that had guided India since independence. The wars with China and Pakistan fostered neonationalism and eventually religious fundamentalist tendencies, and a variety of popular peasant movements began to wage struggles against the central and regional authorities. The international wave of student and anti-imperialist protests also played its part, so that, by the early 1970s, India was a society torn by inner conflict.

Many different strategies of appropriation have since emerged in India, not least from a revived, or reinvented, Hindu fundamentalism. In 1978 Prime Minister Indira Gandhi, after having ruled the country through an unpopular State of Emergency, was defeated by the opposition Janata Party, and later, after her sons were killed, the Nehru dynasty and the rule of the Congress Party came to an end. What has developed in recent years is a reassertive, and militant, form of nationalism that has combined elements of Hindu tradition with a faith in modern technology and science into a kind of "reactionary modernism" (Nanda 2003).

The critiques of Western technology and science that were influential in the 1960s and 1970s remain important in India, however, and as sources of inspiration for the rest of the world, as well. Among the intellectuals at such Indian think tanks as the Centre for the Study of Developing Societies (CSDS), a kind of hybrid discourse of alternative modernity emerged in the 1970s. The political scientist Rajni Kothari, who created the CSDS, had been the chairman of the Social Science Research Council, but he had grown increasingly disillusioned with the path that Indian development had taken. After Nehru's death, he and many other Indian intellectuals began to reconsider the Gandhian legacy and discuss alternative approaches to science, technology, and development. There also emerged, as we have seen earlier, a range of popular movements and environmental protests. There were the so-called people's science movements that were particularly active in southern India. Here the emphasis was on critical popularization, linking science in selective ways to popular myths and traditions and bringing scientific expertise to bear on protests against government-sponsored development projects.

More significant in the long run perhaps were the environmental movements that emerged in the forests of the north, as well as on tribal lands, which helped bring about more ambitious strategies of appropriation. Here critiques of Western science and technology were recombined in the cognitive praxis of environmental activism. As articulated by the physicist-turned-activist Vandana Shiva,

Maldevelopment is intellectually based on, and justified through, reductionist categories of scientific thought and action. Politically and economically, each project which has fragmented nature and displaced women from productive work has been legitimised as scientific by operationalising reductionist concepts to realise uniformity, centralization and control. (Shiva 1988, 14)

Shiva, who in the 1990s became a leading figure of international environmentalism—and, like the KSSP, won an alternative Nobel prize of her own—combined an ecological and feminist critique of Western technology and science with a critical mobilization of Indian cultural traditions.

In her first book *Staying Alive*, Shiva identified alternative feminine principles and a feminine attitude to nature in traditional Indian thought. She has continued to argue in her many writings that projects of (mal)development, such as social forestry and the Green Revolution in agriculture—and, as we saw in the introduction, genetic engineering—are masculine and violent projects that separate women (and men) from their natural roots and destroy valuable natural resources. In the protests of rural women, such as the Chipko movement in northern India, Shiva sees a "countervailing power" of feminine knowledge and politics.

Shiva and other Western-trained scientists who have joined forces with the environmental movements in India also developed a range of research institutions and alternative organizations for the dissemination of their facts and artifacts. Particularly significant has been the Centre for Science and Environment, which has produced a series of reports on *The State of India's Environment* and a magazine titled *Down to Earth*. Started by the journalist Anil Agarwal in 1980, the Centre for Science and Environment has been in the forefront of environmental knowledge making in India, keeping open a kind of hybrid forum for debate and information that can serve to ameliorate some of the more negative aspects of development and modernization. As such, the formations of hybrid identities and institutions continues in spite of the dualism, or bifurcation, that has afflicted India, as it has afflicted China and much of the rest of the developing world, in the neoliberal era of technoscience.

6

ARTISTIC APPROPRIATIONS FROM MORRIS
TO *THE MATRIX*

Our epoch has invented machines which would have appeared
wild dreams to the men of past ages, and of those machines
we have as yet *made no use.* They are called "labour-saving"
machines—a commonly used phrase which implies what we
expect of them; but we do not get what we expect. What they really
do is to reduce the skilled labourer to the ranks of the unskilled.

—William Morris, "Useful Work versus Useless Toil"
(1993, 304)

THE AMBIVALENCE OF THE ARTIST

Throughout his life, William Morris was a contradiction in terms.
He was vehemently opposed to the artistic standards of his time, and
yet he made his living working by them. He dreamed of an egalitarian
society, and yet he lived in luxury and made expensive products that
only the wealthy could afford. He was a successful capitalist businessman who was also an active socialist politician. And perhaps most
important, he was a highly skilled practitioner of sophisticated artistic
techniques who served as a somewhat unwilling leader for a movement
that sought to revitalize the simple arts and crafts. And yet, for all the
contradictions, Morris continues to serve as a multifaceted source of
inspiration for the artistic appropriation of technology and science.

In 1890 this man, who identified himself simply as a designer, wrote a utopian vision of the future titled *News from Nowhere*. Like everything about Morris, the book was a hybrid, combining a love for the past and nostalgia for medieval times with an undeniably modern artistic sensibility. It was meant not to be great literature but rather to contribute to the struggle for socialism, which for Morris was the "education of desire" (Thompson 1955/1977). It was first published in installments in *Commonweal*, the magazine he had helped start a few years earlier, and it was later bound in leather with the full range of engravings and typographical innovations that Morris developed at his Kelmscott Press.

News from Nowhere was written as an answer to the traditionalism that was widespread among many of his fellow British artists and writers and to the futurism that was endemic to most of his fellow socialists. It was meant as a response to the attitudes to technology and industrial society that had been articulated by Samuel Butler in his book *Erewhon* (1872) and by the North American Edward Bellamy in *Looking Backward* (1888). Whereas Butler had imagined the decline of technological civilization and put all machines into a museum so they could no longer cause any damage, Bellamy envisioned the enormous expansion of industrial machinery into ever more areas of life, with production in the hands of an industrial army in which all were expected to serve. For Morris, both visions were fundamentally flawed, the one in its elitist pessimism and the other in its populist optimism. As the artist who believed in the importance of bringing art and beauty into the lives of normal people, Morris in his fantasy brought news from a time when technology and science would be used appropriately, not allowing them to dominate society, as in *Looking Backward*, but certainly not being banished and forbidden as in *Erewhon*.

Morris's decidedly ambivalent attitude to technology and science was formed by experience, and in particular the experience of making beautiful things for a living. Since the 1850s, when he and a few of his friends from Oxford had formed the "Firm"—which later became Morris and Company—he worked in the interior decoration business, and, in the process, he mastered a wide range of practical skills and learned to use a great variety of tools and sometimes even machines. By 1890 his wallpapers, tapestries, carpets, and furniture had become fashionable consumer items in Victorian England, even though he had grown increasingly frustrated by the fact that they were too expensive for the working people to whose revolutionary cause he was committed. Among his other artistic achievements, he was also active in the revitalization of graphic art, not least in the publishing of his own poetry and lectures and the tales of his beloved medieval writers (MacCarthy 1994).

Morris was one of the most outspoken critics of the society that was taking shape around him as a result of the industrial transformation. He especially objected to how art had become vulgarized, reduced to ugly products of poor quality that could be bought and sold on the commercial marketplace. But what continues to make Morris meaningful is that he was so much more than a critic. It was the particular combination of what he termed his "hatred for civilization" and his passion for making beautiful things that makes him so significant in the process that we call the artistic appropriation of technology and science. He epitomizes the ambivalence of the artist.

Morris tried to give art new kinds of social and cultural meanings, and, as such, he has served as an example, positively and negatively, for all of the industrial designers and interior decorators and architects and planners who have continued to try to fashion a popular art and make beauty a natural part of people's everyday lives. In this chapter, we trace some of the trajectories that Morris set in motion, and see what has happened to his vision of a "popular art," as they have confronted the "dominant cultural formation" of commercial capitalism and "residual" cultures of artistic tradition (to borrow a terminology from Raymond Williams [1977]). In particular, we try to identify some of the efforts that have been made to combine the two, to develop hybrid works of art, mixing the old and the new, the innovative and traditional, the dominant and residual, as Morris continually sought to do.

Morris's ideas about the decorative arts and the politics of design informed many of the modernist projects of the twentieth century among artists and architects, as well as within social movements, in Europe and North America. His portrait hung in Hull House in Chicago, where Jane Addams sought to alleviate the distress of the urban poor, and many of the social reformers of the 1930s, the makers of modernity and the welfare state, returned to his lectures and *News from Nowhere*. Even the young J. R. R. Tolkien drew inspiration from the fantasy novels that Morris wrote in the 1890s, after he had left the socialist movement and gave a somewhat freer reign to his literary imagination. But it was especially the artists and architects who designed the technological civilization, in particular all of those who sought to create a meaningful and useful popular art, who carried the legacy of Morris through the twentieth century.

In his lifetime, Morris was a key actor in what came to be called the Arts and Crafts Movement, which led to networks and professional organizations and, not least, creative sites of hybrid identify formation for industrial designers and interior decorators throughout the world (Cumming and Kaplan 1991/2002). In Germany, Austria, and Scandinavia, as well as in Britain and North America, the movements that built on the works and ideas of Morris and his collaborators engineered a kind of revolution in the way in which products are made. Above all else, it was the emphasis on quality—in production as in life—rather than the reduction of quality to a quantitative, mechanical logic that remains the legacy of Morris in our day.

Like all movements, the ones that were dedicated to the promulgation of arts and crafts split into a wide range of disparate groups as they became institutionalized, and the direct influence of Morris on the artistic appropriation of technology and science has long faded into the past. Yet the idea of bringing artistic energy into industrial activities, mixing business with pleasure, so to speak, lives on in many architectural firms, and not least in many designers' workshops. Similarly, Morris's organicism, the artistic representation of natural processes that made his wallpapers and tapestries so appealing in late Victorian England, as transformed by representatives of Art Nouveau and Jugendstil, has continued to exert a significant influence on designers and architects, from Frank Lloyd Wright to Frank Gehry.

For other artists and architects, especially those captivated by technology and its rationality, the example of Morris has taken on an anachronistic, backward-looking meaning. In rejecting the organic and accepting the instrumental imperatives of contemporary life, many modernists have come to see the artisan tradition that Morris epitomized as a barrier to innovation. In the interwar years, the director of the Bauhaus in Germany, Mies van der Rohe, who moved to the United States in the 1930s, came to embrace the possibilities of modern materials and industrial techniques. For many other designers and architects, concrete, glass, and steel provided the basis for a new aesthetic ideal (Misa 2004). *Functionality* became the artistic catchword, but, in becoming established, it has often been connected to a form of hubris, a fascination for building or designing the seemingly impossible. Under the spell of hubris, many modern artists and architects have bestowed upon us the fantastic constructs of their imaginations while they have strayed ever further from their Morrisian roots.

BETWEEN FORM AND FUNCTION

Morris was, of course, not the first person to try to mediate between tradition and modernity. Innumerable artists, artisans, and architects before him had tried—admittedly with mixed results—to make the products of industrial society aesthetically pleasing and to place the achievements of technology and science in an attractive contextual setting. Initially, their strategies were of two kinds: decorative ornamentation and pastoral harmonization.

In his book *Civilizing the Machine* (1976), historian John Kasson documented how many early American manufacturers sought to make their products sublime by adding various artistic touches. Like their European competitors, they equipped their steam engines with Greek columns, applied sophisticated woodwork to their locomotives, and filled their stationery with arabesques and graphic flourishes. Typical patriotic symbols were also used to give a sense of culture to industry. When Thomas Roberts Locomotive & Machine Works of Paterson, New Jersey, built a new locomotive in 1856, the company decorated it with a bald eagle and the Stars and Stripes. Manufacturers of printing presses placed eagles atop their machines, and railroad companies hired painters to show their trains quite literally blending into the countryside.

The painting *Lackawanna Valley* by George Innes, from 1855, is a classic example of this Republican version of what Leo Marx (1964) termed "pastoralism." A toylike train makes its way through a peaceful landscape, leaving an equally toylike factory town behind. Overlooking the scene is a boy, a kind of modern shepherd. The symbolism is clear: there need be no contradiction between modern industry and mechanical means of transportation, on one hand, and the natural landscape, on the other. Like many writers and poets in the nineteenth century, painters and subsequently photographers helped to place the industrial transformation into a familiar imagery and artistic format. Or, in the words of the historian David Nye (1994, 59), "The machine—whether locomotive, steamboat, or telegraph—was considered to be part of a sublime landscape, and at first it was included in pastoral paintings as a harmonious part."

It was not until after the First World War that manufacturers of industrial products began systematically to involve artists more directly in the design and marketing phases of production. Only in the interwar period did leading companies in the United States employ artists—much like they had done with scientists earlier. And when they did make use of artistic assistance, they did so for purely commercial reasons. In an era of mass production and mass consumption, it was increasingly difficult to compete on the basis of price alone. Although it had long been recognized that certain products signal social status and carry cultural capital, such ideas seemed out of date—nonmodern—in an age of standardization and rationalization. When ready-made products superseded custom-made products for a depersonalized and anonymous market, another sort of aesthetic style or principle seemed to be required than those that had worked in the past. As objects became artificial, or what the French art historian Pierre Francastel (1956/2000) termed "plastic," artists needed to find new ways to represent them.

It did not take long before manufacturers understood that market shares could be gained by designing products that were made to seem more attractive than those of their competitors. Although the concept did not emerge until later, "industrial design" became a way to create a sense and sensibility of difference among consumers. The message was obvious to anyone who could read the writing on the wall: mass-produced artifacts also could be imputed with meaning and contribute to the consumer's identity and sense of self. Indeed, as Andy Warhol and the other pop artists of the 1960s made abundantly clear, standardized machine-made products have a beauty all their own.

The automobile industry was a pioneer in the field of industrial design, as in many other areas. In 1913 the Ford Motor Company started assembly-line production, thus laying the foundation for one of the most successful products ever: the Ford Model T. The reason for its success was the car's sturdiness, reliability, and low price. In appearance, however, this world-famous car was unspectacular, and it went through only minor changes during its almost twenty years of production. The Model T symbolized uniformity and simplicity, and it had no unnecessary decorative features. It came in only one color (black) and Henry Ford had hoped it would contribute to the resurrection of the rural United States and of the simple, rural way of life.

As we discuss further in the next chapter, automobiles have always been more than merely means of transportation. From the outset, they served as status symbols and carried with them a wide range of meanings and cultural messages. To meet the Model T challenge, competitors put increasing emphasis on appearance. It was the General Motors Corporation that most ambitiously came to apply artistic elements into its product lines. Although Arthur P. Sloan initially met resistance from the production divisions, his design strategy ultimately carried the day: to aim for "beauty of design, harmony of lines, attractiveness of color schemes and general contour of the whole piece of apparatus" (quoted in Meikle 1979/2001, 13). The General Motors Art and Color Section started concocting breathtaking colors, fashioning smoother automobile bodies, and designing exciting new kinds of paraphernalia on an annual basis. From then on artistic inputs—in the name of industrial design—took on a major importance in regard to innovation and, especially, marketing of commercial products.

Perhaps more than anything else, streamlining, or a general feeling of sleekness, came to represent the main aesthetic principle of industrial design in the ensuing decades. This futuristic-looking form certainly made sense in areas such as automobile and airplane design, where the minimization of air resistance affected performance. But why should pencil sharpeners, vacuum cleaners, and meat slicers be streamlined and sleek looking? From our perspective, it was primarily because such design principles fit into a broader aesthetic program, or cultural mind-set, in which sleekness and, more generally, pure geometrical form came to be associated with progress and with material abundance. Customers found the modernist message attractive, even in relation to more mundane objects of everyday life, where sleekness came to be associated with a new lifestyle of modern living (Nickles 2002).

In the process of providing the technological products of everyday life with cultural capital, which signaled a particular status, or station, in society, a few artists-turned-industrial-designers reached almost legendary status. Raymond Loewy, a French émigré to the United States whose redesign of a mimeograph duplicator machine had given him an entrance ticket into the business world, had a significant influence on the fashioning of mass-produced consumer items. His Coldspot refrigerators, with their round corners and subtle aesthetic touches, for the mail-order firm Sears Roebuck helped usher in the age of artificial obsolescence that the journalist Vance Packard satirized in his books of the late 1950s, *The Status Seekers* and *The Waste Makers*. Loewy was given the task of making small changes, so that each year the very same refrigerator would look a little different and, as with automobiles, the consumer would feel compelled to exchange the old model for the new one. Industrial design became increasingly cosmetic or superfluous, as style replaced functionality as the guiding design principle. As Packard (1960, 72) put it,

> All the emphasis on style tends to cause the product designers and public alike to be preoccupied with the appearances of change rather than the real values involved, and also tends to force more and more extravagance in the design as the designers grope for novelty.

Norman Bel Geddes also made a name for himself in the design of household appliances. His gas stove from 1933 represented a clear break with the engineering-style designs of the past. It had the round corners that by now had become almost compulsory in American manufacturing circles. Geddes systematically removed all inconvenient parts to simplify cleaning, and he did his best to turn this practical item into a work of art. When the stove was marketed, advertisements sold it as promising a "New Deal for the forgotten kitchen" and made the designer a household name (Meikle 1979/2001, 102).

Geddes did not limit himself to individual consumer items. For the New York World's Fair of 1939, he designed the General Motors exhibition building and the so-called Futurama, a miniature urban landscape complete with highways, skyscrapers, and other standard items of the modern urban landscape. In his aesthetic approach, Geddes was directly influenced by the Swiss architect Le Corbusier, the high priest of modernism. Le Corbusier has gone down in history as a person who pursued and developed the rationalist ideals more devotedly than any other person, and his renovation of Marseille and other French cities along modernist lines are well-known. Luckily, his plan to tear down large sections of downtown Paris and replace them with high-rise buildings and wide avenues never materialized. At least on that one occasion, hubris met history and lost.

Modernist designers and architects took the possibilities of mass production, plastic objects, and, not least, new, science-based working materials to a point of no return. In the words of Thomas Misa (2004, 189),

> The materials—inexpensive, available in large quantities, and factory-manufactured—made it economically possible to dream of building housing for the masses, in a way that could not have been achieved with hand-cut stone or all-wood construction. The modern materials were also something of a nucleation point for technological fundamentalists asserting the imperative they felt to change culture in the name of technology.

The fact that modernist architecture and urban planning today find some of their most exorbitant and expensive examples in countries such as Japan and China shows that the appeal of artistic hubris is not limited to the West.

Although Le Corbusier has become famous for calling a residential house a "machine for living," he was not alone in envisioning a future in which all aspects of daily life were organized in accordance with artistic principles. The Austrian architect Joseph Hoffmann had conceived of buildings as "pieces of total art" (*Gesamtkunstwerke*) at the turn of the century, and similar notions came to guide architects for several decades. Unlike Le Corbusier, Hoffmann argued for a kind of design that took its point of departure in basic human needs rather than the demands of an abstract economy or a rational transportation system, or a technological imperative (Noever 2003). The sanitarium in Purkersdorf outside of Vienna is an early example of functional architecture with a flat roof, straight angles, and no unnecessary decoration. The ideal of the building as a *Gesamtkunstwerk* manifested itself in Hoffmann's attention for detail. He was not satisfied to design just the building, and he saw to it that lamps, furniture, and other objects were made to fit into the overall concept.

Hoffmann's main source of inspiration was Morris. In an effort to marry industry and the arts, Hoffmann had founded the so-called Vienna Shops (*Wiener Werkstätte*) together with his companion Koloman Moser. In close collaboration with the School of Handicraft and the Museum of Arts and Industry, this institution soon became a center for Austrian artists and artisans. They worked with various materials— glass and ceramics, metal and textiles—and developed methods that combined high quality and industrial means of production. The slogan "ornamentation is crime," which was coined by Adolf Loos in 1908, captures the state of mind of these reformers. They found the ornamental patterns of Art Nouveau offensive, and instead they aimed at the greatest possible simplicity in their functionalism. The attractive appearance of a material object or a building, as it were, ought never be a goal in itself but always be deduced from its projected functions. Bald eagles and Doric columns were definitely banned from such an artistic appropriation strategy.

MODERN ART MEETS MODERN TECHNOLOGY

One year after Loos published his book *Ornament and Crime* (1908/ 1997), a young Italian issued a pamphlet that marked a turning point in the relations between artists and technology. In Filippo Tommaso Marinetti's *Manifesto of Futurism* (1909/1960), a short but extremely self-conscious document of hubris couched in hype, he called on his readers to embrace wholeheartedly the products of industrial society. Modern technology represented the future:

We shall sing … the nocturnal vibration of the arsenals and the yards under their violent electrical moons; the gluttonous railway stations swallowing smoky serpents; the factories hung from the clouds by the ribbons of their smoke; the bridges leaping like athletes hurled over the diabolical cutlery of sunny rivers; the adventurous steamers that sniff the horizon; the broad-chested locomotives, prancing on the rails like great steel horses curbed by long pipes, and the gliding flight of airplanes whose propellers snap like a flag in the wind, like the applause of an enthusiastic crowd. (Marinetti 1909/1960)

Marinetti's manifesto praised power and violence and rejected everything that was old and traditional in Italian society—be it conventional aesthetic standards, boring museums, or stuffy libraries. The road to the future was paved with victims, and it is not surprising that the futurists, as Marinetti and his followers called themselves, have been accused of preparing the way for Mussolini and Italian Fascism.

Marinetti was fascinated by "roaring cars" and other rapidly moving pieces of machinery, and futurist painters came to be especially concerned with capturing "the beauty of speed" on canvass. Giacomo Balla's pictures of automobiles and bicycles are impressive examples of artistic appropriation, as are Umberto Boccioni's dynamic, expansive cityscapes. Still today, gallery visitors cannot help but be fascinated by the painting techniques that these Italians applied. They were inspired by the cubist method of reducing reality to geometrical forms; their automobiles seem to be overcoming the sound barrier, and their construction machinery breaks through the confines of old city walls.

Unlike the pastoralists of the nineteenth century, who had tried to fashion a harmonious balance between artifact and environment, technology and nature, the futurists unabashedly sold out to the machine. There was no ambivalence here. And, unlike many twentieth-century realist painters, who depicted industrial workers in a heroic fashion or milieus of mass consumption along distracted lines, the futurists were neither romantic nor critical. They were simply enthusiastic and provocative—two traits that they shared with the impressionist painters and sculptors of the late nineteenth century.

Although impressionists might not be, in the first instance, known for their relation to modern technology, the movement definitely came to play an important role in the artistic appropriation of technology and science. With the invention of photography and the proliferation of science-based artifacts into ever more areas of social life, it had become imperative to redefine the social role of the artist, and indeed of art. Rather than providing a pictorial reflection of reality, artists seemed called on to go further or deeper in their efforts at representation. In the middle of the nineteenth century, realist artists had come to turn their attention toward workers, in the countryside and in the factory, but those who came to be called "impressionists"—a term first used by ironic critics—chose another approach to reality. Art should help visualize and interpret other realms of human consciousness than those that were directly accessible to the senses. A painting should not reflect the world like a mirror does, giving an accurate image, but rather transmit a sensation, present a mood. Artists such as Claude Monet and Vincent Van Gogh sought to provide a sort of artistic feeling that psychologists only later began to discover. In the words of Stephen Kern (1983, 163),

> Van Gogh created on canvas an unforgettable dynamic world. His landscapes are visual metaphors for the turbulence in his mind. Roofs undulate with the contours of the terrain, skies flow with surging mountains, and trees grow before our eyes, whipping lines of force into an atmosphere that spirals into stars, eddies around a prominent sun. … His universe was a continuous field of energy circulating through mind, world and art.

Experimentation with new forms of artistic technique and expression was widespread in the late nineteenth century. Monet and Van Gogh, Edouard Manet and Paul Gaugin, Auguste Renoir and Paul Cézanne—to name only some of the more influential members of the impressionist and postimpressionist movements—sought to create a new kind of art that challenged the established routines and the traditional ways of depicting reality. They made space and time, nature and society, object and subject, and, not least, the conscious and the unconscious into central topics of artistic exploration. These artists no longer tried to paint reality as it really was—photographs could do that so much more effectively. Rather, they tried to provide through their art appropriate "structures of feeling" for a technological civilization. Their task was to conjure up meaningful impressions of the world, rather than accurate pictures of the thing itself.

It was together, as a movement—albeit fairly loosely organized—that the impressionists could have the impact they had, giving art a new kind of meaning in the modern world, at one and the same time popular and sophisticated. It was an art that could appeal to highbrow and lowbrow, the masters and the masses, and there was no question about its modernity. These artists also found other spaces for the production of their art than traditional artists had done. Gaugin went to the tropics, Renoir went to the ballet, and they all, at one time or another, went to Provence for inspiration, but also for a sort of communal autonomy. The artists in Scandinavia who gathered in Skagen on the northern coast of Jutland were in search of much the same thing: a creative space of their own. They turned their back to the established academies of art and set up new sites for showing and selling their works. The impressionists contributed to the appropriation process not only with their actual paintings but also with their concern with artistic autonomy and independence, and with reconstituting the public sphere.

Perhaps no single artist contributed to the cognitive praxis of the movement more conscientiously or methodically than Claude Monet, who turned his home and garden into a key site for the artistic appropriation of reality. Like Cézanne, he stayed close to home and painted what was near at hand, and, also like Cézanne, he explicitly distanced himself from what he saw, trying to represent the abstract essence of an image rather than provide an accurate reflection. He carried out his experiments with nuances of light and color in a systematic way, more or less like a scientist, painting the same scene in different moods, varying the conditions to see what the effect would be. From our perspective his paintings of railway stations are particularly interesting—not simply because they depict pieces of machinery and technical structures but also because they suggest the sense of brightness and openness and, not least, possibility that was, more generally, associated with railroad stations in the cultural mood of the time. In France, as elsewhere, engineers had made effective use of iron and glass to design huge stations that gave an expansive feeling of unlimited space. Much like medieval cathedrals, railroad stations took on a kind of spiritual significance in the emerging industrial society, as their structure sought to symbolize the modern spirit, and it was not a coincidence that they were referred to as "cathedrals of our time." Just as writers expressed their fascination at the sight of these bright and airy stations, Monet expressed his impression of light and air on canvass.

From an appropriation perspective, the impressionists provided popular access to, and understanding of, the natural processes that they were investigating in their open-air laboratories. On one hand, the impressionist painters began the transformation of the external world into abstract symbols, into visions of artistic imagination rather than depictions of some immediately recognizable place. By so doing, they served to relativize the physical reality of nature. On the other hand, they expanded the range of artistic representation, taking the objects of everyday life and the typical scenes of everyday environments and turning them into things of beauty. As such, they helped to enhance and enrich the appreciation of technological artifacts. In both respects, the seeds they planted were formative for all the later schools of modern art to come—from cubism to surrealism, from futurism to expressionism, and on to the pop art of the 1960s.

MODERN TIMES

A few decades after photography and impressionist paintings had started to affect how people viewed the world, a new technology emerged that proved to have an unprecedented importance. Audiences were stunned when the French Lumière brothers began to tour European theaters and amusement parks with their movie projectors in 1895. Although the short clips that they and their subcontractors presented initially only showed familiar scenes, the fascination was immediate. Train stations and shipping ports were well-known objects, but they took on a new character when presented on a white screen in a darkened room. Some spectators reportedly jumped out of their seats when a locomotive approached them at high speed on the screen. Letting himself be immersed into the "kingdom of shadows," famous Russian author Maxim Gorkij noted that a coach seemed to be driving "directly toward you" (quoted in Paech and Paech 2000, 20).

In his *Theory of the Film* (1960), German philosopher Siegfried Kracauer later commented on the fact that the world looks different through a camera lens. Cameras and movie cameras do not reflect the world in an objective way but focus and highlight certain aspects of reality. Unlike many other theorists before him, most notably Walter Benjamin, Kracauer was not critical of the cinema. In his pamphlet *The Work of Art in the Age of Mechanical Reproduction* (1936/1968), Benjamin claimed that a movie always gives a distorted view of reality. A talented actor on stage radiates what Benjamin called an "aura," a kind of authenticity that can never be transferred onto the film screen. Kracauer opposed such aesthetic conservatism and instead argued, in an explicit act of cultural appropriation, that film was an art form in its own right. By its ability to focus on detail and reduce the world into smaller units, the camera is a truly modern artistic technique that suits our scientifically and technologically conditioned world perfectly. The industrial era is one in which materiality becomes increasingly important, and Kracauer suggested that the movie camera has an essential role in reminding us of the omnipresence of this "outer reality."

Dziga Vertov's classic documentary *Man with a Movie Camera* from 1929 illustrates Kracauer's argument. Depicting public life in Moscow during one day, the film makes viewers aware of events and objects that are so familiar that we seldom reflect about them. Technical artifacts play a central role in Vertov's film. Trains rush in and out of the city; people get off trams and dash across streets. Modern industrial life is hectic and chaotic, and it is the task of the man with the movie camera to unravel this reality. In other words, a technical instrument expands our realm of experience and our sense of reality.

Throughout the twentieth century the city was also a popular topic for makers of feature films. Fritz Lang's *Metropolis* of 1926 was pioneering in this regard and in the way in which it depicted the factory system. A functionalist city that probably made Le Corbusier green with envy provided the background for a combined love story and critique of industrial technology. The real work in the futurist city was performed by armies of oppressed laborers. Not unexpectedly, the movie's hero not only attempts to improve their lot but also discovers an alternative to the modern city—a *Lebensreform* garden, where the heroine lives in a kind of female paradise.

The workers in Lang's factory were under the control of a ruthless capitalist with sophisticated surveillance cameras, and they had no choice but to submit to the power of the machine. This was also the theme that Charlie Chaplin raised in his *Modern Times* from 1936. In one of the most famous sequences in film history, the Chaplin character is confronted with the pace and rhythm of the assembly line and is literally caught in the cogwheels of mass-production machinery. He dances through the hidden undergrowth of the conveyor belt and is subjected to the hubris of a group of consultants, who have invented an automatic feeding machine that breaks down while being tested on poor Charlie. Although the factory scene is just a minor part of the movie, it has become emblematic for the cultural critique of mass production. "Modern times" has become a label for the inhumanity of factory work in general and the assembly line in particular, and Chaplin's film has played an important part in the appropriation process, by letting us laugh at our troubles. Humor is perhaps the most useful artistic resource in helping to cope with the challenges of technology and science, and no artist ever had more fun at the machine's expense than Chaplin in *Modern Times*.

TECHNOFICTION AND SCIENCE FICTION

Chaplin and Lang might not have been the first to problematize technoscience, but their movies set a framework, within which later filmmakers have continued to operate. In several of Jacques Tati's comedies, especially *Jour de fête* from 1947 and *Trafic* from 1971, he depicted, in his own absurd way, some of the consequences of

Figure 8. Charlie Chaplin in *Modern Times,* 1936. Reprinted by permission of PicturePress, Hamburg, Germany.

technology-induced speed and stress. Tati associated modern life in the first movie with the United States and in the second movie with the automobile, and he showed their devastating effects on traditional life-styles and the human psyche. In *Jour de fête* a postman tried to deliver his mail as quickly as his colleagues in the United States allegedly did, only to drive off the road on his bicycle and end up in a river. In *Trafic* the insanity of the automobile system is portrayed in a wild journey across Europe to a car show in which the new product to be displayed is continually confronted with the limitations of the transportation infrastructure. Modernity for Tati literally drove people mad.

The contrast between the modern city on one hand and rural ways of life on the other that figured so prominently in *Metropolis* continue to inspire filmmakers in our time. In the *Matrix* trilogy, some of the most successful science fiction films in recent years, Zion, the good world of free—that is, nonprogrammed—people, bears close resemblance to the female paradise that Lang had imagined. And the heart of the machine city, where the architect of the mainframe computer that controls the world by means of an almighty program, is not dissimilar to the control room from which the *Metropolis* capitalist oversaw his workers.

Despite these similarities in form and narrative structure, there are clear differences between *The Matrix* and the classic movies from the interwar years. If we analyze them from a historical perspective, then it is striking to what extent they must be regarded as signs, or witnesses, of their times. Whereas *Metropolis* and *Modern Times* commented critically on the inhuman aspects of modernist urban planning and Fordist production methods, *The Matrix* discussed the terrifying outcomes of a fully computerized world. Technology run amok is a theme in all of these films, but the kind of technology that is being problematized is different.

There is, however, a strong continuity when it comes to themes and story lines, as well as in the props and sites that are used. Spaceships and laboratories, robots and extraterrestrials are standard ingredients in most science fiction films, and the mad scientist is a recurring character. Dr. Strangelove, the character played by Peter Sellers in the 1960s Stanley Kubrick film, "loved the bomb" and is not the only scientist to bring hubris alive on the screen. Another mad doctor, namely, Frankenstein, has played the same part in numerous movie versions that have been made of Mary Shelley's novel, from the original in 1931 that featured Boris Karloff to the 1994 version with Robert De Niro. And in several monster films, the creators of the dangerous things that threaten the human population have been biologists, sometimes outright mean, sometimes simply naive. The twist on the theme—making the environmental scientist into a hero in *The Day after Tomorrow*—perhaps heralds the coming of ecofiction films.

Yet the treatment of the theme, no matter how conventional and familiar, has changed with the historical context and local contingencies in which the film was made. Whereas James Cameron's *Titanic* from 1997 made self-conscious engineers responsible for the disaster, a German version of the film, made during the Second World War, put the blame on British capitalists and stock market speculators and featured German engineers trying to persuade the captain to reduce the speed of the ship. Urban dystopias, to take another example, began to appear ever more often on the screen in the 1970s, a time when declining cities were becoming a serious social challenge on both sides of the Atlantic and the environment was becoming a political issue (Tormin 1996). When *Jurassic Park,* with its frightening dinosaurs (born in a scientific lab), was conceived in the early 1990s, it came at a time when wilderness parks had become well-known attractions, and many spectators could be expected to have visited one in real life. Technology out of control is another frequently used topic. Whereas in the early postwar era the technology of reference was likely to be the atom bomb, more recently it has tended to be artificial intelligence or artificial life-forms, cyborgs, or computer software. Whereas nuclear fallout was earlier an extremely common theme in science fiction films, the sinister prospects of global warming and climate change have more recently come to be taken up.

In other words, popular science fiction or, perhaps more correctly, technofiction movies are important barometers that often highlight contemporary problems and reflect current public concerns. They can be regarded as sensitizing instruments that play an important role in the process of cultural appropriation. The success of the *Terminator* trilogy (1985–2003), for instance, cannot just be explained by reference to Arnold Schwarzenegger's muscles or the exciting car chases. It also has to do with the fact that many people are deeply concerned with, or truly fascinated by, the prospects of constructing creatures that have human and nonhuman features. The vision of artificial beings becoming increasingly human seems to be especially challenging. The movie *A.I.* from 2001, in which a robot named David develops such characteristically human feelings as love and affection, brought this theme into the movie houses.

Because science fiction authors and moviemakers often foresee and anticipate developments, they have an important function in providing a kind of cultural assessment of technology and science. We cannot yet create a Terminator or a robot that can express feelings, but we have to think about whether we really want to be able to. It is still not too late to reverse a trajectory that might lead to a situation in which one central computer governs us all. By pointing to the extreme outcomes of hubris, movies—influential as they are in our entertainment age—contribute to assessing the paths that engineers and scientists, corporations and citizens are about to stake out.

Science fiction movies are thus double-edged swords. They often transmit a tragic story line, but they also contribute to the hype and overheated expectations that are associated with the development of new technology. Although the "space odyssey" in the movie *2001* was threatened by an out-of-control computer, moviegoers in the late 1960s were more fascinated by the artistic effects and the intriguing future that the film projected. In so doing, it perfected an aesthetic approach to space travel that had begun even before the first human being was catapulted into orbit in 1961. Vivian Sobchack (1997, 69) wrote the following about a film that had been shot in 1950:

In *Destination Moon* ... the silvery sleekness of Ernest Fegté's single-stage spaceship almost palpably glows against the velvet black and star-bejewelled [*sic*] beauty of a mysterious but non-hostile space; it is breathtakingly beautiful, awe inspiring, and yet warmly comforting like the night light in a child's bedroom.

The citizens of the West might have been shocked that the Soviets were the first to conquer space, but they had been prepared for space travel for at least a decade. When John F. Kennedy in 1961 envisioned placing a man on the moon before the end of the decade, he spoke to an enthusiastic public who more or less knew, or at least thought they knew, what he was talking about. They had read their Jules Verne, and they had watched movies such as *Conquest of Space* (1955) and *Forbidden Planet* (1956). They were ready to go from fiction to action.

THE VARIETIES OF ARTISTIC APPROPRIATION

In general terms, three main strategies, or approaches, can be distinguished in relation to the artistic appropriation of technology and science that have waged a continuing battle with one another from Morris and Monet to *The Matrix*. The one strategy has sought to fashion aesthetic criteria and practices that could appeal to the largest possible audience, or market, whereas a second, or competing, strategy has tried to foster more exclusive attitudes on the part of the artist, designer, or moviemaker. Lowbrow versus highbrow, the idea has been to produce art for the masses or art for the masters, and the battle has affected almost all artists and designers in their attitudes to technology and science.

We suggest that hybridization has been a third approach, representing the attempts to transcend the high–low divide and to combine the demand or pull of the market with the professional skills and competence of the producer. As ideal types of appropriation, the three approaches correspond to the "cultural formations" that Raymond Williams presented in the 1970s when he was seeking to analyze fundamental patterns of cultural transformation. The uses of art vary according to the purpose or task that the artist sets out to accomplish, be it entertainment and promotion, criticism and protest, or some kind of mixture or combination of the two: public education.

A commercial or market appropriation is the approach that is most characteristic of what Williams, in his cultural theory, referred to as the dominant cultural formation. In relation to aesthetics, this approach continually tries to turn art into business, or more generally makes use of art to make products more appealing and thus more successful on the commercial marketplace. Even Morris was subjected to the sorts of commercial pressures that have led to forms of art, design, and moviemaking that are conducive to mass production or, to put it another way, that are appropriate to a mass culture. For the most part, artistic expression becomes a process of making the product fit into the performance criteria and operating conditions of the production technology. This strategy would tend to dominate the field of industrial design, and it is so intimately connected with the cinema that we can hardly imagine it to be otherwise. More than anything else, science fiction films have been used to prepare the cultural ground for new products and new acts of scientific and technological hubris, such as sending rockets into outer space and building ever more complicated weapons.

Traditionalist or handicraft appropriation, on the other hand, is characteristic of what Williams referred to as residual cultural formation; that is, with those actors and institutions who try to live in the past. In the contemporary world, such residual cultures often reject technology and the comforts of modern life with a more austere and traditional set of beliefs. There is an effort to keep alive outmoded traditions of handicraft and artistic practice in the name of one or another kind of authenticity, as many of the latter-day exponents of arts and crafts have tried to do. In the cinema, this kind of appropriation can be found in the rebellious bewilderment that is continually depicted in satiric comedy—from Charlie Chaplin in *Modern Times* and Jacques Tati in *Trafic* to Jim Carrey in *The Truman Show*. Through these comic characters, the hubris of modern technology is shown in all its ruthlessness, mechanically manipulating Charlie and imposing on Carrey's Truman the trauma of a totally artificial and technologically constructed life. In one of its more recent varieties, Sofie Coppola's *Lost in Translation*, it is the American actor Bill Murray, more or less playing himself, who rebels against the high-tech world that he finds transplanted to Japan.

It is in the transcendence, or, at least, in the effort to overcome the dichotomy between these two often polarized extremes, that hybrid, or synthetic, approaches to artistic appropriation have developed. At least the first film in Andy and Larry Wachowski's *Matrix* trilogy exemplified this hybrid approach in that it kept viewers under its spell by means of the most advanced software and film techniques available. Similarly, Peter Jackson's *Lord of the Rings*, using all the wonders of technology to tell a traditional story of good and evil, is an artistic hybrid, mixing fear and foreboding, cultural criticism and commercial marketing in creative combination. In relation to technology and science, both trilogies give expression to ambivalence; that is what makes them work as art, as they turn modernity inside out, questioning its logic while making full use of its techniques. The cultural work that art and design, architecture and film—and even, one might suggest, music and literature—do in relation to technology and science is formed in the field of interaction among these three approaches or strategies of appropriation.

Throughout the world, these appropriation strategies have been filtered through distinctive discursive and institutional frameworks, specific to nations and regions, such as those we discussed in chapter 4. In the United States, the technocratic influence has been significant, whereas in Germany, ideas extracted from the life-reform movement have continued to feature prominently. The alternative green-colored culture that is in just about all German cities is conspicuous for its absence in the United States, where those who would foster an alternative to the dominant technocracy have more or less escaped to the northwestern and northeastern corners and to the southwestern deserts. In both countries industrial design and modern art and cinema were central ingredients in the making of mass society and a mass culture, but there were noticeable differences in the national styles, or trajectories. In Germany a kind of organic engineering aesthetic was manifest in the Bauhaus of the Weimar years and in expressionist art, as artists and engineers sought to naturalize the technological civilization. Later, in such Nazi projects as the building of the *Autobahnen* through the German landscape, the natural environment was given a formative role to play in the construction process. By contrast, the Americans tended to design products and infrastructural projects that, in their artificiality and mechanical perfection, looked like they came directly out of a scientific laboratory. The strong position of realist painting, or "representational art," as Douglas Tallack (1991, 95) called it, in the United States, represented by an artist such as Edward Hopper, testifies to this. Our artificial world—with its gas stations and diners, and now its reality television and shopping malls—has become so natural in its ubiquity that it appears to be the only possible world.

In Sweden and the other Nordic countries, the development of design and modern art were important for national survival, and industrial design and architecture became crucial components in the belated process of industrial transformation and to the formation of national identity. The innovative futurism of Finland, not least as represented by the architecture of Eero Saarinen and Alvar Aalto, as well as the pragmatic functionalism of Sweden, drew on the aesthetic principles of William Morris, but these designers appropriated those principles and practices in different ways. Whereas Finnish artists and architects mobilized the mystique of the forest to create a striking and original art of simplicity and natural beauty, Swedish designers imbued their work with the instrumental practicality that had been fostered in the workshops of the medieval mining communities and the early modern state of the "great power" era. Nokia and IKEA, each in their different ways, make use of these artistic traditions in their commercial appropriation strategies.

THE SITES OF APPROPRIATION

The trajectories set in motion by Morris, Monet, and the other late-nineteenth-century pioneers carried on a kind of cultural competition around the world, as the hybrid artist-engineers of modernity sought publics and audiences and sponsors and markets and eventually established themselves as the arbiters of taste and beauty. In the process, new sites were created for disseminating the artworks but also for educating desire and demand among producers and consumers, the sellers and the buyers. Especially significant were the institution builders, the individuals and organizations that carved out a set of new public spaces: museums and galleries for the display and sale of crafts products and, eventually, modern art, as well, and institutions of higher education and professional association where the artists, designers, and architects could be trained and socialized and, not least, develop projects in which they could combine their talents. The Museum of Modern Art in New York, built in the 1920s, marks in this sense a sort of cultural marker, or exemplar, at one and the same time a new kind of meeting place, a canon-setter, and norm-builder in bringing about an artistic paradigm shift or cultural revolution.

The educational institutions were usually built outside of the traditional universities, at special schools and institutes, where the various sciences and practical skills were brought together into new combinations. New schools for designers and advertisers were established throughout Europe and North America, and many crafts studios and architectural firms came to take on educational functions, providing opportunities for would-be artists to "learn by doing" as apprentices or student interns. Industrial designers, architects, and many artists have required and sometimes received genuinely hybrid educations, with ingredients from engineering and humanities. Instruction, in the best schools, is often primarily conducted through demonstration and example. At places such as the Bauhaus in Dessau, Germany, and the Art Institute of Chicago, where some of the early experiments with these forms of education and training were first carried out, the teaching staff included working artists and architects, as well as academics, and the places became public centers for viewing and exhibiting the new forms of artistic representation.

Others sites were no less important. Although many already existing public spaces were occupied, and given new kinds of meaning by the artist appropriators of technology and science, other sites of appropriation also emerged, where artists could put their ideas into practice. In Barcelona, Antonio Gaudi fancifully reconstructed many private and public buildings, as well as parks and squares, according to his particular version of modernist architecture. The famous cathedral, which he never finished, became an important tourist attraction, as art, in its new modern forms, became a source of competition among cities in attracting profitable visitors. With Gaudi and other practitioners of what came to be called Art Nouveau, designers found new users and new uses for their talents and interests—as illustrators of books and magazines, as decorators of streets and highways, and, not least, as builders and designers and artistic disseminators of the service facilities for the new technological artifacts: train stations, airports, gas stations, and automobile racetracks.

No site has proved to be as culturally significant as the commercial marketplace. In the course of the twentieth century, art has been used, or misused, according to one's perspective, primarily for the marketing of commodities, the selling of products. The showrooms of automobile makers, department stores and shopping centers, and exhibition halls and trade expositions have been made attractive, and, as such, their design and construction have given a great deal of work to the artistically minded. Not least the lighting and redesigning of urban centers, and eventually suburban peripheries, called for technically proficient artists who could transform reality into commercial space. As David Nye (1990, 73) put it, when discussing the electrification of New York,

> In Times Square spectacular lighting had moved far beyond functional necessity. Like the displays at world fairs, it served as an instrument of cultural expression providing symbolic validation of the urban industrial order. Electric advertising signs, intensive street lighting, spotlights, searchlights, and beacons could turn any landscape, from Main Street to Niagara Falls, into a text without words.

Even more significant, however, has been the vast effort and expense that has gone into making the products attractive and appealing. The advertising industry has undoubtedly been the central location in our world where the artistic appropriation of technology and science has taken place. In creating desire, in fostering fashions, and in cultivating taste and style, advertising has formed a "consumer culture." As an industry of its own, advertising has provided aesthetic challenge, inspired creative leaps of the imagination, and, perhaps most important, led to new understandings of human psychology and human needs, as it has brought artists and scientists together into the hybrid forums of the advertising bureau and the market research firm.

As marketing has grown into a science and salesmanship has grown into an art, the cultural appropriation of technology and science has come full circle. Long gone are the times when we did not put our machines to use, as William Morris contended in the late nineteenth century; on the contrary, through the powers of artistic and not-so-artistic persuasion, we are cajoled into using our machines far more than is probably good for us. Television, film, and now, most recently, the Internet have become sites of artistic appropriation where the pull of the market and the call of the past meet in continually intriguing, hybrid combinations. From the Terminator to Spider-Man, from Superman to *The Matrix,* and in comic books, children's toys, and advertising campaigns, as well as in more established forms of artistic expression, hybridization has become embedded into our lifeworlds in a way that Morris could never have imagined. Indeed, we would suggest that hybrid concoctions of the human and nonhuman, the living and the dead have become one of the most important ingredients in the culture of our time and in the making of identity, personality, and lifestyle. As science fiction writer Thomas Disch (1998) put it in the title of his book on how "science fiction conquered the world," art in the contemporary age can provide the "dreams our stuff is made of."

Part 3

Machines and Knowledge in Action

7

MOBILITY MANIA AND ITS MATERIAL MANIFESTATIONS

At first, Bernard drove slowly and sedately. He knew that you mustn't drive a car fast for the first five hundred miles. That was what they had taught him at school, that was what the dealer had told him, that was what it said in the instruction booklet. Still, thirty kilometers an hour seemed like a furious flight to Bernard. He couldn't distinguish hills, trees, or people. Everything flashed by as in the movie-theater. ... Aha, so they were all lying: the dealer and the instruction-booklet. You can drive a new car a lot faster than they said. Well, all the better! He hadn't bought a car just to creep along. He wasn't a turtle.

—Ilya Ehrenburg (1929/1976, 4)

BIGGER AND FASTER

In early April 1912, the largest and one of the fastest ocean liners ever built embarked on its maiden voyage from Southampton, England, to New York City. With its length of 900 feet, its speed of 21 knots, and its capacity to carry almost 2,500 passengers, this ship symbolized the achievements of modern, industrial society. Designed for ultimate safety, the ship was hailed as a historic feat of engineering. It seemed to represent the final solution to the fierce competition for customers on the important North Atlantic route between Europe and North America. During the one-week trip across the ocean, businessmen and well-off tourists could enjoy the luxury and comfort of a culture that was obsessed with what the contemporary economist Thorstein Veblen (1899) called "conspicuous consumption." The ship's name was *Titanic.*

As we all know, a few days after the *Titanic* left England, it hit an iceberg and sank. More than 1,500 passengers and crew followed the ship down into the dark ocean. But, after people on both sides of the Atlantic Ocean had recovered from the initial shock, the dreams of ever faster speed and ever greater size that had inspired the *Titanic* were quickly revived.

In this chapter we discuss some of the material manifestations of what the intellectual historian Stephen Kern (1983) fittingly called "the culture of time and space." Engineers such as Frederick Winslow Taylor were obsessed with time-saving measures in their efforts to speed up the production process; physicists such as Albert Einstein reinterpreted the relationship between three-dimensional space and linear time; philosophers such as Henri Bergson discussed the difference between objective and subjectively experienced time; artists such as Giacomo

Figure 9. Boy on street with sign, TITANIC DISASTER, 1912. Reprinted by permission of Gettyimages, Munich, Germany.

Balla attempted to capture speed and motion on canvas; and athletes tried to run faster and set new records. Although space and time had been organizing principles for the human mind at least since the days of Isaac Newton and Immanuel Kant, turn-of-the-century intellectuals articulated their meaning in new ways. To Filippo Tommaso Marinetti, the Futurist ideologue, speed and motion were the defining values of the times. Unlike the Russian poet Ilya Ehrenburg, whose hero Bernard killed himself by driving his new car too fast, Marinetti never considered the dangers of the mobility mania. In the same year that the *Titanic* went down, Marinetti wrote a "Hymn to Death" (quoted in Schmidt-Bergmann 1993, 274):

> And the open doors creaked
> Steam belching out of its dragon mouth
> Suddenly the ground is shaking. Just a jump
> and we slide blindly down into the waves.
> Hurrah! Hurrah! Death is our beloved!

In the world of engineering, the culture of time and space turned into a kind of speed cult. Well before Taylor wrote his treatise on scientific management he had developed high-speed steel, an alloy that made it possible to lathe a piece of steel four times faster than before. More immediately visible were the achievements in the areas of transportation. Naval architects tried to design ever faster vessels. Locomotive designers, bicycle mechanics, automotive engineers, and airplane builders also contributed to the craze. The results of their efforts were usually considered beneficial and desirable. Ever faster bicycles and automobiles quickly found their way to the market. Guided by visions of progress and powerful performance, users willingly turned the instruments of speed into symbols of status.

New means of transportation fostered new perceptions of reality. Technologies such as the railroad and the steamship, the automobile and the airplane enabled human beings to overcome distance, allegedly save time, and experience new found feelings of freedom. Instead of describing the physical expansion of technological networks such as railroad tracks or telephone lines, we focus on the ways in which these technologies were appropriated into broader discursive frameworks, institutional settings, and daily routines. Transportation can be treated as a kind of "large technical system" (Mayntz and Hughes 1988), but it also can be analyzed in more cultural terms. In the nineteenth century people debated whether the railroad would contribute to economic prosperity and national unification. Simultaneously, however, people of different classes and of both genders took this new technology to heart and developed routines that made it possible for them to include the railroad in their lifeworlds. Mobility became a central concern for society, a kind of mania that had, and continues to have, a wide appeal in spite of the obvious risks and dangers involved.

The transportation technologies fulfilled age-old dreams by enabling human beings to free themselves from the constraints of physical location and the limitations of the bodily senses. With the coming of the train, the poet Heinrich Heine in 1843 claimed to be able to "smell the German linden trees" in his studio in Paris (quoted in Schivelbusch 1977/1986, 37), and the romance of the road is a central theme of twentieth-century culture. When Charles Lindbergh crossed the Atlantic in his little airplane, he became an international celebrity. Technologies of mobility opened up realms of reality that had previously not existed, and they did so in ways that fascinated contemporaries. To enter these realms people had to take on new identities. As train passengers they were propelled through the landscape, and as drivers they could take themselves to places where they had never before ventured. Perhaps more visibly than in many other areas of technology, the hybrid character of mobility is striking. A car in motion is neither a machine nor a human, but a combination of material and corporeal elements. Innumerable are the accounts of airplane pilots, in which they describe the bodily pleasures of flying, and of motorcar racers who thrill us with tales of daring and danger. Through television we have become accustomed to sharing their sensations in the comfort of our living rooms.

The natural landscape was fundamentally transformed as railroad tracks were laid out across fields and along river valleys, and urban space was reshaped as streetcars, automobiles, and buses took over the streets. At the same time, these material systems created places in which people could socialize in new ways. Today we meet neighbors and colleagues and mix with strangers at gas stations and airports, as in the nineteenth century, when train stations became central meeting points in most towns and cities.

PASSENGERS AND PERCEPTIONS

Perhaps more than other areas in the history of technology and science, means of transportation seem to interest broad segments of the general public. The number of coffee-table books that have been published on steam trains, classic automobiles, old ocean liners, and airplanes is enormous. A person looking in the local bookstore for information about technologies of the past probably will be most richly rewarded. Obviously, vehicles and vessels have the power to enthuse not merely a few devotees.

Inside the covers of the most popular books and magazines looms a hardware-centered and iconographic view of technology. On the center stage stands the machine, preferably nicely polished and portrayed in a pastoral setting. Technology, we might say, is being reified. Bracketing out cultural factors and environmental problems, these publications tend to deal almost exclusively with technical matters. Political and economic aspects are, at best, discussed marginally, whereas focus is on themes such as types of engines, brands and models, performance variables, and consumer prices. When writing about means of transportation, many professional historians of technology also deal primarily with hardware and hard facts. Although a purely antiquarian interest in steam locomotives and horseless carriages for their own sake—*l'art pour l'art*—is no longer considered *comme il faut* among serious historians, factors such as size, horsepower, efficiency, and speed still attract attention.

In this chapter we draw on alternative narratives and attempt to fashion a more appropriate story line of the history of transportation technology. John Kasson and Leo Marx, for instance, have showed how the railroad was connected on the discursive level to the American idea of progress. In much the same way as science was regarded as an "endless frontier" in the immediate postwar era, the railroad symbolized for nineteenth-century writers and politicians the white man's manifest destiny to conquer the continent. Wolfgang Schivelbusch's *The Railway Journey: The Industrialization and Perception of Time and Space* (1977/ 1986) also tried to construct a story line that wove things mechanical into a broader cultural tapestry. Already the subtitle reveals that the author's goal was not to write an iconography of locomotives and railroad cars but to analyze the "industrialization and perception of time and space" that accompanied the diffusion of the railway.

The division of passengers into three or four classes shows that the railroad was quickly integrated into well-established social structures and discursive frameworks. To make the new technology acceptable, societies had to create institutions that perpetuated or even reinforced existing interpersonal relations and routines. First-class passengers could enjoy their journey in the comfort that was compatible with their station in life. Upholstery, servants, and well-prepared meals made it possible for them to accept and enjoy the new means of transportation. By contrast, the less well-to-do passengers had to put up with wooden seats and crowded compartments.

To all passengers, the railroad journey was qualitatively different from the stagecoach trip. A stronger sense of anonymity and physical detachment developed. Compared with the coach, the railroad wagon was larger, traveled faster, and carried more passengers. The coach was more intimate, and passengers spent longer stretches of time together. In the railroad compartment, by contrast, there was a higher turnover of passengers. People went on and off more frequently, and it was more difficult to make the acquaintance of one's fellow passengers. Contacts became more superficial, and as a result passengers withdrew into their own minds. Because train riding was smoother than coach riding, it was easier for passengers to read during the journey—an opportunity that booksellers and newspapermen quickly exploited. Instead of getting involved in long conversations, passengers to a larger extent than previously read, beheld their surroundings, or slept.

The growing distance among the passengers was accompanied by an increasing distance between the passengers and the landscape outside the train windows. Before the coming of the railroad, people moved in the landscape. Regardless of whether people were walking, riding a horse, or sitting in a stagecoach, they had the feeling of being part of the surroundings and of nature. Travel diaries testify to the experiences that people had during such journeys. In their contributions to this increasingly popular genre, Carl Linnaeus and J. W. von Goethe, the German writer, in the eighteenth century described in poetic language the intense smells and other sensations of travel. During the frequent

Figure 10. British railway station. Reprinted by permission of Gettyimages, Munich, Germany.

stops, it was possible for passengers to get off, pick some flowers, and chat with the local farmer. Because roads were often in bad condition, passengers had to count on walking long stretches. With the railroad, these experiences largely disappeared. As long as the train kept running, passengers remained pretty much cut off from the outer world, and they had few opportunities to mix with the locals. Instead of smelling the flowers, they were forced to inhale the smoke from the steam locomotive. Because of the relatively high speed of the train, it became increasingly difficult to distinguish one flower from another. In 1837, eight years after George Stephenson's "Rocket" had reached the flabbergasting speed of 35 mph, the French writer Victor Hugo commented, "The flowers by the side of the road are no longer flowers but flecks, or rather streaks, of red or white; there are no longer any points, everything becomes a streak" (quoted in Schivelbusch 1977/1986, 55).

Sitting at the train window, passengers could observe only in passing the trees and meadows along the way. This sensation was also reinforced by the fact that the rails had been built as straight as possible. Unlike the old roads, the rails did not pass each and every village but had been designed to connect larger centers and places in as efficient a manner as possible—much like later motorways. The price that passengers had to pay for this rationality was detachment from the landscape, while the countryside lost its physical presence and reality.

With the rapid diffusion of the railroad, travelers began to exhibit an interest in new destinations. In increasing numbers, Londoners invaded the southern English coast; Parisians discovered the eternal sun of the Riviera; Berliners packed their bags for the Baltic shoreline. The first seeds of today's mass tourism had been sown. For pressed and overworked members of the upper classes, these new opportunities were met with enthusiasm. On Sunday mornings the local train station became a mediating place also for other citizens, who flocked in large numbers to make a day's excursion to the countryside. When more places were integrated into the railroad network, the world literally shrunk.

The railroad's potential expansiveness also fascinated the politically minded. When the technology was in its infancy, it served as a test bed for political and economic projects in various countries. In the German-speaking world, for instance, the political economist Friedrich List gave the railroad a pivotal role in an overarching vision of national unification. At a time when the area that later became Germany still consisted of an array of small states—Prussia being the largest—List argued that the technical construction of an integrated railroad network would enable the political construction of one German Reich. For List, as for many later economists, the railroads were seen as the very engine of industrialization and the archetypical technical system in what later came to be called the second "long wave" of industrial expansion (Freeman and Louçã 2001).

In the United States the railroad played a slightly different political role. Depicted as an engine of civilization, it came to symbolize the joining of the east and the west, the consolidation of the continent. The railroad was described as the key for populating the prairies and turning wild nature into productive farms. Somewhat later a similar vision guided the expansion of the railroad into the northern parts of Sweden. The enormous natural resources of *Norrland* should be made economically useful by extending the railroad lines into areas inhabited by what were considered to be backward reindeer farmers, the Samis. And, in the British framework, the railroad—as a kind of land-based continuation of British sea power—came to be associated with colonial expansion and the creation of a global empire. This ambition was central to the military and economic subjugation of the Indian subcontinent, where one of the world's largest railroad networks had been built by the early twentieth century (Headrick 1988).

As a consequence of this thinking, the planning and operation of most railroad systems became a national enterprise. By the time of the First World War, the German *Reichsbahn* had developed into one of the largest companies in the world. However, the coming of the railroad contributed not only to the unification of geographical space into national units but also to a temporal unification on a national or state basis. To coordinate traffic in enormous areas such as the American or Indian continent, the authorities had to define standard time zones (Landes 1983). In the first half of the nineteenth century, each city and each region had had their own local time. At a particular location, noon had simply been defined as the time when the sun was standing in the south, which meant that only towns situated at the same longitude had the same time. For cows and dairy farmers, this was certainly a rational practice. And, as long as people traveled east or west at a relatively slow pace, it created few inconveniences. Problems appeared only after communication and transportation systems began to speed up and become more tightly integrated. After an initial period, when each railroad company had upheld its own "corporate standard time," national standards were established in most European countries in the second half of the century. Typically, the division of the continental United States into four time zones was introduced in 1883 on the initiative of the railroad companies.

For a cultural history of the railroad—as for a cultural history of the whole industrialization process—unification, standardization, and disciplining are key concepts. Railroads also fostered centralized forms of business, finance, and management (Chandler 1977). Railroads were regarded as instrumental for national unification, and operators forced a time standard on whole countries. Although timetables had previously been employed by stagecoach and shipping companies, they now became more precise and inflexible. Just like the poor maiden traveling fourth class, the distinguished nobleman had to show up on the platform in time for departure. It was certainly possible to allow passengers some latitude as long as the railroad lines remained short and isolated, but this became increasingly difficult as more complex networks developed toward the middle of the nineteenth century. Punctuality and discipline became paramount for keeping the whole system running in a predictable manner. Following James Beniger (1986), we could say that all these phenomena were important elements in a "control revolution." Very few of the sociotechnical systems that we treat in this book would be able to function had not organizations been set up to control machinery and human beings and their natural surroundings. To make such systems work, the material technology has to operate in accordance with preset rules, and the personnel and passengers also have to behave predictably.

BICYCLES AND CARS

For the most part, passengers seem to have accommodated to the demands put on social behavior by timetables and instructions: "Do not lean out of the window!" Although it is possible to find nineteenth-century sources that lament the standardization of movement and the disciplining of action, such criticism has become widespread only after the turn of the century. The reason for this change in attitude toward the railroad had to do with the emergence of alternative means of transportation, such as the bicycle and the automobile, and the spread of a new individualism.

The German author Otto Julius Bierbaum, for instance, in a travel diary of 1903, bemoaned the impersonal and inflexible character of railroad travel and regarded railroad transportation as a form of incarceration, calling the conductor a "prison warden" (quoted in Sachs 1984, 18). Although it has to be kept in mind that some of Bierbaum's trips were sponsored by the automobile industry, this kind of criticism increased significantly in the new century. The railroad had paved the way for the automobile in that it increased the demand and desire for mobility, but it now turned out to have certain drawbacks. The railroad journey appeared suffocating when contrasted with the freedom of the automobile. Those members of the upper classes who could afford to buy an automobile began to redefine the railroad. Having earlier been seen as an efficient means of getting to the seaside, the railroad now began to be associated with a faceless and fearful mass society. The automobile came to symbolize individual autonomy, whereas the train constrained freedom. The railroad might bring passengers from Vienna to Trieste, but with an automobile people could in principle discover the whole of Tuscany at their own pace and according to their own choice of route and direction.

If the railroad contributed to laying the foundation for the automobile by increasing the desire for long-distance mobility, then the bicycle contributed in two very different ways. In contrast to the railroad, the bicycle was in its early years primarily a means of amusement and recreation. The early bikers of both genders used their beloved gadget not to go to work but to show off in public and to revive pastoral ideals by taking trips into the countryside on Sundays. In other words, the bicycle was originally used for leisure-time activities rather than for instrumental purposes. In a literal sense the bicyclists opened up new geographical space, and in a figurative sense they developed new mental maps. Indeed, the bicycle fit very well into the contemporary culture of time and space but also into an age concerned with physical activity and hygienic ideals. The bicycle made its first appearance at a time when the urban middle classes were becoming increasingly intrigued by fresh air and a healthy environment. Because the bicycle made it possible to leave the filthy city behind, it came in very handy.

But this is not the whole story. As the craze spread around Europe, cyclists demanded better paved streets and more constraints on the behavior of pedestrians and horses. They organized interest groups that effectively lobbied for infrastructural improvement and legal reform. By publishing journals and handbooks, and by acting forcefully in the public sphere, bikers' clubs in many countries managed to convince the authorities of the importance of this new technology. In Germany, for example, women bicyclists founded their own associations that helped redefine the position of women in society (Bleckmann 1998). By acquiring a bicycle, women could appropriate new physical spaces, thus making themselves more autonomous in a very concrete sense. The bicycle was used by women as an instrument of physical and cultural emancipation.

As urban streets were paved, bikers began to make the lives of their fellow citizens increasingly precarious. Slowly but surely, grown-ups and children were scared away from the street and up onto the pavement, the so-called sidewalk. With the spread of the bicycle, and somewhat later the automobile, streets lost their old social function and were divided up into different segments. Their very meaning changed. At the same time, the bicyclist took on a new identity, and transportation became an individual activity over which one had control and responsibility. Being a bicyclist became a source of personal autonomy that would be ever more significant with the coming of the automobile.

Like the real, physical nineteenth-century roads, the discursive road toward public acceptance of bicyclists was bumpy, uneven, and curvy. The first recorded attempt at creating a muscle-driven "velocipede" in the 1810s was met with ridicule and laughter. Although (or perhaps because) the patent for a kick-bicycle that the German inventor Karl Friedrich Drais filed in 1817 has to be regarded as an innovative achievement, this artifact was not a success. Instead of being praised for its potential of opening up new perspectives on the world, Drais's wooden bicycle was written off as a "senseless, childish toy," and the inventor was told that he had "lost his mind" (Karl Gutzkow in 1837, quoted in Krausse 1993, 87). Mobility had not yet become a mania, and most roads were of such bad quality that a ride with the kick-bicycle was a pretty bone-shaking experience.

When the bicycle fever finally took off in the last third of the nineteenth century, it did so first in France and Britain—two countries that broke new ground in bicycle design and somewhat later in automotive engineering. In this connection the Frenchman Pierre Michaux and the Brit James Starley were especially significant. After Michaux's fairly heavy, iron-frame bicycle had been exhibited at the Paris World's Exposition in 1867, such interest was sparked that the inventor set up not only a factory with, initially, 300 workers but also a kind of drivers' school to teach his customers how to handle the two-wheelers. Applying light metal spokes, Starley was able to construct a very fast bicycle that was not prohibitively heavy. With Starley's high-wheeler the biker could catch up with the fastest horses. It proved to be particularly conducive to the needs of "young men of means and nerve" who bought it as a kind of status symbol not only to cover ground and have fun but also to impress the female segment of the urban population (Pinch and Bijker 1987).

Races were an integral part of the biking culture from the late 1860s onward. In France, Britain, and elsewhere, individuals and clubs organized competitions that attracted excited spectators. As the working class was creating a form of release by kicking balls in parks and on other urban lots, the middle classes gathered to watch the daring among them ride bicycles at breakneck speed. Although most of these races gave male participants an opportunity to exhibit strength and power, women also competed. Some races were short and required that the biker was able to reach as high a speed as possible. In longer races, by contrast, more demand was put on sturdiness and endurance, both of the vehicle and its driver. It does not take much imagination for one to realize what an adventure the participants of the first seventy-six-mile race from Paris to Rouen in 1869 must have experienced. Such races made the bicycle more familiar to the general public and provided the public with new forms of entertainment and experience.

Women might have admired the courageousness of high-wheel bikers, but the high-wheeler proved to be particularly ill adjusted to women. Long dresses were incompatible with this vehicle. The Victorian idea of women as the sensitive gender in need of protection also contributed to making the high-wheeler a strongly gendered artifact. Women were able to appropriate cycling on a large scale only after the smaller so-called safety bicycle had been engineered in the mid-1880s. Having two wheels of equal size, air tires, and chain drive, this gadget served the interests and needs of different groups of customers. Sportsmen could ride them quickly, older men found the well-functioning brakes and smooth tires attractive, and women did not have to worry about exposing their legs in public.

Once the safety bicycle had become accepted as the standard design, mass-production methods contributed to making it more widely accessible. By acquiring bikes, workers were able to take jobs further away from home, and on weekends they could explore areas that had previously been beyond reach. More important, from the perspective of this chapter, is the ways in which bicycle races contributed to disseminating the cult of speed throughout the population. *Tour de France* was organized the first time in 1904, and it soon came to attract herds of spectators. Boys of all ages, not least in countries such as France, Spain, and Italy, became fascinated by the courage of bicyclists climbing the Pyrenees and the Alps. After the Second World War, commercial interests took over, and, as with motor sports, races gave manufacturers the opportunity to try out new designs under extreme yet controlled conditions. Racetracks became a sort of test site, an experimental space or surrogate laboratory, for producers of bicycles and automobiles.

In the long run the safety bicycle that emerged in the 1880s fostered an interest in personal transportation. It proved to be extremely flexible in creating new demands and crafting new customers. Today companies have created products for new niche markets. So-called mountain bikes, BMX models, racing bikes, and city bikes have—each in their own way—contributed to reproducing and continually reinventing the mobility mania that was born more than a hundred years ago.

The racing culture that had developed around the bicycle was symptomatic for changes that took place at this time. Starting in Britain in the middle of the nineteenth century, a fascination for bodily exercise, sports, and records developed in many countries throughout the world, including the colonies. Each country appropriated the so-called English sports, which primarily had been developed at boarding schools in that country, in its own way (Eisenberg 1999). In Swedish culture, for instance, gymnastics became particularly strong and is to this day associated with the name Ling. At times, this concern with bodily perfection took on extreme forms and often developed into an almost militaristic form of disciplining.

FLEXIBILITY AND FREEDOM

The first automobiles were met with mixed feelings. People were fascinated by these machines that seemed to fulfill the dream of effortless individual mobility. Unlike the bicycle, which still depended on human muscle power, the automobile was propelled in an artificial manner that testified to the power of the human spirit. There had been attempts to replace the horse with a mechanical engine at least since the

Figure 11. Runners, cars, and cyclists on racecourse, Berlin Grunewald, 1920. Reprinted by permission of PicturePress, Hamburg, Germany.

French engineer Cugnot had made the first, not particularly successful, experiments with a steam-powered carriage in the eighteenth century (his machine literally hit the wall). To more critical observers, the horseless carriage was a means of great discomfort and indeed quite frightening. Recalling his first encounter with an automobile in the Bavarian countryside in the early 1900s, Oskar Maria Graf talked about "spooky-looking" drivers and their "roaring monsters" (quoted in Ruppert 1993, 119). The terrible noise that accompanied these vehicles—the gasoline-driven cars, in particular—certainly contributed to scaring fish and fowl, and the smell was disgusting, to say the least. Local gangs in rural areas gave drivers a hard time by throwing stones at cars and poking sticks in the spokes of the wheels. Horse owners mobilized support against reckless drivers who frightened their animals, and victims of traffic accidents and their relatives tried to make their voices heard in the public sphere, among other things by organizing—as in France—societies "against the excesses of automobility" (Merki 1998, 237). The favorite invectives used by working-class representatives and farmers in this debate illustrate the cultural character of the struggle. Drivers had to accept being called "people's enemies" and "speed maniacs," and their cars were distastefully described as "running guillotines" (Merki 1998, 239).

Automobile lovers did not remain passive. They especially hated the British Red Flag Act that required that a person had to walk in front of an automobile, waving a flag to warn horses, children, and pedestrians. Early on, automobile owners decided to organize themselves on the model of the bicycle clubs to fight this law and offer other forms of resistance. Channeling their interests through mediating places such as the British Royal Automobile Club and discursive spaces such as the German *Allgemeine Automobil-Zeitung* (AAZ), the drivers portrayed their vehicles in terms that drew on the grand narrative of modernity and the mythology of progress. When the AAZ in 1906 called the automobile "the foremost personification of the idea of progress," when Bierbaum in 1903 claimed that "the purpose of the automobile is freedom," or when Swiss automobilists told their opponents "not to put sticks into the wheels of time," these actors appropriated it into a well-known discursive framework (quoted in Sachs 1984, 18, 34, 38). In a very concrete way, freedom was being reinterpreted, from a primarily political, social, and economic concept into a notion expressing individual mobility and personal autonomy.

The fight between car owners and their opponents was to a large extent carried out along class lines and the axis town versus countryside. As in the years of the bicycle craze, members of the middle classes were the strongest supporters of the new vehicles. The well-off, primarily urban segments of the population appropriated the bicycle and the automobile for leisure-time activities to cultivate individuality. Soon, they were joined by rural hotel owners and professionals such as medical doctors, for whom the automobile became an important means for securing a steady income and expanding their business. Against these groups stood farmers and craftsmen, often joined by the rural nobility, for whom mechanical novelties represented the dangers of industrial civilization. Interestingly enough, the critics often made recourse to the same key concepts as the proponents. For example, during the twenty-five-year fight over the car's existence in the Swiss canton of Graubünden, critics claimed that the only way for farmers to "retain their freedom" was by banning the automobile from the streets (quoted in Sachs 1984, 34). Both groups referred to the idea of freedom, but they gave it contrasting meanings. As elsewhere in the world, however, the farmers and their associates finally lost the fight in Graubünden—after the tenth referendum had finally given the proponents a small majority.

RACING AND RELIABILITY

After Graubünden there have been very few attempts to ban the automobile and to keep it out of cities or of society in general. With the exception of the creation of pedestrian areas, or so-called walking streets in some city centers since the 1960s and the minor intrusions of bicycle paths along the roads of a few cities, the car has been able to reshape reality in accordance with its needs and renew urban areas in its image. It has been assisted by city planners who have willingly designed what they call "the car-friendly city," and not least by politicians who have come to see the growth of automobiles as an engine, if not the main motor, of economic growth. In certain extreme cases, such as in the planned city of Brasilia or the freeway-driven suburban sprawls of southern California, entire regions have been designed to serve the interests of automotive transportation. As a result, modern society has become so dependent on automobility that there seems to be no way out. The world is one where automobility has become a way of life (Tengström 1991).

The cultural appropriation of the automobile did not take place overnight. As with the safety bicycle in the nineteenth century, the car did not really become embedded in the cultural lifeworld until a stable artifactual form had become universally recognized. It took about a decade of the new century before the internal combustion engine was accepted as the standard propulsion system. When Gottlieb Daimler decided to construct a self-propelled vehicle, he took the existing horse-drawn buggy as his point of departure. In addition to replacing the horses with a gas engine of the Otto four-stroke type, he had to make the carriage sturdier and develop another type of steering system, but by and large the horse-drawn carriage remained the pattern for the first cars. Others, most notably the Frenchman Panhard, soon introduced a structure that reminds us more of modern automobiles: a steering wheel instead of a stick, and four seats facing the frontally placed engine. A decisive step on the way toward freeing the car from the limitation of the past and, more specifically, the carriage type of design was taken in the years around 1900 by Emil Jellinek, an Austrian businessman, and Wilhelm Maybach, chief engineer at the Daimler Motor Company. Their first Mercedes was based on the *Système Panhard* and had a steel-frame chassis with a low point of gravity, which had been developed to fit the needs of racing car drivers. James Flink (1988, 33) said of this design that it "deserves credit for being the first modern motorcar in all essentials."

Why did the Mercedes become a role model for later automotive designs, a golden standard that remains to this day (Hård and Knie 1994)? We argue that the main answer to this question is outside the realm of engineering, on the sites where the automobile was used, and in the discursive spaces where its meaning was settled. This step brings us, not surprisingly, back to the beginning of this chapter and the culture of speed and power, and to the mobility mania fostered by the bicyclists a few decades earlier. But it also takes us to another emerging cultural site of technological civilization; namely, to amusement parks where people could experience the thrills of acceleration and speed.

To escape the strong disciplining power of industrial society, people fled, among other places, to the amusement park. Berliners went to the Luna Park, and New Yorkers went to Coney Island on their new-fangled streetcars. Interestingly enough, this flight did not mean that they left the nervousness and stress that characterized urban life. Rather, the need on the part of the patrons for bodily shaking and mentally shocking experiences seems to have been almost insatiable, and people flocked to such attractions as the Russian Carousel and the Swedish Slide. As a contemporary commentator declared,

> All attractions seem to have been invented only to make us sick. They create artificial seasickness, dizziness, brain anemia,

hallucination, a creeping feeling in the joints, and a kind of crazi-ness—finally ending up in crazy giggling. (quoted in H. Weber 2000, 85)

In the so-called Shoot-the-Chutes, people were able to get dizzy and wet at the same time, and in the Shaky Pot a group of five got physi-cally—and perhaps also mentally—mixed up.

The almost four-mile-long roller coaster in the Luna Park encapsu-lates the main arguments of this chapter. Two years before the sinking of the *Titanic*, this attraction had been designed to transport people at high speed through a fascinating landscape—a huge artificial, hilly landscape that changed each season. Although passengers returned to the point of departure after each trip, they still had a feeling of having traversed a considerable distance in a short time. Mobility mania in miniature! Most of those who visited these amusement parks seem to have been possessed by the power of technology, even if it brought them to the verge of nausea. Whether taking a ride in the elevated carousel, the oversize swing, or the rapid water slide, they were looking for ever more extreme sensations.

The amusement park helps us make sense of the race craze that accompanied the horseless carriage from the very beginning. Its roots lay in the contemporary obsession with achievement and excess in gen-eral and with speed and mobility in particular. Although the body was not used to propel the automobile, in contrast to bicycling, the first car races were certainly not less strenuous. Take, for instance, the Paris-Bordeaux-Paris race that was initiated in 1895: four hundred miles of driving on dusty and bumpy roads, passing angry horses and aggressive farmers, in vehicles that constantly broke down and had to be tempo-rarily repaired on the side of the road. No wonder that most of the starting teams never made it to the end.

It was this racing culture that helped make the Mercedes an icon of progress. With its formidable thirty-five horsepower, impressive top speed of fifty-three miles per hour, reliable performance, and sturdy design, the Jellinek–Maybach creation left the other competitors behind. In the hands of expert drivers, the Mercedes in the early 1900s was able to win one race after the other on the European continent, thereby creating a kind of technological paradigm on which future automobile designers and mechanics would draw. From now on, the car was no longer a horseless carriage but an artifact in its own right. The automobile was born—a vehicle defined by its ability to accelerate quickly, reach high speeds, and keep going for hundreds of miles at a time without having to refuel.

WINNERS AND LOSERS

After society entered what the engineer-historian Friedrich Sass (1962) called "the Mercedes era," the automobile became associated with speed and sturdiness, racing and reliability. What remained to be decided, however, was which power plant would suit these ideals best. The Mercedes was equipped with a gasoline engine, and in the years immediately after its introduction, this technology seemed to be on its way to becoming hegemonic. One can read in an American engineering journal in 1907 that gasoline engineering had reached a stage of maturity and that "there seems to have come a time when radical changes in construction and design are things of the past" (quoted in Volti 1992, 21). Increasingly, contemporary observers were convinced that the future would belong to gasoline. Although steam and electric propulsion remained available well into the 1920s, they were no longer able to threaten the internal combustion engine in any serious way.

The problems that the alternatives to the internal combustion engine met were largely unexpected. The steam carriages that were designed and built in the 1890s had been on the cutting edge of engineering. The Frenchman Leon Serpollet introduced several novelties, such as a flash-type generator and advanced metering techniques, in his steam designs. In shorter races neither steamers nor electrics were inferior to gasoline. What happened as the new century dawned cannot simply be explained by reference to the steam and electric cars' suddenly becoming worse in any purely technical sense. It was rather the meanings that were attributed to them that was the problem. Symbolically, the steam car was not able to escape its historical legacy. Steam engines, which had powered buses and even automobiles for many decades, were at this point in history beginning to be associated in a negative manner with the dirty, coal-based industrial society of the nineteenth century. Manufacturers of steam cars had to fight an image of being old-fashioned; they were seen by many of the new car lovers as representing a bygone era in the evolution of technology. And, as far as the electric car is concerned, it seems to have been the strength of the racing culture that made its diffusion difficult. On decisive sites of appropriation, such as the roads of the long-distance rally track, the electric car could not make its presence felt.

The opponents of internal combustion did not give up easily, however. The emergence of new user cultures in the 1910s promised to usher in an age of pluralism. As the gasoline car made its way onto the racetrack and spread rapidly in urban settings, it encountered vocal critics and to some extent disillusioned drivers. Because of the smell and noise that these vehicles produced, the chief of police in Berlin in

1912 threatened to ban them from the streets of the German capital. Women drivers were apparently not particularly fond of having to use a heavy crank to start the internal combustion engine, and drivers of both genders were not happy about having to put up with "the formidable problem of shifting gears" (Flink 1988, 7). In this situation electric propulsion seemed to be a more appropriate solution. Not only do electric cars not emit any smoke but they are also easy to start and do not require any messing around with clutches and gearboxes. The big drawback was their limited driving range. If the electric car were to have any chance of succeeding, it would have had to find a particular niche in the emerging market, for example, as a city flivver or a fire-brigade truck.

Even Thomas Alva Edison, the heroic inventor personified, put certain effort into developing batteries that would increase the driving range of the electric car, but these attempts remained marginal in comparison to the investments in time and personnel that others were making in internal combustion. To most engineers, internal combustion was considered more exciting. The beginning of the end for the steam and electric cars came as Henry Ford decided to transform the gasoline automobile into a relatively cheap artifact for larger customer groups. The success that the Ford Model T experienced in the 1910s, with production figures running into the hundreds of thousands annually, proved that the alternatives to internal combustion had no future anymore. By means of vertical integration and assembly-line production, combined with mass-marketing techniques and effective exploitation of the labor force, the Ford Motor Company was regarded as the epitome of a new age guided by the ideals of mass production and mass consumption.

Ford's huge Detroit factory site met contradictory reactions. On one hand, journalists, novelists, and moviemakers put their searchlight on the inhuman aspects of assembly-line manufacturing. On the other hand, contemporaries of different political conviction all around the world considered Ford's achievements in the area of production to be a marvel of modernity. Even Vladimir Illich Lenin, the founding father of the Soviet Union, was intrigued, if not fascinated, by what came to be termed "Fordism." In comparison to Highland Park, most other car factories looked like remnants of the past. Steam car manufacturers fared especially badly in this regard. Largely relying on traditional handicraft methods and aiming at an exclusive but small group of customers, producers of steamers drove their machine, so to speak, into a dead end. Take the American brothers F. E. and F. O. Stanley, for instance, two old-fashioned artisans who continued to build their steam cars according to stringent technical and aesthetic standards well into the 1920s. Instead of accepting the principles of mass production, they chose to stick to established, well-tried methods of design and manufacturing, and they prided themselves on not serving a mass market. As a result, they reinforced the association of steam automobiles with the nineteenth century, with past times, even though it was already then realized that the steam car did not pollute the air to the same extent as did the gasoline car (Jamison 1970). On the road and in the minds of people, the future now seemed to belong to the internal combustion engine.

MASS MARKETS AND MASCULINITY

Techniques of mass production, mass distribution, and mass marketing turned the gasoline-propelled automobile into the most attractive and seductive consumer item of the twentieth century. The Ford Model T paved the way for these developments, but in the 1920s, as Henry Ford began to lose touch with the dynamics of the market, the company started to face economic troubles. Competition came from General Motors, which successfully turned novelty into a necessity by introducing the concept of the annual car model and, as we discussed in the previous chapter, new designs and ornamental features. Instead of producing only one model, General Motors offered different models at different prices to different consumers and thus managed to reintroduce status, symbolism, and cultural distinction without giving up the economic advantages of mass production and mass consumption.

Because the economies on the other side of the Atlantic developed more sluggishly, a European mass market emerged only after the Second World War. Whereas companies such as Citroën in France and Fiat in Italy tried to combine creative design with mass production, Volkswagen in Germany chose a more pragmatic approach. Although Ferdinand Porsche's idea of a "people's car" received the support of the National Socialist government in the second half of the 1930s, it was not until the 1950s that the Beetle began to create a mass market. A whole new city, Wolfsburg, had been constructed to manufacture the automobile that the Nazis called the "power-by-happiness-car" (*Kraft-durch-Freude-Wagen*), but as the war approached production had shifted toward military needs. Only during the economic revival of the German Federal Republic could the plant begin to serve a national and an international market.

The Volkswagen did not come alone. Already in the 1930s the car had been regarded as one component in an emerging system of automobility.

For the engineer Fritz Todt, one of Hitler's close collaborators, the goal of the Nazi transportation and traffic policy was to create a modern network of motorways that would connect major cities in the German Reich with each other and with larger cities abroad. This *Autobahn* system had its predecessors. Fascist Italy had invented the *autostrada*, and the first German intersection-free, four-lane motorways had been built outside of Berlin and along the Rhine in the 1920s. But it was the National Socialist regime that materialized this system on a grand scale. Contrary to what often has been claimed after the war, the main rationale for the *Autobahn* system was not military. Rather, Hitler and Todt regarded it as a means to fight unemployment and as a way to make Germany truly modern.

Todt put considerable effort into making the motorways fit into the surrounding countryside. Like Americans had done with their railroads in the nineteenth century, German civil engineers tried to design the *Autobahnen* in such a way that technology harmonized with nature. Painters and filmmakers were assigned the task of documenting the construction sites and the finished roads. Propaganda films show roads laid out between forests, along hillsides, and across valleys. Happy families are sitting at the roadside, enjoying the picturesque view beside their Beetles. No noise, no pollution, no stress.

In the United States highways were also initially embedded in a pastoral framework. Sometimes this framework takes on strong romantic overtones, as in Jack Kerouac's famous novel *On the Road*. In the childhood of automobility, the highway was given a meaning that drew on ideas that had been formulated to appropriate the railroad in the mid-nineteenth century. Literary historian Kris Lackey, in his book *Road-Frames: The American Highway Narrative* (1997), showed how novelists in the early 1900s picked up on perspectives that classical authors such as Ralph Waldo Emerson and Walt Whitman had formulated half a century earlier. Referring explicitly to Theodore Dreiser's novel *A Hoosier Holiday* from 1916, Lackey (1997, 38) wrote,

> Dreiser's advocacy of driving complements independence with pastoral delights. If, in the mid-nineteenth century, some Transcendentalists viewed the railroad as a path to western nature, Dreiser, in 1916, converted their argument to the blue highway. In so doing he relied on the traditional contrast between the machine and the garden. This opposition lodged the automobile squarely in the garden, where it appears to us still, every day, in hundreds of television ads designed to obscure its mechanical nature and industrial origins.

Like Otto Bierbaum in Germany, Dreiser contrasted the noise, dirt, and collective character of the railroad journey with the beauty and liberty of a car trip, thus laying the foundation for a positive symbolism that has been reproduced over and over again ever since.

In postwar Europe the automobile was also applied for means of long-distance travel. As middle-class citizens in Western Europe began to be able to afford their own cars, they slowly but surely began to exploit and appropriate other parts of the continent on an individual basis. Northern Europeans began to cross the Alps on their way to Italy in such large numbers that roads and passes were regularly clogged in the summertime. As a consequence, those who wanted to avoid spending their vacation in traffic jams soon turned to charter flights instead. About the same time as mass motorization began to cause environmental problems in urban areas, mass tourism began to cause other kinds of problems on roads and at overcrowded tourist sites. Mobility mania knew no limits, and ever more hubrislike projects of road building and airport construction have been developed. In a way, one could say that the European Union has been built on highways, *Autobahnen,* and *autostradas.*

Still the future is filled with challenges. Despite endless traffic jams, most people in the industrialized world find it impossible to live without an automobile. We use it to go to work, we need it to take our children to school, and without it we cannot reach our vacation retreats. Whether or not we like it, we find ourselves dependent on the automobile with its inbuilt cult of speed and its intrinsic masculine values. Indeed, the association of automobility with masculinity is as old as the car itself. As with the computer, the automobile has primarily been designed by men, most drivers are men, and a broken-down car is usually repaired by men. Boys, much more strongly than girls, are socialized into a world of mechanics, first by playing with toy cars, then by learning to repair a flat bicycle tire, by driving and trimming a moped, and later by learning how to change a fan belt. Although women increasingly use cars and computers, the ideals that have governed the development of these artifacts all along are primarily masculine.

In their endeavor to cover the earth with asphalt, politicians across the industrial world have made powerful alliances with construction companies, truck and automobile manufacturers, automobile clubs, and transport companies. Still, these groups, at least since the 1960s, have been challenged by an emerging ecological culture that argues for other means of transportation. Inspired by Ralph Nader's book *Unsafe at Any Speed* (1965), the consumer and environmental movements have reacted to the risks and dangers associated with the automobile and to its deleterious effects on the natural environment. There has emerged a new sort of values, or consciousness that the only lasting solution to the problems connected with the automobile is to develop other means of transportation.

Some planners have begun to understand that the gospel of individual mobility might, after all, turn cities into nightmares rather than modernist paradises. And, as a result, collective means of transportation have experienced a sort of rediscovery and revitalization in the past decades. Electric tramlines and subways have a long history, but in the immediate postwar period they did not fare well in the competition with the car. Facing the pressure of congestion and social protest, planners and politicians in city after city, especially in Western Europe and in parts of North America, have begun to consider returning to these collective means of transportation and trying to develop more sustainable transportation policies and practices. At the same time, bicycle paths have entered the urban landscape and high-speed intercity train lines have been constructed. Perhaps the most radical steps have been taken in Asia. Japan experimented with high-speed trains in the 1950s, and Singapore has become a model for planners of public transportation systems from all over the world. But if mobility mania is ever to become a memory of the past, much like the industrial society that fostered it, the expansion of automobility, however "green" the cars and drivers are able to be, will have to be substantially curtailed and the cult of speed reserved for racing tracks.

TOWARD A FEMININE AUTOMOBILITY?

New, more appropriate patterns of mobility might also emerge out of the experimentation with "smart" cars and electric vehicles. Since the oil crisis of the 1970s, there have been several attempts to build electric cars. The French National Electric Corporation unsuccessfully tried to design and get acceptance for an electric car in the 1970s, which has since been seen primarily as an example of insufficient networking on the part of the developers rather than interpreted from the user's point of view (Callon 1987). In the ensuing decades a number of initiatives have been made in several countries—from Norway to the United States. One of the more well-known projects was the Swiss attempt to create a so-called Swatch car. It was the brainchild of the industrialist Nicolas Hayek and was seen as a way to assist Swiss industry in a difficult period, much like the famous Swatch watches had helped the traditional Swiss watchmaking trade out of a crisis a decade earlier.

Hayek envisioned a small electric city flivver, with just enough space for two people and, allegedly, a case of beer.

The project was a turbulent one, but in the end a small, two-seated car eventually materialized. Against Hayek's original intentions, it turned out not to be an electric vehicle. As is well-known, the Smart, as the car came to be called, is equipped with an internal combustion engine. The reason for this fundamental shift clearly has to do with the fact that the project was taken over by representatives of the traditional automobile industry. The car was finally designed and manufactured by the Micro Compact Car Company, a new company with Daimler-Chrysler as its main owner. The alternative path that Hayek had sketched out was not followed, and consumers were never given the opportunity to decide for themselves if they were willing to domesticate a trendy and reliable electric car. There are signs, however, that many people would have been willing to do so.

In the historical literature the electric car is often associated with female users. Henry Ford bought an electric car for his wife, and Grandma Duck drove around the countryside in one. To some extent these associations were reproduced at the end of the twentieth century. Some studies of electric car owners indicate that women are particularly fond of this alternative technology. For instance, professional women without children, who need a vehicle to commute between home and work, express great satisfaction with their little electric cars. As one woman said in an interview, "The car is just great to drive in city traffic. You have extremely good overview, and parking is a piece of cake." She went on to compare it with ordinary, internal combustion automobiles and claimed that the electric car was indeed "much easier to drive" (quoted in Gjøen and Hård 2002).

Although all owners of electric cars agree that the car has its limitations, many argued that all such limitations should not necessarily be seen as drawbacks. Especially those women who had acquired an electric car for environmental reasons realized the advantages of this vehicle. Of course, electric cars do not produce any direct emission, but they also have other positive sides to them. To save the car's battery capacity, drivers should not accelerate quickly. Whereas users of internal combustion cars simply drive to the closest gas station to fill up their tanks, electric car drivers have to be more cautious in traffic and plan in advance which route to take and how far to travel. As one woman expressed,

You learn to drive a car in a very different and more careful way when driving an EV. You get quite a new relation to speed. In the beginning I was somewhat impatient; it was embarrassing to get reactions from other drivers who thought you drove too slowly. Now I take it easy, and whenever somebody honks their horn at me, I just think, "Poor man, you'll soon be killed at that speed." … Everything is relative! I would not like to collide front-to-front in 120 km/h with this automobile, but, on the other hand, that is not possible. I never drive in high speeds with the EV. Besides, it is extremely easy to maneuver and gives you a very good outside view. (quoted in Gjøen and Hård 2002, 271)

The electric car might be able to challenge some of the typically masculine values of power and speed that have accompanied the expansion of automobility. It is a commonplace that a good gasoline car is supposed to be fast and have many horsepower. Because drivers of electric cars seem to develop a sense of "relaxation and enjoyment on the road," they challenge the association of the car with the cult of speed (Knie et al. 1997, 70). They become more sensible drivers and develop a more defensive driving style. In our terminology, the appropriation of the electric car seems to enable a new kind of driving culture to develop. Because owners of electric cars are reported also to give up "needless trips," they also challenge and might help to bring to an end our modern mania with mobility.

in which messages followed preset lines and had to pass a small number of major terminals, were not sufficient. If a bomb, nuclear or conventional, were to hit one of the central units, the coordination of the forces would be impossible. In such a situation it could be possible to use radio communication, but such networks were also vulnerable and prone to attack.

Baran called his solution to this problem "distributed communication." To make sure that a system survived attack from enemy forces, he designed a network that allowed a message to take different routes. A message did not have to follow one preset path on its way from sender to receiver but would be able to choose which way to go. If one line was destroyed, the message would simply take another route.

The military framework of Baran's work is underlined by his second contribution: packet switching. This technique meant that messages were not transferred continuously through the wires. Instead, they were compressed and divided into a number of discrete segments before being sent. Like a postal package, each segment was supplied with a final address and sent on its journey. Once all segments arrived, the message was automatically put together again. At the same time a notice of receipt was returned to the sender, acknowledging safe delivery. The officer could be sure that his order had reached the troops. The goal, to secure safe "control, command, and communication," "3C" for short, appeared within reach (Abbate 1999).

Baran's design, which was originally a purely theoretical construct, was soon tried out experimentally. The so-called ARPANET, one precursor of today's Internet, adopted packet switching. It was set up in 1968 to simplify communication between three universities on the U.S. West Coast and one in Utah, all involved in government-funded research. Its task was indirectly military, in the sense that most of the projects funded by ARPA (the Advanced Research Project Agency) and carried out at these universities had military implications. Indeed, ARPA had been set up in early 1958, only three months after the Soviet Union had launched its first *Sputnik,* to initiate and coordinate research and development projects that would enable the United States to regain international leadership in the areas of technology and science. ARPA and its ARPANET were children of the cold war.

The irony of history ought to be evident at this point. One of the most important parts of our global communications network, that is, the Internet, started out in what used to be called the military-industrial complex. But at the same time this network makes it much easier for terrorists to plan attacks, for computer "crackers" to get hold of classified information, for nongovernmental organizations to coordinate protest marches, and for criminal elements to pursue their activities. E-mail correspondence and the globalization of money transfer certainly made the attacks on September 11, 2001, easier to carry out. It is not only the U.S. armed forces that know how to employ modern technology to implement a 3C strategy.

A POOL OF HUMAN KNOWLEDGE

The history of information and communication technologies cannot be written without paying extensive attention to warfare. Still, it is incorrect to claim that the interests of the military, or, broadly speaking, of kings and generals, have been the only major factors that have shaped these processes. This is also a history of how scientists, businessmen, and civilian users have appropriated and modified technologies of information processing and distribution, as well as communications and media technologies, for their own purposes. In this chapter we sketch some of the processes by which material objects such as books and telephones, computers and cellular phones have been made available to increasingly larger segments of the population, and we discuss some of the dangers inherent in these processes. We acknowledge the democratic potential of publishing and Internet access, but we also point to some of the problems associated with an ever more rapid flow of data and information.

Some twenty years after the ARPANET had been installed, Tim Berners-Lee and Robert Cailliau, two scientists at the European Center for Nuclear Research, designed a computer program that simplified access to net-based information. They wanted computers attached to different networks to be able to communicate with one another. By this time, the ARPANET was just one of hundreds of computer networks worldwide, and it was very difficult to send and receive information between different nets. Scientists working in international settings complained about the fragmentary character of the networks, and they were often frustrated when they tried to get access to documents in other systems. If a European nuclear physicist, for example, wanted to share data with a colleague in North America or simply search for information available in another network, he or she faced a number of obstacles.

Berners-Lee and Cailliau's solution to this problem is nowadays well-known: a program called the World Wide Web. This hypertext-based protocol spread like a forest fire around the world, and together with graphical so-called browsers and search engines it made it possible not only for physicists or computer scientists but for any pedestrian computer user to find and retrieve information from previously incompatible networks from all corners of the earth (Gillies and Cailliau 2000).

In their attempt to connect different networks, Berners-Lee and Cailliau not only tried to address an issue they encountered more or less every day in their office and their laboratory. In fact, the World Wide Web was also the virtual result of a wish to create "a pool of universal knowledge." The actual web was based on an idea that Berners-Lee and Cailliau allegedly got from Ted Nelson (Abbate 1999, 214). In a pamphlet titled *Computer Lib*, published back in the 1970s, Nelson had envisioned a kind of database in which information was easily available to anyone by means of a hypertext-based computer language. Behind the parable looms an age-old dream that has attracted humans through the millennia. Since the days of Babel, mankind has wanted to communicate, regardless of cultural and linguistic differences, and since the days of the Alexandrian library there have been attempts to collect all of human knowledge and make it available at one place. In the twentieth century Nelson's vision was just one of several visions to create what H.G. Wells called a "world brain" (Hellige 2000).

The library of Alexandria was more than a vision. It was a dream come true for any scholar allowed to work there. By means of rather unscrupulous acquisition methods, Demetrios of Phaleron had set out in the fourth century BC to turn this city—that had been newly founded by Alexander the Great—"into a replica of Athens" (Delia 1992). Historians presume that, at its peak around 50 BC, the library housed more than 400,000 papyrus rolls, stored in specially designed stone caskets. The Ptolemaic kings used their military power to steal or borrow rolls from all over the Mediterranean, and they provided students and scientists with attractive scholarships. Most famous of them was probably Euclid, the founder of classical geometry.

Historians and archaeologists argue about how long the Alexandrian library remained in use. Some claim that a fire destroyed it in AD 48, whereas others claim that activities continued well into the third century. In any case, the idea to bring together and systematize all aspects of human knowledge lived on, although on a much more modest scale. In the Middle Ages the pope's palace, monasteries, and emerging universities housed valuable libraries, and several encyclopedias were compiled. Well before the advent of book printing, a group of scholars around Vincent of Beauvais produced an eighty-volume, systematically ordered encyclopedia, *Speculum maius*, including as many as three million words. For readers to find what they were looking for, an alphabetically organized index and a detailed table of contents were at their disposal.

The problem of information overload, which any Internet user is aware of, increased dramatically with the rapid diffusion of book publishing in the second half of the fifteenth century (there were about one thousand printers in Europe half a century after Gutenberg's invention had become publicly known). Books and pamphlets became cheaper, and the number of published works increased dramatically—as did, of course, the number of authors and readers. In a book on what the author called "the media revolution" of the early sixteenth century, historian Johannes Burkhardt (2002) claimed that the Protestant Reformation gave printing an enormous push forward. The printing press is said to have ushered in a new era, as the computer has done in our age. Martin Luther, a prolific writer, knew how to make use of this new technology to spread his ideas. A key event in the Reformation was the market success of Luther's German translation of the Bible, but of equal importance was the strategic dissemination of printed pamphlets and tracts. Indeed, Burkhardt argued that the Reformation would never have come about had the printing press not been invented.

Whether we accept Burkhardt's contention or not, there is no doubt that Luther and his fellow reformers very successfully appropriated printing technology for their own political-religious purposes. Much like nineteenth-century labor leaders made effective use of the rotating printing press and twenty-first-century opposition groups throughout the world apply the Internet to try to undermine existing power structures, Luther was able to use a technology that had been developed to serve the establishment for his own purposes. Early on, the Catholic Church had understood the potential of Gutenberg's invention, and it had used it, for example, to amass support in the war against the godless Turks. As historian Elizabeth Eisenstein (1983, 148) wrote about these early attempts to use media technology,

> Although the anti-Turkish crusade was thus the "first religious movement" to make use of print, Protestantism surely was the first fully to exploit its potential as a mass medium. It was also the first movement of any kind, religious or secular, to use the new presses for overt propaganda and agitation against an established institution.

It did not take long until scientists and engineers began to appropriate printing. The extremely elaborate works of Vesalius, the anatomist, and Agricola, the mining expert, which combined text and illustrations in an unprecedented manner, would hardly have been economically feasible with incunabula. And, as modern science began to institutionalize in the seventeenth century, the continuous publication of theoretical and experimental contributions became an integral part of the academic culture. The Royal Society and the French Academy of Sciences published printed proceedings that summarized discussions that had taken place under their auspices and provided space for the communication of new insights and observations from foreign corresponding members.

With the virtual explosion of publications that followed in the wake of the scientific reformation, it became increasingly difficult for anyone to remain on the research frontier in more than one or two specialty areas. The universally informed renaissance genius became an anachronism. Different strategies were developed to make it possible for natural scientists and philosophers to find their way through the labyrinths of human knowledge. The French *Encyclopédie,* discussed in chapter 3, was one such attempt. Other strategies involved the development of complicated schemes of classification and systematization and the design of intricate retrieval systems undertaken by university librarians. As the sciences became ever more specialized, and the number of new disciplines and subdisciplines grew exponentially, such efforts had a Sisyphean character. Here, the computer came as a kind of a savior, and by the time Ted Nelson envisioned a computerized database, scientists and librarians were on their way to materialize this idea. The first online data storage unit, MEDLINE, had been set up in the 1960s, and in the coming decades libraries in North America and Europe began to digitalize their old card catalogs.

STORY LINE I: COMPUTER LIB

In the counterculture to which Nelson belonged, computing was primarily seen not as a means to rationalize libraries but rather as a means to liberate computer usage from the chains imposed by large and expensive mainframes. By today's standards, the computers of the 1950s were monsters, and they cost hundreds of thousands of dollars. At the end of the 1960s, computers were still bulky and too expensive for most ordinary people. "Computer Lib" became a slogan that helped mobilize a movement, the goal of which was to make computers available to everyone. This loosely organized movement emerged in California in the tumultuous years around 1970. Local associations with typical flower-power names such as the "Homebrew Computer Club" grew up, and a kind of predecessor to later-day Internet cafés provided dope-smoking visitors with an opportunity to try out programming or play games.

Nelson's manifesto summarized the values of this "hacker" culture: "I want to see computers useful to individuals, and the sooner the better, without necessary complication or human servility being required" (quoted in Levy 1984, 175). The goal was to make computer power available to the masses, as it were, an aim that involved several types of appropriation. One of the ideas was to give ordinary users access to mainframes; another idea was to make computers so small and cheap that anyone could afford them; a third idea was to spread knowledge about programming to nonexperts; and a fourth idea was to make programming an open, nonsecretive activity. The last element was a central component in what the activists came to call the "Hacker Ethic." One of the undertakings of the time that has gone down in history was the setting-up of a "Community Memory" in Berkeley, California, in 1973. This was an initiative that allowed several users to work simultaneously, by means of a so-called time-sharing system, with a large, interactive computer so as to be able to exchange information with other users.

The term *hacker* had been coined already a decade earlier on the other side of the American continent, and it originally had very little to do with any kind of counterculture. The first hackers were elite students in the Boston area, most of them male students of electrical engineering at the Massachusetts Institute of Technology (MIT). Because access to the mainframe computers of the institute was expensive, and computer time was a valuable commodity, the hackers had to resort to using the machines for their own purposes at night or weekends. There developed in this environment a kind of subculture around which a number of myths have continually been made and remade. In Sherry Turkle's influential ethnographic study of MIT hackers *The Second Self* (1984), she painted a rather negative picture of these young men. Before going to college most of them had been socially ill-adapted nerds, often outsiders. In the hacker environment they found others of their kind, which made it easier to socialize and develop a common identity. Many of Turkle's interviewees also confirmed that they found it more comfortable to interact with computers than with human beings.

Nowadays, hackers come in all shapes and sizes. Computing is a hybrid activity that involves hammering away at the keyboard for a number of different reasons: profit and problem solving, entertainment and escapism. When the East Coast nerds met the West Coast freaks in the 1970s, a hybrid culture developed that came to form the future of information technology. Business-minded youngsters met up with politically radical libertarians, technically minded personalities got together with fun-loving players, and smart scientists found partners among uneducated basement hobbyists. The outcome, for better or worse, was a highly dynamic culture that was originally held together by a mission to change the world, to create a postindustrial society in which information was to become just as important a resource as soil, labor, and capital. As we are able to tell from hindsight, developments took a path that did not necessarily square with some of the original visions. Instead of living in a society where everyone has free access to information, we nowadays face a situation in which information retrieval and communication channels have become increasingly commercialized. As the printed word became a commodity in the late fifteenth century, information became one in the late twentieth century.

One Boston hacker was the young William Gates. Together with another Harvard student, Paul Allen, Gates in 1975 wrote a BASIC program for the so-called Altair computer, one of the first truly affordable microcomputers. The Altair was a huge success among hobbyists and other computer users for such different things as writing, communicating, and playing games. It seemed as if it would indeed be possible to realize Nelson's vision and liberate computing from mainframes and the military-industrial complex. But, as so often in business history, it did not take long before other forces took over. In 1981 the International Business Machine Company, better known as IBM, launched its Acorn, a personal computer that took the world by surprise. Originally, IBM had produced mechanical office equipment, and in the 1950s it had gotten into the business of making mainframe computers for large firms such as railroad and insurance companies. In the world of business, IBM had made a name for itself by manufacturing high-quality products and for being reliable when it came to maintenance. By offering a personal computer, IBM immediately made computing an interesting alternative for small- and medium-sized offices.

The operating system that came with the Acorn was called DOS, and Microsoft, Gates and Allen's company, designed it. The unholy alliance between the established world of business and the hacker culture was a fact. The rest is contemporary history. The Microsoft Corporation became one of the world's largest companies, and Gates became one of the world's wealthiest persons. To representatives of the postindustrial counterculture, not only had Gates sold out to big business but his software broke with the very essence of the hacker ethic, and his company, which had emerged from a culture of liberation and freedom, became the symbol of arrogance and unscrupulous power. And, to bring this story of the inscrutable paths of history up to date, the main propagator of the libertarian gospel, in the early twenty-first century, is not from California, or even from the United States, but from a small country in northern Europe: Finland. The Linux operating system, a so-called open source to which anyone can contribute, is the creation of Linus Benedict Torvalds, a Finnish student of computer science.

STORY LINE II: DAVID AGAINST GOLIATH

"We'll fight them in the office, at the class-room and the desktop." With these words, and pointing at a blackboard showing three frontlines, an army officer in 1984 explained the task of the 32nd fighting division. Applying their "superior weapon," his enthusiastic troops mounted a devastating attack on the big and powerful enemy from the beachhead they had just secured. Fueled by the order "Let's go get them!" the troops set off on what became a victorious urban guerrilla campaign. The strategy was to infiltrate enemy territory and fight him on his own turf.

This event did not take place in Kabul or any other contested city at the time. The enemy was neither the Soviet Union nor any other national power but—alas—IBM. The rebels were not Afghans but—alas—the allies of the Macintosh computer. The source is not a newsreel but a television commercial that the Apple Company placed with the largest U.S. broadcasting companies when its allegedly revolutionary computer was first announced. According to the short movie clip, made by the famous director Ridley Scott, the superior weapon was the hardware of the Macintosh computer, and its ammunition was its effective software (Friedewald 1999, 400).

The story line of this commercial repeats itself over and over again in computer historiography and in public discourse. Indeed, we argue that—just as in the case of the computer liberation story line—many historians, journalists, and other commentators have uncritically adopted a narrative that was originally constructed by a certain group of actors for reasons of self-glorification. The role of Goliath in this story line is most often played by IBM, "big blue." David, the small and smart challenger, is often Apple, but his name can also be the Digital Equipment Corporation, Micro Instrumentation Telemetry Systems, or Commodore. Historian Brian Winston's book *Media Technology and Society* (1998) reproduced this story line in a paradigmatic manner. In accordance with what Winston called "the law of suppression," attempts to design small and affordable computers for private use were for decades throttled by the military-industrial complex in general and IBM and a few large universities and institutes of technology in particular. Throughout the 1950s and 1960s, the development of computer technology was controlled by a relatively small group of specialists that pursued research along trajectories that effectively marginalized alternative solutions. The result, according to Winston, was a suboptimization of computer resources and substantial delay in the development of what later came to be known as microcomputers and personal computers.

A common feature in most David-versus-Goliath stories in the history of computing is the central role played by certain individuals who sometimes take on heroic proportions. Typical in this regard is Thierry Bardini's book, with the fitting title *Bootstrapping* (2000), on the mathematician Douglas Engelbart and the early years of the personal computer. The author described the deeds of a true pioneer in a romantic manner and mobilized several of the traditional elements of an American success story to give his hero his place in the history of computing. This is the kind of story that we also find in most accounts of the Apple Corporation, in which legendary founders Stephen Wozniak and Steven Jobs are given a hagiographic treatment (e.g., Linzmayer 1999). Wozniak was the brilliant hacker and Jobs the smart businessman, and together they took on the dinosaurs of mainframe computers and fought the arrogance of user-unfriendly software designers. Much of the literature recapitulates in an uncritical manner a view of computer developments that has simply been taken over from the historical subjects.

Apple never managed to beat IBM, and the Macintosh became a niche product only. The indefatigable Jobs did not give up. In 1986 he went on to found another company, Pixar, with the aim of making information technology attractive to the entertainment business. The predecessor of Pixar was Lucasfilm. Filmmaker George Lucas created this company, and it had been experimenting with inserting computer graphics into movies since the late 1970s. When Lucasfilm found itself in economic crisis, Jobs suggested that a new company be set up to make completely animated movies. Instead of drawing and painting an enormous number of pictures on slides as in old-fashioned cartoons, scenes were designed and manipulated on the computer screen. As in the original David-against-Goliath story, Pixar challenged Walt Disney's way of making movies. And, indeed, this time the challenger did succeed. In the new millennium, the computer-animated Pixar movie *Finding Nemo* made more money than any of the Disney Corporation films of the time.

COMPUTERS, MOVIES, AND MALE DRIVES

The incorporation of information technology by the entertainment industry has been a rapid and commercially profitable business.

Information technology has freed itself from its military background, and entertainment has become just as important as the old 3C paradigm. Some of the largest computers of the world are nowadays used to make movies, as are members of new, hybrid professional groups that combine technological skills with artistic talents. Sadly enough, however, substantial amounts of their energy and time go into producing movies that celebrate aggressiveness and glorify violence.

Lucasfilm and Pixar were not the first to try to make information technology relevant for entertainment purposes. Having fun in front of the computer screen had been an integral part of the hacker culture from the very beginning, and the strong affinity of computer games with violence was also established early on. *Spacewar!* was created at MIT in the early 1960s. It featured two spaceships shooting at each other and was a typical product of the *Sputnik* and cold war era. The game was open source and was constantly modified by the gamers. Perhaps unfortunately, already in the second generation of computer games this openness was no longer accentuated. Nolan Bushnell, the designer of *Pong*, one of the first slot-machine games that was installed in a bar, is said to have claimed that he had had to come up with a design that was so easy and robust that any drunkard could understand and play it.

Out of this kind of thinking grew products that were, quite literally, black boxes. Because in those days virtually nobody had a computer at home, but almost everybody had a television set, a winning strategy was to construct a unit that could be connected to the TV screen. One of the classics in this category was Odyssey, which was marketed as "the electronic game of the future" (Lischka 2002, 29). This video console was typical in that users had no possibility to affect or change any of the twelve games that came with it, but it was untypical in that none of the games had anything to do with either violence or outer space. Instead of fighting Soviets or extraterrestrials, happy family members could enjoy a good game of tennis or ice hockey, and children could learn the names of all U.S. states and their capitals by means of a geography application.

The peaceful character of Odyssey and the friendly face of a Japanese character such as Nintendo's Mario never became more than a sideshow in the development of computer and video games. It is a tragic fact that the cultural appropriation of information technology for entertainment purposes has largely taken place within a highly gendered framework of male violence, war, and sex. If a person is good at beating monsters, killing enemies, and saving half-naked women, then he (or she) is sure to make a good computer gamer. Needless to add, such traits are more likely to be found among men and boys, and thus it is not surprising that computing is still primarily a male domain. Men are clearly overrepresented among hackers and crackers, as well as among computer-game addicts.

The rapid diffusion of the Internet after the mid-1990s was accompanied by the same values as was the development of computer games. The World Wide Web allows researchers to gather information from around the globe, but it also allows them and others to consume violence and pornography at an ever faster rate. And, as different information, communication, and entertainment technologies become increasingly connected with each other, it is to be expected that these elements continue to spread into ever more areas of our lives. Unsolicited sex ads bombard our electronic mailboxes, and anyone with an Internet connection can download digitalized X-rated movies.

THE FIRST GLOBAL VILLAGE

This kind of lamentation on our part might seem conservative to the younger generation. And, history indeed shows that the cultural diffusion of new media technologies has always given rise to criticism and doomsday prophesies. When the rotary printing press made it possible to churn out cheap novels and popular magazines in the mid-nineteenth century, intellectuals and self-proclaimed cultural spokespersons began to talk about moral decay. Cinema and, later, television did not fare much better in their early days. The debates that have emerged in the wake of media technologies during the past century and a half exhibit a surprising continuity. What concerned parents used to say about the cinema and radio in the interwar period and about television in the early postwar period, their children and grandchildren today say about computer games and the Internet.

Clear continuities in the history of media technology are not only found on the discursive level. The process of eliminating distance that satellite-distributed television and the World Wide Web more or less completed in the late twentieth century started already in the nineteenth century. The telegraph and the telephone set off this process one hundred years before media analyst Marshall McLuhan (1989) claimed that our world had become a "global village." What McLuhan meant was that we today often tend to be better informed about events that take place in distant places than in our immediate vicinity and that—as a result—a sense of closeness and communality can be expected to develop among the global population. Through the rapid transmission of news we learn more or less directly about important events that take place on the other side of the globe. By implication,

Figure 12. Poster for Telefunken Radios, c. 1930. Reprinted by permission of Landesmuseum für Technik und Arbeit, Mannheim, Germany.

McLuhan argued, people have the impression that they live in a world in which distance hardly plays any role. We often know more about people in faraway countries than about our neighbors—thus the term "global village." Earlier, exciting gossip concerned other village members. Today, it concerns rich VIPs, famous rock stars, and internationally known politicians.

We can trace the roots of this village at least back to the mid-1800s. Although *globalization* was an unknown word in the mid-nineteenth century, the processes that accompanied the expansion of the telegraph are clearly similar to the processes that accompanied the spread of global television and the Internet. Landmarks in this history are the construction of the first North Atlantic telegraph cable in 1858 and the establishment of an intercontinental connection between London and Delhi in 1870. Stock brokers in London could keep themselves informed about developments on Wall Street, and the administrators of the British Empire could handle unforeseen events on distant continents more effectively than before. Business managers could go on trips without having to give up personal control of daily affairs, and rulers could keep their nations unified without necessarily having to visit all parts of their realms. Perhaps even more important for the daily life of the public was the emergence of international news agencies, beginning with that of Paul Julius Reuter. CNN and BBC bring the world into our living rooms today, as newspapers that relied on Reuter's and other news agencies did in those days. A situation emerged in which citizens in many instances were better informed about events in distant countries than in their own hometown. The "global village" is a fitting label that describes a process that took off a century before McLuhan formulated his thesis.

The cultural appropriation of the telegraph and the telephone followed patterns that we discussed in chapter 7. Much like the railroad and the automobile, the telegraph and the telephone contributed in a metaphorical manner to the compression of space and time and the elimination of geographical distance. Companies incorporated railroad transportation and telegraph communication into their daily operations to increase their competitiveness, and ordinary citizens developed new habits of visiting and staying in touch with distant friends and relatives. Had he lived until 1866, the German poet Heinrich Heine would have been able not only to hear the North Sea roaring from his Paris studio but also to read in the local paper about the latest events that had taken place in the United States. Fittingly, Tom Standage talked in his history of early telegraphy, *The Victorian Internet* (1998, 110), about "the telegraph's ability to destroy distance."

To analyze the ways in which the new communication technologies were culturally appropriated, we adopt two concepts that indicate their contextual embeddedness. In much the same way that the neologism "automobility" has been used to discuss the discursive, institutional, and practical ramifications of the artifact "automobile," the concepts of "telegraphy" and "telephony" can be applied to denote the cultural complexity of these two techniques. Whereas the telephone is nothing but the gadget, and the telephone system can be taken to cover individual telephones, wires, and switchboards, perhaps even telephone companies and regulating bodies, we suggest that "telephony" can advantageously be introduced to highlight also the meanings and cultural practices that developed along with this system.

It took considerable time for the electric telegraph to move from invention to what Raymond Williams (1974) called "cultural form." In the late 1830s, when Samuel Morse unsuccessfully tried to convince the U.S. Congress that his mechanical device was not an impractical toy for more or less crazy amateur inventors, the telegraph carried a connotation that made its public acceptance virtually impossible. Only after it had become embedded into a rationalist discourse of efficiency and a media-oriented practice of immediacy in the late 1840s did the telegraph begin to diffuse rapidly, initially in the United States and Europe, but shortly thereafter also to other parts of the globe. In a country such as India, the telegraph proved its efficacy for the military-colonial project, but indigenous governments, for example, in China, also took it up (Baark 1997).

The early history of telegraphy is a history of indifference, even distaste. In Britain, William Cooke initially experienced the same lack of understanding that Morse had felt in Washington, D.C. Although a number of inventors in several countries had been working intensely on the electric transmission of signals for several decades, none of the user groups that after midcentury found themselves more or less dependent on the telegraph showed much interest in this technology before the mid-1840s. Newspapers and businessmen, railroad companies and the military played a waiting game. Considering the—from hindsight—obvious advantages of the instant transmission of important information, this cautious attitude might be surprising. Certain factors indicate, however, that the telegraph's advantages were not all that obvious at the time. On one hand, the technology had its bugs. In the 1820s and 1830s neither hardware nor software appeared fully reliable—nor did, for that matter, all of their propagators. The technical setup was weak, and there was no standard code for the transmission and interpretation of signals. Also the inventors were considered strange and eccentric. On the other hand, one can also ask why actors in the 1830s should at all have been interested in communicating to each other at the speed of light. This was still an era when nobody expected to read about the latest global events in the newspaper, when stock markets did not work on a global scale, and when railroad lines were few and largely insular. After all, when the French Chappé brothers developed the optical telegraph in the eighteenth century, not even the military had been all that interested.

We can suggest that telegraphy could not develop as a cultural form until "the cult of speed" had begun to establish itself. Only after speed and movement, proximity and intimacy had become guiding principles in the leading segments of society could the railroad and the telegraph, so to speak, begin to make sense. Or, to put it another way, the establishment of these and similar technologies contributed to the manifestation of this cult. Once the London public had become accustomed to reading about yesterday's crimes, political events, and royal gossip in their daily paper, it could no longer do without them—and the papers could no longer do without the telegraph and the news items that the various agencies provided. The decision to construct a rudimentary telegraph network in Germany was taken only after the revolutionary events in the years 1848 to 1849 taught the Prussian king that his political future depended on his being continuously updated about important domestic and foreign developments. And, as railroad companies grew in size and complexity, they understood that they could continue growing only if they had rapid and reliable means of communication at their disposal.

The parallels between telegraphy and today's communication technologies are striking. In the areas of industry and commerce, telegraphy spurred colonialism and imperialism, processes that today go under the euphemism of globalization and are supported by global communication networks. In the areas of everyday usage and consumption, telegraphy enhanced the speed by which individuals were able to send messages and place orders, much as e-mail correspondence and e-commerce have done in our time. Still, some differences can be observed. In comparison with the transmission of e-mail messages, the sending and reception of telegrams included several manual steps. The person sending a telegram first had to go to the local telegraph office, where an employee would transfer his or her message by Morse code to an office close to the receiver. If the message had to go a long distance, then it was often necessary that it be retransmitted along the way. And, after having reached its final destination, it had to be reconverted into ordinary language and carried by a messenger to the addressee. Although this might sound complicated, the system was quick and reliable. If a telegram was sent between cities, it usually reached its addressee within a couple of hours. Unlike today, telegrams were used not only for celebratory purposes but also for sending invitations and other short messages, as well as ordering goods and services. Telegraphy was a technology that well suited a society that became increasingly obsessed by overcoming large distances and consuming large amounts of resources. The match between the telegraph and the railroad was indeed perfect. Not only did the railroad companies make use of the telegraph to keep their expanding lines coordinated but also passengers profited by being able to cable their scheduled arrival times to relatives and business companions.

SOCIABILITY AND INTEGRITY

Telegraphy reinforced existing social relations, while simultaneously opening up new social spaces. It enabled people to stay in contact across large distances, and it allowed new kinds of relationships to develop. In her novel *Wired Love* of 1879, Ella Cheever nicely portrayed how members of both genders appropriated this technology for amorous purposes. At the same time, male and female employees of the telegraph offices made extensive use of the cable lines for flirting—more than a century before anonymous chat rooms and e-mails became common phenomena in virtual space. The telegraph was well integrated into the routines of daily life, despite the fact that many users had no idea what made it work. Whereas some are reported to have been thinking of telegraph signals as a kind of fluid, others seem to have believed that the telegraph lines actually transported the telegrams in physical form. The integration of the telegraph into the daily routines of the business world was so strong that most companies stuck to the telegraph even after the telephone began to appear in the late 1870s. Although a telephone call is faster and more direct than the transmission of a telegram, it is more difficult to document. In the world of business, the telegram had some of the advantages that e-mails have today: fairly high reliability and low price; the possibility to reach a desired addressee even though he or she might temporarily be away; and the fact that all communication can be traced and reconstructed afterward. Taken together, these factors gave telegraphy an advantage that did not make it easy for the German Philipp Reis, the American Alexander Graham Bell, and other telephone pioneers to, literally speaking, make their voice heard in the business community. Not even the fact that the telegraph system was occasionally overloaded and at times plagued by message jams at central hubs in the networks helped make the diffusion of the telephone a straightforward affair.

Bell filed his first telephone patent in 1876, after having beat Elisha Gray to the finish line in one of history's most famous patent competitions. Commercialization followed promptly. During a promotional tour in Europe in 1877, Bell visited the small but industrially important town of Drammen in southern Norway. The word about the novelty from the other side of the Atlantic had spread, and the town's business elite had gathered for a demonstration in the Exchange Hall. "You must speak, Mr. Borsch," Bell instructed the bank clerk who nervously said a few words in front of the strange-looking microphone. Although the audience was caught by surprise when they heard the invisible bank director Bang's response in a speaker on the podium, Borsch concluded soberly, "Sirs, this is indeed a very jolly toy, but it will never be of any practical use" (quoted in Dahl, Ellefsen, and Solberg 1993, 21).

The hesitation with which most companies initially approached the telephone came as a disappointment to inventors such as Bell, Edison, and Gray (Pool 1977). Communication between firms had originally played a pivotal role in their sociotechnical scenario, and business had been assigned the role of pathfinder and initiator. In response to the lukewarm interest of representatives of industry, the inventors had to accept other kinds of uses. The initial phase saw different applications: two-way communication and one-way transmission of sound for reasons of command and control. Military establishments and some rank-and-file-organized private companies installed one-way solutions to pass on orders from superiors to subordinates. In some cities telephone lines were drawn between concert halls and other public spaces, where speakers were erected so that an audience could enjoy operas and plays at a reduced rate. Such a connection was set up for public-relations purposes at the International Electricity Fair in Frankfurt am Main in 1891. After having heard a public lecture on the latest developments in telephone technology in the afternoon, the enthusiastic audience went on in the evening to hear a concert broadcast by telephone lines from the city of Wiesbaden, about twenty miles away.

It was not at all obvious in the early years to what ends the telephone would ultimately be applied. Would it primarily become an artifact used for what was considered serious business matters—much like IBM envisioned computer use in the 1950s and 1960s? Or would it become a personal instrument that could be used at home—as the computer did after IBM launched its Acorn in 1981? Would a situation develop in which private chatting and gossiping would fill up the telephone lines, or would industry and commerce readily adopt it? Even after the first local Bell system had been set up in 1878 to connect twenty-one well-to-do subscribers in New Haven, Connecticut, it was still not clear that private usage would carry the day to such a large extent as it has. As long as the number of users remained small, telephones were mostly bought for reasons of prestige. In those days people primarily acquired telephones to signal that they belonged to a privileged segment of the population. As in so many other cases in the history of consumer technology, status played a considerable role in this early phase.

As the number of subscribers grew, the practicality of the telephone became increasingly obvious to various user groups. Medical doctors acquired it to be more easily reachable, and stores installed it to be able to take orders from customers. Other kinds of users quickly learned to appreciate the freedom and security that the telephone provided. The active role that women played is particularly striking. Women eagerly adopted this new means of communication to order goods and services and to maintain social ties across large distances (Fischer 1992). By using the telephone lines' ability to link people, women managed to uphold relationships to friends and relatives in faraway cities and regions. Mothers appropriated it to stay directly in touch with their children, although they might have moved to other areas of the country, and housewives acquired it to sustain their social networks in the immediate neighborhood. Those farmers' wives and urban housewives who could afford it adopted the telephone to escape geographically or socially imposed isolation. Not unexpectedly, this appropriation strategy did not pass unnoticed by commentators concerned with the potential immorality, indecency, and obtrusiveness of this new means of communication. How could a husband control whom his wife was talking to? How could one avoid unwanted and unsolicited contacts between members of different social classes and races?

Although female telephone users might confirm commonsensical wisdom about chatting and gossiping, they clearly falsify other traditional views. One of these concerns women as commercial dopes, and another concern has to do with the allegedly female fear of things technological. It is probably true that many women readily accepted the telephone companies' argument that their personal safety would increase if they had a telephone installed at home: "The modern woman finds emergencies robbed of their terror by the telephone," one firm claimed in an advertisement in 1905 (quoted in Fischer 1992, 157). But it is just as obvious that female users did not sign—or persuade their husband to sign—a telephone contract merely to be prepared for fires, burglaries, or accidents. Social factors seem to have been equally, if not more, important. By adapting this gadget to suit their own needs, women partly acted in a way that had not been foreseen by the telephone companies. The social forms of use posed certain problems for the companies. To avoid lines from being blocked, firms tried to discourage private subscribers from misusing the telephone for simple conversation—to no avail, however. Female users appropriated the telephone as they saw fit and adopted it in ways that squared with their own interests. And, because local calls in most instances followed a flat rate in those days (i.e., the cost of a local call was independent of its duration), they could do so without risking horrendous bills. Rather than rejecting the novel device, women eagerly embraced it: "Mother talked for hours sitting on the piano stool" (quoted in Fischer 1992, 228). No trace of technological fear or conservatism here!

The telephone opened up new mediating spaces between individuals. Compared with earlier means of communication, this faceless but still intimate and immediate way of expressing thoughts and feelings contributed to the reformation of interpersonal relations. This is not to say, however, that telephony was embraced wholeheartedly. Contemporary commentators maintained that these expensive artifacts ought to be used for more important things than meaningless gossip and claimed that the distinction between private and public space began to erode as soon as a telephone was installed in the home. Because this technology enabled anyone to intrude into the private sphere, commentators widely felt that one's integrity was being threatened. A century before the explosion of electronic communication and the diffusion of cellular telephones made this problem ever more pronounced, a discourse developed that to some extent resembles today's discussions. How can one avoid always being accessible and, quite literally, constantly on call without losing contact with the world out there? Eugen Diesel, the son of the famous engineer Rudolf Diesel, described the shock that accompanied the shrill sound of the telephone bell: "With the telephone a demon had found its way into the home and the firm" (quoted in Radkau 1998, 207). The abrupt ringing pierced his very marrow and effectively killed any ongoing activity.

For the German historian Joachim Radkau (1998), who dubbed the decades around 1900 "the age of nervousness," the telephone epitomizes the problematic relationship between technical development and the human psyche in those years. Like trains, automobiles, and ocean liners, telephones had a Janus face. On one hand, contemporaries were fascinated by the increased personal contacts that these technologies enabled, but, on the other hand, they—like Diesel—complained about the hectic and nervous condition that they brought forth. Just as modern technology is characterized by ever higher speed and more power, modern men and women are plagued by higher and more rapid movements. To Radkau, who went to great pains to avoid deterministic arguments, this nervousness was not a pure reaction to technical developments. Rather, the whole turn-of-the-century culture—especially middle-class German culture—was imbued with a sense of irritability and anxiety. Psychiatrists and psychologists enjoyed a booming market, and mental hospitals were filled with people who did not fit the standards and requirements of modern society.

THE IRONIES OF INFORMATION AND COMMUNICATION HISTORY

Computers and telephones are not neutral instruments that simply lie around waiting to be used for reasons of efficiency and profit. A society in which 75 percent of the population owns cellular telephones is different from a society in which there are no such items. Similarly, a world in which almost half the people have access to the Internet differs from a world in which computer-based, electronic communication is not available. And, a culture in which television has largely replaced the printed word is not the same as a culture based on books and journals.

The appropriation of books, telephones, and computers has been a process filled with paradoxes. The history of information and communication technology is indeed a history of ironies. On one hand, there has been a steady increase in the amount of information that can be stored and processed, but, on the other hand, there has been a recurrent danger of information overload. The history of communication technologies indicates that we communicate with an increasing number of human beings, and that telephone communication was accompanied by a sense of growing intimacy. Still, already a century ago critics argued that telephone communication tended to contribute to a growing anonymity in society. Today we observe similar processes taking place in virtual reality. Although it has become easier to search for information, the gap between those who are able to make effective use of that information and those who are not increases all the time. Access to information is a prerequisite for power, but that access is not evenly distributed in society—not even in our so-called information society.

On a macrolevel, it is easy to point to the rapid increase in the amount of information that technologies have been able to process. Gutenberg's printing press increased the speed of book production more than a hundredfold and guaranteed that information could be reproduced in identical form. With the application of punched cards for controlling textile manufacturing and processing census data in the nineteenth century, a qualitative leap was taken, and after the introduction of the integrated circuit (the "chip") and the microprocessor in the 1950s and 1960s, a breathtaking process set in, the end of which is not in sight. Individual computers and computer networks become ever faster and can handle ever more data, as do mobile telephone networks. Perceptive observers, most notably the philosopher Joseph Weizenbaum (1976), warned about the implications of these developments in the 1970s. Their argument was that an increase in data flow does not go along with an increase in human knowledge. Information is one thing, understanding and reason is another. Even if we manage to find and retrieve data by means of Google or other search engines, we cannot necessarily make sense out of this wealth of information and turn it into meaningful, useful, or helpful knowledge.

The same goes for communication technologies such as telephones. We have come a long way from the handful of subscribers who were listed in the world's first telephone directory in 1878. Although the telephone disseminated at different speed in different countries, there was everywhere a steady upward trend. The irony seems to be that as we communicate more with more people, the content of this communication becomes ever more superficial. Cell phones definitely allow greater flexibility and the appropriation of new spaces, but do they really guarantee closer contacts and more intimate relations?

The result of his "displeasure at the considerable deterioration visited upon our good city of Paris and its surroundings" was a series of dictates that prescribed how his Parisian subjects should go about making the capital cleaner and less offensive (quoted in Laporte 1978/2000, 4). They were no longer allowed to dispose of refuse, garbage, and wastewater in the streets. The keeping of domestic animals was forbidden, and each house owner was required to have a cesspool. Even though most inhabitants successfully managed to avoid deferring to these orders, the royal edict indicates that dirt and stench are not just contemporary nuisances (Corbin 1982/1986).

In this chapter we discuss the kinds of ideas and techniques that have been mobilized and the appropriation practices that have emerged in the quest for urban environmental improvement in the modern era. Trying to cope with stench, epidemics, and chaos, medical doctors have prescribed new standards, engineers have constructed more effective equipment, and civil servants have created new kinds of public institutions. We see that not all of these measures were immediately successful. Much like the sixteenth-century Parisians who refused to accept the edict of their king, citizens around the world often have chosen not to change their traditional habits and unhealthy routines. Instead of accepting modern hygienic standards and best-practice techniques, many people have stuck to their established practices. In the industrial world the cleanliness of urban environments improved only slowly, and particularly in developing countries, where megacities proliferate, cities continue to pollute and wreak havoc on their surroundings and on the health of their inhabitants (J. McNeill 2000). In other words, the cultural appropriation of the ideas of sanitation and, as it was later termed, environmental protection has not been a smooth and progressive process.

In the Middle Ages, German city authorities were just as troubled about "muck in the alleys" as was François I (quoted in Bauer 1998, 36). Between the years 1373 and 1509, the city council of Frankfurt am Main issued nineteen laws and commands dealing with cleanliness and public health. It is hard to judge exactly how successful they were. It turned out to be difficult to banish all pigs and to force inhabitants to transport their waste to assigned places outside the city limits. There are indications, however, that the authorities managed to organize sanitary action to some extent. In the historical documents "scavenger" and "privy-sweeper" appear as officially recognized occupations in the Middle Ages, and certain individuals were hired to clean the public wells. In the early modern period, the town executioner was assigned the task of emptying stinking cesspools and throwing their content into the river Main. Considering the low status of this kind of labor, it is not surprising to find many women working as privy-sweepers. With buckets on a yoke and a tallow candle fastened onto their foreheads, these "women of the nocturnal labor"—as they were euphemistically called—carried out their duties in the badly lit streets of Berlin well into the nineteenth century (Hauser 1992, 298).

Some relief came in the second half of that century. Beginning in Britain, water closets became more common in urban residential areas. After having been connected to a citywide sewage system, the water closet definitely contributed to a better urban environment. In the same period the removal of litter and waste from private homes and public places was gradually better organized, and garbage dumps and landfills were set up outside the city limits to take care of the leftovers of urban life. The civilizing process, as described by the German sociologist Norbert Elias (1939/1978), by which the population of the Occident has managed to separate itself from its bodily secretions, took a giant leap forward. Much like handkerchiefs, which enabled individuals to uphold a line between their snot and their hands, sanitary technologies created a border between the city and the countryside. By building sewage systems and organizing waste disposal effectively, urban inhabitants attempted to separate the civilized city from its natural surroundings. Or, in historian Susanne Hauser's (1992, 294) words, they tried to "exclude" nature from the city and to define the environment as a kind of recipient.

It is important to recognize that the vision of a clean city had a dirty side to it: polluted waters and a wasteful use of natural resources. Like all forms of scientific and technological hubris, the solution of one set of problems inevitably created other problems. Water closets, for example, had a number of negative consequences. Their diffusion led to an enormous increase in the use of water, which could in most cases not be met by local wells but required that central waterworks be built. It also meant that human excrements were redefined. In many towns cesspools had been emptied by farmers who used the contents as manure on their fields, but after the water closet was widely domesticated this practice was abandoned. Although there were some experiments with disposing of sewage on fields, excrements ceased to be a resource for agriculture and instead became an environmental burden.

Keeping cities clean, well ordered, and lighted are obviously important tasks for human societies to deal with. Exactly what is considered problematic has changed through the centuries, however—as have the preferred solutions. The French king was concerned about "corruption and stench," but he seems to have been most troubled by the fact that it had become more and more difficult to "journey through [Paris] either by carriage or on horseback without meeting with great peril and inconvenience" (quoted in Laporte 1978/2000, 4). His measures were authoritarian and comparatively simple: giving orders and, in the case of nonconformance, confiscating house and land. Expert knowledge and technical advice were not deemed necessary. In our age this is different. True enough, litter is still removed by hand in many parks and pedestrian areas, but the overall environmental problems of urban life are solved by other means. A striking characteristic of the developments in this area is the growing role played by engineering, scientific, and medical expertise.

In the nineteenth century municipal engineering and public works emerged as important areas of technical development, and urban planning and hygiene became academic subjects. Engineers often played the main role in organizations that were set up to provide the urban population with energy and water and to remove its garbage. Investments were made to come to grips with sanitary and urban environmental problems, to ensure a continuous supply of water and energy, and to provide efficient means of transportation. Public baths and private bathrooms were built, apartments became less humid and unhealthy, the treatment of refuse and waste was made more effective, underground water pipes and sewage systems were put in place, gas and electricity networks were laid out, and streets were made broader and straighter. Medical and scientific knowledge was applied, and administrative power was mobilized. In comparison with medieval and early modern towns, the modern city is indeed a "networked city" (Tarr and Dupuy 1988). Without its many systems, such as gas, electricity, and public transit, it would cease to function.

This process is one of the core projects of modernity, and its history is usually told in a progressive way. In their endeavor to improve public health, medical doctors and teachers successfully enrolled city authorities. Engineers did the same within the area of public works. From the middle of the nineteenth century onward, the growing dependence on technical systems for urban life was in many cities accompanied by what used to be called "municipal socialism," a centralization of power and competence into the hands of the city fathers and their staff. In this process—which began to reverse only in the past two decades—more and more tasks were delegated from the individual citizen to local authorities, a process that generally went further in Europe than in the United States. Following a model that had begun with the erection of energy distribution infrastructures and the establishment of public water works in the nineteenth century, mayors and their administrators tried to draw ever more areas of civic life under their control—ranging from public transport, by means of city planning, to waste disposal. By means of sociotechnical engineering measures, authorities tried to keep chaos at bay.

To be effective, urban infrastructures require that citizens adjust their behavior and patterns of life to the demands of the system. Rather than throwing the dishwater out of the window or urinating in the backyard, we, in our roles as technohuman hybrids, ordinarily use the sink and the water closet. And in most places it is no longer considered acceptable to dispose of garbage on the street. Urban infrastructures have two sides: on one hand, they provide us with obvious comforts, and urban life would be unbearable without them, but, on the other hand, they strongly structure our daily lives. Although, in principle, we can avoid using them, most city authorities in the industrialized countries force house owners to connect to the municipal waterworks and sewage system. And, once the systems have been installed, their sheer existence tends, so to speak, to predispose us to use them: they define appropriate behavior.

PROGRESSIVE AND CRITICAL URBAN HISTORIES

The bridges between urban history and the history of technology and science are weak. Those historians of technology who have studied waterworks and similar structures have seldom been informed about broader cultural patterns, and historians of science have only occasionally addressed intellectual activities in urban settings. Similarly, the contacts between urban history on one hand and historians of public health and environmental historians on the other hand could be closer. A truly transdisciplinary history of urban engineering, health, and environment—what we might call a history of urban ecology—is yet to be written. We attempt in this chapter, as a modest contribution to that history, to identify some of the themes that a history of urban ecology might address and to give some examples of the kinds of stories that such a history might include.

For many decades, scholarly works on the history of urban technologies and of public health suffered from a romantic bias and tended to tell unidirectional, even progressive, stories. Studies of Large Technological Systems usually start with the pioneering experiments, continue with the initial small-scale plants, and close with the establishment of the first integrated systems (Hughes 1987). In the case of electrification, after a pioneer such as Thomas Alva Edison had laid the foundation, entrepreneurs such as Emil Rathenau and Werner von Siemens consolidated the industry, making sure that an irreversible demand for electricity was created and that continuous growth could be maintained. Not dissimilar, the history of public health was for a long time written as a kind of success story (Porter 1999). According to this traditional grand narrative, progress in the areas of medicine, nutrition, and housing contributed to a radical decline in mortality and a considerable improvement of living conditions. Scientific knowledge was for the benefit of humankind, and—in the most enlightened countries—welfare systems were designed for the benefit of the inhabitants.

The emergence of the city as a bundle of large technological systems might appear as the most obvious inroad into a history of urban technology. However, this is just one of several perspectives from which the city can be viewed. The modern city also can be described as a machine, where the circulation of imponderables, artifacts, and humans takes place against the backdrop of architecture and infrastructures that frame urban life in distinct ways. Such mechanistic views have been popular among planners and architects. Contrasting the modern city to earlier periods, when towns and cities had supposedly developed in a more organic manner, these professionals have attempted to create a city that is supposed to function as smoothly as a machine. For Le Corbusier, a key proponent of this perspective, the architect's goal was to create an urban machine, where each unit—the individual home included—functioned as a component part. In this story line the residential house lost its lifeworld character and became a "machine for living."

The history of urban planning is a relatively well-researched field, and several of the works in this area try to give voice to alternative story lines. Progressivism, garden cities, and urban ecology movements have received considerable attention (Stradling 1999). At times, these alternatives have had a gendered aspect. Many women—be they concerned homemakers, feminist activists, or female architects—have criticized the city for being designed by men to cater to male interests. For instance, the separation of residential from commercial areas has been critically examined, as have abstract planning concepts and inhumane traffic solutions. In these tragic narratives urban life takes on a dark and gloomy character. For countermovements and utopian technocrats alike, certain cities have purveyed contrasting symbols. Berlin, for example, has been not only the city of decadence and sin but also "the pioneer technopolis" (Hall 1998).

Alternatives to the traditional, progressive stories have also appeared in the history of public health. Most influential have been the writings of Michel Foucault, the French philosopher. His books on the history of the asylum and the hospital have had a lasting impact on historians in this field (Foucault 1961/1965, 1963/1975). Instead of rehearsing familiar story lines of progress and improvement, Foucault delivered analyses in terms of control, discipline, and exclusion, and he discussed how normality and abnormality have come to be defined. For example, statistics have been seen not as an objective instrument applied to determine the relation between various factors in the area of public health but as a means of defining who is to be considered healthy or sick. Medical doctors and urban reformers have been driven not always by an urge to cure and improve but often by a range of strategic interests—be they economic, scientific, or political. Rather than praising the proponents of urban health reform, historians such as Ute Frevert (1985) have called their achievements a "benevolent siege."

CONTROLLING URBAN LIFE

When conveniences such as running water, paved streets, and central heating—along with, for instance, bacteriological theory—started to spread, they acquired an aura of necessity and inevitability. As is so often the case in appropriation processes, there seemed to be no turning back. Once a technology becomes incorporated into our lives and a fact becomes a part of our way of thinking, they appear natural and are no longer questioned.

After having left the field for the factory, laborers had to resign themselves to another kind of temporal, corporal, and spatial order. Although the foreman might not always have been harsher than the landlord, he had other means at his disposal. By keeping all laborers under one roof, the foreman could control their activities in detail. Not unimportant, the machine required constant attention and thus demanded a certain degree of discipline. Similarly, when leaving the countryside for the city, people faced another kind of order—or, rather, disorder. Apartments were overcrowded, dark, and humid; streets and bars were noisy and chaotic; epidemics abounded. As commentators from Charles Dickens and Friedrich Engels to Jane Addams and Upton Sinclair have noted, circumstances in this urban jungle were inhuman, and it was virtually impossible for a single individual to improve conditions.

In most instances, improvements in the urban environment could be achieved only by means of collective action. Beginning in Britain, the "social question" became an issue for Parliamentary commissions, charity organizations, and workers' unions. Here, as elsewhere, recurrent epidemics spread fear and death in the urban population. Most infamous perhaps were the cholera epidemics, for instance in Hamburg

(Evans 1987). In the United States even such lethal diseases as yellow fever and typhus took their toll. Slowly but surely, doctors and city officials realized that isolation of large segments of the population was not a viable alternative. Construction and hydraulic engineers began to apply their expertise to secure higher health standards and provide clean water and better housing. Often, these professionals became leading figures in various movements of social reform—in some countries known as the "sanitary" movement, in others as the "hygiene" movement. In the United States the so-called progressive movement set out at the end of the nineteenth century to solve what were considered to be some of the most pressing problems of the day. In urban areas, this meant mobilizing engineering knowledge and managerial skills to improve traffic and general living conditions, erect and manage public utilities, and keep streets free from refuse and unwanted persons—minorities and prostitutes among them.

From a sociological point of view, the sanitary or hygiene movement exhibited similarities and dissimilarities with contemporary environmental movements. Both were primarily made up by members of the urban middle class. And initially, the hygiene ideas, like the environmentalism of our time, were largely articulated by established members of society. The most active proponents of the sanitary gospel were medical doctors, teachers, engineers, and professors. Because the members of these professions belonged to the same social circles as the city fathers, they found it comparatively easy to amass public support for progressive action.

In terms of discourses, there are striking similarities between sanitation and environmentalism. Historian Klaus Mönkemeyer (1990, 74) argued that "the environmental debate of the 20th century corresponds to the hygienic debate of the 19th century." Concepts such as "natural," "clean," and "sound" played central roles in both discourses. The sanitarians' ultimate goal was to improve the level of health in the population by means of a more harmonious relationship between nature and human society. In filthy and disorderly surroundings, human beings would not fare well. If society were brought closer to nature—for example, by letting sunlight and fresh air into dark apartments—then citizens would not constantly be sick. Similarly, "purity" was an ideal in the sanitary movement, as it is in environmentalism. Like the terms *sanitation* and *hygiene* a century earlier, *environmental protection* and, more recently, *sustainable development* have become influential political concepts throughout the world. A century ago the corresponding term was *a healthy society*. In a Norwegian magazine an anonymous woman characterized the turn of the twentieth century as "our hygienic era," and in several countries campaigns were launched to create, as it were, a sanitary heaven on earth (*Husmoderen*, vol. 18, 1904, no. 3).

In contrast to contemporary meanings, the connotations of *hygiene* were not limited to areas such as body care and medicine. The word *sanitary* was not only used in connection with bathroom appliances and menstruation napkins. At the Berlin hygiene exhibition of 1883, water closets and medical instruments were placed beside protective clothing and disinfectants. Here, the interested public could inform itself about the latest developments in nutrition, nursing, housing, and water supply. Among the exhibitors were representatives of mental hospitals, fire brigades, and epidemiological laboratories. In Dresden, where an international hygiene exhibition was held in 1911, various aspects of urban life were addressed: from city planning and refuse treatment to epidemic statistics and eugenic ideas (Schubert 1986). In their traditionally instructive tone, representatives of the area of technical hygiene tried to teach visitors how to store provisions, how to install water pipes, and how to plan their apartments and houses and keep them bright, clean, and well ventilated.

Basically everything that had to do with the protection and well-being of human beings and their belongings was in those days subsumed under the label of *hygiene*. In the sad case of eugenics, this cognitive praxis was carried one step further to include the betterment of human beings. The Department of Hygiene at the University of Uppsala, Sweden, arranged an exhibit on racial differences at the Dresden exhibition.

The growing public awareness of sanitary issues was reflected in academia. Physicians began to realize that diseases spread faster if living conditions and nutrition standards are poor, and they opted for the creation of hygiene professorships at medical schools. To follow courses in social hygiene became compulsory for medical students; in Germany this step was taken in 1883. Typical urban issues such as the supply of pure water and the design of effective sewage systems entered philosophical faculties and technical colleges. Subjects such as "hygiene and medical chemistry," "technical hygiene," "school hygiene," and "building hygiene" were being taught toward the end of the nineteenth century. At the University of Giessen, for instance, professor of hygiene Georg Gaffky lectured on such different topics as alcoholism, ventilation, slaughterhouses, and water filtration (Wolff 1992). More famous was Max von Pettenkofer, who had received a chair for hygiene at the Munich University in 1865 and made a name for himself as an expert on public health, nationally and internationally.

Like environmental studies today, hygiene was a truly transdisciplinary subject, and it was closely related to practical life. Textbooks and handbooks summarized sanitary knowledge in an almost encyclopedic fashion, and they usually included detailed descriptions of various applications. Rudolf Abel's *Handbook of Practical Hygiene* (1913) is typical in this regard. For this publication Abel, who headed the Berlin Board of Health, had gathered around him a group of scientists, physicians, and engineers—university professors and practitioners. Typically, bacteriological or pathological theory played a marginal role in the section on epidemic disease. Emphasis was instead on how epidemics spread and how they could most effectively be avoided and contained. The state and the citizens were assigned important tasks in this fight—the former by controlling ports and working places and by setting up vaccination programs, the latter by clean living and by joining societies such as the "German Society for Combating Venereal Diseases" (Abel 1913, 10).

The mixture of themes that were included under the heading of hygiene and sanitation is, at least at first sight, somewhat bewildering (see Table 6). The representatives of the subject aimed at mastering all aspects of the human environment—be it disease, urban pollution, or living conditions generally. In contrast to modern environmentalism, its main objective was not to protect or sustain nature as such but to protect and sustain human beings. By developing knowledge about the relationship between individuals on one hand and their natural and artificial surroundings on the other, it was possible to control these surroundings and thus improve the human condition. Medical knowledge was considered a prerequisite for the repression of epidemics, technical knowledge was deemed necessary for the management of the built

TABLE 6. The Manifestations of Hygiene and Sanitation in the Public Sphere

Elements of the Sanitary Discourse	Parts of the Field of Hygiene	Material and Social Manifestations (Examples)
Pure water	Hydraulic engineering	Waterworks
Rapid removal of debris	Municipal engineering	Sewage systems
"Back-to-nature"	Urban planning	Parks and garden cities
Discipline	Social hygiene and social work	Public baths
Public health	Statistics and demography	Education
Combating disease	Epidemiology	Vaccination
Human improvement	Eugenics/racial hygiene	Sterilization and euthanasia
Normality	Psychiatry	Mental hospitals

environment, and biological and chemical knowledge was regarded essential for the regulation of physiological processes.

The successful translation of this knowledge into action depended on the willingness of the population at large to internalize the sanitarians' ideas. The hygienic program required a considerable degree of self-control on the part of the citizens, and this did not come about automatically. It was easier to acquire public support if the demands squared with already existing values and belief systems. An important precondition for the cultural appropriation of sanitary technologies in the nineteenth century was that values such as self-discipline and cleanliness had begun to make their way into the urban middle classes already in the eighteenth century. Public morality prescribed that excessive feelings be kept under control. Children were taught to repress their impulses, and adults were taught to check their natural instincts. Along with diligence, thrift, and order, cleanliness and hygiene began to establish themselves as paramount civic virtues in the age of Enlightenment. Doctors recommended bathing for health and cosmetic reasons, and educators taught parents the importance of having their children keep their bodies and clothing clean and tidy.

The gradual assimilation of sanitary ideas was a central element in a more general process of social mobility and aspiration, in which cleanliness was established as a kind of "mother virtue" (Frey 1997, 156). Because cleanliness was strongly associated with frugality, beauty, and health, it lay close at hand to broaden hygiene to encompass a wide array of measures and activities (see Table 7).

TABLE 7. The Manifestations of Hygiene and Sanitation in the Private Sphere

Elements of the Sanitary Discourse	Parts of the Field of Hygiene	Material and Social Manifestations (Examples)
Bathing	Plumbing	Bathrooms and heaters
Cleanliness/washing	Chemistry and mechanical engineering	Detergent and washing machine
Fresh air	Technical thermodynamics	Air conditioning
Sunshine	Building construction	More windows and healthier materials
Order and frugality	Home economics	Rational kitchen
Control	Technical hygiene	Fire protection
Healthy food	Nutrition and food chemistry	Refrigeration and diet plans

THE CLEAN AND SOUND BODY

The strengthening of the human body was a paramount concern to the sanitarians; they heartily recommended people to take cold baths and eat raw fruit and vegetables. Wincenz Priessnitz managed to attract patrons of both genders to his natural-well shower establishment deep in the German forests. Understandably, many persons were still more prone to put up with a warm bath or a hot shower. Nineteenth-century inventors displayed a certain ingenuity in this field. In his book *Mechanization Takes Command* (1948), Sigfried Giedion documented a number of bathtubs, steam baths, and showers that were designed for individual use. One of the most curious solutions was a wave bath—a small bathtub with a rounded bottom in which the bathing person was able to rock back and forth, thus creating small waves. Indeed, the Jacuzzi of those days! Steam baths came in various designs, and they were often portable. Typically, the user wrapped his or her body in a thick fabric, lay down on a bed, and had the enveloping fabric filled with steam. The Swiss industrialist Arnold Rikli described one of his inventions as follows:

> This portable steam-bath has the great advantage over the Russian or the Turkish bath that it can be taken in any room, that it leaves the head free and allows the lungs fresh air to breathe ... and has the advantage of Priessnitz's dry packing in so far as it takes much less time. (quoted in Giedion 1948, 666)

Medical doctors also came up with ingenious designs. On the basis of hydrotherapeutic ideas they developed various types of devices, all of which aimed at healing and strengthening the body by means of pure water. For instance, a French medical handbook from the 1860s illustrates how showers could be used for gynecological and other treatments. Under the supervision of properly dressed male doctors, nude female patients were submitted to more or less dubious forms of treatment. Or in the words of a contemporary doctor, "It is no rare thing to see a subject who at this first shower betrays actual terror, shouts, struggles, runs away, experiences frightening suffocation and palpitation" (Giedion 1948, 678). The end obviously justified the means.

In those days private houses generally had neither water conduits nor proper sewage, and it was subsequently not easy to install showers at home. Because, furthermore, bathrooms were rarely found only in ordinary dwellings, permanent installations were usually not possible. In this situation, the keen customer was happy to acquire a portable

Ce n'était pas assez d'un lavage ordinaire ;
Les malheureux parents ne savaient plus que faire.

Figure 13. "The Compulsory Bath," illustration for *Les Defauts Horribles*, c. 1860. Reprinted by permission of Gettyimages, Munich, Germany.

shower that did not need to be connected to any pipes or sewers. With a hand pump, cold or preheated water was led from a barrel to the shower and afterward collected in a tub. Even more practical under these circumstances was the closed system of the steam bath. Here, not much water was needed, and the amount of condensing water that had to be gathered was comparatively small.

These gadgets were not widely adopted. Most people—even those members of the bourgeoisie who were convinced of the healthy effects of washing—stuck to the traditional wash table. As bedrooms became more intimate and secluded from the rest of the house or apartment, they also became the place where the daily wash took place. The wash table contained a jug and hand basin, and it can be regarded as a precursor of modern washbowls and bathroom cabinets. They included towel hooks and offered some space for soap and other utensils. Discretely placed underneath the table was the essential chamber pot.

Bathrooms became a standard component of the modern home soon after water had been laid on. The technical prerequisites for a rapid diffusion of baths and showers developed in the second half of the nineteenth century. In Europe and North America, these were the pioneering decades of sanitary engineering and plumbing. Like the modern, mechanized kitchen, bathrooms developed into what Onno de Wit et al. (2002) called "innovation junctions." In these rooms a number of technical novelties come together, and engineers, technicians, and craftsmen had to coordinate their actions. Sanitary engineers cooperated with electricians and carpenters. Manufacturers of boilers provided the market with devices that could be connected either to gas pipes or to coal stoves. Plumbers had to keep themselves informed about the latest toilet and bathtub designs. If we add central heating systems to this list, it becomes obvious to what extent technology came to permeate the modern home. The driving forces behind this development were not only ideas about how to organize housework more rationally. Clearly, hygienic ideas and demands for comfort played an important role in this domestication process. In the home, the "pursuit of cleanliness" was transformed into a craze for modern technology (Hoy 1995).

Following Ruth Schwartz Cowan's book *More Work for Mother* (1983), those historians of technology who have treated the dissemination of domestic technologies tended to discuss this ironic process in terms of rationalization and professionalization. According to this story line, kitchen appliances and other household machines were, in the first instance, introduced to make housework more efficient and to contribute to increasing housewives' status and upgrading their tasks, but, as it turned out, in the end they seldom lived up to the promises that had been associated with them. Without questioning the validity of this interpretation, we want to stress the importance of sanitary ideas and of hygiene movements for the appropriation—or, perhaps better still, the domestication—of these technologies. Washing machines were introduced not only to save time but also to increase the level of hygiene and cleanliness.

It is possible to discern national differences in the ways in which the new technical possibilities were assimilated. In Germany, for instance, the water closet was usually not placed in the bathroom at all, but in a separate, small room: the lavatory. British bathrooms were often lavishly decorated and furnished. Upper-class families turned this new space into something that looked almost like a living room, complete with upholstery armchairs, thick curtains, and even Oriental carpets. By literally embedding cold metal faucets and polished ceramic appliances in a familiar environment, these groups managed to make the new technology acceptable and appropriate. Because, at the same time, this kind of decoration and furniture was difficult to keep clean, this fashion, paradoxically, made the traditional British bathroom less hygienic. Although thick wall-to-wall carpets later became common in the United States, the American middle class originally preferred simpler solutions and tried to keep building costs down.

The working and rural classes did not immediately climb on the bandwagon of personal hygiene. When we consider the firm place the shower has in our routines nowadays, it is difficult to imagine how reluctant most people were to subject themselves to this kind of self-discipline a century ago. The ritualization of the daily bath or shower did not take place overnight. The public baths were not an immediate success, and frustrated sanitarians even went so far as to discuss the possibility not only of using "the strong authority of education" but also of forcing the members of the lower classes to keep themselves clean (quoted in Spieker 1996, 116, 134). Thereby they had two powerful institutions at their disposal: the school and the military. One of several measures toward the end of the nineteenth century to increase personal hygiene and public health was to have showers installed at public schools, and the children were obliged to use them on a regular basis. During military service most young men had to accept the same treatment. We can, of course, doubt that the strategy to force the soldiers to take an ice-cold shower at five o'clock in the morning contributed to the popularity of the sanitarians' cause.

Not only were the proponents of hygiene driven by feelings of benevolence toward other groups in society but also, in their endeavor to improve public health, they also followed their own interests. If the members of the proletariat did not learn the elementary rules of hygiene, one middle-class observer wrote at the turn of the century, then not only they were at peril but also "we and our children" (quoted in Spieker 1996, 114). The sudden and indiscriminate outbreaks of epidemics in many urban centers had made it clear that they did not follow class lines. In their fight against miasmas and bacteria, medical doctors and nurses entered schools and other institutions with a triple mission: to force their patrons to undergo certain health programs, to teach them proper behavior, and to make sure that assigned norms were followed.

As we already indicated, the hygiene propaganda did not reach all of its target groups. Public baths were simply too expensive for many workers. Also, for a lack of time women in particular tended to avoid them. Even after bathrooms had begun to become standard in a majority of households, there was no guarantee that these were used as prescribed. A bathtub, for instance, was a perfect place to store coal.

Not surprisingly, the propaganda was more effective in reaching the urban upper and middle classes. As a reaction against the conceived unhealthy conditions in the modern city, those who could afford to change them developed different strategies. Dissatisfied with the efforts of sanitary reform and progressivist politics, many well-to-do people turned their back on the city altogether. Most notably in the United States, a process of suburbanization set in at the turn of the twentieth century, and this process was directly connected with the emergence of more efficient means of transportation: railroads, tramways, steamers, and, later, automobiles. And, at the same time, health resorts and spas mushroomed at convenient distances from major urban centers.

One of the most well-known American health resorts was Hot Springs, Arkansas. Although not placed so strategically as John Harvey Kellog's famous spa in Saratoga in upstate New York, Hot Springs's beauty and the alleged healing powers of its waters had a magnetic impact on the public. The first establishments in Hot Springs had been simple and anything but luxurious, but they soon gave way to more expensive and elaborate hotels. From the point of view of the history of technology and science, it is interesting to note that electrical and mechanical therapies—more or less scientifically founded—were with time given increasingly more room at these establishments. When Samuel Fordyce reopened his hotel in 1915, he packed it with new devices. Massage machines, electric oscillators, and different types of showers treated the patrons' bodies in various ways. The "mechano-therapy room" looked much like today's workout centers and was equipped with a number of machines and gadgets. The so-called "Zander machines put the body through a series of physical exercises, including horseback riding, bicycling, rowing, and getting punched in the stomach" (Peña 1999, 765). Self-discipline and self-control seem to have been perverted into kinds of flagellation and self-humiliation. For many patrons, this must have been their first truly physical approach with mechanically moving instruments. Previous natural relationships between human beings and, for instance, horses were, in this artificial environment, replaced by a hybrid relationship between humans and machines.

CLEANING THE HOME AND THE STREETS

Not surprisingly, Fordyce adhered to the ideals of hygiene. To combat bacteria and dirt, he banned upholstery and large carpets in the workout rooms. This practice was not limited to Hot Springs. House-wives followed a similar strategy in their war against dust and debris. Because—as the author of a contemporary housekeeping manual stated—"carpets, plush covers, curtains, etc. are absolutely impossible to keep free of dust," the most diligent housewives removed them or replaced them with materials that were easier to handle (quoted in Berner 1998, 324). The private home had to be protected from alien particles (Breuss 1999). The martial language that accompanied this fight is remarkable, and it testifies to the seriousness of the matter. An invisible line was drawn between the chaotic and dangerous public areas outside the home and the harmonious atmosphere inside. The home is my castle, and no dirt and dust should be allowed to pass its threshold!

Middle-class housewives made use of typical low-tech and soft, social solutions in their struggle to keep the home clean, neat, and orderly. The zealous housewife had a number of tools at her disposal: wall brushes, carpet sweepers, upholstery beaters, and mitten dusters, for example. Those who could afford it appointed craftsmen to varnish the wooden floors or to cover them with linoleum. Apartments were constantly aired, also in the cold season. In women's journals a debate blazed up between those who recommended sweeping the floor with wet rags and those who stuck to using brushes and dry cloth. To ensure that the program was successfully carried out, all members of the household had to be educated. Children, husbands, and servants had to be taught how to behave in accordance with the ideology of hygiene. Because servants usually had grown up in rural areas or came from a working-class milieu, they were particularly difficult to deal with. Complaints about undisciplined behavior and sloppiness on their part were an integral part of conversation among middle-class women.

In their fight against filth, housewives slowly appropriated technical and scientific solutions of another kind. Engineers invented vacuum cleaners and washing machines, and chemists developed new antiseptic agents and detergents. In traditional history of technology, we find heroes such as H. Cecil Booth, whose "Puffing Billy" was so large and heavy that it had to be operated from the street outside the house, and W. H. Hoover, who developed the first small-size vacuum cleaner that could be used by women in their own apartments. As Boel Berner (1998) pointed out, the heroines of daily cleaning—whom she called "domestic engineers"—remain anonymous in these stories.

The large-scale diffusion of vacuum cleaners and washing machines had to wait until after the Second World War. Only a small minority of households had access to these mechanical gadgets before the war.

Figure 14. Poster for Johns Volldampf washing machines, nineteenth century. Reprinted by permission of Landesmuseum für Technik und Arbeit, Mannheim, Germany.

When the sanitary movement peaked in the decades around 1900, other technical systems were more important. Electric light made dusting and sweeping easier (alas, it also made the dust more visible), but even more important was probably the installation of water and sewage pipes in ordinary dwellings. Thereby, not only could the family members be washed more regularly but also their clothes could be too. On wash day, all textiles had previously been carried to the nearest washhouse or jetty, by either domestic servants or professional so-called washwomen. For those who could afford it, commercial steam laundries also had emerged as a possibility (Mohun 1999). When water had been laid on in residential areas, the whole washing process moved inside, often into the basement of the apartment house. Like so many other activities that used to be carried out collectively, washing was privatized and individualized. With water being led directly into the house, the nice chatting breaks at the neighborhood well disappeared.

Housewives and city fathers were happy to get rid of gossiping servants at the public wells. Just as the middle-class woman tried desperately to keep her home tidy and harmonious, progressive town authorities—vocally supported by women's societies and clubs—attempted to make the urban environment clean and orderly. The extreme case is New York City, where three thousand street sweepers in white uniforms were employed in the mid-1890s. Responsible for this undertaking was the legendary Colonel George E. Waring, whom historian Martin Melosi (1981) called "the apostle of cleanliness." Waring was driven not so much by scientific knowledge, which he largely lacked, as by a strong almost religious conviction about the potential threat posed by litter, dirt, and decaying organic substance. His military background seemed to have been conducive to the successful organization of this formidable enterprise, which involved minute planning and required absolute discipline on part of the employees. After all, who could be better suited than a colonel to lead the war against dust?

Aiming at removing everything that they considered misplaced from the streets of the Big Apple, Waring and his supporters took on not only nonhuman leftovers but also human debris. Unwanted individuals were forced away from the streets and had to move to other neighborhoods. This program of exclusion and separation spread to other cities. To tackle filth and chaos, urban centers were organized in accordance with established civilizing values of hygiene and discipline. Progressive societies carried out propaganda campaigns, and schools and other institutions organized litter-collecting drives. Architects and urban planners suggested that cities ought to be structured in new ways. Parks were given important tasks as a kind of sanctuary in the middle of a chaotic urban machine. By creating Central Park the pioneering landscape architect Frederick Law Olmsted became immortal among New Yorkers. Even more all encompassing was the vision of so-called garden cities, which partly materialized in several British and German cities. On a more mundane level, engineers developed and implemented new technologies. Several types of horse-drawn garbage and latrine collector wagons were available on the market toward the end of the nineteenth century. Streets were paved with asphalt or set with cobblestone to make street cleaning more effective—and to cater to increased traffic.

Engineers also began to address the critical issue regarding where to ultimately dispose of the immense amounts of waste that a large city produced. Since time immemorial the established practice had been to burn the refuse, use simple garbage dumps, or dispose of wastes in the nearest river or offshore. As cities grew in size, landfills became more popular. To create additional building land, some coastal cities even used their wastes to construct artificial land or islands—New York City is a case in point. Toward the end of the nineteenth century, mobile refuse burners could be seen in the streets, and some cities invested in incineration plants. British engineers and municipal authorities led the way. Incineration might not appear to be particularly high-tech, but it turned out to be a difficult task to burn urban garbage. Especially problematic from a technical point of view was the high humidity content of household waste, which resulted from the practice of mixing organic with inorganic components.

Despite all of these attempts to make cities cleaner and to bring nature into the urban environment, better housing was probably the most important of all the improvements that were made in urban living conditions. As long as workers and the lower middle class resided in badly isolated, offensively dirty, and overcrowded apartments, the sanitarians would not be successful in their cause. As a reaction to the misery in many quarters, municipal authorities began to regulate building construction. Earlier, fire protection had been the main reason for requiring wider streets and a maximum building height, but in the second half of the nineteenth century, social and hygienic aspects became equally important. "More air! More light!" became the slogan of the day (Rodenstein 1988). In Berlin it was required by law that the courtyards of the so-called tenement barracks (*Mietskaserne*) be of a certain minimum size, and in Hamburg the construction of windowless sleeping rooms was forbidden. To some extent, these directions were based on scientific findings. Physiologists had estimated that an adult person needed at least ten cubic meters of fresh air per night, and they also meant to have proved the healthy effects of sunlight and ozone (which is formed in the presence of sunlight). With its abhorrence for bad air, the miasma theory delivered a convincing rationale for improving ventilation and trying to get people out of musty apartments. Primarily in the United States, humidity became a topic of intense discussion, and around 1900 several engineers set about to control the inner environment by means of air conditioning.

One of the persons who invested the most energy in improving the lot of the poor was the legendary Jane Addams, a Nobel Peace Prize laureate. Her Hull House in Chicago, founded in 1889, became a center for urban and social betterment. In her youth Addams had toured Europe, and like so many other reformers in turn-of-the-century America, she was appalled by the disastrous conditions in large European cities and inspired by some of the organized attempts to make urban life human on that side of the Atlantic. On her return home to the United States, she decided to take on the urban situation head-on. Garbage collection, sewage treatment, housing quality, child rearing, working conditions, and public health were some of the topics that this indefatigable woman set out to improve.

Unlike many similar efforts in this era, Hull House was not in the first instance a charity organization but an institution that took initiatives on the basis of thorough scientific investigation, a precursor to today's action research. It became a magnet for reform-minded medical doctors, teachers, and social workers, many of whom were women. Alice Hamilton was one of the most vocal and active ones. She had studied medicine at the University of Michigan and later became the first female professor at Harvard University (Gottlieb 1993). Her specialty was what in those days was called "industrial hygiene." During her sojourn in Chicago, she carried out influential studies of workers' conditions and public health. She found out that there was a connection between a typhoid epidemic and a poor sewage system, and she contributed actively to the harsher legislation in the area of occupational health.

THE DILEMMAS OF HYGIENE

The hygienic practices that we have discussed in this chapter depended to a large extent on the gradual expansion of technical networks and engineering expertise, as well as initiatives on the part of local governments. The area of water supply and sewage is perhaps the most obvious example. Comparing the situation at the end of the nineteenth century with the time when most cities drew their water from a large number of small wells, Gerrylynn K. Roberts (1999, 143) wrote,

Wells ... were small-scale and localized facilities, and installing them required little technical expertise. By contrast, constructing a central [water] supply involved surveying a considerable area of land, employing engineering experts and using technically sophisticated materials such as hydraulic cement; it also required substantial funds.

Considering how far the cultural appropriation of water and sewage systems has gone in our time, the difficulties that surrounded their introduction might be surprising. Although, in the late 1700s, a yellow fever epidemic had given the impetus to the rapid construction of a waterworks in Philadelphia, citizens preferred to continue using well water. In Berlin forty years elapsed between when the first serious suggestion to install water pipes had been made in 1816—incidentally, not for private or industrial purposes but for street cleaning and fire protection—and when the actual installations were made in 1856. As in Philadelphia success was not immediate; only three hundred households were initially connected. Making conscious use of hygienic and moral arguments, the Berlin Waterworks Company successively pushed for its new product—allegedly pure running water—in advertisements and brochures.

Political debate and economic problems accompanied the establishment of waterworks in many towns and cities. Not least for financial reasons, caution was certainly wise. Many cities had to borrow substantial amounts of money to finance these projects—which might explain why many waterworks and water towers were designed in such an imposing manner (Goubert 1988). Typical topics of debate in city halls and local newspapers were the exact location of the waterworks, forms of ownership, and the general advantages of a centrally managed water network as compared with a decentralized system of individual wells. Although, initially, private initiatives were common in this sector, a trend toward municipal socialism is clearly visible, not least in France. Even in the United States, more than half of all waterworks were publicly owned at the turn of the twentieth century.

Once a town had decided to take the step toward a common water supply system, it usually did not take long before the sewage question got onto the agenda. Because the improved availability of water resulted in a rapid increase in usage, more water now had to be led away. Furthermore, in several cities an unhappy relationship developed between the freshwater source and sewage recipient. Chicago is a case in point. As the amount of sewage that was piped into the Chicago River began to reach excessive levels, the city's water supply in Lake Michigan was threatened (Cain 1978). The solution vividly illustrates the hubris character of much civil engineering work. Instead of constructing a sewage treatment plant, the city decided to dig a canal about the size of the Panama Canal and in this way channel the city's sewage by means of two smaller rivers into the Mississippi. It is no wonder that citizens of St. Louis and other affected towns were not amused.

In Berlin other solutions were debated. In support of their opposing views, farmers and municipal engineers could mobilize different kinds of experts. Justus von Liebig, probably the most famous German nineteenth-century chemist, forcefully argued against all kinds of sewage pipes. To him, human excrement was too valuable an economic resource to be led into rivers or spread onto a few fields at the outskirts of a city. Instead, Liebig recommended that urban municipalities develop a modernized system for the emptying of privies and the transportation of their contents from urban areas to farms. Against him stood the well-known physician Robert Koch, who made a name for himself as one of the main proponents of the bacteriology theory and the fight against cholera. Because Koch's main concern was individual and public health, he was a vehement opponent of privies. Human excrements contained bacteria that could be lethal, and they had to be removed from residential areas as quickly as possible. Therefore, he considered water closets to be the only truly hygienic solution. With this line of argument, he was supported by colleagues who still adhered to the traditional miasma theory. To them, the rapid removal of all kinds of waste was necessary to avoid the development and spread of "bad air" and other dangerous gases.

Once the struggle had been settled in favor of large-scale, central solutions, the initiative and responsibility moved from physicians and medical doctors to those in the engineering profession. To solve the technical problems caused by urbanization, municipal engineering emerged as a new specialty. It became the task of the municipal engineer to implement the strategies developed by the proponents of the sanitary gospel. Although a colonel might have been well suited to organize herds of manual laborers, the design of huge public works called for another kind of expertise. Sure enough, managerial skills were required also for the construction of waterworks or sewage systems, but, in addition, knowledge about materials, statics, and geology was necessary.

The ideology and daily practice of the hygiene movement were in many ways inconsistent. If we compare its visions with its effects, we are struck by a number of paradoxes—or, at best, unintended consequences. By focusing so strongly on the urban environment, the sanitarians at times lost sight of the natural environment. As in the case of Chicago, they often did nothing more than move the problem from one place to another, from the city to its surroundings or from one city to another one downstream. The huge garbage dump outside the city seems to have been a lesser evil than a piece of paper on the pavement. From hindsight, this is all the more astonishing, as original nature was considered an asset in itself. As we have seen, the sanitarians aimed at bringing more fresh air and pure water into cities, apartments, and houses, and they recommended that people leave the city for vacation and recreation. Also, the emerging practice of mixing all kinds of waste, rather than separating various components from each other, meant that valuable resources were eliminated, or at least withdrawn from the circulation of nature and the economy. With the introduction of large-scale sewage systems and water closets, human excrements became a problem rather than a resource.

If we look critically at the sanitarians' program, we have to conclude that it has to be regarded as one of the main factors behind our contemporary environmental problems. When cities constructed central waterworks, they also had to make sure that these huge investments paid off. Consequently, tariffs were designed in such a way that there was little if any incentive to save water. The same goes for the sewage system. Once connected, house owners and tenants had no reason to keep the amount of fluid waste down. What to do with the sewage at the end of the pipe became a problem for municipal engineers. The easy way out—to channel it into the nearest river—often hit back. Although the Berlin system of spreading the sewage onto the surrounding fields might have had short-term benefits, the rapid growth of the city and the increasing amounts of industrial waste made this system increasingly problematic.

As in many other areas of engineering, the development of urban technologies has all too often been guided by delusions of grandeur and greatness. The development of power plants and citywide electricity networks are paradigmatic examples of the steady expansion of so-called large technological systems, what Thomas P. Hughes (1989) termed "technological momentum." Many electricity systems were initially designed to serve only a few downtown office blocks, but, as soon as demand was awakened, aggressive plans were made for much more grandiose schemes. Extrapolations were made, and future, often exponential, growth rates were projected. The same goes for waterworks and sewage systems, which were, and still are, often vastly overdimensioned. Bigger is better, larger is more exciting, greater is more economical! Historian Dirk van Laak recently analyzed this engineering ideology of gigantism in a book called *White Elephants* (1999). Economies of scale surely play a role when projects are conceived, but—as we argue throughout this book—hubris is perhaps the main driving force. In the areas of urban technology and municipal engineering, a kind of megalomania has certainly played a role. As we have seen in this chapter, such a strategy often leads into a blind alley. The soil and ground water on which we depend get polluted in the process.

Part 4
Coping with Technoscience

Indochina. They tried to imagine together other uses to which their knowledge and expertise could be put that were not intrinsically destructive (Allen 1970). Like many of their contemporaries at other universities across the country—and for that matter around the world—they were seeking to come to terms with the military manifestations of technological and scientific hubris that had engulfed academic life since the Second World War.

Among the speakers on March 4 were Nobel Prize-winning scientists, such as the Harvard biologist George Wald, who argued that the war in Vietnam was merely a part of a deeper malaise in American academic life, by which military interests had been allowed to impose their own particular form of rationality onto the overall values and norms of science and engineering. Another speaker was the MIT professor of linguistics Noam Chomsky, who had recently begun to challenge the new forms of American power and the rise of what he termed the "new mandarins" within the U.S. political culture (Chomsky 1969). Chomsky had become famous a few years earlier for developing a theory of "generative grammar" by which he imputed an inborn capacity for making sense of words as central to what it is to be a human being. His theory challenged those who argued that human behavior could be likened to the workings of a machine and questioned whether intelligence in any meaningful sense could be artificial. Chomsky became one of the main critics of the emerging American empire during the following decades, a soft-spoken academic man who found the subservience of MIT and other universities to the military morally repugnant in its unthinking acceptance of the will to power.

As was the case at most American elite universities, MIT had become fundamentally integrated into what President Eisenhower, in leaving the White House in 1960, referred to as a "military-industrial complex." The former general had been in command during the 1950s as academic institutions were brought into line, into the world of big science with its secret projects and bureaucratic values. But at the end of his term in office, he warned of the risks involved in having institutions of higher learning and industrial development so intimately connected to the needs of national defense. Eisenhower argued that if the military-industrial complex was not restrained, other uses of technology and science would become secondary, even marginalized. And as the speakers pointed out on March 4, defense could easily become offensive and accelerate into the spiral of aggression that was so evident in the war in Vietnam.

The students and teachers at MIT also considered ways to reform the curriculum and, more broadly, the educational and research agendas of

MIT. Members of the Union of Concerned Scientists, which had been formed as part of the moratorium, presented ideas for new sorts of courses for science and engineering students so that they might be able to exercise, or at least to think about, social responsibility in their future careers. What seemed to be lacking in the education of scientists and engineers, many of the participants contended, were appropriate frameworks for linking technology and science to broader public concerns. Two cultures had emerged in contemporary societies, as the British chemist turned novelist C. P. Snow put it some years before in a speech at neighboring Harvard. The humanists, or what Snow termed the literary culture, had become far too estranged from the dominant scientific-technical culture, and it was important for institutions of higher learning to find ways to reconnect them (Snow 1959).

In part as a result of the day's deliberations, and the more general spirit in which they were conducted, MIT became one of the many technological universities around the world during the next few years to establish courses and eventually research programs in science, technology, and society, or STS. In retrospect, the activities of March 4 represented the initial phase of an appropriation process by which new sorts of hybrid identities, institutions, and discourses transcending the boundaries between technology and culture, or science and society, began to be carved out of the academic and broader political culture.

MAKE LOVE, NOT WAR

In this chapter we connect the broader politics of technology and science to the more circumscribed worlds of science and technology policy. In particular, we want to connect the critical movements that emerged in the 1960s to shifts in what Michel Foucault (1980) termed regimes of power and knowledge, and to what can be characterized as changing agendas of science and technology policy (Elzinga and Jamison 1995). In the 1940s, as an integral part of wartime mobilization, technology and science were also mobilized, and a regime was installed that transformed the relations between the producers of knowledge and the elites of power. Governments took responsibility for formulating policies and making decisions about science and technology, and a range of new political practices and institutions were put in place to hold them accountable for the policies that were made. From the 1970s to the present, those relations have come to be reconstituted, as a global regime of knowledge and power has taken form, by which transnational corporations and transnational organizations have taken over much of the responsibility for setting the policy agenda. A good deal of the substantive content of the new modes of knowledge production that have emerged during the past thirty years is derived from the protest movements of the 1960s, even though those connections are seldom examined explicitly.

In mounting their protests, student activists mobilized the traditions of dissent and resistance that had emerged in previous periods of social and cultural critique: the civil disobedience that Henry David Thoreau had written about in the nineteenth century as part of the abolitionist movement against slavery, the strikes that the labor movement had developed in the late nineteenth century, and the "experiments with truth" that Mahatma Gandhi had practiced in India in the struggle for independence. In 1968 the "whole world was watching" the new wave of critical social movements, and the spirit of protest manifested itself in Paris, Berlin, Prague, and Mexico City, as well as in a number of U.S. cities and college campuses (Kurlansky 2004).

In Paris the protests were primarily against the national government's educational policies and the regime of knowledge and power that had come to rule France after the Second World War. President Charles de Gaulle had appropriated the postwar arms race within a

Figure 15. Hippies taunting police during the trial of the Chicago Seven, a group of radicals arrested during the protests against the Vietnam War at the Democratic National Convention, 1968. Reprinted by permission of Gettyimages, Munich, Germany.

distinctively French discursive framework, drawing on the positivism of Comte and Saint-Simon to envision a new age of national glory that could help his nation recover from the traumatic loss of its colonies in Asia and Africa. The students in Paris objected to the militarist vision and to its practical implications for their education. Like their counterparts in other parts of Europe, the new left in France combined what Herbert Marcuse called a "great refusal" to take part in the technocratic projects of the government with a conscious display of international solidarity for the Vietnamese and other victims of imperialist oppression.

In Prague and elsewhere in Eastern Europe, the protests were primarily directed against the imposition of an authoritarian logic on the countries under Soviet domination and the use of technology and science in a kind of internal war of repression. The alternative vision that was promulgated in the 1960s was a "socialism with a human face" that included alternative uses of scientific and technological creativity. In Czechoslovakia a team at the Academy of Sciences from a wide range of fields, headed by the philosopher Radovan Richta, investigated the "social and human implications of the scientific-technological revolution" and produced the multivolume report *Civilization at the Crossroads* in 1968 (Richta et al. 1968). In the Richta report the scientists offered a detailed blueprint of a socialist humanism that sought to redirect science and technology to the satisfaction of basic human needs, rather than to the costly and unproductive arms race. The new kinds of automation technologies and cybernetic sciences, they argued, offered opportunities for socialist countries to develop much more sophisticated and sensitive forms of social and economic planning than were currently being used. But the Soviet Union answered their vision by sending tanks into Prague, and, as in other Eastern European countries, the scientists and technologists who had taken part in the study either were forced underground or fled to the West.

In North America and Western Europe, the protests of the 1960s focused on the use of technology and science in the war of external aggression in Southeast Asia. Although technical artifacts or instruments of destruction had been used to kill people since time immemorial, never had they been used so rigorously, so systematically, so *scientifically* as in Vietnam and, for that matter, in the repressive apparatus of the Soviet Empire. Although the political systems differed, there was nonetheless what some called at the time a convergence between communism and capitalism, not least in relation to the social functions of technology and science (Bell 1960). Napalm and many of the other instruments of destruction used in Vietnam were systematic applications of science and represented the mixing of theoretical speculation and controlled experiment by well-funded researchers.

In both systems the weapons were made in scientific institutions; in the West they were conceived and developed at universities or at public and private research laboratories on contract to the military, and in the East they were conceived and developed within the seamless webs of centralized bureaucracies and newly created science cities, such as Akademgorodok in Siberia (Josephson 1997). In both systems the pursuit of ever more advanced and sophisticated weaponry was the central story line of the cold war era. Military competition had set the agenda for science and technology policy since the end of the Second World War, in terms of discursive frameworks and practical projects and programs.

The policies pursued by the U.S. government in Vietnam were also products of science; more specifically, of social or political science. The expertise on which those policies were based came from so-called think tanks, such as the Rand Corporation in California, or centers for strategic studies or international relations at universities, where experts in operations research and political science combined forces to develop theories to justify the war effort and increase its effectiveness. The war games that these scientists played led to the development of powerful instruments of calculation and simulation that, in the 1950s, started to be called computers.

Through its computer laboratories, its multiple military research programs, and the involvement of some of its faculty members in military committees and other intelligence activities, MIT was in many ways the very center of what had become a military-industrial complex. As the 1960s progressed, it seemed to many people that the military-industrial complex had gotten out of control and that its hold on technology and science had become too strong (Wisnioski 2003). Alternative visions emerged in the so-called counterculture: visions of liberatory, mind-expanding technologies and holistic, spiritual sciences. The young rebels followed one of their main sources of inspiration—the Nobel Prize-winning German novelist Hermann Hesse—and took "journeys to the East" in search of mystical enlightenment and peace of mind. They read writings by those who had grown up under the yoke of colonial oppression, learning how lives were lived among those whom the Algerian doctor Frantz Fanon called "the wretched of the earth." They followed their own cultural heroes in asking fundamental questions of their elders, their masters of war, as in Bob Dylan's protest anthem "Blowing in the Wind" from 1962: "How many times must the cannon balls fly before they're forever banned?"

It was in a "dialectics of liberation" (Cooper 1968) that the revolts of the 1960s had their cognitive core. German intellectuals such as Hannah Arendt, Erich Fromm, and Herbert Marcuse, who had fled to the United States to escape Nazi oppression, had planted intellectual seeds for the protest movements in the 1950s by reinterpreting earlier traditions of resistance and dissent (Jamison and Eyerman 1994). Technology and science, or what Arendt called the "life of the mind," could be used and should be used for other things than waging war in Southeast Asia or in repressing freedom in the Soviet Empire. Out of the protests of the 1960s emerged new approaches to the use of technology and science. But, as in previous eras, the visions were fundamentally transformed as they came to be put into practice.

THE NEW MEN

The second half of the 1960s was a turning point in the relations between science, technology, and society, in much the same way as the Second World War is often seen as marking a turning point in the relations between science, technology, and political power. On both occasions there were fundamental shifts in the regimes of knowledge and power. The shifts in regime reflected changes in regard to agency, that is, to who is in charge of making decisions and exercising authority, and in regard to accountability, that is, the procedures by which the agents are made to take responsibility for their actions. In much the same way that agency and accountability shifted to the military and to the state in the course of the 1940s, there has been a noticeable shift during the past three decades to assigning the main authority and responsibility to the private sector and the commercial marketplace when it comes to the political appropriation of technology and science.

During the Second World War, scientists and engineers were mobilized to an extent they had never been before. They were given the resources and the opportunity to help produce more effective weapons, from radar to atom bombs and rockets, and to provide expert advice and secret intelligence that could be of value for the war effort. Even social and human scientists were engaged: anthropologists such as Ruth Benedict to help understand the enemy's way of life, and philosophers such as Herbert Marcuse to help understand the linguistic codes of the enemy. In the struggle against Nazism, all sorts of knowledge could play its part, and engineers and scientists willingly joined the fight. From an appropriation perspective, the mobilization of technology and science for war can be seen to have initiated a broader transformation of the intellectual regime, a new political contract between

TABLE 8. Changing Regimes of Power and Knowledge

	Industrial "Little Science"	Military "Big Science"	Commercial "Technoscience"
	Before WWII	*1940s–1970s*	*1980s–*
Type of Knowledge	Disciplinary	Multidisciplinary	Transdisciplinary
Organizational Form	Individuals or small research groups	R&D departments and institutions	Ad hoc projects and networks
Dominant Values	Academic	Bureaucratic	Entrepreneurial

power and knowledge. From the 1940s through the 1960s, internally derived approaches to the production of technology and science, based on disciplinary identities and academic values, were transformed into externally imposed institutional forms and bureaucratic values. As Derek de Solla Price (1963) colorfully put it, when he summarized his statistical analysis of rates of increase in money and manpower devoted to research and development, little science had given way to big science as the dominant mode of knowledge production (see Table 8).

During the past thirty years, big science has gradually given way to what Michael Gibbons and his coauthors (1994) influentially characterized as a new mode of knowledge production: a "mode 2" of technoscience that has replaced the "mode 1" of traditional, discipline-based science. Entrepreneurial and commercial values have tended to replace bureaucratic and academic values in many fields of research and development, and the ideals of knowledge have shifted from an industrial model to a postindustrial model. At the same time, technology and science have come to be organized increasingly in ad hoc projects, and temporary networks, that are determined by what Gibbons and his collaborators termed "contexts of application." One's competence as a scientist or engineer is continually combined with others in transdisciplinary undertakings. As a result, the distinction between technology and science has lost much of its meaning in many of the arenas of knowledge production in the contemporary world, particularly in the so-called fields of high technology. In a postindustrial era, a term such as *technoscience* seems to make better sense.

As we saw in chapter 4, a range of ideas were promulgated in the wake of the First World War about the political implications of the emerging technological civilization. Technocratic modernists, who believed in the powers of technology and science to transform human capacities and, for that matter, human identities, debated with those who were more skeptical to the wonders of modern technology and science. Debaters agreed that the state needed to take on new tasks, either to serve as a more effective agent of technocratic planning or to function as a cultural savior in response to the inherent nihilism of modernity. Left to the invisible hand of the commercial marketplace, technology and science were likely to cause more social problems than they solved. Left to their own internal devices, scientists would inevitably choose topics to investigate that were too narrow and did not take broader social interests sufficiently into account. There was thus a need, whether one accepted modernity or felt disenchanted by it, for the state to take on a new role in relation to the production of technology and science.

At the same time, the young Soviet Union provided ample evidence that science and technology could be significantly strengthened by state support and encouragement. The Soviet leaders propounded and sought to practice what they called "scientific socialism," which they argued was far superior to capitalism in stimulating technology and science. On the basis of a selective reading of the writings of Marx and Engels, the Soviet leaders characterized modern technology and science as the key production factors, or productive forces. But they needed to be controlled and directed by the state if they were not to become counterproductive or counterrevolutionary. During the economic depression of the 1930s, with many scientists out of work in the West, the Soviet Union exerted a strong attraction, not just on the relatively few who were card-carrying communists but also for many more progressives who felt that science and technology were not being adequately used and supported in the capitalist countries.

Although there were certain attempts to increase the resources channeled to science and technology in relation to some of the programs of sociotechnical reform that emerged in the 1930s, many progressive scientists and engineers did not think that those efforts went far enough. They were limited to specific regions, as in the case of the Tennessee Valley Authority in the United States, or to specific types of technology, as in the case of electricity distribution, which was one of the few areas where technology and science had come to be governed by public authorities. The critics claimed that public planning and coordination were inadequate, and politicians needed a better base on which to make decisions about how to spend the public funds that were allocated for science and technology.

In Britain, John Maynard Keynes developed his economic ideas urging a much stronger role for the state in managing the affairs of private industry. At the same time, a group of socially minded scientists sought to promote an increased role for the state in relation to science and technology (Werskey 1978). As John Desmond Bernal put it in his book of 1939 *The Social Function of Science,* science had become too important to be left to the whims of the commercial marketplace. Science needed to be planned and organized for the public good, and not as the case was at the present time, primarily for private gain. His book provided historical analysis, and a great deal of statistical information, about the social relations of science. Bernal argued that decisions about the funding, organization, and coordination of scientific research and technological development needed to be brought under some sort of overall political control.

Bernal was a distinguished experimental physicist, whose use of x-ray photographic techniques provided some of the crucial evidence for the double-helix model that his Cambridge colleague Francis Crick constructed with the visiting American James Watson in the 1950s. In the 1930s Bernal had already achieved the reputation as a hardworking creative scientist and a political activist, a not untypical form of hybridization during the Depression. His breadth of knowledge had earned him the nickname "Sage," and with some authority he could speak for the scientific community in suggesting that there was a need for an entirely new modus operandi for making effective use of science, another kind of political regime for appropriating facts and artifacts.

It was not until the outbreak of war, however, that politicians in the leading industrial countries began to take the call for a science policy seriously. The Manhattan Project—which led to the dropping of atom bombs on Hiroshima and Nagasaki in 1945—was only one of many initiatives taken by the belligerent governments to sponsor scientific and technological development. And even the Manhattan Project had not been decided quickly or easily by the politicians in Washington: it had been instigated by a letter sent to President Roosevelt by Albert Einstein, which had actually been written by the Hungarian refugee Leo Szilard, who feared that the Nazis were attempting to construct an atom bomb. Szilard was one of the main contributors to the fundamental research on atomic fission that had been carried out in the 1930s, and he knew that many of the scientists who were still in Germany were well informed about the possibility of making a powerful new weapon. But even after the letter was sent, it took almost two years for the project to be organized, and it proved difficult then, as now, to mix the academic approach of the scientists with the needs for secrecy and confidentiality imposed by the project's military leadership.

Radar, computing, chemical warfare, and, not least, aircraft design and strategic bombing were major areas in which technology and science were successfully mobilized for the war effort. In the process a number of new councils, committees, advisory boards, and other decision-making bodies were created, as the state took on a new role in relation to knowledge production. After the war, science policy became an established concern for politicians and national governments, and it came to be seen as an important strategic resource in the waging of the cold war. In the words of the MIT professor Vannevar Bush, who, after serving on a wartime government commission, was asked by President Roosevelt to suggest how the U.S. government should best carry out this new role, science was characterized as the new frontier. And in a typical display of hubris, the frontier that was science was considered to be "endless" (Bush 1945/1960).

The report by Bush was one of a number of proposals after the war about how the experiences of appropriating science and technology for the war effort could be applied to peaceful purposes. On the discursive level, Bush and his counterparts in other countries fashioned a strategic narrative: science should be a national priority in the world of international competition. What had been achieved on the battlefields should now be achieved in the marketplace. For strategic reasons, substantially larger public funding ought to be channeled to science and substantially more political authority should be given to scientists. In return, Bush presented a glorious vision of unimagined prosperity and wealth based on applying science to human needs, a sort of contemporary version of Bacon's *New Atlantis*. What Bernal before the war had derived from a socialist belief system and an admiration for the Soviet Union, Bush appropriated into the value system of republican government and the new frontier of global domination.

At the institutional level, a range of new research councils were created; in the United States, Bush's report led to the creation of the National Science Foundation. They were financed by public funds but largely controlled by scientists. Major research institutions were also deemed necessary, particularly to develop civilian uses of atomic energy. These state-supported facilities complemented those already established by the military and provided a new set of large-scale, multidisciplinary sites for carrying out research and development activities that neither traditional universities nor private corporations could afford. These national laboratories came to be operated along industrial lines, and it was at one such institution—at Oak Ridge, Tennessee—that the director Alvin Weinberg coined the term *big science* as a way to distinguish the kind of knowledge produced at such places from the *little science* of the past, a distinction that would then be used by academic analysts such as Derek de Solla Price (Weinberg 1967). Similar developments took place in Europe, in countries with strong, centralized governments, such as France and Sweden, and in countries such as Britain and Italy, where national laboratories in atomic energy and state ministries of science were established in the immediate postwar period.

At these institutions scientists were expected to take on new kinds of social roles, at the interface between science and society. On one hand, they were expected to take part in the policy process and serve on committees to advise politicians on scientific and technical matters. On the other hand, they were to assess applications for funding from their academic peers and disseminate their knowledge in more popular formats. Combining traditional academic values with the demands of large-scale bureaucracies proved to be easier said than done, and there was a great deal of discussion as the 1950s progressed about the resultant cultural tensions and the new kinds of hybrid identities that were being formed in the lifeworlds of big science. As they were characterized in the title of one of C. P. Snow's postwar novels, these were the "new men" who walked the corridors of power and served a new set of paymasters.

One of the main tensions concerned competing claims on the loyalty of the knowledge producers. The so-called Oppenheimer affair of the early 1950s, when J. Robert Oppenheimer, who had led the Manhattan Project, was stripped of his security clearance and his place on the Atomic Energy Commission because of his alleged contacts with communists, brought out some of the less desirable implications of the new regime. Especially in the United States, where Senator Joseph McCarthy unleashed a kind of anticommunist witch hunt, the new contract between science, technology, and the state was challenged by émigré scientists, such as Leo Szilard and Eugene Rabinowitch. They were active in starting the *Bulletin of Atomic Scientists* and initiating the Pugwash conferences, where scientists from Western Europe and North America could meet with their counterparts in the Soviet Empire. These scientific activists felt that the traditional values of internationalism and freedom of expression were threatened by the new order, and thus they planted some of the seeds that grew into the movements of the 1960s, on both sides of the iron curtain.

HUBRIS GOES INTO ORBIT

As the 1950s wore on, it became clear to politicians in the West, as well as to the general public, that for all the money being spent on science, the promises of endless prosperity were still to a large extent unfulfilled. Science certainly contributed to ever more awesome weapons of mass destruction, but the Soviets seemed to be keeping pace. Now that the

Federal Republic of Germany and Japan were rebuilt and their economic structures reestablished, many American companies were facing intensified competition. At the same time, many of the foreign scientists who had fled to the United States in the 1930s had returned home, and Americans were no longer the undisputed world leaders in all technological and scientific fields. In other capitalist countries, as well as in the Soviet Union, the state did not merely support basic research but also applied technology and science to industrial development. The shock of the *Sputnik* satellite, which the Soviets sent into orbit around the Earth in 1957, thus triggered important changes in the discourses of science and technology policy and in the practical and institutional dimensions.

For one thing, it seemed to be insufficient to support scientific research and technological development if there was not attention given to the links between them; that is, how new ideas were actually turned into new products. And for another thing, it was not enough for each country to pursue its own science and technology policies; to meet the Soviet challenge, it would be necessary to cooperate. In the 1960s the U.S. government commissioned two studies—HINDSIGHT and TRACES—that examined the relations between basic science and industrial innovation (Salomon 1977). Whereas the first study investigated what role basic research had played in the development of successful innovations, the second study asked which research programs, if any, had resulted in terms of marketable products, or spin-offs. Elsewhere, others were beginning to explore the different aspects of the innovation process, in terms of the management of projects within companies and the diffusion of innovations in society. From such studies, it was clear that technological innovations not merely were a matter of applying science but required a more sophisticated understanding of market demand and corporate selection processes.

It was also in the early 1960s that the leading industrial nations established the Organization for Economic Cooperation and Development (OECD) to help them more effectively make use of technology and science for economic growth. The OECD invited the young French philosopher Jean-Jacques Salomon to set up a division on science policy to provide a scientific basis, in terms of statistical surveys and policy analysis, for the policy makers in the member governments. Salomon went on to create a more academic Society for Science Policy Studies with colleagues in Eastern Europe and in large developing countries, such as India, as a way to create a new sort of expertise, a "science of science" that could be of interest to policy makers and to academics. What seemed to be especially important for the new hybrid men of science policy—the politicians and their expert advisors—was to begin to bring economists into the emerging sites of knowledge production, so that the crucial links between the "R" of scientific research and the "D" of technological development could be more effectively connected into an innovation chain.

In the United States the National Aeronautics and Space Administration was given the task of taking on the Soviet space challenge, but it had another, tacit purpose: stimulating technological development. What could be done openly and explicitly in other countries, namely, using the state apparatus and the organs of government to support the private sector, was, for ideological reasons, difficult to justify in the American political culture. As such, the story line of development and growth that was so central to the policy initiatives of the 1960s was couched in the United States in the grammar of space exploration, star wars, and rocketry. Hubris went into orbit.

The political discourse of economic growth and international development that began to be articulated within OECD and national governments in the 1960s was informed by academic discourses that focused, among philosophers and historians, on the conditions of scientific growth and, among economists and management scientists, on the dynamics of technological development. The central text by Thomas Kuhn, *The Structure of Scientific Revolutions,* which was published in 1962, presented science as a thoroughly social activity but, even more significantly, as an activity that had its own developmental logic or rationale. As opposed to those philosophers who had characterized science as a continuous or cumulative pursuit of truth, Kuhn presented a picture of discontinuous growth, by which science progressed not in a neat pattern of expansion but in a more cyclical pattern of paradigm shifts. Kuhn's book helped to usher in what the historian Jerome Ravetz later called "post-normal science"—or in the term used by Gernot Böhme and his collaborators in Germany, "finalized science" (Schäfer 1983). In the age of science policy, the internal development of knowledge had come to a final point: state intervention was necessary so that society could make most effective use of its technological and scientific resources.

Among economists and management consultants there emerged a similar concern with processes of growth, and with the role of technical change in longer-term patterns of economic development. A particularly influential text of the early 1960s was *The Stages of Economic Growth* by W. W. Rostow (1960), one of President Kennedy's policy advisors. Rostow argued that industrial development was something like going into space; what was crucial for a country or an industrial branch, or, for that matter, a particular company or firm, was making use of technical improvements so that production could take off into another previously unimagined dimension. That, Rostow contended, was what the English had done in their industrial revolution, and the stages that England had passed through were what developing countries needed to reproduce and emulate.

We can consider economic and scientific growth central figures of thought in the story line of development, which exerted a powerful influence over policy makers throughout the world in the 1960s. The goal was to transform modernity into an ongoing process of "modernization" and to redefine technology and science as component parts in a process, or chain of innovation, from basic research through application, or applied research, into technological and industrial development. As the economist John Kenneth Galbraith (1968) characterized it, industrial society and its corporations were no longer seeking to maximize profit and produce goods and services for which there was a recognizable demand on an identifiable market; rather, modern corporations were in the business of producing technological development and pursuing growth as an integral part of the primarily military projects of the new industrial state.

FROM PROTEST TO ASSESSMENT

In 1970 an OECD committee, headed by Harvard engineering professor Harvey Brooks, produced the report *Science, Growth and Society.* The report signaled the coming of a new era, in which the relations between science, technology, and society were to be fundamentally reconstituted, from serving the interests of a military-industrial complex to constructing what might be termed medical-commercial ensembles. It was one of the most explicit attempts to transform the critical spirit of protest that was so strong in the late 1960s into constructive new kinds of policies. The Brooks report signaled a shift of policy attention from serving what Galbraith termed the bureaucratic "technostructure" of big science to improving the relations between science, technology, and society. On a more practical level, the regime shift was characterized by a range of new hybrid identities and hybrid sites for the making of one or another kind of science and technology assessment and for the fostering of what has come to be called scientific entrepreneurship.

To facilitate these changes, a new conception emerged of the state and of the exercise of political power, from representative government to what is sometimes called "deliberative governance" (de la Mothe

2001). Rather than defining the policy task primarily in terms of national security and military defense, the state took on a somewhat more amorphous role in relation to technology and science, generating expert knowledge to diagnose the ills, or risks, that have befallen society, and encouraging the technoscientific provision of cures and remedies for those ailments. On one hand, the new regime sought to assess the consequences of technological and scientific development and, on the other hand, to redirect technology and science toward the interests of life rather than death.

There were many makers of science and technology policy who in the 1970s recognized the need for new kinds of activities and sites within the corridors of power, which could serve to mediate between the concerns of the public and the formal decision-making process (Dickson 1984). Technology assessment, as it came to be organized in the United States, was primarily an early warning system, which sought to identify the different types of social, economic, and political consequences of particular technological developments. The staff of the Office of Technology Assessment, founded in 1972, included legal and social experts and natural scientists and engineers and produced reports in a wide variety of scientific and technical fields up to its closure in 1994. Governments in Europe and international organizations instituted assessment activities, sometimes under the rubric of future studies, or futurology, and by the end of the 1970s, they had become a recognized part of the policy process. The general ambition was to provide balanced background information for policy decisions, in a variety of areas, ranging from information technology and biotechnology to energy, health and environment, and more traditional scientific fields.

In addition to these undertakings, there emerged a number of more bottom-up or grassroots initiatives. In the Scandinavian countries, there was a range of more action-oriented approaches to information technology policy, as labor federations and unions collaborated with sympathetic academics to carry out assessments of particular technical applications. Occupational health was another area that was focused on in the first phase of technology assessment in many European countries, as was the issue area that came to dominate all others as the decade progressed: energy in general and atomic energy in particular. New sites also emerged. Particularly in the Netherlands and Denmark, there were efforts made to develop participatory forms of assessment, which could play a more proactive, or constructive, role in the development of technology and science. In the Netherlands technology assessment was consolidated at an institute, named after Walter

Rathenau, whom we discussed in chapter 4, whereas in Denmark technology assessment was supported as part of the programs that were established in relation to energy technology, information technology, and biotechnology.

In Denmark the cultural tradition of popular education that had been institutionalized in the nineteenth century in the people's high schools and played an important role in the industrialization process was mobilized in the development of technology assessment. Nongovernmental organizations, and people's high schools, were brought into various assessment activities. Eventually a new method of consensus conferences was created to bring concerned citizens directly into the science and technology policy process. A state technology council was established to stage organized events at which laypeople were brought together with experts and political officials to discuss issues of public concern (Baark and Jamison 1990).

Technology assessment was only one component of a broader process of readjustment in the world of technology and science that took place in the wake of the movements of the 1960s, and what Salomon (1977) called the "period of questioning" in science policy. In the United States perhaps the most significant element was the rise of new academic subjects and university departments that grew out of the cognitive concerns of the movements. Among those that most forcefully tried to make modern technology and science accountable was the women's movement. Feminist theory emerged in the humanities and the social sciences, and, in the 1970s, female scientists and engineers began to explore the gender aspects of the natural and engineering sciences as well. Women's studies departments represented an important addition to many U.S. universities, even though they were slower to emerge in Europe and the rest of the world. And beyond women's studies, feminism or gender theories provided another dimension to the political discourses of science and technology.

The women's movement opened up new themes and topics for investigation and helped change research priorities and agendas across the entire realm of technoscience. In many technological universities, female scientists and engineers developed research programs on technologies of everyday life and on the relations between women and technology. In particular, reproductive technologies and issues related to genetic testing became an area where feminist scholars made seminal contributions (Wajcman 1991). On a more theoretical or conceptual level, feminist theorists, such as Evelyn Fox Keller, helped direct attention to the metaphors and, more generally, the linguistic conventions of science, especially in genetics (Keller 1985, 2002). The writings of

Sandra Harding and Donna Haraway have exerted a strong influence on the philosophy of science and helped bring about an awareness among philosophers to gender issues (Harding 1998). Haraway has been particularly important in conceptualizing hybrid forms of reality, or what she famously termed *cyborgs*, and for developing approaches to philosophy that attempt to break the old dichotomies between subject and object, the personal and the social, and, not least, the human and the nonhuman (Haraway 1997).

In the 1970s the view of a unified or universal science, based primarily on physics, that had dominated the theory of knowledge since the nineteenth century was challenged by what might be termed pluralism: *Science* with a capital letter became a multiplicity of *sciences*. And this was to have major significance for the politics and policy of technology and science. Throughout the world, the hegemony of the natural sciences and the leading role of physics were threatened by the emergence of new fields within the social and human sciences. Even more important, the dominant perception of Western science as the only legitimate form of knowledge production was questioned by various "ethnosciences" from other parts of the world, as well as from minorities within the industrialized, Western world.

On an institutional level, these discursive developments were complemented by the efforts to establish a new international scientific and technological order. Within the United Nations, and, in particular, the specialized agencies, such as UNESCO (United Nations Educational, Scientific and Cultural Organization) and UNDP (United Nations Development Program), representatives from the newly independent developing countries sought to redistribute the financial and human resources devoted to technology and science. To counter what was referred to as a highly deleterious "brain drain" to the industrialized world, the United Nations deemed it necessary to strengthen the technological capacity of developing countries. Throughout the 1970s, at a series of meetings and conferences, the international relations of science and technology were debated, but at the end of the decade, there was relatively little to show for the efforts.

More or less unaffected by these critical debates, a handful of developing countries joined Japan to compete with the industrialized countries in many branches of industry, particularly in information technology. These so-called newly industrializing countries—South Korea, Taiwan, and Singapore in particular—showed that it was possible to develop successful export industries, not so much by developing links to science, along the lines of the growth and development story line of the 1960s, but by focusing on particularly promising areas, and, as the

Japanese had systematically tried to do, picking the winners by means of technological forecasting (Irvine and Martin 1984).

Such selective, or market-oriented, industrialization strategies, which the West took over from Japan, broke with the doctrines that had guided science and technology policy up to the 1970s. They were driven not by security or military interests but rather by purely economic concerns. With the coming into power of conservative governments in Britain and the United States around 1980, they helped bring a new kind of commercial, or neoliberal, discourse into the world of technology and science. A market orientation came to dominate the politics of technology and science in the years to come. Especially in the biomedical field, and in the broader areas of health and agriculture, powerful alliances were created between transnational corporations and transnational organizations to reinvent knowledge in the name of life sciences.

LIFE GOES TO MARKET

During the big science era, many countries had built up sizeable research and development efforts in particular areas of biology and medicine, usually based at universities or, as in the United States, at national institutes of health. They had generally been conceived as specific missions, of which the so-called cancer mission had been the most substantial. In comparison to the mobilization of technology and science for military purposes, the support to biomedical technoscience was not subject to the same sorts of bureaucratic procedures, because there was not the same need for secrecy, surveillance, and control. Rather, it seemed more desirable to encourage cross-fertilization of scientific and technical ideas, to explore the interfaces between biology and medicine, between understanding processes of life and practicing treatment of disease.

The genetic breakthroughs of the 1950s and, in particular, the double-helix model of Watson and Crick served to catalyze this hybridization process. The scientific minded could use the code as a starting point for exploring the connections between particular kinds of genetic traits and particular kinds of diseases and plants, whereas the technically minded could try to build apparatuses by which to transfer genetic material from one organism to another. There was a clear potential relevance both for agriculture and medicine. During the 1960s molecular biology was one of the fields of science that attracted creative people who wanted to do something other than work for the military, and it was also a field that had obvious significance for many other actors—from the food industry to the health business, and especially for seed companies and pharmaceutical corporations. Some of the research carried out by university scientists in the 1960s was supported by companies interested in the results, but there were bureaucratic rules and behavioral norms that served as barriers. In particular, the rights to what has come to be called "intellectual property" were complicated: should the universities where scientists worked be able to earn money on the results of the research, or were the scientists more to be regarded as the employees of the companies?

In 1972, when a group of researchers at a public research institution in Asilomar, California, succeeded in transferring genetic material from one organism to another, thereby launching the biotechnology industry, these issues came to a head. In addition to the economic aspects, genetic engineering raised fundamental questions of ethics and morality—was it right to play God and alter the genetic composition of living beings (Goodfield 1977)? There also were risks involved and questions of laboratory safety, at least according to many of the scientists who were actively involved. How could the communities surrounding the high-risk laboratories where the research was conducted be protected from the release of genetic material into the environment? Was it dangerous to work in such laboratories? Who should set the rules for such activity? Especially in cities where research was concentrated—Cambridge, Massachusetts, in particular—local review boards were created to deal with these controversial implications of genetic engineering (Krimsky 1982).

Already by the late 1970s, however, it was clear to many observers that biotechnology had enormous economic potential, and many of the scientists involved began to establish companies where they could try to develop commercially viable products (Yoxen 1983). When Ronald Reagan was elected president, bringing with him an ideological distaste for bureaucratic rules, such entrepreneurial activity received government encouragement, as did other kinds of efforts to improve the relations between universities and industries. Some universities created offices for technology transfer and hired patent lawyers, and biotechnology companies joined information technology companies at the new science parks that became a recognizable feature of many university towns. As a sort of Silicon Valley fever spread around the world in the 1980s, biotechnology companies in these hybrid sites became one of the main areas where the new regime of power and knowledge was put into place (Rogers and Larsen 1985). In many European countries there were state-support programs for biotechnology research and development, and, as with information technology, technology assessment and foresight activities increasingly focused on these new areas of high technology.

In the 1990s there were many attempts to clone Silicon Valley, as David Rosenberg put it, not least in the expansive newly industrializing countries of Asia (Rosenberg 2002). The international diffusion of cellular telephones and other communications technologies contributed to an intensification of contacts between universities and technology firms and to an increase in attention to entrepreneurship and other aspects of knowledge management and product development. The story line of economic innovation became the dominant narrative trope of the high-tech culture, and in some of the newcomers, such as Finland and Singapore, a kind of hypermodernism developed in relation to design and architecture. In Finland and other high-user sites, the Internet also became a health problem, as young users found themselves addicted to it, in much the same way as earlier generations had become addicted to drugs.

From the mid-1990s onward, several biotechnological products began to reach the marketplace, in the food and health areas, ushering in a new stage in the multifarious processes of cultural appropriation. In the words of Dorothy Nelkin and M. Susan Lindee (1995), the gene became a "cultural icon," the focal point of enormous public and media attention—as well as stimulating the formation of hybrid identities and institutions, from genetic counselors to ethical councils and consensus conferences. With these efforts, the world of policy making and the broader policy discourse has tried to accommodate the concerns of the public, particularly in terms of ethical and moral aspects of genetic engineering. And as cultural icons, genetics, and genetic technologies have fostered a wide variety of artistic appropriation in science-fiction films and stories and in such serious literature as Margaret Atwood's critical novel *Oryx and Crake*.

The cultural appropriation of biotechnology has been highly contested. In many parts of the world, not least in developing countries, there has been a great amount of criticism of the new, genetically modified products, particularly in relation to food and agriculture, whereas the medical applications have generally but not universally been received more positively. As with many other drugs and clinical treatments, genetically engineered medications were shaped by a new set of social relations and new networks of interaction between universities, business, and government. Medical technology and life sciences became big business under the control of the large biotechnology companies, such as Monsanto and Dow Chemical. And yet, in a curious way, for all of the new cures and remedies, artificial plants and hybrid foods, the majority of the people who populate the planet are not healthier or, for that matter, less hungry. Rather, as is the case in many other areas, biomedical and agricultural technologies, or techno-sciences, are extremely skewed in their appropriation (Shiva 2000). As with the green revolution, the new seed varieties have mostly come to benefit those who are already well off, whereas in the medical field, those who are most in need cannot afford to be treated, as pharmaceutical companies produce ever more drugs directed to those who can afford to buy them.

At the same time, the very health of science and technology, according to many knowledgeable observers, is threatened by this process of commercialization (Krimsky 2003). In breaking down the boundaries between an academic culture devoted to a disinterested pursuit of truth and an economic culture devoted to a vested interest in particular applications of truth, technology and science and their traditional home, the university, have become fully embedded into a regime that some social scientists refer to as the "knowledge society" (Stehr 1994). In the words of Derek Bok (2003, 207), former president of Harvard,

> Commercialization threatens to change the character of the university in ways that limit its freedom, sap its effectiveness, and lower its standing in the society. … The problems come so gradually and silently that their link to commercialization may not even be perceived. Like individuals who experiment with drugs, therefore, campus officials may believe that they can proceed without serious risk.

In the contemporary regime of power and knowledge, hubris goes under the name of globalization, extending its reach into ever more domains of public and private life. Everywhere we go we can eat the same hamburgers, we can buy the same drugs, and, for that matter, we can see and hear the same technologically enhanced forms of entertainment.

The regime has proved remarkably resilient and has shown itself to be extremely difficult to challenge. There are movements of opposition that have begun to react to the most visible manifestations: McDonald's hamburger stores have been attacked, fields of genetically manipulated soybeans have been destroyed, animals confined in laboratory cages have been released, and the stem cells of human beings have been defended from commercial exploitation. And yet the greedy grasping of the globalizers goes on, continually opening up new frontiers, new bridgeheads for the combinations of fear and fantasy that make up the main streams of contemporary life—real and imagined, actual and virtual.

Transnational organizations, be they intergovernmental or nongovernmental, have been charged with the task of making the regime politically accountable, as national governments have sold their rights to govern to the market, as simply one more form of intellectual property. Appropriate forms of global governance have yet to take hold, as the potential agents—whether at the United Nations and the European Union or among the so-called nongovernmental organizations—are either incorporated into the dominant culture of transnational capitalism or captured by the traditional cultures of the victims and the losers.

In the following chapter we suggest that the hybrid discourses, identities, and institutions that might one day be able to restrain the hubris of globalization have begun to emerge within the quest for what has been termed "sustainable development." Whether we call them environmental movements or subpolitical networks, a wide range of contemporary critics of technology and science have been making forms of green knowledge out of which an alternative to the commercial regime of knowledge and power might eventually be fostered. Whereas many of them have succumbed to the temptations of the dominant culture, others have sought to connect the ecological to the social and, in the quest for sustainable development, to begin to link environmental concerns to those of global justice and solidarity. It is to the historical trajectory of this emerging ecological culture and to the dialectics of environmentalism that we turn our attention.

development project. Like everything about the Tvind schools, the wind power plant was built for highly ideological reasons, although there was the practical ambition, as well, to provide electricity for the schools and the neighboring village. It was built to show that wind energy was a viable alternative to fossil fuels and to atomic energy, which at the time large numbers of the Danish population were opposed to quite vociferously. The plant was also built to show that advanced technology could be made by amateurs, by the "people" (Jamison 1978).

Although the first message—that wind energy was viable—came to be accepted by the majority of the Danish population, and by people throughout the world, during the ensuing decades, the second message came to be challenged. Indeed, it was challenged already at the time, when it was disclosed that much of the design and construction work that was involved in the Tvind mill had been carried out by experts at the Technological University in Copenhagen, not by local amateur technicians. Still, the populist idea that the people knew more than experts has remained strong in Denmark. In 2002 a liberal-populist government appointed the self-proclaimed environmentalist Bjørn Lomborg, who admitted to knowing very little about environmental science and technology, director of a Danish state-sponsored institute for environmental assessment. His main qualification was the diatribe against environmental experts that he had published the year before in Britain and the United States, *The Skeptical Environmentalist* (2001).

The stories of Tvind and Lomborg encapsulate a good deal of the processes by which environmentalism—and the vision of a sustainable technology and science—has come to be appropriated into Danish society. Emerging as an integral part of the student protests of the 1960s and 1970s, the environmental movement was transformed in the ensuing decades into a number of acceptable, and often profitable, forms of green business, such as wind energy and organic agriculture. In the course of its short history, the movement also came to be subjected to a kind of ideological corruption. According to their original propaganda, the Tvind schools aimed at starting a revolution and, in particular, transferring some of the teachings and experiences from Mao Tse-tung's Great Proletarian Cultural Revolution from China to the Danish countryside. But what was not known at the time was that the Tvind teachers—and all the other teachers who worked at the many other schools and companies that were set up in the so-called Tvind Empire—were pooling their salaries and giving most of them away to their charismatic leader Amdi Pedersen. Lomborg, on the other hand, launched a profitable media career by articulating a widely felt skepticism toward environmentalism on the part of many Danes, especially those in the rural areas, who saw their way of life, and not least their livelihoods based on chemically dependent agriculture, threatened by new-fangled environmental experts.

THE PROFESSOR PROTESTS

In neighboring Norway, at about the same time that the Tvind mill was starting to produce electricity, a man in his late sixties was practicing civil disobedience on behalf of the environmental cause. He made an unlikely activist, but there he was, demonstrating with hundreds of others at a construction site, trying to stop the building of a hydroelectric dam on the Alta River in the far northern reaches of the country. Arne Næss had been an internationally renowned professor of philosophy at the University of Oslo, but he was also a passionate mountaineer and a longtime admirer of Mahatma Gandhi, and that combination of interests helped turn him into an environmental activist in the 1970s and join in the protests at Alta (Eyerman 1994).

The Alta struggle was a major political event in Norway and a moment of transition for the environmental movement, which, as elsewhere, had reached a significant societal presence by 1980, when the confrontation took place. The conflict at Alta was the most important battle in public between the ruling Social Democratic government, with its strong commitment to the industrial exploitation of natural resources, and a loosely organized alliance of activists seeking to defend certain regions and their resources from being exploited. The protests brought to a climax a decade of active opposition to the government's plans to build hydroelectric dams on some of the previously untouched northern rivers, and it proved to be a turning point in the life cycle of the environmental movement. In the 1980s many of the movement's members left protesting behind in pursuit of more constructive types of activity, carrying the environmentalist cause into other social forums: government, universities, and even the business world.

The Norwegian shade of green politics was fueled by the campaign against European integration, which in the early 1970s had mobilized a majority of the population to vote against joining the European Economic Community, as the European Union was then called. Rather than continuing on the path of science-based economic development and the further expansion of industry, which the European project seemed to imply, Norwegian environmentalists envisioned an alternative development path instead. They called for a more small-scale or appropriate technology that could fit into the decentralized and largely self-contained structure of the Norwegian economy. Their calls for a more holistic and experiential science resonated well in a country where the active enjoyment of nature played a large role in many people's identities. In the course of the 1970s, an environmental consciousness had served to awaken interest in alternative ideas and techniques for interacting with nature, as part of a collective effort to create a more ecological society.

Although by 1980 the protection of the environment had grown into a worldwide concern, protests and debates followed different trajectories in different countries. In Norway the main struggles were directed toward hydroelectric power plants and the erection of oil platforms in sensitive waters. In Germany and Sweden campaigns against atomic energy played a major role, as in the United States, whereas in a country such as France this was almost a taboo topic. The peaceful use of atomic energy had been one of the main symbols of postwar science-based progress and one of the highest priorities of postwar science and technology policy on both sides of the iron curtain. In relation to atomic energy, there were the direct, short-term dangers from possible explosions and accidents, as well as the longer-term dangers associated with the disposal of waste products from the plants. There were also political dangers, because atomic energy required a range of experts and forms of decision making that were difficult to control with established democratic means. In its large-scale and centralized character, atomic energy epitomized the new forms of political power that had accompanied postwar scientific and technological progress. For the political scientist Langdon Winner (1980), atomic energy proved that artifacts "have politics." Winner's contention was that the development of large-scale technological projects embodied the political values and commitments of those who planned and designed them.

Opposing the further development of atomic energy and proposing ecological alternatives had helped to forge a sense of collective identity among those who questioned the dominant discourses of socioeconomic development in general and the dominant policy doctrines for the development of technology and science in particular. The energy debates of the 1970s served to bring environmental concern out of the margins and into the mainstream of political and social life. Almost as soon as it had been established, however, that sense of collective identity started to dissipate. The broad social movements and mass mobilizations that had been formed proved to be short-lived and difficult to sustain. But many of their ideas and practices came to be appropriated in the ensuing decades by more established social actors and institutions.

The dam at Alta was eventually built, and the protesters went home. In Norway, as elsewhere, people started to drift away from active involvement in the environmental movement, but the struggle was certainly not forgotten. As in other countries where the atomic energy issue was resolved by phasing out further development and thereby removing the issue from the political agenda—or in Sweden and Austria by means of referenda—the ecological critique of technology and science that had been articulated did not disappear in Norway. The minister of the environment at the time, a medical doctor named Gro Harlem Brundtland, who had defended the construction plans, went on to become prime minister and later head a UN commission on environment and development. The commission became identified with the doctrine of "sustainable development" that was widely disseminated around the world when the commission published its report *Our Common Future* in 1987. Some of the Sami people, who had joined with the young and old protesters from the cities, entered into alliances with indigenous peoples in other parts of the world to see to it that the Alta struggle would not have to be replicated, at least not in northern Scandinavia. Like Native Americans and other indigenous groups, the Sami people went on to develop their own cultural identity—in their case, with schools, literature, music, and not least technological aids appropriate for their primary economic activity of reindeer herding: snowmobiles and improved forms of meat distribution. And Arne Næss continued, as a sort of learned elder in the ensuing decades, to contribute to the spreading of a worldwide environmental consciousness.

In an article written in 1973, Næss coined a phrase that has since become one of the more popular terms used by radical environmentalists as their ideas have come to be appropriated—and, to a large extent, diluted—by the surrounding society during the past thirty years. It was necessary, Næss wrote, to develop a "deep ecology"—a more profound way of thinking about the environment that could counter the superficial ways of thinking that, then as now, were so prevalent. He argued that the environmental challenge either could be met by means of instrumental measures and policies—which inevitably proved to be insufficient; that was what he termed "shallow" ecology—or could be met by thinking harder about the nature of environmental problems and developing a more ecological way of life (Næss 1973).

For Næss, as for many other "fundamentalists," as they came to be called in Germany, who took part in the oppositional movements of the 1970s, environmental problems had moral and material dimensions. Not only was the problem the increased amounts of waste and pollution that accompanied mass consumption, or the intensified exploitation of nonrenewable energy sources and other natural resources that was an intrinsic part of industrial development, but it was also a moral or spiritual problem, due to the dominance in modern societies of a particular mind-set, a science-driven technological or instrumental rationality: what Herbert Marcuse in the 1960s influentially characterized as "one-dimensional thought" (Marcuse 1964). Technological development and mass consumption had become surrogate religions, which lacked effective public control and thereby threatened the survival of other approaches to knowledge and the natural environment.

It was not enough, Næss contended, to develop techniques for controlling pollution and making more efficient use of energy and other resources to "save the earth," as a popular slogan ran in those days. It was also crucially important to question the dominant assumptions about humanity's relations to nature and to think deeply about the overall consequences of continuous science-based technological expansion. It was also necessary to formulate alternative, ecological criteria and procedures for pursuing science and engineering, which respected the integrity of the nonhuman world and the moral responsibilities of humankind in relation to sustaining the life-support systems of the planet.

A year later, in a book that was first published in English in 1989 as *Ecology, Community and Lifestyle,* Næss suggested that traditional philosophical ideas about solidarity and community, as well as about nature and science, needed to be reexamined in the light of the environmental crisis. He proposed the concept of "species egalitarianism" as a central element in the ecophilosophy that he outlined in the book to designate the idea that humans should think of themselves as equal, and by no means superior, to all the other species with which we share the planet. The exploitative attitude to nature, which had been the worldview of modern technology and science since the seventeenth century, needed to be replaced by an ecological or systemic worldview. Like other ecological thinkers, Næss criticized the reductionism of modern science, the dominant tendency of scientists to break nature down into its fundamental elements, be it particles, genes, molecules, or individual organs. And he discussed the need for more holistic ways of thinking about, and interacting with, nature that focused attention on other units of analysis: systems, communities, patterns, and life cycles.

It has been a seesaw struggle ever since, as the ideas and practices, the philosophies and the politics of environmentalism have come to be appropriated for different purposes in different settings. For most people, environmental concern has been seen primarily as something to incorporate into already established institutional and cognitive frameworks, scientific disciplines and legal procedures. For others, who periodically mount campaigns against environmental protection, the ideas and practices of environmentalism have been portrayed as dangerous transgressions from civilized behavior, and environmentalism has given rise to many "backlashes" from defenders of established ideologies and ways of life, not least from those in positions of power (Beder 1997). As Lomborg argued, the environment should be protected in such a way that "we can get the most environment for our money." Applying the traditional methods of cost accounting to attack every conceivable environmental proposal, Lomborg claimed that most of the money spent on environmental protection could be much better spent for other things (Lomborg 2001).

And yet, for all the newfound friends and old-fashioned foes who have come along during the decades to try to take it over or bring it down, an environmental consciousness continues to embed itself in our societies and impinge itself on our identities. We have become familiar with terms derived from ecology and other environmental sciences; words such as *biosphere, ecosystem, energy efficiency, biodiversity,* and *sustainability* have become part of a normal educated person's vocabulary. A wide range of professional roles, academic careers, and business opportunities now exist for people who take environmental concern seriously. Environmental protection agencies and environmental interest organizations have become fixtures of public life, even though there are those who would like to turn back the clock and act as if the environmental movement had never existed.

At an institutional level, environmental concern has become a part of our decision-making and administrative structures. International negotiations and agreements over such matters as biodiversity and climate change are routine political events, whereas efforts to "green" industry and apply environmental criteria into planning and governance procedures are fostered by governmental and intergovernmental bodies. In practical terms most universities now have departments or centers for environmental science, and most technological universities have projects and sometimes even degree programs in environmental management, as well as more traditional forms of environmental engineering. In recent years, many business firms, in such branches as cosmetics, household appliances, home furnishings, and apparel, as well as in food and agriculture, have sought to prevent waste and pollution from their production processes. Some have even tried to develop green, or ecological, products. And as consumers around the world have become concerned with the environmental quality of the products they purchase, elaborate labeling systems have been established to provide ecological seals of approval on many consumer items. It is this uneven, and still highly unfinished, process of cultural appropriation that we trace in this chapter.

A CRITIQUE FROM WITHIN

The idea of protecting something called the "environment" emerged in the course of the 1960s, as a fourth long wave of economic growth and expansion began to draw to a close (see chapter 2). As had been the case with the previous waves, when the slowing down in rates of productivity and in the so-called diffusion of innovations was accompanied by the rise of new social actors and issues, the environmental debate represented a broad societal assessment of technology and science. The emergence of environmentalism was an intrinsic part of a critical evaluation in public of the dominant ideas and practices of socioeconomic development and of the ways in which technoscience was carried out (Jamison 2001).

The initial environmental debate in the 1960s took place primarily in the United States and the countries of northern Europe, which were the leading industrial powers of the time and whose chemical and automotive industries had perhaps benefited most from the kinds of technological and scientific advances that had characterized the fourth wave of industrialization. In those countries there had been a growing awareness, throughout the postwar economic boom, that the kinds of development that were taking place had some serious and rather problematic side effects (Mishan 1969). It was also in those countries that there were discursive and institutional frameworks, particularly in relation to nature conservation, that could provide congenial cultural contexts for addressing the new kinds of environmental problems. In other countries, particularly those of southern and eastern Europe, as well as in most of the so-called developing world, an environmental consciousness was more of an import item, and this affected the subsequent processes of appropriation in terms of timing and substance. Other idea traditions were mobilized, and other kinds of hybrid identities were created. But when the oil price increases of 1973 and 1974 helped give environmental issues a central political importance throughout the world, all countries were forced to find ways to take on the environmental challenge.

At the outset environmentalism represented the articulation, or identification, by scientists, public officials, nature lovers, and a good many concerned citizens of a new range of problems for science, technology, and society to try to solve. In certain places the air had begun to take on the appearance of a permanent haze, or smog, due primarily to emissions of exhaust fumes from automobiles, and there were calls in some of the most afflicted places, particularly Los Angeles, for new approaches in policy making and technological development to control the pollution. In other areas, the water was so contaminated that fish were beginning to wash up dead on the shores, and there were those who called for harsher laws and more effective technologies so that rivers and lakes could support life once again. In countless other places, where the chemicals that were used in agriculture were spreading unintentionally across the landscape, the coming of the spring, in Rachel Carson's telling metaphor, had become ominously silent (Carson 1962). An organic, or ecological, approach to agriculture—what Carson termed "the road not taken"—was called for. In general terms, the modern world had become afflicted with a new set of ailments, the side effects of science-based prosperity and affluence: an environmental crisis.

The specific problems had not, of course, emerged all of a sudden. Smog had been a matter of concern in Los Angeles before the Second World War, and water pollution and waste had been a component part of industrialization from the very beginning. What had changed were the scale, intensity, and proliferation of environmental deterioration. The range of problems had increased, but perhaps, even more serious, the worsening environmental situation seemed to be systemic, an integral feature of the scientification of production that took place in the postwar era. The vocabulary that had been appropriate for comprehending and dealing with specific, delimited problems needed therefore to be replaced by more generic and systemic concepts. Rather than there being particular instances of waste and pollution in our surroundings, there was now an all-encompassing environment that needed to be protected. As the biochemist Barry Commoner put it in his book *Science and Survival,*

In the past, the risks taken in the name of technological progress ... were restricted to a small place and a short time. The new hazards are neither local nor brief. ... At the same time the permissible margin for error has become very much reduced. ... Modern science and technology are simply too powerful to permit a trial-and-error approach. (Commoner 1966, 32)

Environmentalism first emerged as an open-ended process of public education. It was, to a large extent, the popular writings of scientists— Rachel Carson, Barry Commoner, Paul Ehrlich, Georg Borgström, and others like them—that served as catalysts in the formation of the environmental movement. And it was the internalization of the crisis into their identities, and into the identities of many of those who read their books, that established the new, hybrid identity of the environmental activist. These were natural scientists exercising what they took to be their social responsibility, and in addition to writing popular books, they also created new kinds of institutional sites for public information and counterexpertise. Unlike previous critics of technology and science, who had served to initiate processes of cultural appropriation, the pioneering environmentalists were insiders rather than outsiders, professional scientists and science writers rather than rebels. They did not object to science and technology as such, and they did not challenge the rigorous methods of scientific inquiry or the importance of technological ingenuity for dealing with social problems; what they objected to was the direction, the dominant path, that technoscience had taken.

After the Second World War, scientific research, and the technological applications of scientific research, had come to play an increasingly important role for economic development. As Carson and Commoner showed in their writings, however, many of these science-based products had dangerous consequences, in that they could not be effectively used or recycled into natural patterns. They became waste, or pollution, and, as such, they caused diseases for humans and nonhumans and serious disruptions in natural processes. By seeking to replace natural products with artificial ones, and by trying to tap into previously unused resources and sources of energy, scientific and technological hubris had come to threaten what came to be termed the "carrying capacity" of the planet.

In the late 1960s and early 1970s, a worldwide environmental movement carved out a space in society for developing alternative approaches to science and technology. There were grassroots engineering activities that went under the name of appropriate, alternative, or radical technology (Pursell 1993; Harper and Boyle 1976). And there were places in which these ideas and practices could be learned and disseminated: local action groups, amateur workshops, new organizations and magazines, production collectives, and even some university departments or environmental programs. Among other things, the environmental movement served to translate a scientific terminology into socioeconomic discourses; the holistic concepts of systems ecology inspired political programs, according to which an ecological worldview was to govern social and political interactions. Technology was to be developed under the general perspective that "small is beautiful," as E. F. Schumacher (1973) put it, with the underlying assumption that large-scale, environmentally destructive projects were to be opposed and stopped.

In the course of the 1980s and 1990s, the environmental movement was decomposed into a disparate cluster of organizations and individuals, networks and companies, academic fields and consulting firms. It was transformed into various kinds of professions and institutions, on one hand, and disenchanted critics and countercritics, on the other. Parts of the movement's ideas and practices were incorporated into the established culture, as green parties entered parliaments and even governments, and some of the alternative technical projects proved commercially viable—organic agriculture and wind energy, in particular. More generally, in the name of sustainable development, environmental ideas came to be appropriated by business interests and by established scientific disciplines. And the hybrid identities that had started to be formed in the 1960s—the activist scientist (e.g., Commoner), the scientific generalist (e.g., Næss), the amateur engineers at places such as Tvind, the poetic biologist (e.g., Carson)—were transformed into more socially acceptable professional roles and identities: environmental managers in companies, green product developers, industrial ecologists, and green party politicians.

We can trace the cultural appropriation of environmentalism through three main phases, by which the ideas and practices that were originally formulated in the 1960s have come to be embedded into our societies and economies. In each phase there were contending approaches, or strategies. Some people have sought to incorporate environmental concern into the dominant institutional and discursive frameworks, whereas others have sought to use the environmental cause primarily to further other political or social interests. Still others have sought to stay true to the original visions and ambitions and develop synthetic forms of appropriation. As we recount the conflicts and contentions over environmentalism, we should remember that this is a history that is still very much in the making and that the processes that we are discussing are ongoing and thus remain uncertain in their meanings and implications (see Table 9).

PHASE ONE: PUBLIC EDUCATION

Environmentalist consciousness had at least three main sources. In other words, there were at least three different traditions that came to be combined and reinvented in the environmental movement: nature conservation, scientific ecology, and human geography. They had

TABLE 9. The Cultural Appropriation of Environmentalism

Phase One: 1960s
Public education, making a movement
Criticizing technoscience
Phase Two: 1970s–1980s
Institution building, the greening of politics
Appropriate technology
Phase Three: 1990s–
Professionalization, green business
Environmental innovation and marketing

developed independently from each other in the course of the nineteenth and twentieth centuries and had formed separate sorts of discourses, institutions, and practices in previous stages of appropriation. Environmentalism drew on these traditions while simultaneously transforming them into a new kind of composite, or hybrid culture, bringing together the compassion of the conservationist, the rigor of the ecologist, and the exploratory methods of the geographer.

The tradition of nature preservation and resource conservation had emerged as part of earlier critiques of technology and science. In the romantic revolt, a kind of organized "nature loving" had developed among biologists and artists, as well as among people who simply found city life too constraining and chaotic. As we discussed in chapter 2, Henry David Thoreau sought to create a romantic science, based on what he called true Indian wisdom, and throughout the nineteenth century, adventurers and aesthetes followed the call of the wild and, in theory and practice, invented a tradition of nature admiration that inspired the establishment of institutions and organizations for the conservation, or protection, of nature. The Scottish immigrant John Muir was one important source of inspiration, as he founded a club to fight to save particularly beautiful parts of the Sierra Mountains in California from further exploitation. In other countries the example of the Sierra Club were emulated, and the establishment of special agencies within national administrations to protect natural resources and administer nature reserves and national parks also spread from the United States to other parts of the world.

The science of ecology also had emerged in the nineteenth century, but its roots went further back, to the systematic biologists and, in particular, the Swedish taxonomist Carl Linnaeus. Ecology became the science of the productive relationships in nature—a "nature's economy," as it was referred to in the early part of the twentieth century, when Charles Elton developed the concept of "ecosystem" to characterize the specific forms of producer-consumer relations that existed among plants and animals (Worster 1977). In the 1940s and 1950s, a more technocratic form of ecology was created in the United States, by which a cybernetic language of feedback mechanisms and energy flows was applied to Elton's ecosystems, and there were efforts among ecologists to simulate the relations that existed in the natural world in the laboratory, and eventually on computers. The main proponents of this systems ecology, the brothers Howard and Eugene Odum, brought their ideas to the public and to the larger society in a number of writings in the 1960s (Söderqvist 1986).

Finally, there was a geographical tradition, or, more generally, a tradition of exploration, with deep roots in the modern culture that was mobilized in the making of an environmental consciousness. Trodding in the footpaths of explorers, geographers had developed methods of regional surveying, and they had created physical and cognitive maps that were essential tools for environmental protection and the still emerging professions of environmental management and environmental planning. But even more important perhaps was the discursive framework that geography, and, for that matter, urban planning, provided for the fledgling movement, especially the idea of "human ecology," which had previously been used by some sociologists, anthropologists, and historians. Human ecologists, such as the cultural historian Lewis Mumford and the urban sociologist Robert Park, had been among the first to consider the relations between nature and society in practical and theoretical terms.

The seeds of what grew into an environmental movement had been planted in the 1940s by some of the leading figures in these older idea traditions, such as Aldo Leopold, Julian Huxley, and Fairfield Osborn. The new environmentalism differed from the older traditions, however, in terms of the specific issues being addressed and the ways in which they were discussed. Particularly important was the recognition that the exploitation of natural resources and the destruction of the nonhuman world had taken on enormous proportions during and after the Second World War. Fairfield Osborn, director of the New York Zoological Society and founder of the Conservation Foundation, referred to the new situation as "man's war with nature" in his book *Our Plundered Planet*, which came out in 1948, and in the course of the 1950s, the particular weapons of that warfare became ever more refined and the damage ever more visible. In a very real sense, nature had ceased to exist as a realm of reality outside of human intervention.

The new challenges reached a broader public primarily through the eloquent prose of the biologist-turned-science-writer Rachel Carson. She portrayed the situation in words that were familiar to anyone who had taken a walk in the woods or felt the slightest sympathy for the health of the natural environment. "Over increasingly large areas of the United States," she wrote, "spring now comes unheralded by the return of the birds, and the early mornings are strangely silent where once they were filled with the beauty of bird song" (Carson 1962, 97). She had already found an audience in her books of the 1950s, *The Edge of the Sea* and *The Sea around Us,* in which she had mixed some environmental reporting into her natural history, but in *Silent Spring,* the book that she published the year before she died, she managed to establish what came to be the environmental movement's characteristic form of expression: reasoned and impassioned, objective and engaged. It was by critically evaluating the consequences of specific instances of industrialized science, as Carson did in her book with the chemical insecticides used in agriculture, that the environmentalist critique was able to reach a wider audience and create a new venue for collective identity formation. Carson's achievement, her cultural innovation, was to direct the analytical methods of science against the projects of technoscience.

We can think of the 1960s primarily as a period of public education, a time when people were made familiar with the new problems, and a time when at least some people internalized the problems and their solutions by becoming environmentalists; that is, by changing their identities. What was involved was the dissemination, through the media, of a new range of issues and eventually the emergence of a more all-encompassing ecological critique. As the awareness about the problems grew, the dimensions of the perceived dangers also grew, so that by the late 1960s when Paul Ehrlich published *The Population Bomb,* a kind of doomsday mentality had taken shape, giving the problems not only an urgency that they had previously not had but also a political importance that even Carson could never have imagined. A cluster of new societal problems was identified, from chemical risks to automotive air pollution, which gave rise to widespread public debates and eventually to a number of policy responses.

By the early 1970s there had emerged a range of new activist groups, such as Friends of the Earth, which David Brower, the director of the Sierra Club, created as a way to challenge what he had come to see as the conservatism of the older organization. There was, as well, a process of policy reform and institution building. Most of the industrialized countries established state agencies to deal with environmental protection, and environmental research and technological development were organized in new locations in the private and public sectors. Many national parliaments enacted more comprehensive environmental legislation, and the UN Conference on the Human Environment in Stockholm in 1972 brought the issue area into the intergovernmental arena.

The manned landing on the moon in 1969 had provided the symbol for the Stockholm conference, the blue planet viewed from space: small, fragile, and strikingly beautiful in its shape and color. Biologist René Dubos and economist Barbara Ward collaborated on the book *Only One Earth* that set the conference agenda.

Now that mankind is in the process of completing the colonization of the planet, learning to manage it intelligently is an urgent imperative. Man must accept responsibility for the stewardship of the earth. … The planet is not yet a centre of rational loyalty for all mankind. But possibly it is precisely this shift of loyalty that a profound and deepening sense of our shared and inter-dependent biosphere can stir to life in us. (Ward and Dubos 1972, 25, 298)

In the early 1970s a range of initiatives was taken to put the emerging environmental consciousness into practice. In the United States a group of self-proclaimed "new alchemists" moved from the university out to the country to experiment with organic agriculture and renewable energy technology. In many European countries projects in alternative or radical technology were conducted at production collectives, people's high schools, and movement research centers. Like the windmill builders at Tvind, they were trying to turn the enthusiasm and engagement of amateurs into new forms of appropriate technology. Among UN agencies, this became an important priority area, and in a country such as India, an extensive network of local workshops developed in the countryside, showing, in George MacRobie's (1981) words, that "small is possible." In retrospect, we can see that the environmental movement opened a public space for experimentation with collective engineering in relation to energy, agriculture, housing, and transportation. The particular technical interests have diffused widely into society, whereas the collective creativity has largely dissipated.

The first phase of appropriation was also characterized by efforts, on the part of established scientific and technological experts, to develop more sophisticated techniques of pollution control and waste treatment. Environmental protection became, throughout the industrialized world, a new sector for scientific research and technological development, and departments of environmental studies were founded at many universities. The environmental challenge was thus appropriated in a variety of ways, or according to a number of different strategies or approaches along a continuum from incremental, so-called end-of-pipe approaches at one extreme to the more radical, alternative approaches to technology and science among movement activists on the other. These tensions became exacerbated by the oil crisis in the winter of 1973.

PHASE TWO: POLITICIZATION

It was the raising of oil prices by the Organization of Petroleum Exporting Countries (OPEC) that served to alter the character of the processes of cultural appropriation. For one thing, the oil crisis propelled energy issues and especially nuclear energy to the center of politics and public debate throughout the world. For another thing, the dramatic increase in the cost of oil mobilized interest in alternative, renewable sources of energy and in techniques of energy conservation. A wide range of expertise—in fields ranging from energy planning to nuclear reactor safety and solar heating—was suddenly in demand, and the broader social and political implications of energy and resource use were also subjected to ambitious research and analysis. In Denmark renewable energy experimentation, particularly wind power, became a social movement of its own and fairly quickly led to new industrial firms and major government funding programs.

In general terms the energy debates served to professionalize and institutionalize environmental concerns and contribute to a differentiation of roles and identities within the fledgling environmental movement. New scientific disciplines and subdisciplines developed in relation to energy and environmental issues: energy systems analysis, human ecology, environmental studies, environmental history, and even environmental economics. In the Netherlands, environmental science became an established discipline at several universities, and national research funding programs provided support for new departments and research institutes. Environmental research tended to become a sector of its own within the broader systems of research and development. As a result of these developments, many of the academic scientists, who had been active in the formation of new groups and organizations, as well as in the broader dissemination of environmental concern in the initial stages, eventually drifted away from activism, as opportunities for professional research careers opened up at universities and in government and industry.

The environmental movement was, as such, a temporary, short-lived phenomenon. As a popular front, or campaign, against nuclear energy, the different idea traditions that had been mobilized in the 1960s could be combined for a time. But the integrative *cognitive praxis*—with a visionary ecological philosophy guiding a range of practical experiments in settings that were largely outside of the formalized organizational frameworks—did not remain intact (Eyerman and Jamison 1991). For a brief time, the movement provided an organized learning experience, in which theory and practice were combined in pursuit of a common goal. When the issues that had inspired the movement seemed to have been resolved, the different component parts of the movement tended to split apart and fragment.

In India and other parts of the third world, protests against hydro-electric dams, industrial forestry projects, and the so-called green revo-lution in agriculture forged new connections between scientists, engineers, and local populations, as the environmental consciousness was appropriated into a very different set of cultural contexts. In the opposition to the Silent Valley dam, a "people's science movement" came into being, whereas in the Chipko movement, in the foothills of the Himalayas, a local ecology of diversified resource use was pitted against the monocultural, managerial ecology of professional forestry. These new forms of environmentalism were difficult to contain within one and the same movement. While the environmental movement was growing, expanding, and diversifying, the seeds were being sewn for a kind of fragmentation process that would become ever more noticeable and apparent as the 1980s progressed.

The 1980s also brought with them an ideological shift, a veritable counterrevolution in many of the leading industrial nations. "Thatch-erism" in Britain and "Reaganomics" in the United States represented the most visible manifestations of a neoliberal corporate offensive, which opposed much of the substantive program of environmentalism and the other new social movements, such as the women's movement. In regard to science, technology, and the environment, neoliberalism led to a more explicitly economic orientation. A new language of deregulation, market liberalization, and strategic research—and new programs that stressed the importance of university–industry col-laboration and academic entrepreneurship—came to replace societal relevance and technology assessment. The broad public space that environmentalists had carved out was thereby circumscribed and con-strained, and the ambitions to produce an alternative knowledge and an alternative approach to politics were significantly reduced in scope. What began to emerge instead was a new kind of professional environ-mentalism, in business and government, as well as in the environ-mental movement, as the neoliberal ideology spread into the broader society.

Like technoscience, environmentalism was transformed for better or worse into more commercial activities. Many former activists set themselves up in business, creating consulting firms or small companies that specialized in new market niches, such as energy conservation, waste recycling, ecological construction and design, and environmental impact assessment. By 1981 several of the Danish wind energy companies had created their own interest organization, and the government was providing financial and technical support to what was to grow into a highly successful industrial branch. Wind technology was a particularly good example of how alternative visions came to be realized by more commercially minded actor-networks. By making it possible for people to invest in and thereby share the ownership of local wind energy plants and by making arrangements so that the power that was generated could be easily connected to the already established energy distribution networks, Danish policy makers created an exemplary story of cultural appropriation (Jamison et al. 1990). Compared with other countries, such as Germany and Sweden, where large wind energy plants had encountered economic and technical problems and even cultural resistance from those who had vested interests in other types of energy technology, wind energy in Denmark became a national object

Figure 16. Wind turbines and service roads dissecting a hillside, aerial, United States, c. 1990. Reprinted by permission of Gettyimages, Munich, Germany.

of pride, a project that had political and economic benefits and that eventually became a significant export industry (Heymann 1998).

A few larger corporations also began to establish environmental departments, and, particularly in the United States, the idea of "pollution prevention" first practiced at Minnesota Mining and Manufacturing (3M) grew into an influential corporate slogan in the 1980s. Efforts to eliminate pollution at its source were shown to be effective and profitable in relation to many production processes, and they were often more technically challenging for engineers than the so-called end-of-pipe approaches to pollution control that had been developed earlier. New technical ideas in the areas of industrial ecology, cleaner technologies, and waste minimization began to be discussed and even implemented in experimental projects, and consulting firms with expertise in the various techniques and practices started to grow in importance—not least in countries such as Germany and the Netherlands, where an environmental consciousness had been strong in the 1970s.

The emergence of these more constructive activities was accompanied by the spread of a dramatically innovative, professional environmental activism spearheaded by Greenpeace and by the reemergence, in many countries, of the older conservation societies. Greenpeace was a pioneer in what might be termed "high-tech environmentalism," making use of computers and sophisticated communications techniques to raise awareness about a few highly charged topics: nuclear fallout, seal and whale hunting, and oil pollution. As the energy issue lost its media interest, and the ideological counteroffensive of Thatcher and Reagan pushed environmentalists onto the defensive, Greenpeace signaled the coming of a more politically strategic kind of activism. The organizational ambition was to carry out a limited number of campaigns that were internationally coordinated and that combined direct, dramatic forms of action with highly focused information and lobbying efforts.

Finally, the 1980s witnessed the widespread entrance of environmentalism into the parliamentary arena, as green parties, under the inspiration of the West German *Die Grünen,* were formed across Europe and North America. The formation of green parties was controversial and was perhaps the main factor that led to splits and conflicts within national environmental movements. Many were the activists who contended that movements could not operate as formal political parties and that the establishment of green parties would be counterproductive. By the mid-1980s the environmental movement had thus lost whatever coherence it might once have had. It was divided into distinct branches, and in most places the branches were subdivided along sectorial lines. With professionalization came also a kind of specialization that affected the particular issues that were dealt with.

PHASE THREE: INTEGRATION

The late 1980s marked the beginnings of a third, more structural stage of cultural appropriation. On the discursive level, a range of global environmental problems—climate change, ozone depletion, biodiversity—replaced local problems as the main areas of concern and public debate, and the solution to these problems came to be characterized in the vocabulary of *sustainable development,* following the report of the World Commission on Environment and Development in 1987.

The discourse of sustainable development served to redirect environmentalism in three main ways. There was an internationalization of the environmental political agenda and with it an emphasis on trade and development assistance, and there was an opening to new actors and social constituencies. The Brundtland report had been written by a committee composed of scientists and government officials that also included representatives of nongovernmental organizations and business firms. The quest for sustainable development was thus a mission that challenged the autonomy, or specialized identity, of the environmental movement. In calling for the integration of economics and ecology and for the linking of environmental problems to issues of income and resource distribution, poverty alleviation, and gender equality, the Brundtland commission reframed the ecological problematic. Finally, the quest for sustainable development opened environmentalism to the social sciences. To provide the knowledge base for the comprehensive program of global recovery that was enunciated in the report, all sorts of experts, and not just the natural scientists and engineers who had previously occupied that role, needed to make contributions.

Because of its generality and all inclusiveness, the quest for sustainable development inspired vastly different kinds of social actors and thus led to a range of conflicting interpretations. In relation to technology and science, there developed a bifurcation, or polarization, between green business, on one hand, and a range of critical ecologies on the other. Whereas one side seeks to incorporate programs of sustainable development into established routines and institutions, the other seeks to integrate environmental concern with issues of global equity and justice (see Table 10).

For the proponents of green business, the appropriation of environmentalism has been primarily a process of commercialization. By using

TABLE 10. The Dialectics of Sustainable Technology and Science

Green Business	Critical Ecology
"Ecological modernization"	"Environmental justice"
Instrumental rationality	Communicative rationality
Environmental management	Environmental ethics
Commerical orientation	Community emphasis
Expert solutions	Public engagement

concepts such as ecological modernization, environmental management, and ecoefficiency, the environmental challenge has been incorporated into an acceptable or familiar discursive framework: business as usual. In such a way, it is hoped that green innovations, and even green products, can become a significant part of a new wave of technological and economic development. But there are important differences among the proponents of green business in terms of the way they think about technology and science.

In ideal-typical terms, three main conceptual frameworks have emerged, as the critical ideas of the 1970s have been transformed into various programs or strategies of technological change. First, there is the adaptive approach of *ecoefficiency,* which has been promulgated primarily by large transnational corporations and supported by such organizations as the World Business Council for Sustainable Development, which was established in 1989 (DeSimone and Popoff 2000). Here the idea is to use existing technology as much as possible and to make production processes more effective. In relation to technological development, this idea can be considered a strategy of incremental change and calls for little alteration in organization. The principles of ecoefficiency are, among other things, to reduce material and energy intensity of goods and services, reduce toxic dispersion, enhance material recyclability, extend product durability, and increase the service intensity of products: in other words, to reform or redesign the technologies that already exist so that they can make more effective use of energy and natural resources.

A second approach to green technology is that of "ecological modernization," which signals a shift from pollution control and so-called end-of-pipe technologies to more preventive and precautionary approaches. It provides an influential story line for several governments and policy makers in Europe, as well as for many of those working in the areas of environmental and technological policy at the intergovernmental level, especially within the European Commission (Hajer 1995). Here the main emphasis is on changing organizational routines and production networks rather than on making specific technical "fixes" (Mol and Sonnenfeld 2000). So-called ecomodernists tend to stress the importance of more deliberative forms of regulation and policy making and so-called market instruments: green taxes and other tax reforms, environmental accounting, and environmental management. What has been proposed, and to a certain extent implemented, are flexible or so-called soft regulation regimes, by which companies are given subsidies and technical support for developing cleaner technology projects and instituting environmental management systems. In general, there is an emphasis in the discourse of ecological modernization on more proactive rather than reactive approaches to technology, science, and policy.

Ecoefficiency and ecological modernization can be contrasted to more radical approaches to sustainable technology that have been given labels such as "ecological economics," "industrial ecology," and "natural capitalism." The idea of natural capitalism presented by Paul Hawken, Amory Lovins, and Hunter Lovins in a book published in 1999 encompasses many of the more fundamental or systemic transformations that are proposed by green engineers. In terms of the dynamics of change, these more radical strategies call for the creation of new companies and social as well as technological innovations. Rather than the incremental strategy of ecoefficiency, or the organizational strategy of ecological modernization, natural capitalism can be said to involve a transformative strategy (Hawken, Lovins, and Lovins 1999). What is involved is a radical improvement in resource productivity. In his own engineering consulting work (based at the Rocky Mountain Institute in the United States), Amory Lovins has designed "hypercars" for American automotive firms that are said to have no negative impact on the environment, because of the extremely high levels of resource productivity that are applied. Another principle of natural capitalism, in relation to technological development, is the notion of biomimicry, which means the redesigning of industrial production systems along biological lines. As in other approaches to ecological economics, what is envisioned is a service and flow economy, locating production closer to the resources that are used and developing much more interaction between the actual production processes and the users of the products.

For many critical ecologists, who, in recent years, have joined the protest movements against globalization, sustainable development has been given substantially different meanings. The main challenge has come to be seen as linking environmental concern with other political concerns for justice, gender equality, antiracism, and ethnic diversity, so that the quest for sustainable development can be appropriated into more specifically defined local campaigns. Public participation, by which is often meant an engagement of ordinary people into environmental activities and sustainable development programs, is an important element of the critical ecology discursive framework. But their inability to join forces effectively has helped foster much antienvironmental backlash. As recent opposition to wind energy plants well illustrates, environmental concern means very different things to different people. Whereas in the 1970s wind energy was seen as a part of the transition to an ecological society, its appropriation by business firms has inspired at least some traditional nature-loving environmentalists to rise up in protest.

Like the other ideas and artifacts that we have discussed in preceding chapters, environmental facts and artifacts have been appropriated into our contemporary societies in an uneven manner. At each of our different levels—the discursive, the institutional, and the practical—ideas, routines, and behavior have certainly been transformed by environmentalism, but the process, in a more general sense, remains unclear and uncertain. Has environmental protection, like hygiene before it, become a permanent feature of scientific and technological activity? Or will environmentalism be so taken over by other interests that its ultimate meaning will be a "greener, cleaner" production, as mobility has more or less been reduced to automobility and communication has been reduced to information processing?

12
CONCLUSIONS: HISTORY AS CULTURAL ASSESSMENT

The idea of culture describes our common inquiry, but our conclusions are diverse, as our starting points were diverse. The word, culture, cannot automatically be pressed into service as any kind of social or personal directive. Its emergence, in its modern meanings, marks the effort at total qualitative assessment, but what it indicates is a process, not a conclusion.

—Raymond Williams (1958/1971, 285)

APPROPRIATING THE PAST

History is always written after the event, *post facto*. It is a process of recollecting, by which we try to make a coherent story out of disparate pieces of evidence. The stories that historians tell are filtered through their experiences and structured by their professional training and, more specifically, by their socialization into one or another academic tradition. Their writings, we might say, represent an appropriation of the past. But all too often those appropriations are overly selective and specialized. Most historians of technology and science have in recent decades tended to write ever more detailed accounts of ever more limited scope. With this book we have tried to counter that trend and present a broader approach.

As is the case with all other historical accounts, those that deal with developments in technology and science are inevitably attempts to fit stories about the past into some kind of discursive framework (Hård and Jamison 1998). At the same time, the writing of history, like all other forms of knowledge making, is shaped, or conditioned, by the times in which it is written. A past exists—events have most certainly taken place—but history, which is the telling of stories about the past, is made in the present. The writing of history can never be freed from the contemporary situations, interests, and concerns of the historians who are telling the stories. These contextual conditions influence the implicit assumptions and explicit biases that enter into all historical accounts, no matter how objective and impartial the historian attempts to be. They affect the questions that historians ask of the past and the evidence that is collected to try to answer those questions.

Of all the many possible ways to tell stories about the past, historians choose those that they find most attractive, for reasons of philosophy, politics, or personality. The past can be remembered only in the present. And that remembering is always done within a certain framework, or tradition, and presented according to a particular kind of story line. The story line that we have developed in this book is one of cultural appropriation. Our goal has been to contribute to a broader cultural assessment of technology and science, whereby we might use history to get some help in taming the forms that hubris has taken in the contemporary world.

THE FOUNDATIONAL NARRATIVES

As we have argued throughout this book, a historically oriented cultural assessment of technoscience requires that we tell new stories of the past, stories that can transcend the polarization between romance and tragedy. A story line of cultural appropriation is one of critical appreciation. We have tried to balance a respect for the hubris that lies behind our scientific and technological achievements with an awareness of the need for dealing with the hybrid implications of those achievements. As such we have tried to transcend the heroic story line that has been so dominant in the historiography of technology and science.

The dominant perspectives on the technical and scientific past can, in large measure, be traced back to what Eric Hobsbawm (1962) called the "age of revolution," when Europe was shaken by major transformations in the realms of politics and economics. The French Revolution of 1789, on one hand, and the English Industrial Revolution, on the other hand, represented a dual revolution that Hobsbawm and many others have seen as "probably the most important event in world history" (Hobsbawm 1962, 62). It was a period of transition from one kind of society to another, a moment in time when manifestations of the mechanical arts and applications of the experimental philosophy appeared to be creating fundamentally new conditions for human life.

In an age of social transition, the remembrance of the past took on a new importance. Across Europe, there emerged a more self-conscious and ambitious approach to the writing of history to help make sense of the situation. In particular, there was an effort to find some deeper meaning in the changes that the dual revolution was bringing about. Where had this Promethean urge, this interest in newness and change come from? What driving forces had unleashed the sources of creativity, ingenuity, and systematic scientific investigation that were so central to the emerging industrial society? What role had previous revolutions—in politics, religion, and science—played in the making of these industrializing forces? And, underlying all the others, was there a logical explanation for the changes taking place, did the chaotic and unnerving signs of the times fit into a larger pattern of some kind?

The questions were new because the experiences were new. The situation appeared to be unprecedented, and so the early chroniclers sought to provide meaningful precedents and reference points for the contemporary experiences. In the late eighteenth century, German scholar Johannes Beckmann coined the concept of *Technologie* as he traced the emergence of different fields of engineering and saw, behind the various technical improvements, something broader and more general. We can consider Beckmann's writings, along with the *Encyclopédie* of Denis Diderot and his colleagues, the first systematic attempts to write a history of technology and science. But they remained within a classificatory or taxonomic "episteme" (Foucault 1966/1970). Their approach to technology and science was systemic rather than historic; they were concerned primarily with a cataloging of human accomplishments rather than attempting to understand the underlying processes of change. The historians of the Enlightenment could still only envision a technological society; they were not yet living within one. It was not until technological innovations imposed themselves more directly on human societies that a new kind of discursive framework developed among the historically minded.

The first explicit histories of technology and science were imbued with the spirit of positivism. Whether they focused on the achievements of scientists and engineers or on the broader social and economic repercussions of those achievements, most of the historical accounts of the nineteenth century tended to tell tales that described developments in technology and science as progressive and heroic. In so doing, they reflected the dominant ideology of the emerging industrial society, which placed scientific-technological progress as one of the central figures of thought. Progress, we might say, was the central story line in the narratives that were fashioned.

Many of the early histories of technology and science tended to be congratulatory and were often part of the struggle for social status on the part of the scientists and engineers who wrote them. William Whewell, the Cambridge don, who coined the term *scientist* and was one of the founders of the British Association of the Advancement of Science (BAAS) in 1831, was also one of the earliest historians of science. His historical writings were meant to help justify public expenditures on scientific research and scientific education and promulgate heroic stories of truth's conquering superstition. In keeping with liberal ideology, the focus was on the individual genius and his contributions to the cumulative development of knowledge. Science in Whewell's metaphor was a river flowing through the landscape of civilization, gathering up the tributaries composed of the ideas of brilliant individuals (Yeo 1993).

Thomas Carlyle and other early-nineteenth-century writers signaled the coming of a more specifically historical approach. Carlyle emphasized change and dynamism as the "signs of the times," and his historical philosophy, with its emphasis on great men and individual accomplishment, became a source of inspiration for historians of technology and science. Portraying the past feats of engineers as momentous accomplishments, Samuel Smiles, for example, saw in their applications of human ingenuity models of the utilitarian values of the Victorian age. In the United States, Jacob Bigelow, a Harvard professor, in his 1829 lectures on technology argued that the wedding of knowledge to the useful arts was the characteristic feature of modern society. Technological development came to be seen, for indigenous writers such as Emerson and foreign observers such as Tocqueville, as the epitome of American republican ideals, combining craftsmanship and democracy in a shared progressive project (Kasson 1976).

In their underlying teleological assumptions, Whewell's, Carlyle's, and Emerson's approach to history corresponded with the idealist philosophy that was being most ambitiously formulated at the time by G. W. F. Hegel in his writings about the unfolding of the human spirit. Hegel emphasized the collective nature of human advancement through Reason, carrying the visions of the Enlightenment into the industrial era. For Hegel, and, to an even greater extent, for his rebellious disciples Karl Marx and Friedrich Engels, *Wissenschaft* (the more all-encompassing German term for science) had a socially transforming mission. Although retaining the spirit of positivism, Marx and Engels brought Whewell down to earth and stood, as they once put it, Hegel on his feet.

In keeping with the positivist discourse, Marx sought to develop a scientific understanding of industrial society. Marxism eventually served as the guiding ideology for the ill-fated experiments in the twentieth century with scientific socialism, but it also provided one of the main sources of inspiration for those who later wrote the history of technology and science (Jamison 1982). The extremely influential Marxian story line added to the internal accounts of scientific and technical progress an appreciation of the broader external social and economic contexts in which facts and artifacts developed. But it shared the progressive assumptions that dominated the history of technology and science until the First World War made such assumptions difficult to sustain, when, as Lewis Mumford later put it, "the unthinkable had happened, and from now on nothing would be quite unthinkable" (Mumford 1982, 377). As a result, at least some of the historically minded, such as Mumford, began to fashion narratives depicting alternative and even tragic story lines about the history of technology and science.

HISTORY OF SCIENCE AND TECHNOLOGY AS A VOCATION

Few of the influential writers of the early nineteenth century were professional historians. By the end of the century, and partly as a result of the expansion of universities, the writing of history was gradually institutionalized into academic departments, disciplines, and subdisciplines. The history of technology and science became integrated into other historical subfields, such as history of ideas, literary history, and economic history, or into the teaching of the natural and engineering sciences. Ernst Mach, for instance, was one of many physicists who pursued the history of physics as a part of his scientific research career (Kuhn 1977).

The professionalization of many scientific and engineering fields led to a need for providing what might be called an official past, a kind of collective memory for the new professionals. With the founding of the *Deutsches Museum* in Munich, and the subsequent establishment of similar places throughout Europe and North America, the achievements of the past were also given a new function in cultural life. Telling stories about the history of technology and science became a way to encourage young people to make career decisions, and it also played a role in fostering national pride and competition. As such, the dominant narratives tended to be heroic and idealistic.

The Belgian George Sarton is generally considered the first person to seek to carve out a particular niche in the academic world for the history of science (Thackray and Merton 1972). Before moving to the United States, where he settled after the First World War, Sarton had established *Isis*, a special journal for the history of science, and throughout the interwar period, he took many initiatives to try to make the history of science a legitimate academic pursuit. Engineering societies and technical museums provided the main sites for the early efforts at developing a historiography of technology. Yearbooks and journals often written for an audience of engineers and amateur technology freaks offered opportunities for would-be historians to practice their not-yet existent trade.

In keeping with what might be called the dominant story line of modernity, the history of technology and science was broken down into romantic tales of adventure, describing how engineers and scientists, and eventually entrepreneurs and captains of industry, had conquered nature by means of some particular technical improvement or scientific accomplishment. Sarton and the early historians of technology shared a faith in progress that, if anything, was strengthened by the Great War and its tragic aftermath. Although politics and ideologies, and even economic competition, had led to disaster, science and technology continued to grow and expand human capabilities. For Sarton, the history of science was the "only history which can illustrate the progress of mankind" (quoted in Thackray and Merton 1972).

Despite the efforts of Sarton and others to win academic recognition and legitimacy for the history of science, it was not until after the Second World War that a particular disciplinary identity was established in most countries. An interesting exception was in Sweden, where Johan Nordström in Uppsala, educated as a literary historian, created a separate academic subject, the History of Ideas and Learning. In Sweden the history of science and technology has often been told according to a kind of patriotic story line, as historians have sought to identify the particular contributions that Swedish scientists and engineers have made or how foreign ideas have been appropriated into Sweden. The history of science and technology has been seen to be an important component of the national identity, and histories and biographies of scientists and engineers have been written more for a general public than for fellow academic historians.

In Britain and the United States, history of science emerged as a discipline amidst the general postwar enthusiasm for science. At Harvard the university's president James Conant initiated special courses for undergraduates and an ambitious research program in the history of science, which were linked to the university's efforts in general education. At several other universities in the United States, courses and eventually graduate programs were created in the 1950s and 1960s; in Britain, history of science was institutionalized at Oxford and Cambridge. The general orientation of the new discipline was intellectualist. The history of science was told primarily as an adventure of the mind. It was in its relations to philosophy and as a part of a general Western process of enlightenment that the scientific past was remembered. Especially influential were the writings of Alexander Koyré in France and Herbert Butterfield in Britain, which offered detailed scrutiny of scientific ideas and provided methods and conceptual frameworks for tracing the progressive development of scientific ideas.

These historians drew on the positivist discursive framework of the nineteenth century. Theirs was an approach to history that celebrated and glorified the scientists of the past and fit well into the mood of scientism that was so characteristic of the immediate postwar era. This celebratory story line was propagated in the United States by Melvin Kranzberg, the longtime editor of *Technology and Culture,* the journal that was founded in 1959, and by Daniel Boorstin, the longtime director of the Smithsonian Institution in Washington, whose works on U.S. history focused, to a large extent, on the important role that inventors and engineers had played in the "democratic experience" (Boorstin 1987).

For Boorstin, the United States was the very "republic of technology." At the core of the national identity was a fascination with things technical that had become one of the defining features of American history. Boorstin helped to make popular a particularly American story line in the history of technology, in which the westward expansion, the taming of the frontier, and various technical projects in transportation and communication—railroads and the telegraph, automobiles and the telephone, airplanes and television—that had been initiated by Americans were combined into triumphant tales of inventive passion and commercial expansion. Like the intellectualist history of science, the celebratory history of technology regarded scientists and inventors as the heroes of our time, white men whose efforts changed the course of history (Smith and Marx 1994).

The history of technology continued, well into the 1950s, to be a marginal subject in most countries, practiced primarily by engineers turned historians or as a component of economic and business history. There was an antiquarian interest in the past that was fostered by the Newcomen Society in Britain and was given textbook treatment in the multivolume *History of Technology* edited by the Cambridge professor Charles Singer. As in the history of science, the development of technology was primarily seen as following a kind of cumulative, even evolutionary, story line. One development had prepared the way for the next, and it was the tracing of those linear paths of discovery in separate areas of invention and industry that became the chosen task for the historian of technology.

A different approach to the history of technology and science developed within economic history and among historically minded economists. At the turn of the century, Thorstein Veblen identified technology as the fundament of economic development, and he argued in his writings that economic history should focus much more explicit attention on the development of machinery and the institutions in which such innovations had taken place. His theoretical approach to history was complemented, in the 1920s, by the work of Abbott Payson Usher, who looked in detail at the history of particular mechanical inventions (Usher 1929).

Usher sought to derive from his historical studies some general principles about the inventive process, which were further developed by Joseph Schumpeter in his many works in economic history. Schumpeter focused attention on the key role played by entrepreneurs in bringing new ideas and inventions to market. It was not sufficient for scientists and engineers to fashion new materials or discover new properties or processes in nature. To be economically important, inventions needed to be commercialized; that is, transformed into profitable innovations. The story lines in the narratives that were recollected were of entrepreneurship and strategic management, and the heroes were the businessmen, who were able to turn technology and science into profitable commercial undertakings.

These approaches were from the outset applied to the particular concerns of the business world. There was a generally positive attitude to technology, and the history of science and technology was here treated in explicitly commercial terms. Technology and science were seen as tools, or means, for the achievement of economic success and the accumulation of wealth. This historical interest in the uses of scientific-technical knowledge in economic activities reflected what might be termed an underlying material, or instrumental, bias.

The history of science was also affected by the changing contexts in which research was carried out in the postwar era. The transformation of little science into the big science of atomic energy, aerospace, and telecommunications served to redirect at least some historical attention to the science of the twentieth century. Often less celebratory, the history of more recent science tended also to adopt more of an institutional, and less of an individual, focus. The age of big science also led to historical studies on the interface of science and government and of national and international scientific organizations.

The growing importance of technology and science in society had, by the 1960s, also led to the emergence of separate courses and eventually programs and departments in the history of technology, particularly in the United States, the Soviet Union, and the German Democratic Republic. Focusing originally on the lives of inventors and engineers, historians of technology gradually carved out an academic niche, or speciality area, that was somewhat separate from economic history. As practiced, for instance, by Thomas Hughes, emphasis turned to the technological networks, or systems, in their own right and not merely as part of commercial or broader economic developments.

There had previously been a certain sociological influence on the historiography of science and technology. On one hand, Max Weber's notion of the "iron cage" provided a key story line for many of the tragic tales that were told about the victims of progress, especially in relation to industrialization. And on the other hand, Weber's emphasis, throughout his writings, on the relations between science and social interests contributed, in the 1920s, to an explicit "sociology of knowledge" by which the development of ideas was linked to the interests of particular social groups.

This sociological understanding of modern science was given a somewhat sharper focus in the late 1930s by, among others, Edgar Zilsel and Robert Merton. As science and rationality were seen to be threatened by the extremisms of the left and the right, it became important to identify the specific social conditions that have given rise to modern science and what Merton called the "institutional imperatives" that were essential for its health and vitality (Merton 1973). Zilsel explored, in a series of articles that combined history, philosophy, and sociology of science, the connections between the new ways of practicing science that emerged in the early modern period and changes in the economic, political, and cultural spheres (Zilsel 2000). He also traced the emergence of new mediating concepts, such as laws of nature and probability, which were shared by scientists and nonscientists. And he tried to deconstruct the various components of what he termed the "scientific spirit," which combined the social norms or ethical attributes that Weber had identified with particular aspects of scientific practice: experimentation, calculation, and observation.

As the institutions of science, and state policies for scientific research, developed in the years after the Second World War, the socio-logical understanding of science largely fell into disrepute, a victim of anticommunism and cold war ideological disputes. On one hand, there were those who wanted to keep science, as well as its funding and orga-nization, free from the society that had shaped it; these were the defenders of academic freedom and the open society and what might be termed the myth of pure science (Fuller 2000). On the other hand, there were those, such as the British physicist John Desmond Bernal and other defenders of Soviet communism, who tried to show how sci-ence and society had been inextricably intertwined. Although the one side wrote one kind of history of science—focusing on the great, noble figures, such as Newton, Descartes and Huygens, who freed humanity from ignorance by the power of their minds—the other side developed an external history of science, which was largely disregarded by profes-sional historians (e.g., Bernal 1954). The internalist–externalist dispute was as much a battle over contemporary issues of science policy and the contemporary status of science as it was about what actually hap-pened in the past. With the closing of the cold war, it has become easier to transcend the external–internal dichotomy, as many historians have taken what might be termed a cultural turn and concerned themselves, as we have done in this book, with the broader cultural dimensions of technology and science.

A CULTURAL TURN

The intertwining of the social and the cultural in the history of tech-nology has been a rather peripheral theme for most of the formative figures in social theory and social history. Marx, who tended to see technology and science as primarily "forces of production," did give attention to the other, more cultural uses of artifacts. In the first chap-ter of *Capital* (1867/1976), he developed the idea of "commodity fetishism" as one way to discuss these social, or contextual, aspects of technology and science. He contended that throughout history, human-made artifacts had been infused with meanings and values that rendered invisible the underlying social relations of power and hierar-chy. It is insufficient to comprehend human goods solely in economic and functional terms, or, as Marx put it, in terms of their "use value" alone. Cultural values, social inequalities, and ideological frameworks must be taken into account if we are to understand fully the complexities of our artifactual landscape. In this landscape, a chair is not just a thing to sit on but an object that is interpreted in relation to its age, designer, place of manufacture, previous owner, and aesthetic form.

Because of the long-standing positivist focus and economic bias of the history of technology and science, it used to be quite difficult for scholars to make serious use of these insights. In the 1960s and 1970s, however, a critical interest in technology and science emerged as part of the new social movements of feminism, environmentalism, and anti-imperialism. Reappraisals of the history of technology and science started to appear, often mixing serious scholarship with polemical critique. Particularly influential were Harry Braverman's *Labor and Monopoly Capital* (1974), which described the uses of technology in particular U.S. industries from a Marxian perspective; David Noble's *America by Design* (1977), which examined the rise of corporate research and management science in a highly critical fashion; and Carolyn Merchant's *The Death of Nature* (1980), which provided an ecofeminist reading of the scientific revolution.

The publication of the anthology *The Social Shaping of Technology* by Donald MacKenzie and Judy Wajcman in 1985 (the second, expanded edition was published in 1999) served to bring these and other social historical writings into the emerging field of science, technology, and society studies. Primarily dealing with the design and production of artifacts and technological systems, this book clearly established that "artifacts have politics." Thus, it was quite consequential that Langdon Winner's (1980) article with this title was reprinted as the volume's first chapter. That technologies are not neutral was brought out further by Tine Bruland's discussion about the initial attempts to design half-automatic spinning machines in the nineteenth century and by David Noble's analysis of the development and introduction of numerically controlled machine tools after the Second World War; rather, they reflect power relations, economic interests, and cultural values.

Material objects are constantly being loaded with meaning. Things are not just instruments that simply lie around for us to use when we see fit. Rather, they convey symbolic meanings and purport values and norms. As long as the sewing machine is defined as a female object, men will be more reluctant to use it than women. Anthropologists have been particularly sensitive to the symbolic character of objects. In a classic article, Lauriston Sharp (1952) half a century ago analyzed the religious and social connotations of axes in an aboriginal Australian culture. The Yir-Yiront people studied by Sharp traditionally employed stone axes when chopping wood or making tools and weapons. These stone axes not only were used for such instrumental purposes but also played a central role in religious ceremonies and totemic rites. Like other totems, such as spears and corpses, stone axes were vehicles for getting into contact with the ancestors. In contrast, steel axes, introduced by European missionaries, carried no religious meaning of this kind. Unlike stone axes, which were considered masculine, steel axes were, furthermore, not gendered. Instead of social stability and cultural continuity, steel axes came to define a new social order that the Europeans were imposing and that threatened the traditional harmony within the group.

Because there had existed a kind of consensus about their meaning and modes of application, stone axes had, in Sharp's functionalist analysis, contributed to the unification of the aboriginal culture. In our society such consensus about the signification of objects also exists. The use of forks for eating is usually not seriously contested in our parts of the world. Although eating without utensils might be approved of in a hamburger bar, it is ordinarily considered filthy and distasteful. Forks symbolize cleanliness and accepted behavior. Not seldom, however, artifacts and systems are subject to intense discussion and diverse opinion. In the 1970s and 1980s, for instance, the controversy around nuclear power shook the political system of many countries, and today genetic engineering is a cause of great concern for large segments of the population.

The establishment on a large scale of a certain technology in a society requires that a considerable proportion of the population be convinced of its advantages. Although technology is in our culture strongly associated with terms such as *novelty* and *future*, it is still the case that it is often represented by means of traditional symbols and discussed by means of familiar concepts. When, for example, Swedish conservatives in the decade preceding the First World War began to make peace with modern industry, they did so by making recourse to age-old images and ideas. The revolution concept seems to lend itself particularly well to the creation of histories that aim at mobilizing the past for contemporary purposes. From the history of technology and science we are all familiar with the traditional narratives about the scientific revolution and the first and second industrial revolution. Told as they usually are in a progressive and uncritical manner, such narratives are intended to celebrate the pioneering accomplishments of Western science and technology in the post-Renaissance era. Cultural historians, however, tend to be highly critical toward such all-encompassing and congratulatory stories. In contrast, they attempt to uncover alternative stories, "small narratives," that not only view the past from other perspectives but also represent less grandiose, more mundane events.

As we have tried to show in the preceding chapters, the history of technology and science has become far richer than it once was, peopled by a wider range of actors and institutions, and made up of an array of discourses and practices. It has given a richer pool of material to draw on, and in this book we have tried to provide a more all-encompassing story line. The optimistic prognostications of Francis Bacon about the marvelous future of scientific-technological progress, for example, was shared by many in the seventeenth century, especially as those visions materialized in the instruments and methods of experimental philosophy. But there were other voices that situated technical improvement and scientific inquiry within a fundamentally religious project. In the mid-seventeenth century, Baconianism was highly variegated, and among the more radical Puritan groups, there were already warnings about the risks that were inherent in too much tinkering with God's order and in imputing too much power to human agents. In the nineteenth century, as industrial technologies spread around the world, there were also victims and critics, whose stories have tended to be neglected in the historical literature. From the Luddite machine-breakers to the socialist and populist movements, there were those who challenged the dominant meanings that were given to science and technology. Similarly, in our century, among environmentalists, feminists, anti-imperialists, and other political groups, alternative visions for knowledge making and for technical development have been articulated. Especially now, when the wonders of technology are of benefit to merely a small minority of the world's population, and when the proliferation of risks and uncertainties is increasingly recognized as one of the central defining features of our age, a more balanced view of the historical record seems to be called for.

TOWARD CULTURAL ASSESSMENT

When Raymond Williams (1958/1971) in the 1950s began to develop what has since grown into the field of cultural studies, his notion of culture was primarily intellectual. Culture concerned meanings and interpretations, and it was the task of the cultural historian to try to bring to life those people—William Morris and George Orwell, among them—who had contributed to a kind of cultural critique of the industrial system and modern society. We also received our historical training within the discursive framework of what one might call an intellectual history of technology and science. In this book, however, we have tried to go beyond this narrower notion and present an approach to culture as ways of life and as institutions, in addition to ideas and discourses.

For us, culture includes not only what certain intellectuals have said and thought but also the routines and practices that users develop in relation to machines. In addition, culture involves the institutional arrangements that are set up to manage and control further developments. As we argued in the introductory chapter, a cultural history of technology and science should concern itself with all levels of reality, which we have characterized ideal-typically as discourses, institutions, and practices.

Because history writing is never a mere collection of past events or a recollection of past experiences, it remains for us to explain why such a history is important. What role can a cultural history of technology and science play in our contemporary world? What is the task, even responsibility, of the historian, and of history, in an era of technoscientific hubris and technological hybrids? How might history contribute to what we call a "cultural assessment of technology and science"? As Williams indicated in the quote at the beginning of this chapter, such an assessment is a qualitatively oriented process not a quantitative or pseudoscientific evaluation.

When the U.S. sociologist William Ogburn (1922) in the 1920s coined the term *cultural lag*, the underlying argument was one of (too) slow adaptation. The modern society, he contended, had not yet fully realized the revolutionary impacts that modern technology and science would ultimately have on culture, and his concept was meant to improve and speed up that process of adaptation. Such deterministic ideas are still around. Opening any paper today, one finds stories that tell how we, inevitably, are on our way into a world in which genetic engineers create larger and tastier tomatoes, nanotechnologists develop environmentally friendly plastics, and microbiologists come up with a cure for cancer. Hubris is all around.

One of the tasks of a cultural assessment of technology and science is to unravel, or deconstruct, such hype, to critically comment on the interest-driven promises that the dominant cultural formation and its propagandists bombard us with. In this book we have tried to show how hubris often goes too far, that outlandish visions have seldom materialized—and, when they have done so, as in the case of the atomic bomb or the modernist city, they have ended up as nightmares rather than dreams come true. Francis Bacon's "New Atlantis" was not a democratic society, and few, if any, technocratic visions in history have been.

It is important to realize, of course, that a complete rejection of everything modern is just as foolish as a mindless glorification. Fundamentalist reaction is just as dangerous as technocratic excess. Our task as historians is to dig out of the past successful cases of cultural appropriation, processes in which human needs have been met and the human condition been improved. The consolidation of hygienic standards of living and the integration of new communication devices into our ways of life are such cases. Urban reformers might have had a tendency to patronize the poor, but many of them certainly contributed to improving their lot. And users were able to appropriate the telephone to fit their own needs against the wise guys of the telephone companies.

Still, we warn readers not to make instrumental use of the stories we tell in this book. We are convinced that it is possible, as it were, to learn from history, but because history never repeats itself, historical knowledge cannot be predictive or prescriptive in any absolute sense. For historians, the relationship between the past and the future is not the same as it is for physicists and engineers. Rather than being prescriptive, a cultural history of technology and science can be a source of reflection and inspiration. A qualitatively oriented assessment process ought to draw on historical experiences as a mirror through which we might look at our own age. And those experiences, in turn, might provide inspiration for dealing with the glaring contrast between scientific and technological abundance on one hand and spiritual poverty on the other hand, which Martin Luther King so eloquently identified in his famous speech "I Have a Dream" in 1963.

More than forty years later, the tension between technoscience and the uses to which it is put remains enormous, and it might be hoped that the stories in this book can help, in some small way, in our collective efforts to make better use of our technologies and our sciences. But it is not our task to tell our readers what to make of the stories we have told in this book. James Watson can serve as a warning example and Vandana Shiva as a role model for some, but this is merely one possible reading. Bruno Latour (1987, 19) said, "The fate of what we say and make is in later users' hands"; similarly, the fate of our text is in the hearts and minds of our readers.

BIBLIOGRAPHY

Aase, Monica, and Mikael Hård. "'Det norske Athen.' Trondheim som lärdomsstad under 1700-talets andra hälft." *Lychnos: Annual of the Swedish History of Science Society* (1998): 37–74.

Abbate, Janet. *Inventing the Internet.* Cambridge, MA: MIT Press, 1999.

Abel, Rudolf, ed. *Handbuch der praktischen Hygiene.* Jena: Gustav Fischer, 1913.

Adas, Michael. *Machines as the Measure of Men: Science, Technology, and Ideologies of Western Dominance.* Ithaca, NY: Cornell University Press, 1989.

Addams, Jane. *Twenty Years at Hull-House.* New York: New American Library, 1910/1961.

Alcock, J.F., and H.S. Glyde. "The Practice of Research: The Equipment Provided and Methods in Use at the Works of Messrs. Ricardo." *Aircraft Engineering* (September/ October 1930).

Allen, Jonathan, ed. *March 4: Scientists, Student, and Society.* Cambridge, MA: MIT Press, 1970.

Ambjörnsson, Ronny, et al., eds. *Från Aten till Los Angeles—idéhistoriska miljöer.* Malmö: Liber Hermods, 1986.

Baark, Erik. *Lightning Wires: The Telegraph and China's Technological Modernization, 1860–1890.* Westport, CT: Greenwood, 1997.

Baark, Erik, and Andrew Jamison. "Biotechnology and Culture: Public Debates and Their Impact on Government Regulation in the United States and Denmark," *Technology in Society* 12 (1990): 27–44.

———. "The Technology and Culture Problematique." In *Technological Development in China, India and Japan: Cross-Cultural Perspectives,* edited by Erik Baark and Andrew Jamison. New York: St. Martin's, 1986.

Bacon, Francis. *The New Organon and Related Writings.* Indianapolis: Bobbs-Merrill, 1620/ 1960.

Balazs, Etienne. *Chinese Civilization and Bureaucracy: Variations on a Theme.* New Haven, CT: Yale University Press, 1964.

Bardini, Thierry. *Bootstrapping: Douglas Engelbart, Coevolution, and the Origins of Personal Computing.* Stanford, CA: Stanford University Press, 2000.

Barloewen, Constantin von, and Kai Werhahn-Mees. *Japan und der Westen.* Vol. 2, *Wirtschafts-und Sozialwissenschaften, Technologie.* Frankfurt am Main: Fischer, 1986.

Bates, Marston. *Man in Nature.* Englewood Cliffs, NJ: Prentice Hall, 1961.

Bauer, Thomas. *Im Bauch der Stadt. Kanalisation und Hygiene in Frankfurt am Main 16.-19. Jahrhundert.* Frankfurt am Main: Waldemar Kramer, 1998.

Beck, Ulrich. *Risk Society: Toward a New Modernity.* London: Sage, 1986/1992.

Beder, Sharon. *Global Spin: The Corporate Assault on Environmentalism.* Totnes, Devon: Green Books, 1997.

Beer, John Joseph. *The Emergence of the German Dye Industry.* Urbana: University of Illinois Press, 1959.

Bell, Daniel. *The End of Ideology: On the Exhaustion of Political Ideas in the Fifties.* Chicago: Free Press of Glencoe, 1960.

Bellamy, Edward. *Looking Backward, 2000–1887.* Boston: Ticknor, 1888.

Ben-David, Joseph. *The Scientist's Role in Society: A Comparative Study.* Englewood Cliffs, NJ: Prentice Hall, 1971.

Bender, Thomas, ed. *The University and the City: From Medieval Origins to the Present.* Oxford: Oxford University Press, 1988.

Benedict, Ruth. *The Chrysanthemum and the Sword: Patterns of Japanese Culture.* Boston: Houghton Mifflin, 1946.

Beniger, James. *The Control Revolution: Technological and Economic Origins of the Information Society.* Cambridge, MA: Harvard University Press, 1986.

Benjamin, Walter. "The Work of Art in the Age of Mechanical Reproduction." In *Illuminations*, edited by Hannah Arendt. New York: Harcourt, Brace & World, 1936/1968.

Berg, Maxine. *The Machinery Question and the Making of Political Economy.* Cambridge: Cambridge University Press, 1980.

Bernal, John D. *Science in History.* London: Watts, 1954.

———. *The Social Function of Science.* London: Routledge and Kegan Paul, 1939.

Berner, Boel. "The Meaning of Cleaning: The Creation of Harmony and Hygiene in the Home." *History and Technology* 14 (1998): 313–52.

Bijker, Wiebe E. "The Social Construction of Bakelite: Toward a Theory of Invention." In *The Social Construction of Technological Systems: New Direction in the Sociology and History of Technology*, edited by Wiebe E. Bijker, Thomas P. Hughes, and Trevor J. Pinch. Cambridge, MA: MIT Press, 1987.

Bijker, Wiebe E., Thomas P. Hughes, and Trevor J. Pinch, eds. *The Social Construction of Technological Systems: New Direction in the Sociology and History of Technology.* Cambridge, MA: MIT Press, 1987.

Bleckmann, Dörte. *Wehe wenn sie losgelassen! Über die Anfänge des Frauenradfahrens in Deutschland.* Gera, Leipzig: MAXIME–Verlag Kutschera, 1998.

Böhme, Gernot, et al. *Die gesellschaftliche Orientierung des wissenschaftlichen Fortschritts.* Frankfurt am Main: Suhrkamp, 1978.

Bok, Derek. *Universities in the Marketplace: The Commercialization of Higher Education.* Princeton, NJ: Princeton University Press, 2003.

Bollenbeck, Georg. *Bildung und Kultur. Glanz und Elend eines deutschen Deutungsmusters.* Frankfurt am Main: Insel, 1994.

Boorstin, Daniel. *Hidden History: Exploring Our Secret Past.* New York: Harper & Row, 1987.

Borish, Steven. *The Land to the Living: The Danish Folk High Schools and Denmark's Non-violent Path to Modernization.* Nevada City, CA: Blue Dolphin, 1991.

Bourdieu, Pierre. *Distinction: A Social Critique of the Judgement of Taste.* New York: Routledge and Kegan Paul, 1979/1984.

Bowler, Peter. *Evolution: The History of an Idea.* Berkeley: University of California Press, 1984/2003.

Braverman, Harry. *Labor and Monopoly Capital: The Degradation of Work in the Twentieth Century.* New York: Monthly Review Press, 1974.

Bray, Francesca. *The Rice Economies: Technology and Development in Asian Societies.* Berkeley: University of California Press, 1986.

Breuss, Susanne. "Die Stadt, der Staub und die Hausfrau. Zum Verhältnis von schmutziger Stadt und sauberem Heim." In *Urbane Welten. Referate der Österreichischen Volkskundetagung 1998 in Linz*, edited by Andrea Euler. Vienna: Selbstverlag des Vereins für Volkskunde, 1999.

Briggs, Robin. *Witches and Neighbors: The Social and Cultural Context of European Witchcraft.* New York: Viking, 1996.

Broberg, Gunnar, and Mattias Tydén. "Eugenics in Sweden: Efficient Care." In *Eugenics and the Welfare State: Sterilization Policy in Denmark, Sweden, Norway and Finland*, edited by Gunnar Broberg and Nils Roll-Hansen. East Lansing: Michigan State University Press, 1996.

Buch, Leopold von. *Leopold von Buchs Resa igenom Norrige åren 1806, 1807 och 1808, jemte ett bihang ur Hausmanns resa genom Skandinavien åren 1806 och 1807, en tabell öfver Norriges befolkning år 1801 samt författarens rese-charta ifrån Christiania till Nord-Cap.* Stockholm: Strinnholm och Haeggström, 1810/1814.

Burke, Peter. *A Social History of Knowledge: From Gutenberg to Diderot.* Cambridge: Polity Press, 2000.

Burkhardt, Johannes. *Das Reformationsjahrhundert: Deutsche Geschichte zwischen Medienrevolution und Institutionenbildung 1517–1617.* Stuttgart: Kohlhammer, 2002.

Bush, Vannevar. *Science, the Endless Frontier: A Report to the President on a Program for Postwar Scientific Research.* Washington, D.C.: National Science Foundation, 1945/1960.

Butler, Samuel. *Erewhon, or, Over the Range.* London: Trübner, 1872.

Butterfield, Herbert. *The Origins of Modern Science 1300–1800.* New York: Free Press, 1965.

Cain, L.P. *Sanitary Strategy for a Lakefront Metropolis: The Case of Chicago.* DeKalb: Northern Illinois University Press, 1978.

Callon, Michel. "Society in the Making: The Study of Technology as a Tool for Sociological Analysis." In *The Social Construction of Technological Systems: New Direction in the Sociology and History of Technology*, edited by Wiebe E. Bijker, Thomas P. Hughes, and Trevor J. Pinch. Cambridge, MA: MIT Press, 1987.

Calvert, Monte. *The Mechanical Engineer in America, 1830–1910: Professional Cultures in Conflict.* Baltimore, MD: Johns Hopkins University Press, 1967.

Cannadine, David. "The Past and the Present in the English Industrial Revolution, 1880–1980." *Past and Present* 103 (1984): 131–72.

Carson, Rachel. *Silent Spring.* Boston: Houghton Mifflin, 1962.

Centre for Science and Environment. *The State of India's Environment, 1982: A Citizen's Report.* Delhi: Centre for Science and Environment, 1982.

Chandler, Alfred D. Jr. *The Visible Hand: The Managerial Revolution in American Business.* Cambridge, MA: Belknap Press of Harvard University Press, 1977.

Chang, Richard T. *From Prejudice to Tolerance: A Study of the Japanese Image of the West, 1826–1864.* Tokyo: Sophia University, 1970.

Childs, Marquis. *Sweden: The Middle Way.* New Haven, CT: Yale University Press, 1936.

Chomsky, Noam. *American Power and the New Mandarins.* New York: Vintage Books, 1969.

Christianson, John R. *On Tycho's Island: Tycho Brahe and His Assistants, 1570–1601.* Cambridge: Cambridge University Press, 2000.

Cipolla, Carlo M. *Before the Industrial Revolution: European Society and Economy, 1000–1700.* London: Methuen, 1976.

Commoner, Barry. *Science and Survival.* New York: Viking Press, 1966.

Cooper, David, ed. *The Dialectics of Liberation.* Harmondsworth: Penguin, 1968.

Corbin, Alain. *The Foul and the Fragrant: Odor and the French Social Imagination.* Cambridge, MA: Harvard University Press, 1982/1986.

Cowan, Ruth Schwartz. *More Work for Mother: The Ironies of Household Technology from the Open Hearth to the Microwave.* New York: Basic Books, 1983.

Crosby, Alfred. *The Measure of Reality: Quantification and Western Society, 1250–1600.* Cambridge: Cambridge University Press, 1997.

Cumming, Elizabeth, and Wendy Kaplan. *The Arts and Crafts Movement.* London: Thames and Hudson, 1991/2002.

Dahl, Tor Edvin, Terje Ellefsen, and Anne Solberg. *Hallo?! Norges telefonhistorie.* Oslo: Gyldendal, 1993.

Dalton, Dennis. *Mahatma Gandhi: Nonviolent Power in Action.* New York: Columbia University Press, 1993.

Dann, Otto. *Nation und Nationalismus in Deutschland 1770–1990.* Munich: C.H. Beck, 1993.

Darnton, Robert. *The Literary Underground of the Old Regime.* Cambridge, MA: Harvard University Press, 1982.

Daston, Lorraine, and Katherine Park. *Wonders and the Order of Nature, 1150–1750.* New York: Zone Books, 1998.

Delia, Diana. "From Romance to Rhetoric: The Alexandrian Library in Classical and Islamic Traditions." *American Historical Review* 97 (1992): 1449–67.

DeSimone, Livio, and Frank Popoff. *Eco-efficiency: The Business Link to Sustainable Development.* Cambridge, MA: MIT Press, 2000.

Dessauer, Friedrich. *Streit um die Technik.* Frankfurt am Main: Josef Knecht, 1956.

Dickson, David. *The New Politics of Science.* New York: Pantheon Books, 1984.

Disch, Thomas. *The Dreams Our Stuff Is Made Of: How Science Fiction Conquered the World.* New York: Touchstone, 1998.

Dutta, Krishna, and Andrew Robinson. *Rabindranath Tagore: The Myriad-Minded Man.* New York: St. Martin's, 1995.

Ehrenburg, Ilya. *The Life of the Automobile.* New York: Urizen, 1929/1976.

Eisenberg, Christiane. *"English Sports" und deutsche Bürger: Eine Gesellschaftsgeschichte 1800–1939.* Paderborn: F. Schöningh, 1999.

Eisenstein, Elizabeth L. *The Printing Revolution in Early Modern Europe.* Cambridge: Cambridge University Press, 1983.

Elias, Norbert. *The Civilizing Process: The History of Manners.* Oxford: Basil Blackwell, 1939/1978.

Elzinga, Aant. "Universities, Research, and the Transformation of the State in Sweden." In *The European and American University since 1800: Historical and Sociological Essays,* edited by Sheldon Rothblatt and Björn Wittrock. Cambridge: Cambridge University Press, 1993.

Elzinga, Aant, and Andrew Jamison. "Changing Policy Agendas in Science and Technology." In *Handbook of Science and Technology Studies,* edited by Sheila Jasanoff et al. Thousand Oaks, CA: Sage, 1995.

———. "Making Dreams Come True: An Essay on the Role of Practical Utopias in Science." In *Nineteen Eighty-Four: Science between Utopia and Dystopia,* edited by Everett Mendelsohn and Helga Nowotny. Dordrecht, the Netherlands: Reidel, 1984.

Evans, Richard J. *Death in Hamburg: Society and Politics in the Cholera Years, 1830–1910.* Oxford: Clarendon, 1987.

Eyerman, Ron. *Between Culture and Politics: Intellectuals in Modern Society.* Cambridge: Polity, 1994.

Eyerman, Ron, and Andrew Jamison. *Social Movements: A Cognitive Approach.* Cambridge: Polity, 1991.

Feenberg, Andrew. *Alternative Modernity: The Technical Turn in Philosophy and Social Theory.* Berkeley: University of California Press, 1995.

Ferruolo, Stephen C. *"Parisius-Paradisus:* The City, Its Schools, and the Origins of the University of Paris." In *The University and the City: From Medieval Origins to the Present,* edited by Thomas Bender. Oxford: Oxford University Press, 1988.

Fischer, Claude S. *America Calling: A Social History of the Telephone to 1940.* Berkeley: University of California Press, 1992.

Flink, James J. *The Automobile Age.* Cambridge, MA: MIT Press, 1988.

Foucault, Michel. *The Birth of the Clinic: An Archaeology of Medical Perception.* New York: Vintage Books, 1963/1975.

———. *Discipline and Punish: The Birth of the Prison.* London: Allen Lane, 1975/1977.

———. *Madness and Civilization: A History of Insanity in the Age of Reason.* New York: Random House, 1961/1965.

———. *The Order of Things: An Archaeology of the Human Sciences.* New York: Random House, 1966/1970.

———. *Power/Knowledge: Selected Interviews and Other Writings, 1972–1977.* Edited by Colin Gordon. New York: Pantheon Books, 1980.

Fox, Robert, and Anna Guagnini, eds. *Laboratories, Workshops, and Sites: Concepts and Practices of Research in Industrial Europe, 1800–1914.* Berkeley: University of California Press, 1999.

Francastel, Pierre. *Art and Technology in the Nineteenth and Twentieth Centuries.* New York: Zone Books, 1956/2000.

Frängsmyr, Tore, ed. *Science in Sweden: The Royal Swedish Academy of Sciences, 1739–1989.* Canton, MA: Science History Publications, 1989.

———, ed. *Solomon's House Revisited: The Organization and Institutionalization of Science.* Canton, MA: Science History Publications, 1990.

Freeman, Christopher. *Technology Policy and Economic Performance: Lessons from Japan.* London: Pinter, 1987.

Freeman, Chris, and Francisco Louçã. *As Time Goes By: From the Industrial Revolutions to the Information Revolution.* Oxford: Oxford University Press, 2001

French, Cecil. "Ricardo at Shoreham." *Sussex Industrial History* 25 (1995).

Frevert, Ute. "Fürsorgliche Belagerung. Hygienebewegung und Arbeiterfrauen im 19. und 20. Jahrhundert." *Geschichte und Gesellschaft* 11 (1985): 420–46.

Frey, Manuel. *Der reinliche Bürger. Entstehung und Verbreitung bürgerlicher Tugenden in Deutschland 1760–1860.* Göttingen: Vandenhoeck und Ruprecht, 1997.

Friedewald, Michael. *Der Computer als Werkzeug und Medium. Die geistigen und technischen Wurzeln des Personal Computers.* Berlin: Verlag für Geschichte der Naturwissenschaften und der Technik, 1999.

Fuller, Steve. *Thomas Kuhn: A Philosophical History for Our Times.* Chicago: University of Chicago Press, 2000.

Galbraith, John K. *The New Industrial State.* New York: New American Library, 1968.

Gandhi, Mohandas Karamchand. *An Autobiography: Or the Story of My Experiments with Truth.* Ahmedabad: Navajivan, 1927.

Gay, Paul de, et al. *Doing Cultural Studies: The Story of the Sony Walkman.* Milton Keynes: Open University Press, 1997.

Gibbons, Michael, et al. *The New Production of Knowledge: The Dynamics of Science and Research in Contemporary Societies.* London: Sage, 1994.

Giedion, Siegfried. *Mechanization Takes Command: A Contribution to Anonymous History.* New York: Oxford University Press, 1948.

Gillies, James, and Robert Cailliau. *How the Web Was Born: The Story of the World Wide Web.* Oxford: Oxford University Press, 2000.

Gillispie, Charles Coulston. *Science and Polity in France at the End of the Old Regime.* Princeton, NJ: Princeton University Press, 1980.

Gittings, John. *Real China: From Cannibalism to Karaoke.* London: Simon & Schuster, 1996.

Gjøen, Heidi, and Mikael Hård. "Cultural Politics in Action: User Scripts in Relation to the Electric Vehicle." *Science, Technology, and Human Values* 27 (2002): 262–81.

Golinski, Jan. *Making Natural Knowledge: Constructivism and the History of Science.* Cambridge: Cambridge University Press, 1998.

Goodfield, June. *Playing God: Genetic Engineering and the Manipulation of Life.* New York: Random House, 1977.

Gottlieb, Robert. *Forcing the Spring: The Transformation of the American Environmental Movement.* Washington, D.C.: Island Press, 1993.

Goubert, Jean-Pierre. "The Development of Water and Sewerage Systems in France, 1850–1950." In *Technology and the Rise of the Networked City in Europe and America,* edited by Joel A. Tarr and Gabriel Dupuy. Philadelphia: Temple University Press, 1988.

Gouldner, Alvin. *Against Fragmentation: The Origins of Marxism and the Sociology of Intellectuals.* New York: Oxford University Press, 1985.

Grafton, Anthony. *Leon Battista Alberti: Master Builder of the Italian Renaissance.* New York: Hill and Wang, 2000.

Grafton, Anthony, and Ann Blair, eds. *The Transmission of Culture in Early Modern Europe.* Philadelphia: University of Pennsylvania Press, 1990.

Grell, Ole Peter, ed. *Paracelsus: The Man and His Reputation, His Ideas and Their Transformation.* Leiden: Brill, 1998.

Habermas, Jürgen. *The Structural Transformation of the Public Sphere: An Inquiry into a Category of Bourgeois Society.* Cambridge: Polity, 1962/1989.

Hajer, Maarten. *The Politics of Environmental Discourse: Ecological Modernization and the Policy Process.* Oxford: Clarendon, 1995.

Hall, Peter. *Cities in Civilization: Culture, Innovation and Urban Order.* London: Weidenfeld and Nicolson, 1998.

Haraway, Donna J. *Modest_Witness@Second_Millennium. FemaleMan©_Meets_OncoMouse™: Feminism and Technoscience.* New York: Routledge, 1997.

———. *Simians, Cyborgs, and Women: The Reinvention of Nature.* London: Free Associations Books, 1991.

Hård, Mikael. *Machines Are Frozen Spirit: The Scientification of Refrigeration and Brewing in the 19th Century—A Weberian Interpretation.* Frankfurt am Main and Boulder, CO: Campus Verlag and Westview Press, 1994.

———. "*Mechanica* och *mathesis.* Några tankar kring Christopher Polhems fysikaliska och vetenskapsteoretiska föreställningar." *Lychnos: Annual of the Swedish History of Science Society* (1986): 55–69.

Hård, Mikael, and Andrew Jamison, eds. *The Intellectual Appropriation of Technology: Discourses on Modernity, 1900–1939.* Cambridge, MA: MIT Press, 1998.

Hård, Mikael, and Andreas Knie. "The Ruler of the Game: The Defining Power of the Standard Automobile." In *The Car and Its Environments: The Past, Present, and Future of the Motorcar in Europe,* edited by Knut H. Sørensen. Bruxelles and Luxembourg: The European Commission, 1994.

Harding, Sandra. *Is Science Multicultural? Postcolonialisms, Feminisms and Epistemologies.* Bloomington: Indiana University Press, 1998.

Harper, Peter, and Godfrey Boyle, eds. *Radical Technology.* London: Wildwood House, 1976.

Hauser, Susanne. " 'Reinlichkeit, Ordnung und Schönheit'—Zur Diskussion über Kanalisation im 19. Jahrhundert." *Die alte Stadt* 19 (1992): 292–312.

Hawken, Paul, Amory Lovins, and L. Hunter Lovins. *Natural Capitalism: Creating the Next Industrial Revolution.* Boston: Little, Brown, 1999.

Headrick, Daniel R. *The Tentacles of Progress: Technology Transfer in the Age of Imperialism, 1850–1940.* New York: Oxford University Press, 1988.

———. *The Tools of Empire: Technology and European Imperialism in the Nineteenth Century.* New York: Oxford University Press, 1981.

Nader, Ralph. *Unsafe at Any Speed: The Designed-in Dangers of the American Automobile.* New York: Grossman, 1965.

Næss, Arne. *Ecology, Community and Lifestyle: Outline of an Ecosophy.* Cambridge: Cambridge University Press, 1989.

———. "The Shallow and the Deep: Long-Range Ecology Movement." *Inquiry* 16 (1973): 95–100.

Nakayama, Shigeru. *Science, Technology and Society in Postwar Japan.* London: Kegan Paul International, 1991.

Nanda, Meera. *Prophets Facing Backward: Postmodern Critiques of Science and Hindu Nationalism in India.* Piscataway, NJ: Rutgers University Press, 2003.

Nandy, Ashis. *Traditions, Tyranny and Utopias: Essays in the Politics of Awareness.* Delhi: Oxford University Press, 1987.

Needham, Joseph. *The Grand Titration: Science and Society in East and West.* London: Allen and Unwin, 1969.

———. *Science in Traditional China: A Comparative Perspective.* Hong Kong: Chinese University Press, 1981.

Nelkin, Dorothy, and M. Susan Lindee. *The DNA Mystique: The Gene as a Cultural Icon.* Oxford: Freeman, 1995.

Nelson, Richard, ed. *National Systems of Innovation: A Comparative Analysis.* New York: Oxford University Press, 1993.

Nelson, Richard, and Sheldon Winter. *An Evolutionary Theory of Economic Change.* Cambridge, MA: Belknap Press of Harvard University Press, 1982.

Nickles, Shelley. "'Preserving Women': Refrigerator Design as a Social Process in the 1930s." *Technology and Culture* 43 (2002): 693–727.

Noble, David F. *America by Design: Science, Technology, and the Rise of Corporate Capitalism.* New York: Knopf, 1977.

———. *The Religion of Technology: The Divinity of Man and the Spirit of Invention.* New York: Knopf, 1997.

———. *A World without Women: The Christian Clerical Culture of Western Science.* New York: Knopf, 1992.

Noever, Peter, ed. *Der Preis der Schönheit. 100 Jahre Wiener Werkstätte.* Ostfildern-Ruit: Hatje Cantz Verlag, 2003.

Northrop, F.S.C. *The Meeting of East and West: An Inquiry Concerning World Understanding.* New York: Macmillan, 1946.

Nowotny, Helga, Peter Scott, and Michael Gibbons. *Re-thinking Science: Knowledge and the Public in an Age of Uncertainty.* Cambridge: Polity, 2001.

Nye, David. *American Technological Sublime.* Cambridge, MA: MIT Press, 1994.

———. *Electrifying America: Social Meanings of a New Technology.* Cambridge, MA: MIT Press, 1990.

Ogburn, William. *Social Change with Respect to Culture and Original Nature.* New York: Viking Press, 1922.

Orange, Derek. "Rational Dissent and Provincial Science: William Turner and the Newcastle Literary and Philosophical Society." In *Metropolis and Province: Science in British Culture, 1780–1850,* edited by Ian Inkster and Jack Morrell. Philadelphia: University of Pennsylvania Press, 1983.

Osborn, Fairfield. *Our Plundered Planet.* Boston: Little, Brown, 1948.

Osietzki, Maria. "Die Gründungsgeschichte des Deutschen Museums von Meisterwerken der Naturwissenschaften und Technik in München 1903–1906." *Technikgeschichte* 52 (1985): 49–75.

———. "Weiblichkeitsallegorien der Elektrizität als 'Wunschmaschinen.'" *Technikgeschichte* 63 (1996): 47–70.

Outram, Dorinda. *The Enlightenment.* Cambridge: Cambridge University Press, 1995.

Ovitt, George Jr. "The Cultural Context of Western Technology: Early Christian Attitudes toward Manual Labour." *Technology and Culture* 27 (1986): 477–500.
———. *The Restoration of Perfection: Labor and Technology in Medieval Culture.* New Brunswick, NJ: Rutgers University Press, 1987.
Pacey, Arnold. *The Maze of Ingenuity: Ideas and Idealism in the Development of Technology.* London: Allen Lane, 1974.
———. *Technology in World Civilization: A Thousand-Year History.* Oxford: Basil Blackwell, 1990.
Packard, Vance. *The Waste Makers.* New York: Pocket Books, 1960.
Paech, Anne, and Joachim Paech. *Menschen im Kino. Film und Literatur erzählen.* Stuttgart: Metzler, 2000.
Parameswaran, M.P. "Significance of Silent Valley." *Economic and Political Weekly,* July 7, 1979.
Pells, Richard. *Radical Visions and American Dreams: Culture and Social Thought in the Depression Years.* New York: Harper and Row, 1973.
Peña, Carolyn Thomas de la. "Recharging at the Fordyce: Confronting the Machine and Nature in the Modern Bath." *Technology and Culture* 40 (1999): 746–69.
Phillipson, Nicholas. "Commerce and Culture: Edinburgh, Edinburgh University, and the Scottish Enlightenment." In *The University and the City: From Medieval Origins to the Present,* edited by Thomas Bender. Oxford: Oxford University Press, 1988.
Pinch, Trevor J., and Wiebe E. Bijker. "The Social Construction of Facts and Artifacts: Or How the Sociology of Science and the Sociology of Technology Might Benefit Each Other." In *The Social Construction of Technological Systems: New Direction in the Sociology and History of Technology,* edited by Wiebe E. Bijker, Thomas P. Hughes, and Trevor J. Pinch. Cambridge, MA: MIT Press, 1987.
Pool, Ithiel de Sola, ed. *The Social Impact of the Telephone.* Cambridge, MA: MIT Press, 1977.
Popper, Karl. *The Logic of Scientific Discovery.* London: Hutchinson, 1959.
Porter, Dorothy. "The History of Public Health: Current Themes and Approaches," *Hygiea Internationalis* 1 (1999): 9–21, http://www.ep.liu.se/ej/hygiea/ (accessed January 2005).
Porter, Roy, and Mikulás Teich, eds. *The Scientific Revolution in National Context.* Cambridge: Cambridge University Press, 1992.
Prakash, Gyan. *Another Reason: Science and the Imagination of Modern India.* Princeton, NJ: Princeton University Press, 1999.
Price, Derek J. de Solla. *Little Science, Big Science.* New York: Columbia University Press, 1963.
Pursell, Carroll. "Government and Technology in the Great Depression." *Technology and Culture* 20 (1979): 162–74.
———. "The Rise and Fall of the Appropriate Technology Movement in the United States, 1965–1985." *Technology and Culture* 34 (1993): 629–37.
Pye, Lucian W. *Asian Power and Politics: The Cultural Dimensions of Authority.* Cambridge, MA: Belknap Press, 1985.
Pyenson, Lewis, and Susan Sheets-Pyenson. *Servants of Nature: A History of Scientific Institutions, Enterprises and Sensibilities.* New York: Norton, 1999.
Radkau, Joachim. *Das Zeitalter der Nervosität. Deutschland zwischen Bismarck und Hitler.* Munich and Vienna: Carl Hanser, 1998.
Rathenau, Walther. *Zur Kritik der Zeit.* Berlin: S. Fischer, 1912.
Reich, Leonard S. *The Making of American Industrial Research: Science and Business at GE and Bell, 1876–1926.* Cambridge: Cambridge University Press, 1985.
Ricardo, Harry R. "Applied Research." *Proceedings of the Institution of Mechanical Engineers* 152 (1945): 143–48.
———. *Memories and Machines: The Patterns of My Life.* London: Constable, 1968.

Richta, Radovan, et al. *Civilization at the Crossroads: Social and Human Implications of the Scientific and Technological Revolution.* Prague: Academy of Sciences, 1968.

Ringer, Fritz. *The Decline of the German Mandarins: The German Academic Community, 1890–1933.* Cambridge, MA: Harvard University Press, 1969.

Roberts, Gerrylynn K. "Technologies of Water, Waste and Pollution." In *American Cities and Technology: Wilderness to Wired City,* Gerrylynn K. Roberts and Philip Steadman. London and New York: Routledge and Open University Press, 1999.

Roberts, Gerrylynn K., and Philip Steadman. *American Cities and Technology: Wilderness to Wired City.* London and New York: Routledge and Open University Press, 1999.

Rodenstein, Marianne. *"Mehr Licht, mehr Luft." Gesundheitskonzepte im Städtebau seit 1750.* Frankfurt am Main: Campus Verlag, 1988.

Rodgers, Daniel T. *Atlantic Crossings: Social Politics in a Progressive Age.* Cambridge, MA: Belknap, 1998.

Rogers, Everett, and Judith Larsen. *Silicon Valley Fever: Growth of High-Technology Culture.* London: Allen and Unwin, 1985.

Rohkrämer, Thomas. *Eine andere Moderne? Zivilisationskritik, Natur und Technik in Deutschland 1880–1933.* Paderborn: Ferdinand Schöningh, 1999.

Rosenberg, David. *Cloning Silicon Valley: The Next Generation High-Tech Hotspots.* London: Pearson Education, 2002.

Rostow, W.W. *The Stages of Economic Growth: A Non-communist Manifesto.* Cambridge: Cambridge University Press, 1960.

Ruppert, Wolfgang, ed. *Fahrrad, Auto, Fernsehschrank. Zur Kulturgeschichte der Alltagsdinge.* Frankfurt am Main: Fischer Taschenbuch Verlag, 1993.

Russell, Colin. *Science and Social Change 1700–1900.* London: Macmillan, 1983.

Ruth, Arne. "The Second New Nation: The Mythology of Modern Sweden." *Daedalus* 113 (1984): 53–96.

Sachs, Wolfgang. *Die Liebe zum Automobil. Ein Rückblick in die Geschichte unserer Wünsche.* Reinbek: Rowohlt Verlag, 1984.

Said, Edward. *Culture and Imperialism.* New York: Knopf, 1993.

Sale, Kirkpatrick. *Rebels against the Future: The Luddites and Their War on the Industrial Revolution: Lessons for the Computer Age.* Reading, MA: Addison-Wesley, 1995.

Salomon, Jean-Jacques. "Science Policy Studies and the Development of Science Policy." In *Science Technology and Society: A Cross-Disciplinary Perspective,* edited by Derek de Solla Price and Ina Spiegel-Rösing. London: Sage, 1977.

Sass, Friedrich. *Geschichte des deutschen Verbrennungsmotorenbaues. Von 1860 bis 1918.* Berlin: Springer-Verlag, 1962.

Sassower, Raphael. *Technoscientific Angst.* Minneapolis: University of Minnesota Press, 1997.

Schäfer, Wolf, ed. *Finalization in Science: The Social Orientation of Scientific Progress.* Dordrecht, the Netherlands: Reidel, 1983.

Scheler, Max. *Problems of a Sociology of Knowledge.* London: Routledge, 1924/1980.

Schelling, F.W.J. *On University Studies.* Athens: Ohio University Press, 1802/1966.

Schivelbusch, Wolfgang. *The Railway Journey: The Industrialization and Perception of Time and Space.* Berkeley: University of California Press, 1977/1986.

Schmidt-Bergmann, Hansgeorg. *Futurismus: Geschichte, Ästhetik, Dokumente.* Reinbek: Rowohlt, 1993.

Schubert, Ulrich. *Vorgeschichte und Geschichte des Deutschen Hygiene-Museums in Dresden (1871–1931).* Dresden: Medizinische Akademie, 1986.

Schumacher, E.F. *Small Is Beautiful: Economics as If People Mattered.* London: Blond and Briggs, 1973.

Schumpeter, Joseph. *Capitalism, Socialism and Democracy.* New York: Harper and Brothers, 1942.

Schwentker, Wolfgang. "Barbaren und Lehrmeister. Formen fremdkultureller Wahrnehmung im Japan des 19. Jahrhunderts." In *"Barbaren" und "weiße Teufel." Kulturkonflikte und Imperialismus in Asien vom 18. bis zum 20. Jahrhundert*, edited by Eva-Maria Auch and Stig Förster. Paderborn: Ferdinand Schönigh, 1997.

Science for the People, eds. *China: Science Walks on Two Legs.* New York: Avon Books, 1974.

Shapin, Steven. *The Scientific Revolution.* Chicago: University of Chicago Press, 1996.

Sharp, Lauriston. "Steel Axes for Stone-Age Australians." *Human Organization* 11 (1952): 17–22.

Shelley, Mary. *Frankenstein, or The Modern Prometheus. The 1818 Text.* Oxford: Oxford University Press, 1818/1993.

Shiva, Vandana. *Staying Alive: Women, Ecology and Development.* London: Zed Books, 1988.

———. *Stolen Harvest: The Hijacking of the Global Food Supply.* Cambridge, MA: South End, 2000.

Sieferle, Rolf Peter. *Fortschrittsfeinde? Opposition gegen Technik und Industrie von der Romantik bis zur Gegenwart.* Munich: Beck, 1984.

Skinner, Quentin. *Machiavelli.* Oxford: Oxford University Press, 1981.

Smith, Bonnie G. "Gender and the Practices of Scientific History: The Seminar and Archival Research in the Nineteenth Century." *American Historical Review* 100 (1995): 1150–76.

Smith, Merritt Roe. *Harpers Ferry Armory and the New Technology: The Challenge of Change.* Ithaca, NY: Cornell University Press, 1977.

Smith, Merritt Roe, and Leo Marx, eds. *Does Technology Drive History? The Dilemma of Technological Determinism.* Cambridge, MA: MIT Press, 1994.

Snow, C.P. *The Two Cultures and the Scientific Revolution.* Cambridge, MA: Harvard University Press, 1959.

Sobchack, Vivian. *Screening Space: The American Science Fiction Film.* New Brunswick, NJ: Rutgers University Press, 1997.

Sobel, Dava. *Galileo's Daughter: A Historical Memoir of Science, Faith, and Love.* New York: Walker, 1999.

———. *Longitude: The True Story of a Lone Genius Who Solved the Greatest Scientific Problem of His Time.* London: Fourth Estate, 1996.

Söderqvist, Thomas. *The Ecologists: From Merry Naturalists to Saviors of the Nation.* Stockholm: Almqvist and Wiksell, 1986.

Sombart, Werner. *Deutscher Sozialismus.* Berlin: Buchholz and Weisswange, 1934.

Sörlin, Sverker. *Framtidslandet. Debatten om Norrland och naturresurserna under det industriella genombrottet.* Stockholm: Carlssons, 1988.

Spence, Jonathan. *The Search for Modern China.* London: Hutchinson, 1990.

Spengler, Oswald. *The Decline of the West.* London: Allen and Unwin, 1918/1922.

Spieker, Ira. "'Jedem Deutschen wöchentlich ein Bad!' Die Popularisierung von Volksbädern um die Jahrhundertwende und ihre Einrichtung im ländlichen Raum." In *Reinliche Leiber—Schmutzige Geschäfte. Körperhygiene und Reinlichkeitsvorstellungen in zwei Jahrhunderten*, edited by Regina Löneke and Ira Spieker. Göttingen: Wallstein, 1996.

Standage, Tom. *The Victorian Internet: The Remarkable Story of the Telegraph and the Nineteenth Century's Online Pioneers.* London: Weidenfeld and Nicolson, 1998.

Stehr, Nico. *Knowledge Societies.* London: Sage, 1994.

Stradling, David. *Smokestacks and Progressives: Environmentalists, Engineers and Air Quality in America, 1881–1951.* Baltimore, MD: Johns Hopkins University Press, 1999.

Suzuki Daisetz Teitaro. *Zen and Japanese Culture.* Princeton, NJ: Princeton University Press, 1938/1970.

Takezawa Shinichi. "Arbeitsmotivation und technoloigscher Wandel." In *Japan und der Westen.* Vol. 2, *Wirtschafts-und Sozialwissenschaften, Technologie,* edited by Constantin von Barloewen and Kai Werhahn-Mees. Frankfurt am Main: Fischer, 1986.

Tallack, Douglas. *Twentieth-Century America: The Intellectual and Cultural Context.* Harlow, Essex: Longman House, 1991.

Tanizaki Jun'ichirō. *In Praise of Shadows.* New Haven, CT: Leete's Island Books, 1933/1977.

Tarr, Joel A., and Gabriel Dupuy, eds. *Technology and the Rise of the Networked City in Europe and America.* Philadelphia: Temple University Press, 1988.

Taylor, F. Sherwood. *The Alchemists.* London: Heinemann, 1952.

Teich, Mikuláš, and Robert Young, eds. *Changing Perspectives in the History of Science: Essays in Honour of Joseph Needham.* Dordrecht, the Netherlands: Reidel, 1973.

Tengström, Emin. *Bilismen, i kris? En bok om bilen, människan, samhället och miljön.* Stockholm: Rabén och Sjögren, 1991.

Thackray, Arnold. "Natural Knowledge in Cultural Context: The Manchester Model." *American Historical Review* 79 (1974): 672–709.

Thackray, Arnold, and Robert K. Merton. "On Discipline Building: The Paradoxes of George Sarton." *Isis* 63 (1972): 473–95.

Thomas, Donald E. Jr. *Diesel: Technology and Society in Industrial Germany.* Tuscaloosa: University of Alabama Press, 1987.

Thomas, Keith. *Religion and the Decline of Magic: Studies in Popular Belief in Sixteenth and Seventeenth Century England.* New York: Scribner's, 1971.

Thompson, E.P. *The Making of the English Working Class.* New York: Victor Gollancz, 1963.

———. *William Morris: Romantic to Revolutionary.* 2nd ed. London: Merlin Press, 1955/1977.

Tichi, Cecilia. *Shifting Gears: Technology, Literature, Culture in Modernist America.* Chapel Hill: University of North Carolina Press, 1987.

Tönnies, Ferdinand. *Community and Civil Society.* Edited by José Harris. Cambridge: Cambridge University Press, 1887/2001.

Tormin, Ulrich. *Alptraum Großstadt. Urbane Dystopien in ausgewählten Science Fiction-Filmen.* Alfeld: Coppi-Verlag, 1996.

Turkle, Sherry. *The Second Self: Computers and the Human Spirit.* New York: Simon & Schuster, 1984.

Turner, R. Steven. "The Prussian Universities and the Concept of Research." *Internationales Archiv für Sozialgeschichte der deutschen Literatur* 5 (1980): 68–93.

Uglow, Jenny. "Introduction." In *Cultural Babbage: Technology, Time and Invention,* edited by Francis Spufford and Jenny Uglow. London: Faber and Faber, 1996.

———. *The Lunar Men: Five Friends Whose Curiosity Changed the World.* New York: Farrar, Straus and Giroux, 2002.

Usher, Abbott Payson. *A History of Mechanical Inventions.* New York: McGraw-Hill, 1929.

Veblen, Thorstein. *Absentee Ownership and Business Enterprise in Recent Times: The Case of America.* New York: B.W. Huebsch, 1923.

———. *The Engineers and the Price System.* New York: B.W. Huebsch, 1921.

———. *The Instinct of Workmanship and the State of the Industrial Arts.* New York: Macmillan, 1914.

———. *The Theory of the Leisure Class: An Economic Study in the Evolution of Institutions.* New York: Macmillan, 1899.

Volti, Rudi. "Alternative Internal Combustion Engines, 1900–1915." In *Automobile Engineering in a Dead End: Mainstream and Alternative Developments in the 20th Century,* edited by Mikael Hård. Gothenburg: Gothenburg University, 1992.

Wad, Atul, ed. *Science, Technology and Development.* London: IT Publications, 1988.

Wagner, Michael. *Det polytekniske gennembrud. Romantikkens teknologiske konstruktion 1780–1850.* Århus: Aarhus Universitetsforlag, 1999.

Wajcman, Judy. *Feminism Confronts Technology.* Cambridge: Polity, 1991.

Wallace, Anthony F.C. *Rockdale: The Growth of an American Village in the Early Industrial Revolution.* New York: Knopf, 1978.

Walls, Laura Dassow. *Seeing New Worlds: Henry David Thoreau and Nineteenth-Century Natural Science*. Madison: University of Wisconsin Press, 1995.

Ward, Barbara, and René Dubos. *Only One Earth: The Care and Maintenance of a Small Planet*. London: Andre Deutsch, 1972.

Watson, James. *The Double Helix: A Personal Account of the Discovery of the Structure of DNA*. New York: Atheneum, 1968.

Weber, Heike. "Technisiertes Vergnügen: Unterhaltung im kaiserzeitlichen Berlin." Master's thesis, Berlin Technical University, 2000.

Weber, Max. *The Protestant Ethic and the Spirit of Capitalism*. London: Routledge, 1904/1992.

———. "Science as a Vocation." In *From Max Weber: Essays in Sociology*, edited by H.H. Gerth and C. Wright Mills. New York: Oxford University Press, 1919/1958.

Webster, Charles. *The Great Instauration: Science, Medicine and Reform 1626–1660*. New York: Holmes and Meier, 1975.

Weinberg, Alvin M. *Reflections on Big Science*. Cambridge, MA: MIT Press, 1967.

Weiss, Sheila. "The Race Hygiene Movement in Germany." *Osiris* 3 (1987): 193–236.

Weizenbaum, Joseph. *Computer Power and Human Reason: From Judgment to Calculation*. San Francisco, CA: W.H. Freeman, 1976.

Wendt, Ulrich. *Die Technik als Kulturmacht in sozialer und geistiger Beziehung*. Berlin: Reimer, 1906.

Werskey, Gary. *The Visible College: A Collective Biography of British Scientists and Socialists of the 1930s*. London: Allen Lane, 1978.

White, Hayden. *The Content of the Form: Narrative Discourse and Historical Representation*. Baltimore, MD: Johns Hopkins University Press, 1987.

White, Lynn. *Medieval Religion and Technology: Collected Essays*. Berkeley: University of California Press, 1978.

———. *Medieval Technology and Social Change*. London: Oxford University Press, 1962.

Whitehead, Alfred North. *Science and the Modern World*. New York: Macmillan, 1925.

Wiener, Martin. *English Culture and the Decline of the Industrial Spirit, 1850–1980*. Cambridge: Cambridge University Press, 1981.

Wigforss, Ernst. *Från klasskamp till samverkan*. Stockholm: Tiden, 1941.

Williams, Raymond. *Culture and Society 1780–1950*. Harmondsworth: Penguin, 1958/1971.

———. *Television: Technology and Cultural Form*. London: Fontana and Collins, 1974.

———. *Keywords: A Vocabulary of Culture and Society*. Croom Helm: Fontana, 1976.

———. *Marxism and Literature*. Oxford: Oxford University Press, 1977.

Winner, Langdon. "Do Artifacts Have Politics?" *Daedalus* 109 (1980): 121–36.

Winstanley, Gerrard. *The Law of Freedom and Other Writings*. Edited by Christopher Hill. Harmondsworth: Penguin, 1652/1973.

Winston, Brian. *Media Technology and Society: A History: From the Telegraph to the Internet*. London: Routledge, 1998.

Wisnioski, Matt. "Inside 'the System': Engineers, Scientists, and the Boundaries of Social Protest in the Long 1960s." *History and Technology* 19 (2003): 313–33.

Wit, Onno de, et al. "Innovation Junctions: Office Technologies in the Netherlands." *Technology and Culture* 43 (2002): 50–72.

Wolff, Claudia. *Georg Gaffky (1850–1918). Erster Vertreter der Hygiene in Gießen von 1888–1904*. Giessen: Wilhelm Schmitz Verlag, 1992.

Worster, Donald. *Nature's Economy: The Roots of Ecology*. San Francisco: Sierra Club Books, 1977.

Wright, Georg Henrik von. *Myten om framsteget. Tankar 1987–1992. Med en intellektuell självbiografi*. Stockholm: Bonniere, 1993.

Yates, Frances. *Giordano Bruno and the Hermetic Tradition*. London: Routledge and Kegan Paul, 1964.

———. *The Rosicrucian Enlightenment.* London: Routledge and Kegan Paul, 1972.

Yeo, Richard. *Defining Science: William Whewell, Natural Knowledge and Public Debate in Early Victorian Britain.* Cambridge: Cambridge University Press, 1993.

Yoxen, Edward. *The Gene Business: Who Should Control Biotechnology?* London: Pan Books, 1983.

Zilsel, Edgar. *The Social Origins of Modern Science.* Edited by Diederick Raven, Wolfgang Krohn, and Robert S. Cohen. Dordrecht: Kluwer Academic Publishers, 2000.

———. "The Sociological Roots of Science." *American Journal of Sociology* 47 (1942): 245–79.

INDEX

A

Abel, Rudolf, 228
Académie des Sciences, 39, 42, 79
academy, 40
academy of science, 21, 26, 42, 202
Accademia del ciemento, 79
Addams, Jane, 104, 107, 147, 219, 225,
  238–239
Agarwal, Anil, 143
agora, 77
Agricola, Georgius (Georg Bauer), 201
agriculture, 277, 279, 282–283
air condition, 238
alchemy, 35
d'Alembert, Jean le Rond, 76
Alexandria, 200
Allen, Paul, 204
alternative technology, 194
ambivalence, 7
amusement park, 187
Apple Company, 205–206
appropriate technology, 122, 271, 278, 283
Arabic, 27
Arendt, Hannah, 251
Aristotle, 77
arms race, 249
ARPANET, 198–199
art, 147, 152, 155–157, 162–166
arts and crafts, 145, 147–148, 163
Asia, 127–129, 193, 265
atomic bomb, 160–161, 306
atomic energy, 255, 260, 272–273, 284

Atwood, Margaret, 7, 265
Austria, 148, 273
automobile, 159, 179–187, 192–193, 234

B

Babbage, Charles, 60
Bacon, Francis, 6, 19–20, 40–41, 255,
  305–306
bacteriology, 241
Bakunin, Mikhail, 66
Balazs, Etienne, 136
Balla, Giacomo, 154, 172–173
Baran, Paul, 197–198
bathroom, 130, 232–233
bathtub, 230, 234
Bauhaus, 148, 164–165
BBC, 210
Beck, Ulrich, 7
Beckmann, Johannes, 295
Beer, John J., 91
Bell, Alexander Graham, 213–214
Bellamy, Edward, 64, 146
Ben-David, Joseph, 39
Benedict, Ruth, 134, 251
Beniger, James, 179
Benjamin, Walter, 157
Berg, Maxine, 52
Bergson, Henri, 172
Berlin, 240
Bernal, John Desmond, 254–255, 302
Berner, Boel, 235

Berners-Lee, Tim, 199–200
Bernstein, Eduard, 67
bicycle, 180–183, 190
Bierbaum, Otto Julius, 179, 184, 192
big science, 252, 255–256, 263, 301
Bigelow, Jacob, 61, 296
biotechnology, 2, 264
Birmingham, 84
Black, Joseph, 80
Blake, William, 45, 59
Boccioni, Umberto, 154
Böhme, Gernot, 258
Bok, Derek, 266
Boorstin, David, 299
Booth, H. Cecil, 235
Borgström, Georg, 277
Boulton, Matthew, 84
Bourdieu, Pierre, 111
Boyle, Robert, 21, 25
Brahe, Tycho, 35–38
Braverman, Harry, 303
brewing industry, 89
Britain, 52, 58, 61, 64, 68, 81–84, 87, 99,
    114, 140, 148, 181–183, 211, 221, 225,
    253, 256, 263, 270, 285, 299–300
British Association of the Advancement of
    Science (BAAS), 61, 296
Brooks, Harvey, 259
Brower, David, 282
Bruland, Tine, 303
Brundtland, Gro Harlem, 273
Bruno, Giordano, 33, 38
Burkhardt, Johannes, 201
Bush, Vannevar, 255
Bushnell, Nolan, 207
Butler, Samuel, 146
Butterfield, Herbert, 23, 299
Byron, Lord (George Gordon), 46

C

Cailliau, Robert, 199–200
Campanella, Tomaso, 6, 38
car (see automobile)
Carlyle, Thomas, 296
Carson, Rachel, 277, 282
Cézanne, Paul, 155–156
Chaplin, Charlie, 158, 163

Chicago, 240
Childs, Marquis, 115
China, 27, 31, 124–131, 135–139, 143, 152,
    211, 270
Chomsky, Noam, 246
cinema (see film)
civilization, 108, 178, 185
cleanliness, 220, 229, 232
cloning, 7
CNN, 210
cold war, 207, 250
colonization, 139
commercialization, 266, 288
Commoner, Barry, 277
computer, 199–206, 217, 250
Comte, August, 43, 64, 249
Conant, James, 299
Cooke, William, 211
Coomaraswamy, Ananda, 140
counterculture, 250
Cowan, Ruth Schwartz, 12, 232
Crick, Francis, 1, 254, 263
cultural approaches, 9
cultural appropriation, 4, 13–14, 22, 26–27,
    34, 48, 54, 56–58, 63, 84, 100, 167, 185,
    207, 210, 220, 229, 239, 265, 276–278,
    284–288, 294, 307
cultural assessment, 4, 8, 60, 107, 161,
    293–294, 305–306
cultural critique, 54, 56, 107
cyborg, 3, 161, 262
Czechoslovakia, 249

D

Daimler, Gottlieb, 186
Dalton, John, 84
Darwin, Charles, 51, 62, 66, 99
Darwin, Erasmus, 51
Denmark, 61, 63, 68, 261, 269–271, 284,
    286
Descartes, René, 25
design, 147, 163
Deutsches Museum, 112, 297
Dewey, John, 104, 138
Dickens, Charles, 60, 225
Diderot, Denis, 76, 295
Diesel, Eugen, 216

Diesel, Rudolf, 89, 216
Diggers, 19–21, 25, 40
Disch, Thomas, 167
discipline, 225, 229, 237
Disney, Walt (Walter Elias), 206
DNA, 1
domestication, 232
Drais, Karl Friedrich, 181
Dreiser, Theodore, 191–192
Dubos, René, 283
Durkheim, Émile, 68
Dylan, Bob (Robert Allen Zimmerman),
    250

E

ecoefficiency, 289
École Polytechnique, 43, 87
ecology, 273–275, 278, 280
Edinburgh, 80–81
Edison, Thomas Alva, 68, 91–92, 102, 189,
    214, 223
Ehrenburg, Ilya, 173
Ehrlich, Paul, 277, 282
Einstein, Albert, 172, 254
Eisenhower, Dwight D., 246
Eisenstein, Elizabeth, 201
electric car, 188–189, 193–195
electric light, 130
electricity, 222, 242
Elias, Norbert, 9, 221
Eliot, T. S., 106
Elton, Charles, 281
e-mail, 212–213
Encyclopédie, 76, 80, 202, 295
energy, 123, 222, 283
Engelbart, Douglas, 206
Engels, Friedrich, 24, 57, 63, 225, 297
England, 11, 19–20, 25, 45–46, 60, 64, 67,
    71, 146, 148, 171–172, 259
Enlightenment, 42
entertainment, 206–208, 266
environment, 123–125, 154, 211, 237, 241
environmental movement, 271, 273, 275,
    278–279, 281–282, 284, 287
environmentalism, 226, 228, 267, 270,
    274–281, 285–288, 291, 303
Erasmus of Rotterdam, Desiderius, 34
Euclid, 200

eugenics, 99, 120, 227
European Commission, 289
European Union, 267, 271
experimental philosophy, 39, 42

F

Fanon, Frantz, 250
feminism, 23, 56, 142, 261, 303
film, 157–164, 167, 208
Finland, 164, 205, 265
Ford Motor Company, 150, 189
Ford, Henry, 101, 189–190, 194
Fordyce, Samuel, 234
fork, 304
Foucault, Michel, 11, 39, 42, 224, 247
Fourier, Charles, 64
France, 57, 68, 88, 181, 249, 256, 272
Frankenstein, 60, 160
Franklin, Benjamin, 42, 73
Freeman, Christopher, 55
French Revolution, 42, 80
Frevert, Ute, 225
Fromm, Erich, 251
futurism, 153, 157, 164

G

Gaffky, Georg, 227
Galbraith, John Kenneth, 106, 259
Galilei, Galileo, 22, 38
Galton, Francis, 99
Gandhi, Indira, 123, 141
Gandhi, Mahatma (Mohandras
    Karamchand), 139–141, 248, 271
garden cities, 237
gas, 222
Gaskell, Elizabeth, 60
Gates, Bill, 6, 204
Gaudi, Antonio, 166
Gaugin, Paul, 155
de Gaulle, Charles, 248
Geddes, Norman Bel, 151–152
gender, 87, 189, 288
General Electric, 92
General Motors Corporation, 150, 152, 190
genetic engineering, 264–265
Geoffrin, Marie Thérèse, 75

German Edison Company, 112–113
Germany, 35, 59, 68, 72, 83, 87–88, 99,
    101–103, 108, 111, 114, 148, 164–165,
    177, 180, 190–192, 212, 227, 232, 254,
    257–258, 272–273, 286–287
Gibbons, Michael, 252
Giedion, Sigfried, 8, 230
Giessen, University of, 87, 92, 227
globalization, 133, 209, 212, 266
Goethe, Johann Wolfgang von, 63, 176
Golinski, Jan, 32
Gorkij, Maxim, 157
Gray, Elisha, 213–214
Greenpeace, 287
Gresham College, 36
Grundtvig, N. F. S., 61–63
Gunnerus, Johan Ernst, 72
Gutenberg, Johann (Johannes Gensfleisch),
    201, 217

H

hacker, 203
Hamilton, Alice, 239
Haraway, Donna, 3, 262
Harding, Sandra, 262
Hauser, Susanne, 271
Hayek, Nicolas, 193–194
health resort, 234
Hegel, G. W. F., 296–297
Heine, Heinrich, 174
Hesse, Hermann, 250
Hill, Christopher, 10, 36
Hitler, Adolf, 191
Hobsbawm, Eric, 294
Hoffmann, Joseph, 152–153
Hoover, Herbert C., 106
Hoover, W. H., 235
Hopper, Edward, 164
Horkheimer, Max, 110
housewife, 235
hubris, 2, 6, 24, 30, 36, 53, 60, 88, 98, 100,
    107, 122–126, 136, 152, 153, 160, 161,
    163, 221, 240–242, 246, 255, 256, 258,
    266, 278, 294, 306
Hughes, Thomas P., 51, 97, 102, 242,
    301
Hugo, Victor, 177
human ecology, 281

Hume, David, 80–81
Huxley, Julian, 281
hybrid, 3, 82, 122, 134–135, 141, 143, 146,
    147, 163, 165, 167, 203, 223, 234, 257,
    294, 306
hybrid identity, 29–30, 36, 40, 62, 79, 88,
    107, 127, 147, 247, 256, 259, 265, 276,
    278–279
hybridization, 28, 31, 138, 162, 167, 254,
    263
hydroelectricity, 121–122, 272
hygiene, 227, 229, 233, 235

I

Icarus, 5, 98, 100
Iida Kenichi, 131
imperialism, 58–59, 139
impressionist, 155–156
India, 2, 27, 121–129, 139–143, 211, 257,
    283, 285
industrial design, 150–151, 163–164
industrial heritage, 47
industrial revolution, 49, 52, 54, 65, 194
industrialization, 51–52, 54, 56, 58–59, 69,
    188, 276
International Business Machine Company
    (IBM), 204–206, 214
Internet, 3, 198–199, 201, 208, 217, 265
iron production, 132
irrigation, 136
Italy, 59, 153–154

J

Japan, 55, 127–135, 152, 193, 257,
    262–263
Jellinek, Emil, 186
Jennings, Humphrey, 53
Jobs, Steven, 206
Just, Adolf, 108

K

Kant, Immanuel, 76, 80, 173
Karloff, Boris, 160
Kasson, John, 149, 175

Keats, John, 60
Keller, Evelyn Fox, 11, 261
Kennedy, John F., 162, 258
Kepler, Johannes, 36
Kern, Stephen, 172
Kerouac, Jack, 191
Keynes, John Maynard, 253
King, Martin Luther, 1, 307
Kjellén, Rudolf, 118
Klages, Ludwig, 109
Koch, Robert, 241
Koyré, Alexander, 299
Kracauer, Siegfried, 157
Kranzberg, Melvin, 299
Kropotkin, Petr, 66–67
Krupp, Friedrich, 98
Krutch, Joseph Wood, 106
Kubrick, Stanley, 160
Kuhn, Thomas S., 10, 258

L

laboratory, 86–87, 91–93
Lang, Fritz, 158
Latour, Bruno, 12–13, 307
Le Corbusier (Charles Jeanneret), 152–153, 224
Leiden, 80–81
Lenin, Vladimir Illich, 189
Leopold, Aldo, 281
Liebig, Justus von, 87, 92, 240–241
Lindbergh, Charles, 174
Linde, Carl von, 88–89
Lindee, M. Susan, 265
Linnaeus, Carolus (Carl von Linné), 42, 72, 83, 176, 280
Linux, 205
List, Friedrich, 177
Loewy, Raymond, 151
Lomborg, Bjørn, 270, 275
London, 26, 36, 39, 42, 75, 79, 210–212
Loos, Adolf, 153
Los Angeles, 277
Lovins, Amory, 290
Lucas, George, 206
Ludd, Ned, 45
Luddites, 46–48, 56–57, 60, 118, 305
Luther, Martin, 34, 201

M

Mach, Ernst, 297
Machiavelli, Niccollò, 133–134
machine-breakers, 46
Macintosh, 206
MacKenzie, Donald, 303
MacRobie, George, 283
magic, 24, 30–31, 33–34, 38
Manchester, 85
Mandel, Ernest, 57
Manhattan Project, 254, 256
Mao Tse-tung, 124, 138–139, 270
Marcuse, Herbert, 39, 251, 257
Marinetti, Filippo Tommaso, 153–154, 173
Marx, Karl, 24, 57, 63–67, 297, 302
Marx, Leo, 9, 149, 175
masculinity, 192
mass production, 57, 102, 149, 152, 163, 190
Massachusetts Institute of Technology (MIT), 203, 207, 245–247, 255
Maybach, Wilhelm, 186
McCarthy, Joseph, 256
McLuhan, Marshall, 208–209
mechanical philosophy, 22–23
mechanization, 63
media, 199, 201, 207
medicine, 35, 40, 263
Melosi, Martin, 237
Mercedes, 186–188
Merchant, Carolyn, 23, 39, 303
Merton, Robert, 26, 301
miasma theory, 238, 240
Michaux, Pierre, 181
Micro Compact Car Company, 194
Microsoft Corporation, 204
Middle Ages, 5, 23
military, 57–59, 197–200, 207–208, 211, 233, 245–246, 250, 255
military-industrial complex, 246, 250
Miller, Oskar von, 112
modernism, 152
modernity, 13, 33, 40, 100, 102, 115–116, 120, 126, 134, 148, 155, 159, 164–165, 184, 189, 253, 259, 298
Molin, Adrian, 118
monasticism, 28
Monet, Claude, 155–156, 162, 165

Monge, Gaspard, 87
Mönkemeyer, Klaus, 226
More, Thomas, 31, 34
Morris, William, 64, 67, 145–148, 153, 162, 164–165, 167, 305
Morse, Samuel, 211
motorway, 191
movie (see film)
Muir, John, 280
Müller, Adam, 114
Mumford, Lewis, 8–9, 21, 104–105, 107–108, 281, 297
Munich, 88–89
municipal engineering, 222, 241
Musil, Robert, 112
Myrdal, Alva and Gunnar, 118

N

Nader, Ralph, 192
Næss, Arne, 271, 273–274
narrative, 5, 13, 21, 23, 33, 51, 175, 184, 205, 224, 255, 265, 296, 304
National Aeronautics and Space Administration (NASA), 258
national park, 280
nationalism, 59
native Americans, 13, 23, 51, 59
natural philosophy, 24
Naturphilosophie, 62–63
Needham, Joseph, 31, 135
Nehru, Jawaharlal, 121–122, 140–141
Nelkin, Dorothy, 265
Nelson, Ted, 200–202
Netherlands, 260, 284, 287
Neumann, Friedrich, 86
New York, 104, 106, 152, 165–166, 171, 234, 237–238, 281
Newton, Isaac, 21–23, 173
Nietzsche, Friedrich, 53
Nishida Kitar, 133
Nobel Prize, 1
Nobel, Alfred, 134
Noble, David, 99, 303
Nordström, Johan, 6, 29, 92, 106, 303
Nordström, Ludvig, 298
Norström, Vitalis, 118
Northrop, F. S. C., 128

Norway, 71, 80, 103, 116, 213, 271–273
Nye, David, 149, 166

O

Odum, Eugene, 281
Odum, Howard, 107, 281
Ogburn, William, 306
Olmstead, Frederick Law, 237
Opium War, 137
Oppenheimer, J. Robert, 256
Organization for Economic Cooperation and Development (OECD), 257–259
Organization of Petroleum Exporting Countries (OPEC), 284
Ørsted, Hans Christian, 62
Orwell, George, 305
Osborn, Fairfield, 281
Outram, Dorinda, 80
Owen, Robert, 60, 64

P

Packard, Vance, 151
Paracelsus (Theophrastus Bombastus von Hohenheim), 34–36, 41
Paris, 73, 74, 78, 249
Park, Robert, 281
Pasteur, Louis, 89–91, 94
pastoralism, 149
Pedersen, Amdi, 270
Pettenkofer, Max, 91, 227
Philadelphia, 80
photography, 157
Pixar Animation Studios, 206
Plato, 77
Polhem, Christopher, 84, 117
pollution, 277, 278, 282, 283, 287
Popper, Sir Karl, 39–40
populism, 67, 68
Porsche, Ferdinand, 190
positivism, 64–66, 249, 295, 297, 299
postindustrial society, 204
power, 247, 251–252, 259, 264
pragmatism, 120
Prague, 249
Price, Derek J. de Solla, 252, 255

Priessnitz, Wincenz, 230
Priestley, Joseph, 51, 84
printing, 201, 217
progress, 25, 298, 301
progressive movement, 226
pseudoscience, 25
public health, 224, 233, 239

R

Rabinowitch, Eugene, 256
radio, 198, 208
Radkau, Joachim, 216
railroad, 175–179, 212, 234
railway station, 156, 177
Rand Corporation, 197, 250
Ranke, Leopold von, 86
Rathenau, Emil, 223
Rathenau, Walther, 112–115, 260–262
Ravetz, Jerome, 258
reactionary modernism, 120, 142
Reagan, Ronald, 264
reductionism, 274
Reis, Johann Phillip, 213
Renaissance, 4, 6, 23, 32, 34
Renoir, Auguste, 155
Reuter, Paul Julius, 210
Ricardo, Harry R., 93–94
Richta, Radovan, 149
Rikli, Arnold, 230
risk society, 7
Roberts, Gerrylynn K., 239
Rohe, Mies van der, 148
Rohkrämer, Thomas, 109
romantic, 56, 60–63, 280, 298
Roosevelt, Franklin D., 254–255
Rosenberg, David, 265
Rostow, W. W., 258–259
Royal Society, 21, 39–40, 42, 79, 202

S

Saint Simon, Comte de (Claude Henry de Rouvroy), 43, 64, 249
Sakuma Shôzan, 132
Sale, Kirkpatrick, 47
Salomon, Jean-Jacques, 257, 260

sanitation, 220, 226, 228
Sarton, George, 298
Schallmayer, Wilhelm, 98–99
Schivelbusch, Wolfgang, 175
Schumacher, E. F., 122, 279
Schumpeter, Joseph, 49, 54, 300
science fiction, 158–161, 163
scientific method, 25
scientific reformation, 21, 27
scientific revolution, 21–22, 24, 26, 33
scientism, 141
seminar, 86
Serpollet, Léon, 188
sewage, 221, 222, 236, 239–240, 242
Shapin, Steven, 22
Sharp, Lauriston, 303
Shelley, Mary Wollstonecraft, 7, 60, 160
Shiva, Vandana, 2–3, 7, 142–143, 307
shower, 231, 233
Siemens, Werner von, 223
Sierra Club, 280, 282
Silicon Valley, 264–265
Sinclair, Upton, 225
Singapore, 193, 262, 265
Singer, Charles, 300
Skinner, Quentin, 133
Sloan, Arthur P., 150
Smiles, Samuel, 296
Smith, Adam, 80
Snow, C. P., 247, 256
Sobchack, Vivian, 161
Sobel, Dava, 26
Socrates, 77
Sombart, Werner, 115
Soviet Union, 198, 249, 253–255, 257
Spence, Jonathan, 137
Spengler, Oswald, 110
Sputnik, 198, 207, 257
Sri Lanka (Ceylon), 140
Standage, Tom, 210
standardization, 57, 149, 179
Stanley, F. E. and F. O., 189
Starley, James, 181
steam car, 188–190
Steiner, Rudolf, 108
Stockholm, 82–83, 283
stone axe, 304
story line, 5, 10
Sun Yat-sen, 137

sustainability, 124, 275
sustainable development, 267, 273, 279,
  288, 290–291
Sweden, 115–120, 164, 178, 256, 272–273,
  286, 298
Szilard, Leo, 254–256

T

Tagore, Rabindranath, 140
Takezawa Shinichi, 131
Tanizaki Jun'ichir, 130
Tati, Jacques, 158–159, 163
Taylor, Frederick Winslow, 101, 172–173
technocracy, 134, 164
technology assessment, 108, 260–261, 264,
  285
telegraph, 208–213
telephone, 208, 210, 213–217, 307
television, 208, 217
Tennessee Valley Authority (TVA), 253
theology, 28, 31
Third Reich, 94, 120
Thompson, E. P., 10
Thoreau, Henry David, 61, 140, 248, 280
Thorwalds, Linus Benedict, 205
time zones, 178
Titanic (1997 film), 160
Titanic (ship), 172
Todt, Fritz, 191
Tönnies, Ferdinand, 114
tourism, 177, 192
Toynbee, Arnold, 49, 65, 68
train station (see railway station)
transportation, 174–175
Trondheim, 71–72, 82
Turkle, Sherry, 203

U

Uglow, Jenny, 84
Union of Concerned Scientists, 245, 247
United Nations, 262, 267
United States, 11–12, 57–61, 64–68, 87, 91,
  99–107, 113, 116, 132, 134, 148–151,
  159, 164, 178, 191, 193, 198, 204,
  210–211, 222, 226, 233–234, 238–240,
251, 253, 255–263, 270, 272, 276,
  280–287, 290, 296, 298–299, 301
university, 78, 85–86
Uppsala, 83
urban planning, 152, 222, 224, 281
Ure, Andrew, 60
useful knowledge, 24, 37, 41–42
Usher, Abbott Payson, 300

V

vacuum cleaner, 235
Van Gogh, Vincent, 155
Veblen, Thorstein, 68, 105–106, 172, 300
Verne, Jules, 162
Vertov, Dziga, 157
Vesalius, Andreas, 201
Vivano, Vincenzio, 79

W

Wajcman, Judy, 303
Wald, George, 246
Wallace, Anthony, 12
war, 57–59, 137, 207, 245–246, 251, 254
Ward, Barbara, 283
Warhol, Andy, 237
Waring, George E.,
wash table, 231
washing machine, 232, 235–236
waste, 238, 278, 283
water, 222, 236, 240
water closet, 221, 227, 232, 242
water supply, 239
Watson, James, 1–3, 6, 254, 263, 307
Watt, James, 50–51, 84
Weber, Max, 1, 25, 39, 42, 68, 92–93, 102,
  301–302
Wedgwood, Josiah, 51, 84
Weinberg, Alvin, 255
Weizenbaum, Joseph, 217
Wells, H.G., 200
Whewell, William, 60, 296–297
White, Hayden, 3
White, Lynn, 9
Whitehead, Alfred North, 60
Wigforss, Ernst, 119